**PSYCHOLOGY and
COMMUNITY CHANGE**

The Dorsey Series in Psychology

Consulting Editor   GERALD C. DAVISON
State University of New York at Stony Brook

PSYCHOLOGY and COMMUNITY CHANGE

KENNETH HELLER
Professor of Psychology
Indiana University

and

JOHN MONAHAN
Assistant Professor of Social Ecology
University of California, Irvine

1977

The Dorsey Press Homewood, Illinois 60430

Irwin-Dorsey Limited Georgetown, Ontario L7G 4B3

ISBN 0-256-01941-X
Library of Congress Catalog Card No. 76–49320
Printed in the United States of America

To Audrey and Linda

PREFACE

IN 1920, WINSLOW, a famous physician of the day, defined public health as "the science and art of (1) preventing disease, (2) prolonging life, and (3) promoting physical and mental health through organized community efforts."[1] Transposed to psychology, this early definition captures a great deal of the current emphases in community psychology and community mental health. To be sure, the field has moved beyond a simple public health model, but the ideas suggested by Winslow—prevention and promotion of health and well being through the medium of organized community efforts—form the foundation upon which other topics of interest have been built. For example, at the National Training Conference on Community Psychology held in Austin, Texas in 1975, community psychology was said to emphasize the amelioration of situational and social forces which contribute to problem behavior while enhancing those factors conducive to psychological strength and competence. There was a call for psychologists to give up their exclusive focus on the individual and learn more about processes of community change. Other recent interests include a concern for the interaction between individuals and their physical and social environments (e.g., person-environment interaction theories and developments in social ecology) and the psychological effects of disruptive social conditions. Thus, while the field has expanded, elements in the original Winslow definition are germane to the unresolved issues in community psychology.

We mention this historical example because throughout the book we will emphasize the historical antecedents to current beliefs and practices. We are impressed by the extent to which ideas originate and

---

[1] B. S. Brown, "Philosophy and scope of extended clinic activities," in A. J. Bindman and A. D. Spiegel (eds.), *Perspectives in community mental health* (Chicago, Ill.: Aldine, 1969), pp. 41–53.

flourish as a function of changes within the political and social milieu. Good ideas in the sciences are not the exclusive reflection of experimental rigor. While rigorous research is important, so too is the social support and reward structure to which the scientist is exposed and which encourages the pursuit of some topics and the neglect of others. For any field to develop systematically, there need to be rewards for sustained scholarly activity.

There is a lesson here for community psychology. Several years ago, Rappaport and Chinsky[2] described community psychology as a new orientation or point of view, rather than a new substantive body of knowledge. What is required for community psychology to move beyond this stage and become more than ideology is good research and sustained commitment from scholars and those who reward scholarly activity. Zeal alone cannot carry a field beyond its initial formative stages.

Over the last several years, we have been sustained personally by a network of professional colleagues who shared our concerns for expanding the knowledge base of community psychology. Kenneth Heller began formal training in community mental health in 1968 with a special research fellowship (NIMH #40,558) at the Laboratory of Community Psychiatry, Harvard Medical School. Gerald Caplan, the director of the laboratory, was a stimulating and challenging teacher. Subsequently, other colleagues provided continued stimulation by their willingness to exchange ideas. Bruce Denner, Arnold Goldstein, Philip Mann, Richard Price and Robert Wolosin are a few of those who deserve special mention for their support, challenge, and feedback. Richard Price, who has become a close personal friend, was particularly willing to make himself available for extended discussion. Robert Wolosin introduced Heller to the literature in community sociology and the social psychology of organizational change. Also, he provided valuable consultation and feedback during the development of the concepts used in Chapter 9. Special thanks is extended to Robert Arnove, who made available his detailed file on alternative schools.

Colleagues in the Program in Social Ecology at Irvine were most helpful to John Monahan in the development of his ideas concerning community psychology. In particular, Ralph Catalano, Raymond Novaco, Joseph DiMento, David Dooley, Carol Whalen, Peter Scharf, and Daniel Stokols gave generously of their counsel. Arnold Binder

---

[2] J. Rappaport and J. M. Chinsky, "Models for delivery of service from a historical and conceptual perspective," *Professional Psychology*, 1974, 5, 42–50.

arranged summer teaching for Heller at Irvine in 1973 so that planning the manuscript could be expedited.

The contribution of graduate students and former graduate students to the ideas of their professors often is underrated. In reality, information flows in both directions, and if the proper atmosphere has been cultivated, the teacher can benefit as much as the students. The stimulation received from our students is gratefully acknowledged. Since several students read and commented on sections of the manuscript, their help should be specifically mentioned. This group includes Andrea Klein, Steven J. Lynn, Howie Markman, Mary Munchel, Ralph Swindle, and Michael Markowitz. Robert Schwartz wrote a term paper on the social history of the treatment of the mentally retarded that was so exceptional that with revision it has been included as part of Chapter 2 (see pp. 42–67).

Helpful suggestions were provided by Dorsey Press editorial consultants: James Kelly, Robert Calsyn, and Donald Tasto.

Much of the manuscript was typed by Judy Jerkich, who also provided editorial and technical assistance. Her work represented secretarial professionalism at its best; and her dedication and patience were indispensible to the production of the final manuscript. Juanita Melgoza and Diane Langmack also provided expert secretarial help.

During the more than five years of manuscript preparation, our families showed an unusual patience and adaptability to our demanding work schedules. Audrey and Linda supported us during difficult periods while pursuing professional careers of their own. Their encouragement and devotion is appreciated more than they may know. Carolyn, Daniel, and Emily tolerated fatherly eccentricities in good humor.

This project is best described as a joint effort of two friends and colleagues. While each of us was responsible for the final draft of different parts of the book, the planning and execution of the text involved a process of mutual interchange and interaction that provided intellectual stimulation of equal value to both of us.

February 1977   KENNETH HELLER
                                                   JOHN MONAHAN

CONTENTS

PART TWO

Basic concepts

PART THREE

Perspectives in community change

PART ONE

The development of a
community orientation:
Historical and research issues

1

INTRODUCTION

THERE has been a quiet revolution occurring within the behavioral sciences. The environmental context of behavior has been rediscovered and psychological theories are once again grappling with the problem of how best to describe the factors associated with person-environment interactions. At the same time a parallel development has been occurring in the helping professions that use psychological theories as their conceptual base. Clinical interventions derived from intrapsychic formulations have come under attack for their restricted utility in dealing with the real-life concerns of troubled individuals. To properly understand these criticisms and why the conceptual changes are occurring requires us to adopt a historical perspective, and focus on post–World War II events as they affect the behavioral sciences and the mental health professions.

In May of 1965, a conference was held in Swampscott, Massachusetts, that has been described as the event that marked the official birth of community psychology. The conference did not just "happen" but reflected the unrest in psychology that had been brewing for at least a decade. The work of the conference was to review the state of the field and to plot a future course of development for the place of psychology in the community mental health movement. It was not difficult for the conference participants to achieve consensus concerning the problems; however, agreeing on the definition of community psychology and the direction the field should take was another matter.

3

Issues of concern

Overtaxed treatment facilities

One problem that needed attention was the trend toward "ware-housing" increasing numbers of patients in public mental hospitals. Through the mid 1950s, the resident population rose to include over 500,000 patients a year. Approximately two out of every five hospital beds were for mental patients and in the 1950s the numbers seemed to be continually rising. The actual number of hospitalized mental patients finally peaked in 1955, at which time maintenance expenditures were over $600 million per year. Despite this huge monetary outlay, quality of care left much to be desired. According to one estimate, per capita expenditure for patients in state mental hospitals was only one seventh that spent in community general hospitals. The difference was not just due to the high cost of medical care, but represented the low priority given by the states to the treatment of mental disorders. According to one estimate, state mental hospital expenditures were about two thirds less than the amount spent in psychiatric hospitals administered by the Veterans Administration (Joint Commission on Mental Illness and Health, 1961).

Beginning in 1956 and continuing thereafter, the resident population of mental hospitals began to drop, reversing what had been an upward trend that had persisted for over 50 years. The reversal of this upward trend began immediately after the introduction of the major tranquilizing drugs, which quite naturally are given credit for stopping the upward spiral of mental hospital prevalence rates. However, the situation is somewhat more complicated because at about that same time there was a shift toward better hospital care and more liberal parole and discharge policies. While the number of resident patients dropped steadily after 1956, total cost and cost per patient actually increased. Part of the increase represented economic inflation but another important reason for the increased expenditures was a more concerted effort at treatment. Still, while the tranquilizing drugs revolutionized the management of psychotic patients by no longer requiring the need for physical restraints, lobotomy operations, etc., other treatment alternatives were desperately needed. How could the newly accessible patients be helped to resume constructive lives in the community? Surely it was unrealistic to expect that medication alone could do the job.

Dissatisfaction with psychotherapy as the exclusive mode of psychological intervention

Another problem becoming apparent at about this same time involved an increasing dissatisfaction with traditional psychotherapy, which had become the major psychological helping modality. In 1952, Hans Eysenck began an attack on the effectiveness of traditional psychotherapy that was to continue throughout the decade (Eysenck, 1952; 1961), influencing the thinking of many mental health professionals. The general form of Eysenck's argument was to assert that the base rate for spontaneous improvement (i.e., improvement without therapy) among neurotic patients was about 66 percent. Since psychotherapy-outcome studies generally reported a similar two thirds improvement rate, Eysenck claimed that psychotherapy does not have more beneficial effects than that obtained from the base rate for spontaneous improvement.

There were many attempts to refute Eysenck's argument (De Charms, Levy, & Wertheimer, 1954; Luborsky, 1954; Rosenzweig, 1954) for he was attacking the very heart of psychological and psychiatric activity, but these presentations were never given the publicity of Eysenck's original claim, which over time became part of the accepted lore of the field. It was not until 1971 that the original data upon which Eysenck based his arguments were systematically reanalyzed. That herculean task was performed by Alan Bergin (1971), who was able to show the ambiguity of the original data and how Eysenck ordered the data according to his own biases. One example from Bergin's reanalysis can be used to illustrate the problem of bias. Eysenck cites data from the Berlin Psychoanalytic Institute that described improvement in terms of four categories (cured, very much improved, improved, and uncured). The first two categories of improvement are clear, but how should the third category, "improved" be treated? How should outcome in this category be classified when calculating improvement rates? Bergin was able to demonstrate that Eysenck recoded these cases as "slightly improved" and *excluded* them from the reported improvement rate. Another issue concerns premature dropouts and whether they should be counted as therapeutic failures. Though patients can drop out of psychotherapy for a number of reasons, only some of which are related to treatment, Eysenck included *all* dropouts as unimproved.

Table 1–1 presents a summary and recoding of this example of the

TABLE 1–1
Psychotherapeutic-improvement rates as a function of improvement categories and classification of premature dropouts: A summary of Bergin's reanalysis of the effects of psychoanalysis as practiced at the Berlin Psychoanalytic Institute 1920–1930

	"Improved" cases classified as failures	*"Improved" cases classified as successes*
Dropouts counted as failures	44%	60%
Dropouts excluded	62	83

ambiguity in Eysenck's original data. Eysenck chose to report the most pessimistic interpretation of the effects of psychoanalysis (44 percent improved). A proponent of psychoanalysis could choose an opposite alternative at each decision point, and from the same data could report an improvement rate for psychoanalysis almost double that reported by Eysenck (i.e., 83 percent). Bergin was able to show similar deficiencies in Eysenck's claim that neurotics generally showed a two thirds spontaneous-improvement rate. Bergin presented new data to indicate that the median spontaneous-remission rate "appears to be in the vicinity of 30 percent" (Bergin, 1971, p. 241). Thus, depending upon one's attitude toward the data, differing psychotherapy-outcome and spontaneous-remission figures can be obtained.

The point of this discussion is to indicate that while the effectiveness of psychotherapy is still an open question, Eysenck's attack on psychotherapy was generally accepted as valid. Eysenck was believed, not because he presented the field with impeccable data, but because many in the field were looking for evidence to bolster their skepticism about psychotherapy. There was a growing dissatisfaction with an exclusive reliance on this treatment modality for solving the country's mental health problems.

Even if psychotherapy were 100 percent effective for those individuals capable of staying with the treatment, its utility could still be questioned. It is a lengthy and exclusive method applicable to only a restricted set of problems. Its greatest strength is in dealing with the type of problems for which it was originally developed—neurotic inhibitions in otherwise socially competent and effective individuals. Granted that this area of greatest strength has importance, still, relying on psychotherapy as an *exclusive* treatment modality is the point at issue. Table 1–2 summarizes the deficiencies of the psychotherapeutic model.

TABLE 1–2
Psychotherapy as a "waiting" mode of delivering mental health services

Characteristics of the Waiting Mode (adapted from Rappaport and Chinsky, 1974):
1. Service is rendered by an "expert" or authority who is highly educated in a mental health profession.
2. Service is rendered in the expert's office or in a hospital.
3. The expert passively waits for the client to find him. The expert does not initiate contacts.

Deficiencies of the Traditional Psychotherapeutic Model:
1. *Selection of clients.* The overwhelming majority of psychotherapy clients fall into the YAVIS syndrome—Young, Attractive, Verbal, Intelligent, and Successful. Mental health treatment in the waiting mode has become almost exclusively the province of the white and wealthy.
2. *Selection of treatment providers.* Since it relies on experts and highly educated professionals to perform almost all contact with clients, the traditional style of delivering mental health service has always suffered from an acute manpower shortage.
3. *Selection of problems.* The majority of outpatient psychotherapy deals with "neurotic" problems (e.g., self-understanding, relationship difficulties). Mental health treatment in the waiting mode has largely ignored the more difficult—but more socially relevant—problems of alcoholism, drug abuse, violence, etc.
4. *Selection of treatments.* Mental health treatment in the waiting mode tends to be very lengthy and hence, very expensive. In addition, most of the forms of mental health treatment are geared to the type of clients mentioned in #1 and the type of problems mentioned in #3.
5. *Selection of point of intervention.* Because it relies on waiting until the client's difficulties are severe enough to motivate him to seek expert help, the traditional style of delivering mental health care only deals with full-fledged psychological problems. There is rarely the opportunity to intervene early in the development of a problem, and even more rarely the chance to prevent problems from occurring.

The implication of this position, as seen in the Table, is to reinforce the need for a distinction to be made between the effectiveness of psychotherapy and its social utility. Even if psychotherapists perform with maximal effectiveness, psychotherapy may still be lacking in social utility. Too many troubled individuals do not meet the "entrance requirements" for treatment; their troubles are not amenable to a treatment focus emphasizing insight and understanding; and the intervention occurs too late to be of maximal benefit in altering the development of entrenched difficulties.

The need to consider environmental variables

Overtaxed treatment facilities, inadequate mental health manpower, and a questioning of traditional psychotherapy were some of the issues and problems of concern addressed by the advocates of community mental health and community psychology in the 1960s. One further issue of at least equal importance involved the increased awareness of social and environmental problems as they impinged upon the lives of people. An awareness of the tragic waste of human potential associated with poverty and racial discrimination was part of the climate of the times. Psychologists were not immune to recognizing the urgency of this country's neglected social problems. Many wanted to increase the scope and relevance of psychological intervention, but how should increased relevance take place? The participants at the Swampscott conference felt that the time had come for psychology to step out of its long-standing immersion in strictly clinical medical settings by expanding the scope of its inquiry and action (Bennett, et al., 1966). While social problems had complex determinants, there were psychological components to these problems to which the field could respond as long as there was a clear understanding that psychological solutions were not inherently better than social or political ones. As Cowen pointed out, mental health professionals could have an expanded voice in the solution of social problems, but they would certainly not "stand alone as the 'chosen' ones or even the front-runners in the quest for solutions" (Cowen, 1973, p. 453).

Was the conceptual framework within which psychology operated adequate for dealing with complex social problems? A serious indictment of the ability of the behavioral sciences to respond to urgent problems of the day came from those who attacked the inadequacy of psychology's conceptual framework. Caplan and Nelson (1973) noted that despite the fact that much of behavior is best understood as an interaction between persons and their environments, the bias in psychological research is on "person centered" characteristics. When psychologists investigate social problems, they are more likely to focus on variables that lie within the individual, while ignoring situationally relevant factors. What this leads to is a "person blame" causal attribution, that is, "the tendency to attribute *causal* significance to person-centered variables found in statistical association with the social problem in question" (Caplan & Nelson, 1973, p. 199). An example of psychology's overemphasis on person-centered variables is provided by Caplan and Nelson in their examination of a six-month section of the 1970 *Psychological Abstracts*. The *Abstracts* is a compendium of all published research in psychology, categorized according to specific topics. Caplan and Nelson looked at all the research dealing with *black Americans* and classified the research as emphasizing either person or situation-oriented variables. They found that 82 percent of classifiable psychological research on this topic emphasized person characteristics to the neglect of environmental components.

Caplan and Nelson discovered that the *Abstracts* revealed other evidence of the field's person-centered bias:

> As with telephone books, reading *Psychological Abstracts* can be instructive in ways not intended by those who compiled or organized it. Some peripherally relevant observations: *(a)* Although *Psychological Abstracts* abstracts articles from the journal *Social Problems* . . . there is no category by that name or any variation of it in the subject index. *(b)* In the format outline used by *Psychological Abstracts,* the areas of crime, juvenile delinquency, and drug addiction are among those grouped under the subheading of Behavior Disorder within the division of Clinical Psychology—again illustrating the bias of the field. *(c)* Perhaps reflecting their missionary zeal, Mental Health and Psychological Services listings can be found under the index heading Social Movements. *(d)* Even in the act of trying to select social problem areas with which to illustrate our thesis, our assertion was substantiated. Almost all "problems" listed are those of individuals or conventionally defined categories of persons. One searches in vain for serious treatment—whether as dependent, independent, or merely correlated variables—of social *system* variables as they may relate to those psychological variables with which psychologists ordinarily concern themselves. (Caplan & Nelson, 1973, p. 205)

The implications of the Caplan and Nelson argument is that it is not enough to be interested in social problems. The bias that a discipline's conceptual framework imposes on natural phenomena must also be recognized. Some distortion is inevitable since a conceptual framework can only present an approximation to reality. Some variables will be ignored while others are highlighted in the attempt to make sense out of complex, intertwining real world problems.

Actually, neither "person blame" nor "system blame" explanations are adequate by themselves. Just as a person-blame orientation can reinforce the status quo, so too can a system-blame perspective become an excuse for inaction. If individuals are simply passive "victims" of their environments, personal responsibility and accountability for one's own behavior can be avoided. A fuller perspective would indicate that environmental influence is not a one-way process—environments influence behavior, but persons also have the capacity to shape environments. What is needed is a more complex and sophisticated view of causality.

Models and perspectives in community psychology

The preceding discussion highlighted the importance of conceptual frameworks as guides to relevant action. At this point, we should offer some additional comments concerning the nature of models and perspectives in psychology. As we have tried to indicate, scientific investigation, or for that matter any attempt to make sense out of natural phenomena, involves the application of conceptual templates that are only approximations to nature. As Kuhn has argued, science is not simply the accumulation of facts, but also involves attempts "to force nature into conceptual boxes supplied by professional education" (Kuhn, 1962, p. 5). There are several implications that flow from this point of view.

Most basic is the need to avoid the reification of concepts, that is, the tendency to regard an idea or abstraction as if it were a real object, a "thing." For example, concepts like "unconscious," "ego," "drive," "motive," and so on, do not have an external reality, but refer to ideas about mental functioning. They may be useful in some contexts but deceiving in others. For example, suggesting to a psychotherapy patient that his "unconscious" is blocking his ability to act appropriately reifies the concept by giving it a reality it does not have, and in addition, takes responsibility for action away from the person (It's not your fault you can't do better, your unconscious is keeping you down). George Kelly (1958) described his experiences as a school psychologist in a similar manner. A teacher might refer a child for "laziness" and ask the psychologist to choose up sides in making a differential diagnosis—Was the child lazy or not? It soon became apparent to Kelly that "the teacher's complaint was not necessarily something to be verified or disproved by the facts in the case, but was, rather, a construction of events in a way that . . . made the most sense to her at the moment" (Kelly, 1958, p. 44). Often, more progress could be made by working with the teacher to broaden her perception of the child than by trying to "cure" the child's laziness.

It is important to keep in mind that we are dealing with perspectives that are constructions of events. This is important for all fields but has special relevance for the behavioral sciences. Levine and Levine (1970) take the position that concepts concerning psychological functioning are very much influenced by events of the day. Knowledge derived from empirical research is but one source of psychological theories. As Levine and Levine (1970) have documented, over the decades, theories about psychological dysfunction and the procedures necessary to remediate that dysfunction have emphasized either social or intra-psychic determinants of behavior. The thesis presented by the Levines is that mental health theories emphasizing environmental determinants flourish during periods of political or social reform, while intra-psychic theories that assume the "goodness" of the environment are prominent during periods of political and social conservatism.

The thesis presented by the Levines makes sense if we think of ideas as reflecting the construct system of the theorist, who in turn is very much influenced by the prevailing *Zeitgeist,* or spirit of the times. Thus, we need to look for support for our ideas beyond their simple popularity and should not mistake popularity for validity. A popular idea if untested to determine its validity is easily replaced as changes occur in the social climate—abandoned not because the idea was disproved, but because it may no longer be considered fashionable.

There is no one viewpoint within the community field but rather several distinct orientations, each of which leads to different assumptions about the nature of psychological functioning and its enhancement in community settings. Implicit in each is a view of persons in society, which includes basic assumptions about the nature of psychological well-being and how it is to be achieved, as well as assumptions about the role of society and social institutions that impinge upon and influence individual behavior. Following the lead of Price (1972) we will refer to orientations toward community processes as *perspectives.* There has been a trend in psychology to use the term *model* to characterize one's theoretical viewpoint. Thus, terms such as *the medical model, the psychoanalytic model, the learning model,* etc., find widespread use. As Price points out, while the term *model* may have special appeal because of its scientific sounding character, it does lead to some confusion. The basic character of a model is that it is a conceptual analogy that allows us to construe behavior that we do not yet understand in terms that are more familiar. In Price's words:

> The basic character of the model is that it is an *analogy*. When we are confronted with a set of events or a structure we do not understand, we may attempt to give an account of the events or structure that relies upon analogy. Thus we may conceive of the brain *as if* it were a computer, or may think of the heart *as if* it were a pump. In each case we attempt to understand the puzzling events or structures that confront us by thinking of them as if they were other events or structures with which we are more familiar. Of course, we may use analogies to help us understand events that are much more broadly conceived or problems that are less well defined than our examples of the heart or brain. For example, we may think of abnormal or deviant behavior as if it were an illness or disease. In using illness as an analogue or model, we are attempting to understand a set of events and behaviors which are puzzling to us (that is, abnormal behavior) by assuming that it is analogous to events we understand in more detail (that is, disease or illness). (Price, 1972, p. 8)

This analogue, or "as-if," character of models can be misleading, particularly as applied to complex community phenomena. Words like *sick society* (medical model), *repressive institutions* (psychoanalytic model) or *reinforcing environments* (learning model) confuse more than they clarify. As Price notes, models are incomplete representations that invite generalization beyond the scope originally intended.

Discussing community orientations as *perspectives* allows us to emphasize that differences between them are a function of how events are interpreted and understood. In part, these viewpoints were developed through observation of different phenomena. However, more likely is the possibility that the differing advocates of community change view the same events, but from quite different perspectives.

The changing fields of clinical and community psychology

Earlier in this chapter, we noted that developments in community psychology came about as a reaction to prevailing attitudes and practices within clinical psychology. Still, we must point out that in actuality, both fields have been steadily changing over time. The 1950 status and thrust of the mental health fields to which those with a community orientation were reacting does not capture or do justice to current thinking. Clinical psychology of the 1950s was very much tied to psychiatry and psychiatric theories. The influence of psychological knowledge in areas such as child development, social psychology, and the psychology of learning had not yet been felt. In contrast, what we see today in clinical psychology is a diversity of psychological perspectives from which new forms of practice have been derived. Just as one cannot speak of a single community perspective, so too would it be misleading to describe clinical psychology as if it represented a monolithic ideological structure.

At this point it would be appropriate to describe some of the shifts in emphasis that have been occurring in clinical psychology. It should become apparent that community perspectives do present new conceptual challenges to *traditional* clinical thinking. Appreciating the impact of the new points of view will make it difficult to operate clinically with a "business as usual" attitude. However, it would be wrong and ultimately divisive to suggest that advances in community psychology would not be welcome and incorporated by many clinical practitioners. To suggest that one field has a monopoly on the desire or ability to achieve substantive improvements in the human condition, reflects a provincialism that the human service professions can ill afford. Just as some aspects of psychoanalytic and behavioral thinking have become fused and integrated into the general body of psychological knowledge, we would not be too surprised to see a similar phenomenon occurring with regard to some community ideas and practices.

While some degree of fusion between the clinical and community fields may take place some time in the future, at the present time it would be more helpful to clearly articulate the differences between the two by focusing on the major themes unifying community perspectives. We should then be able to develop intervention implications from these ideas and put them to empirical test. More than continued rhetoric, what is needed is systematic analysis, conceptual clarity, and empirical verification. It is with this spirit that we now offer a framework within which community intervention can be viewed.

It seems to us that the assumptions upon which intervention strategies depend can be described as varying along three dimensions:

Theoretical perspective: deficit ↔ competency orientations

Ecological level: individual ↔ organizational ↔ community levels

Intervention point: early in development ↔ later in development

The traditional orientations to change within psychology can be characterized in *deficit* terms. The targets for intervention are viewed as possessing deficits or problems that need to be prevented or remedied. Traditionally, most clinical interventions were derived from a deficit orientation—the clinician's job was to remedy existing problems. The point of intervention for most clinicians occurs *late* in the development of a psychological disorder, since clients tend to come to clinicians primarily when their problems are well entrenched. Furthermore, clinical intervention tends to focus on the *individual*, rarely considering intervention beyond the small group or family levels.

As community perspectives developed, the deficit orientation was initially retained as interest shifted from treatment and rehabilitation to prevention. The primary focus moved toward the development of interventions that could be used at earlier points in time to *prevent* or avoid the occurrence of anticipated deficit. The goal of prevention activities is on reducing the risk for disorder among community members. Although the concept was new to mental health, prevention was long accepted in public health practice. As used in that field, prevention involves lowering the rate of new cases of disorder "by counteracting harmful circumstances before they have a chance to produce illness" (Caplan, 1964, p. 26). The intent is to reduce the risk for disorder for whole populations, not just for specific individuals.

A concern for prevention provides a major conceptual shift for the mental health fields. Intervention is required at an earlier point in time before disorder can develop, and more careful attention must be given to environmental factors that support or hamper adjustive capacity. Prevention activity can take place at a number of ecological levels, focusing either on persons or on broader community-wide factors. Preventive interventions can be designed to ameliorate harmful environmental conditions or to support the resistance of populations to unavoidable future harmful experiences.

Table 1–3 presents examples of deficit-oriented interventions occurring at different ecological levels and intervention points. At the individual level, early deficit-oriented preventive interventions would include screening children to determine those at risk for later maladjustment and providing early therapeutic intervention to prevent the appearance of suspected problems. Cowen's project, "red-tagging" children in the Rochester school system (discussed in Chapter 4), is one example of this approach. Another example of an individual early deficit-oriented intervention would be crisis intervention in which persons in acute psychological distress are provided immediate help to prevent the development of more severe maladjustments.

TABLE 1–3
Strategies for change: A deficit orientation

Ecological level	Point of intervention		
	Earlier	Later
Individual or small group	1. Identify high-risk children 2. Crisis intervention 3. Polio vaccination	1. Much of individual psychotherapy 2. Much of group therapy 3. Medication
Organizational	1. Staff sensitivity groups 2. Case-centered consultation 3. Special education programs	1. Remedial reading classes 2. Hospital token economies 3. Continuation schools
Community	1. Media program on the "early warning signs of mental illness" 2. Streetlighting to reduce crime 3. Seatbelts in cars	1. Welfare programs 2. Building mental hospitals 3. Building prisons

Sensitivity sessions with staff of an organization beginning to experience morale problems represents an early deficit-oriented intervention at the organizational level. Similarly, special education programs in schools represent an organizational analogue to the problem of high risk children. Here the intervention is not earmarked for individual children but represents an organizational programmatic response to this form of educational deficit. Case-centered consultation (discussed in Chapter 6) to care-givers of high-risk children (e.g., teachers and parents) to provide better classroom or home management would also fall in this category.

At the community level, messages in the television or print media to be on the lookout for the "early warning signs" of mental illness, or messages that urge citizens to be compassionate toward alcoholics since they have "a disease like any other" are early deficit-oriented interventions. Examples of early deficit-oriented interventions at the community level that are not related to mental health would include streetlighting to reduce crime, and campaigns to encourage wearing seatbelts.

Change strategies that are invoked *after* a deficit has already manifested itself can also be thought of as on three levels (see Table 1–3). On the individual or small group level, much of psychotherapy and behavior therapy, as well as drug treatment would fall into this cell. Intervention is applied late in the sequence of problem development, and is conceptualized in terms of remedying individual deficits. At the organizational level, setting up remedial reading classes in a school system, or establishing a token economy program in a mental hospital would illustrate late deficit-oriented interventions. Finally, on the community level, late interventions keyed to perceived deficits would be exemplified by the construction of prisons or mental hospitals, and by the creation of traditional welfare programs.

Thus we see that two of the themes that community ideology brings to the mental health fields are a concern for prevention and a need to focus on broader ecological levels than the level of exclusive treatment of individuals. These two themes can be found in modern public health theories in which disease is seen as an end product of an interaction between host, pathological agent, and environment (Bloom, 1965). Effective prevention can result from the modification of one or several of these factors. For example, in public health medicine, prevention of disease can be effective by immunizing the host (e.g., immunizing an individual against smallpox); or by modification of the environment (e.g., spraying mosquito-infested areas to reduce the incidence of malaria) (Bloom, 1965). In a similar manner, mental health prevention-oriented activities could include techniques for strengthening the resistance of persons, such as anticipatory guidance (e.g., preparing patients for the stress of surgery, discussed in Chapter 4) or techniques aimed at environmental modification (e.g., program consultation in schools, administrative consultation, and community organization).

Another important change in psychological thinking in the last few decades has involved a growing dissatisfaction with the emphasis on the pathological. Personality theorists have long been concerned with the problem of defining normality in more meaningful ways than simply the absence of disorder (Shoben, 1957; Smith, 1959; Wallace, 1966); yet it was difficult to talk about *positive* mental health because of the inevitable disagreement as to what "normality" should encompass. It proved easier to circumvent this value-laden question by concentrating on pathology—after all, everyone could agree that the grosser forms of psychological disorder were "evils" to be avoided (Smith, 1959). Therapists were more comfortable describing their work in terms of removing symptoms and reducing discomfort. It was assumed that increased productivity and competence would automatically result from a lifting of pathological processes.

An alternative to a deficit or pathology emphasis is one that focuses more directly on psychological *strengths* and *competencies*. This change is not simply a semantic shift but has implications for how one conceptualizes behavior and designs helping interventions. Consider a category of behavior that is almost always thought of in deficit terms—schizophrenic behavior. One could say that "Patient A is schizophrenic" or "Patient A is capable of schizophrenic behavior" (Wallace, 1966, p. 133). In the first instance, the implication is that the patient will continuously show deficit behavior and that if he appears capable, it is only because his disorder is temporarily in remission. On the other hand, describing a person as capable of schizophrenic behavior does not preclude the possibility that he is also capable of many other behaviors as well. The capabilities conception should lead the psychologist to study the situations that seem to differentially call forth schizophrenic and non-schizophrenic behaviors in order to maximize the occurrence of the latter.

"Competence" refers to the development of psychosocial strengths; it can occur at a number of levels and intervention points. Table 1–4 illustrates the variety of interventions possible from a competency orientation. A good example of early, competence-based intervention at the level of the individual or small group would be Parent-Effectiveness-Training (P.E.T.) classes, in which parents attend not because of their inadequacies or deficits as parents, but rather because they recognize the need for specialized training in how to relate to their children. A variety of other examples would fall under the rubric of "skill building," and would include athletics, public speaking, dance—anything that would help a person develop a sense of self-esteem and task competence.

At the organizational level, consultation focused on providing skills and information to consultees such as teachers, welfare workers, or other agency personnel (i.e., consultee-centered consultation discussed in Chapter 6), is a form of early competence-oriented intervention. Here, a mental health professional attempts to educate caregivers so as to increase their own competence in handling cases. Sex

TABLE 1–4
Strategies for change: A competency orientation

Ecological level	Point of intervention	
	Earlier	*Later*
Individual or small group	1. Well-baby clinics 2. Parent effectiveness training 3. Skill building (athletics, public speaking, etc.)	1. Behavior shaping 2. Occupational therapy 3. Women's or gay support groups
Organizational	1. Police selection and training 2. English-as-a-second-language programs 3. Sex education classes in schools 4. Consultee-centered consultation	1. Achievement Place 2. Fairweather's Lodge program (Chapter 7) 3. OD training groups (Chapter 6)
Community	1. Community development programs 2. Fostering support networks 3. Anticipatory guidance through community-wide media	1. Social advocacy strategies 2. Job banks for displaced workers

education classes in schools is another example. Children are provided with competent knowledge about sexual functioning to replace misconceptions that can lead to later psychological difficulties.

Media programs that attempt to build immunity to stressful psychological events constitute early competence-based intervention on the community level. The technique here is called anticipatory guidance and involves presenting an optimum solution to a crisis before the crisis arises, so that the person will have a ready response to stress. The "Bernard St. Bernard" puppet series (Chapter 4) is a case in point. Community development programs that attempt to build pride and responsibility for the local community are other examples.

Competence-based interventions also can occur late in the sequence of problem development. At the individual level, "support groups" for various minority populations (women, gays, ex-mental patients, prisoners, etc.), in which the emphasis is not on therapy but rather on a banding together and pooling of strength, often against common enemies (e.g., discrimination, repressive laws), are good examples of the competence orientation. The emphasis in these groups is not on "what is wrong with us that we can change" but rather on "what strengths and untapped potential do we possess that can be employed to improve our lot." Occupational therapy is another example, the purpose being to increase a patient's sense of self-esteem and personal competence by virtue of learning a craft.

At the organizational level, late competence-oriented interventions would include those community treatment programs that emphasize training in skills necessary for independent living. "Achievement Place" (Fixsen et al., 1973), where children referred by a juvenile court are rewarded for competence in pro-social behavior is one example. Those organization development strategies (Chapter 6) that diagnose an organization's strengths as well as weaknesses, and attempt to augment the former while circumventing the latter, may also be placed in this cell.

Finally, on the community level, late competence-oriented interventions would be exemplified by the social advocacy approach of Saul Alinsky (1946; 1971). Alinsky entered communities usually at a time of turmoil and unrest, and organized the populace to place pressure on those institutions that had it in their power to provide for community needs. The emphasis in the Alinsky approach (discussed in Chapter 8) is on the power that resides in a local community, and that needs to be organized and mobilized for effective action. The "Great Society" Job Corps program is another example of late competence-based intervention on the community level. Thousands of "hard core" unemployed persons were given training to enhance their chances of securing a job in the future.

To summarize: the impact of the community perspectives can be conceptualized best in terms of emphasis and orientation that highlight a few key concepts: prevention; intervention at organizational and community levels; and procedures to foster skills and competencies. In contrast, the traditional perspectives in clinical psychology emphasize the remediation of deficits in individuals that are developed sufficiently to warrant a visit to the office of a mental health professional—the helping resource usually called upon last in time of trouble. The distinctions between the two orientations are important.

We have been operating from the traditional clinical perspective for so long that it is easy to assume that the only way to be psychologically helpful is to adopt the traditional stance. It is important to recognize that conceptual shifts have been occurring as well within the clinical fields, primarily among psychologists with social and behavioral perspectives (Price, 1972). It was no accident that most of the participants at the Swampscott conference that gave birth to community psychology were "converted clinicians" (Bennett, 1965). We hope to be able to show that the new emphases can lead to productive areas of psychological inquiry and eventually to new forms of intervention that can provide greater social utility.

Community psychiatry, community psychology, and community mental health: A terminological note

A brief word can be said about the labels that can be applied to the subject of this book. To some, the labels "community psychiatry," "community psychology," and "community mental health" are synonymous and interchangeable. Others have a strong preference for one of the three. While conceptual advances are not likely to hinge on a semantic issue, we consider the nuances and implications of the various terms sufficiently important to warrant a brief discussion.

Both the terms *community psychiatry* and *community psychology* are tainted with closed-shop disciplinary connotations. Community psychiatry hints that the hierarchical, psychiatrist-on-top relationships that have led to so much dissension in clinical work will be carried over to the community. At a time when progress toward more equitable professional relationships in clinical work is being achieved, the term *community psychiatry* appears to be a step in the wrong direction.

There are problems with *community psychology* as well. Cook (1970) holds that "community psychology shares many of the concerns of community mental health. But community psychology goes beyond community mental health in its concern with non-mental-health problems, e.g., the functioning of individuals within social units, organizations, and communities. Community psychology represents a mixture of mental health, behavioral science, social science, psychology, sociology, and other areas. It is the application of behavioral science principles to the understanding and solution of a variety of problems and community situations, and not just those problems related to mental health and mental illness" (p. 2). While we agree with Cook's description, especially with his emphasis that the field should deal with problems that have not traditionally been considered "mental health" problems, we find it somewhat ironic that a field that explicitly sets out to be multidisciplinary would immediately choose a name that relates to only one discipline.

Some psychologists wish to avoid the term "community mental health" to dissociate themselves from psychiatrists. Thus Bennett (1965) states that "Medicine itself—and psychiatry in particular—is expanding its own conceptions of medical responsibility to encompass preventive and societal intervention. One wonders, however, whether the physician's indoctrination to prescribe with authority is compatible with the psychologist's concern for self-actualization and self-management." We wish to dissociate ourselves from what could be viewed as professional provincialism. Self-actualization and self-management are hardly the province of any one discipline, even the one to which the authors of this book happen to belong. Nor has the experimental method been copyrighted.

What is ideally needed is a term whose connotations suggest: (a) a community and ecological focus; (b) a concern with problems of human functioning that includes a focus on the prevention of disorder, but that also goes beyond problems traditionally designated in "mental health" terms; (c) a stance that includes a concern for coping, adaptation, and competence, not just an emphasis on disorder; (d) a willingness to promote multidisciplinary, collaborative research, since no profession has a monopoly on interest in community change; (e) a commitment to an empirical, experimental approach to social intervention; and, (f) an avoidance of inappropriate medical overtones.

If this book is every published in German, perhaps the translator can supply us with one of the famous German word-sentences that would hit on all of the above points. For our English readers, we must reluctantly conclude that there is no one best term. As much as possible, we will talk about community *perspectives* to emphasize the divergence of views that exists among those with community viewpoints.

As psychologists, we are concerned with developments within our own field and hope that we can play a small part in shaping psychology's future. It is for this reason that at times we may address issues of primary concern to psychologists. We recognize our psychological heritage and purposely have chosen a title for this book to alert the reader to the fact that we write as psychologists approaching the problems of community change. We hope the reader will recognize our biases and regardless of whether he or she shares them, can still find value in following our content discussions.

Some further thoughts about values and community intervention

Any field whose practice touches the lives of others is confronted with value choices. Such decisions are not always apparent to the professional in day-to-day work, but are implicitly made nonetheless. The choice of problems considered legitimate for study and the imposition of intervention technologies to solve these problems reflect social values, not just "scientific" findings (Rappaport, 1975). The private practitioner who accepts clients on a voluntary basis may not be aware of any particular value decision on his or her part, but implicit in clinical work is the value that individuals should be helped to adjust to the goals and norms of the groups and organizations of which they are a part. Implicit also is the expectation that social institutions are basically benign and that improved adjustment follows from individual change. Thus, while value decisions may not be explicit, clinical work is not value-free.

Articulating values can be extremely difficult because values are not static—they shift with continued thought and discussion and with changing events. Also, focusing on values can produce discomfort because value discussions may suddenly call into question long-established beliefs and practices. In 1968, one of us (KH) provided consultation to a school system in a large city. A common practice at that time was for practitioners in mental health clinics to accept referrals from schools and social agencies and write lengthy reports about the psychological deficits found in children so referred. It was dismaying to see that such reports were written routinely even when the clinic was not prepared to offer follow-through consultation to help the referring agent or parent deal more constructively with the child's officially diagnosed psychological problem. It seemed to be assumed without question that diagnosis without treatment was an ethically acceptable and professionally valuable enterprise.

Unfortunately, clinic reports written to schools could be used to deny children access to regular classroom contacts. The schools were required to provide an educational opportunity for all children, but the law allowed special arrangements to be made for children officially diagnosed as "emotionally disturbed." In the school system in question, emotionally disturbed children who disrupted regular classroom routine and who could not be placed in the few special classrooms available were provided with one hour a day of individual home tutoring. Tutoring met the educational requirements of the law but it was hardly an appropriate substitute for the educational and socialization experiences available in the regular classroom.

Without providing therapy or consultation that could eventually aid in returning the children to full participation with their peers, the clinics became part of a procedure that eventually hurt the children the reports were written to help. Restricted to one hour a day of individual tutoring, the children fell behind both educationally and socially. However, for clinic professionals to become aware of the problem would have required basic reorientations in theoretical perspective and work styles. As long as their model of practice suggested that effective psychological change could only come about through intensive intra-psychic psychotherapy, there was no point in their talking to teachers of children not in treatment, or to parents of children for whom long-term intensive therapy was neither acceptable nor appropriate.

Consider the following case of a nine-year-old boy for whom home tutoring was provided. The child's official diagnosis was "school phobia." The parents did not follow through on the clinic's offer of intensive psychotherapy, dropping out after one session. From information provided by the tutor a fresh perspective could be gained about the situation, one in which it would appear that despite the official diagnosis of the child's "problem," he may have been responding reasonably well to an unfortunate family situation. An elderly and sick grandmother lived in the home while economic circumstances forced both parents to assume full-time jobs. The parents were very worried about leaving their sick mother alone all day and freely communicated their concern to family members. They would say things like: "Grandma could fall downstairs and be killed if she were left alone with nobody to care for her." Was it any wonder that a child in this family developed fears of going to school, anticipating what might happen to a beloved grandmother in his absence?

What sort of "therapy" should be provided for a school "phobia" of this sort? Should the helping professionals in this case sit by impotently because the parents did not accept the plan for intensive psychotherapy—knowing all the while that the child was a victim of a situation he did not create. Not acting, that is, not providing an alternative treatment plan is as much a value decision as would be a strategy that would call for putting greater pressure on the parents to remedy the situation. Should a treatment be devised to desensitize the child's fear so that he would feel less responsible for his grandmother's fate and could accept a possible accidental death without guilt? Desensitization techniques to accomplish such a goal already exist; their use again requires a value decision. Should an attempt be made to convince the family to hire a companion for the grandmother—a move they had already considered but unfortunately could not afford? Whether to divert funds from food to home care or whether to apply for welfare assistance again are value choices.

Until now, the choices presented have stressed person-centered interventions of a kind that might be consistent with the usual operating styles of many mental health professionals. However there are other alternatives that could be suggested that would require greater conceptual shifts. For example, communities could devise better ways to provide for elderly citizens so as to encourage more constructive pursuits in the "golden" years. There is no reason why grandmothers need sit at home, lonely and useless. Constructive work could be provided for senior citizens that could be accomplished through group effort. A somewhat feeble grandmother might still help out in a community nursery school where she could read to small groups of children, while at the same time being "supervised" herself. If the grandmother were completely immobile, she could still be involved in a neighborhood-based helping network—visited and cared for by other elderly citizens, while she in turn might have responsibility to maintain phone contact with others in similar restricted circumstances. Strategies such as these require a shift in conceptual analysis to give greater emphasis to the importance of group support and usefulness to others as key ingredients in maintaining psychological well-being. Providing continued productive opportunities for the elderly also requires a shift in values toward greater humanistic concern for all citizens. We can stop treating the elderly as useless cast-offs if we are willing to undertake a change in social priorities.

It is difficult to talk about values abstractly for such discussions can degenerate into a long catalog of virtues to be optimized that too often become Barnum-like statements about improving "the quality of life." However, in any one particular situation it is much easier to be specific. In the example just provided, value choices were embedded in each intervention strategy but were *not* made explicit by the professionals involved. Consider another example in which one of us (JM) provided consultation to a local police department and did specify his personal values as part of the initial agreement. After numerous meetings and in the context of a growing and friendly professional relationship with the police chief, but before any formal agreements were reached as to the nature of the consultant's role, a memo was sent to the chief that read in part:

> I would like to be explicit about the values that will guide our future interaction. I see them as three:
>
> *a. Autonomy.* A primary function of the local police force shall be to guarantee every citizen the right to live a life free of unnecessary state interference in their decision-making.
>
> *b. Safety.* A primary function of the local police force shall be to guarantee every citizen the right to lead a life free of fear for his or her physical safety.
>
> *c. Justice.* The value by which competing claims for individual autonomy and community safety shall be mediated is that of justice. In its most basic sense, justice can be defined as "fairness" to all citizens in the application of the law.

To be sure that the implications of these values were clear, six operational principles were specified that would guide the consultant's involvement in the formation of police policy:

> 1. *Community input.* The citizens of this community should have maximum input at every stage of the policing process.
>
> 2. *Openness.* Police policies and procedures should be open to public review. Secretiveness is to be avoided wherever possible.
>
> 3. *Least forceful alternative.* When several courses of police action are available, the least forceful alternative consistent with community safety shall be chosen.
>
> 4. *Legal rights.* Whatever action is taken, the maximum protection of the individual's legal and psychological rights shall be afforded.
>
> 5. *Diversity.* The local police force shall show a high degree of respect to cultural and subcultural diversity within the community.
>
> 6. *Experimental social innovation.* The explicit philosophy of the department shall be one of responsible experimentation with ways to maximize the values of autonomy, safety, and justice. Policies are made to be changed by empirical data on their effectiveness.

Subsequently the consultant was asked by the Police Chief for advice on procedures for police selection and promotion in the agency (cf. McDonough & Monahan, 1975), and many proposed departmental policies were forwarded to him for input before being acted upon.

We are suggesting that value discussions need to have a higher priority in training programs for helping professionals. One way of beginning such discussions is to raise ethical issues in books such as this. Thus, throughout this text, we will emphasize value choice points that occur as different strategies of community intervention are considered.

In most general terms, our own (ever changing) values lie in the direction of a more equitable, just, and fair society. We believe that this will require substantial change in the American social and political structure, so that every citizen is guaranteed the right to a living wage, to good health care (including mental health care), and educational opportunities. We also believe that such change can be wrought through a democratic framework. Our preference is for the reform of society and not its revolutionary overthrow.

Our only hesitancy about putting personal values in print is an awareness of how transitory value commitments can sometimes be. Events of the day have a way of making value statements appear outdated. What may be considered appropriate ethical behavior in one generation may appear naïve in the next. In the spring of 1976 (when this material was written) the United States had just passed through a crisis of confidence in government. A president had been forced out of office who sanctioned spying on an opposition political party, secretly tape-recorded conversations between himself and all visitors to his office, and repeatedly lied about these activities to the American public. Partly in reaction to these events, pessimism about government intervention and concerns about officially sponsored secrecy and spying have increased. The legacy of Watergate has included increased concern for the protection of individual rights and calls for a retrenchment in government-sponsored intervention in the lives of private citizens. These events as well as psychological and military withdrawal from an unpopular foreign intervention in Vietnam are the backdrop for our comments about values. The extent to which they influence our values—or those of our readers—is difficult to say, and probably can only be accurately judged from the perspective of history.

The events of the day also affected the community-oriented psychologists of the 1960s. They were not just searching for better methods of psychological service delivery. They were aware of the burning, unresolved social issues that were prominent at the time and were dismayed by psychology's apparent impotence in addressing these problems. The plight of the poor, urban violence, and racism all pointed directly to major inequities in the fabric of society. These problems could not be overlooked and at the time seemed remediable only through direct social action and major institutional change. Social action was justified on the basis of moral rightness. Whether the changes advocated were acceptable to the American public or whether social action was always a feasible alternative was too often deemed unworthy of discussion.

Today, we are still faced with the legacy of society's unfinished business. The social issues that were discussed so eloquently in the 1960s are still with us in full intensity. The complex, multidimensional problems of the poor are no less a cause for concern now than they were a decade ago when we declared a national "War on Poverty." That our beginning efforts to reduce the adverse effects of poverty produced only small successes should not blunt our interest in the continued importance of the problems. We must overcome a national tendency to think that solutions are best achieved by "throwing money" at a problem. Unfortunately, too many of us are unwilling to work on complex social problems that are not amenable to quick solutions. Interest lags, giving the appearance of either unsolvability or of diminished need for concern. In actuality, the problems remain at full strength, perhaps capable of solution if we would only approach our task more systematically and with greater sustained commitment.

Campbell (1971) has described an ideal stance that society should take in working toward solutions of its major social problems. His "experimenting society" captures a value commitment to social innovation and its evaluation that we wholeheartedly endorse.

> The experimenting society will be one which will vigorously try out proposed solutions to recurrent problems, which will make hard-headed and multi-dimensional evaluations of the outcomes, and which will move on to try other alternatives when evaluation shows one reform to have been ineffective or harmful. (Campbell, 1971, p. 1)

The experimenting society is committed to properly evaluated action research as a way of solving pressing social problems. It should be one in which there is public access to the records on which social decisions are made. Recounts, audits, reanalyses, and reinterpretation of results all should be possible. Citizens, not part of the government bureaucracy, should have the means to communicate their disagreements with official analyses and to propose alternative experiments. Within limits determined by the common good, the experimenting society should be voluntaristic, providing for and en-

couraging citizen participation, but not mandating participation by
those who freely choose to remain uninvolved.

The above points reflect our own values with extraordinary accuracy. We would like to see a continued thrust toward properly evaluated social innovation. Empirical data on the effects of social policies
should be important for citizens as well as government decision makers. An individual's political persuasion—whether "conservative" or
"liberal"—should not determine the need for or willingness to use verified data. On the other hand, *unevaluated* demonstration projects
probably have little *long-term* useful purpose, being essentially political responses to public pressure to "get something done."

There is one area in which we do disagree somewhat with
Campbell's recommendations. Campbell would relegate the social
scientist to a passive role in helping society decide upon its social
priorities. He feels that the role of the social scientist is not to say what
should be done, but rather to say "what has been done" (Campbell,
1971, p. 8), i.e., to document how effectively social goals have been
realized. Campbell is pointing to a danger that when government officials ask scientists what they should do, scientists may answer "with
an assurance quite out of keeping with the scientific status of their
fields" (Campbell, 1971, p. 9). We agree that there is a danger of
"overadvocacy," in that the political system can pressure well-
meaning and otherwise careful scientists to exaggerate claims for their
proposals in order to get them adopted. The antidote for this problem
need not be to refrain from advice, but to present one's ideas tenta-
tively as hypotheses to be tested. While social scientists may not have
definitive answers, they often do have partial knowledge that can increase the value of their "hunches." The danger to be avoided is the
exaggeration of claims of effectiveness in order to get proposals
adopted by slow-moving bureaucracies.

We are not advocating a society ruled by a "social science priest-
hood." In a democracy, any proposal for social action should be debated freely and ultimately decided by the people through their
elected representatives. We are advocating that these decisions should
be based on evidence. We recognize that social policy decisions cannot
be made on the basis of evidence alone, in that they often reflect an
accommodation to competing political pressures. Such political responsiveness is necessary in a pluralistic democracy. However, we
feel that it is socially irresponsible to suggest that such decisions
should be made without evidence. It is our obligation to develop the

best possible scientific evidence and to actively publicize our results—with full knowledge that our data will not always be used when final decisions are made.

In later sections of this book we will discuss alternative strategies of community intervention and will present some rational bases for making choices between them. Again, personal values will undoubtedly affect the way in which we discuss intervention strategies. By now it should be clear that we are distressed by the social inequities that continue to plague our society and believe that the social sciences should be more active in the search for solutions to these problems. Thus, we would count ourselves among those who are advocates for significant social change. On the other hand, we do not see ourselves as revolutionaries. We think that society can and should be improved, but that it need not be torn down to accomplish this goal. We wish social change were a simple process. Unfortunately, it is not—and our righteous indignation will not make it so. A greater equity in social life can be achieved, but there is no *one* "royal road" that will automatically lead to its accomplishment.

Plan of the book

Chapter 1 began with a historical review of the post–World War II surge of interest in community approaches to psychological problems. The important events leading to a search for a new point of view were: overtaxed treatment facilities and the inability to finance the manpower needed for expanded treatment services; a basic questioning of the social utility of traditional psychotherapy; and a renewed interest in understanding the contribution of environmental variables to the etiology, treatment, and prevention of psychological disability. The reawakened concern for the environment reflected changes in the climate of the times that produced shifts in the focus of popular interest.

Neither clinical nor community psychology are static fields. In responding to similar pressures, both have been changing in orientation. Current developments within both fields are marked by an interest in strengthening coping skills and capabilities. This new competency orientation need not be restricted to individual work and can be used in planning multilevel intervention at individual, organizational, or community levels. Thinking about behavior in multilevel terms is one characteristic of the community approach. A second is the emphasis on seeking out opportunities for early intervention to enhance psychological well-being. We have finally recognized that there are more acceptable psychological alternatives than waiting for disability to become manifest before planning treatment or remediation.

To some extent, the goals of all forms of psychological intervention reflect value choices; hence, there is a general need for more explicit value discussions. This need is more acute for community intervention programs since so many citizens are potentially affected. For example, one cannot seriously discuss problems of poverty, delinquency, or drug use without becoming involved in value-tinged debate. There is no need to be apologetic about the need to consider values; the danger is in the opposite extreme, namely, embarking on programs of community intervention with values hidden by the "objective" language of science. As we shall note throughout the text, the values that surface in the behavioral sciences do not represent just the objective pursuit of knowledge. The problems that become emphasized as worthy of most scientific attention are in part determined by ideas dominant in the cultural milieu.

Chapter 2 continues the discussion of the effects of the climate of the times on ideas about etiology and treatment. The historical swings in mental health ideology are illustrated by a detailed discussion of the changing views of mental retardation. What was true of retardation is also true for other developments within the mental health professions. The rise and fall of "moral therapy", the growth and recent abandonment of custodial mental hospitals, the changes in focus of child guidance clinics and special education classes—are all examples of innovations in mental health practice that were influenced by the changing climate of the times. Swings in the social and political climate will always occur; however one way of reducing their impact on psychological theory and practice is through empirical research. While it may be difficult to resist appealing and fashionable ideas, the fate of social innovations should depend on more than faddishness.

Ways to overcome faddish swings in the social climate are the concern of Chapter 3. Research and program evaluation are seen as necessary in establishing lasting social innovations as well as in building a scientific discipline of social change. Research and program evaluation are seen as differing not in methodology or sophistication but only in the intent of the empirical investigator. Needs and priorities in community research are outlined, with emphases upon investigations at levels higher than the individual, and upon studies aimed at social environments and their effects on behavior. Several research methodologies particularly appropriate for organizational and community research are detailed, including management information systems, cost-effectiveness analysis, social indicators, and epidemiology. Whatever methodologies are employed, the purpose is the same: to empirically narrow the range of hypotheses capable of explaining community phenomena.

Chapters 4 and 5 constitute Part Two, which we have labeled "Basic Concepts." Together they represent two of the themes that are the hallmarks of the community approach: early intervention and a concern for the effects of environmental variables on behavior. How much is known in each of these areas? Are there developing substantive areas of knowledge that can form the basis of a new intervention technology? These are the questions that motivated our chapter reviews.

In Chapter 4 we point out that, at the present time, the mental health professions do not have a prevention language or technology. Historically, as these fields developed their primary mandate was treatment. Prevention originated in public health medicine where it referred to efforts oriented toward reducing the incidence of illness in populations. For example, swamp drainage virtually eliminated malaria in many countries. Similarly, the Salk and Sabin vaccines have prevented the occurrence of the polio epidemics that were so prevalent until a few decades ago. However, the analogy to the prevention of infectious diseases implied by the public health model can be misleading when applied to psychological disorder. Infectious diseases tend to be associated with clear-cut unitary causes. Such is not the case for psychological disorder in which etiology is either unknown or associated with multiplicative predisposing factors. Genetic, constitutional, familial, and environmental factors have all been described as contributing to eventual disability. Thus, while prevention programs might be oriented toward only one factor, no one factor by itself holds the key to complete elimination of disorder. Prevention activities should probably involve multipronged efforts aimed at reducing excessive stress, while at the same time strengthening the capacity of populations to deal with the negative psychological concomitants of stress that become apparent.

There are several variables associated with the ability to resist the deleterious effects of stress. One often neglected variable in stress-resistance research is the availability of supportive social structures. While the evidence is sparse there is reason to believe that social support from others can moderate the impact of stressful life events. This suggests an alternative helping strategy. If most people do not go to formal psychological helpers in time of need, the effects of unavoidable stress can be moderated by the encouragement of natural helping networks in communities.

In writing the prevention chapter, a purposeful decision was made to forego a comprehensive review of the prevention literature. Such reviews can be found elsewhere. In addition, because of conceptual and/or methodological inadequacies, many prevention studies leave the reader with a disappointing sense of ambiguity and incompleteness. We have chosen a different strategy to present our thoughts about prevention. We review only selected studies—those most suited to a discussion of important conceptual issues in prevention, or those that are illustrative of methodological points whose correction would aid in realizing more definitive tests of intervention hypotheses. We have chosen this approach because, despite the problems, we would like to see prevention activity encouraged. Preventing disorder and enhancing psychological well-being are relatively new concepts for psychology. If carried to fruition, they have the potential for stimulating a revolution in psychological thought and practice.

The effect of the environment upon human behavior is the subject of Chapter 5. Since most professionals have come to community work from clinical practice or research, there is a noticeable tendency to use analogies drawn from the study of individuals in order to understand community phenomena. In this chapter, an alternative to the use of individual analogies is presented in the concept of ecology.

The roots of the term *ecology* lie in the biological sciences. Sociologists borrowed ecological concepts from biology to explain the development of cities and founded the study of human or social ecology. Later, psychologists such as James Kelly refined the basic principles of ecology and applied them to a range of community phenomena. The central tenet of ecology, in all fields, is that of interdependence, that "everything is connected to everything else." Changes in one social system, therefore, are bound to effect changes in others. While this realization of the complexity of relationships between community systems suggests that intervention efforts be mounted cautiously, lest unforeseen negative consequences occur far from the target problem, it should not lead to paralysis. It is impossible to know if a problem can be solved without trying.

The field of environmental psychology complements that of social ecology. It derives from a renewed appreciation of Kurt Lewin's dictum that behavior is a function of both personal and environmental variables. A great deal of research suggests that noise, density, and certain architectural arrangements, for example, may have adverse effects upon the behavior of many people. All of these factors are subject to remedial intervention. More to the point, community workers could become actively involved in the planning of future physical projects so that they might be designed with a view toward preventing sources of environmental stress. In this regard, recent research has focused on the effect that changes in the society's economy have on social indicators such as commitment rates. When a social stressor occurs that cannot be prevented by mental health professionals (such as a negative change in the economy), the role of the professional lies in mitigating its adverse effects. Several methods of achieving that goal are presented.

Finally, Chapter 5 considers the psychosocial environment and the methodologies that are being developed to measure the social climate of community institutions. The potential for employing "environmental feedback" as a stimulus for community change is just beginning to be tapped. All three areas considered in this chapter—the physical, economic, and psychosocial environments—provide evidence that the ecological approach to community problem-solving may provide community work with the systems-level analogies it so urgently needs.

Part Three of this book deals with psychological approaches to community change. Three differing approaches are compared: the enhancement of change within social institutions through *consultation* with institutional personnel (Chapter 6); replacing unresponsive systems with *alternative* structures and personnel (Chapter 7); and generating political pressure through *organized* citizen constituencies (Chapter 8). The advantages and limitations of each approach are discussed, and the community and institutional factors favoring each are outlined (Chapter 9).

In Chapter 6, three consultation perspectives are described and compared: mental health consultation, behavioral consultation, and organization development. While there are a number of important differences between each of these perspectives, there are basic assumptions about community change that all have in common. As a set of "within system" strategies, consultation aims at institutional renewal and self-improvement. The emphasis is on helping institutional workers improve their job functioning, which in turn is expected to result in more effective and sophisticated service delivery. Consultants are supportive of attempts at self-improvement by providing workers with increased psychological knowledge and improved interpersonal and behavioral skills; and by helping workers analyze personal, institutional, and community constraints that may impinge upon job performance. Understanding impediments to job functioning is the first step in learning how to cope with them more effectively. Ultimately, an important goal of consultation is to insure that the agency's programs are being performed in a manner that articulates best with current knowledge of psychological development.

One difficulty facing consultants is deciding how to deal with personal problems of agency workers (consultees) that may interfere with their work. The issue is whether to confront these problems directly. Mental health personnel are quite accustomed to dealing with personal problems in psychotherapy, but consultation is not psychotherapy and difficulties arise if the two are confused. The problem is made more difficult when the consultee does not seek referral for personal help because he or she is unaware of the intrusion of unresolved personal problems into the work setting. The ethical issues surrounding this consultation problem are discussed and one technique, "theme-interference reduction," is described in some detail. We have included material on theme interference because of its prominence in the field, although we recognize that opportunities for classical theme-interference reduction are extremely rare. In our discussion, the technique is separated from its psychoanalytic rationale and is reconceptualized as an attitude change strategy, of some utility for dealing with overgeneralized stereotyped attitudes.

A major difficulty for all consultation perspectives involves situations in which the needs of some groups are being neglected, but the majority community refuses to recognize that problems exist. Without some degree of community arousal or "strain," there is little motivation for community change. In this situation, care-givers, recognizing community sentiments, also will be unresponsive to the consultant's efforts to focus on generally ignored problems. When social problems are generally ignored or when there is active resistance to their examination, other strategies are needed.

Bypassing existing social institutions by developing community alternatives is one such strategy. Proponents of the alternatives approach believe that institutional self-renewal (change from within) rarely occurs voluntarily. Institutions are too bureaucratic, self-serving and "resistant." Furthermore, since many communities are marked by great diversity among their citizens, it is unrealistic to expect a single institution (e.g., a single high school) to serve a plurality of community needs. Alternatives should provide the best vehicle for encouraging an optimal fit between persons and environments. Groups with unmet needs can fashion more suitable institutional arrangements. With several parallel structures available, citizen groups can choose those deemed most appropriate.

Of course, a major problem for alternatives is potential cost. Duplicating services can be inefficient and wasteful. However, note that there is active debate on this point. Advocates of alternatives point out that it is more costly to provide only one form of service (e.g., a structured academic curriculum) that would then also require remedial services for those unable to meet the program's demands, as well as policing services to control those who might rebel against the imposition of a program that they find unsuitable.

Cost must be distinguished from access to resources, since alternatives do require the latter. Access to resources usually involves some form of input into the resource allocation process. When school boards decide about program priorities and what programs will be funded, they respond in part to input from various community groups. Disorganized groups, those without an effective political voice, are likely to be unrepresented in the resource allocation process. Without input into allocation decisions, and without resources of their own, the groups with the greatest problems (e.g., disorganized poverty groups) are least likely to be represented in the development of community alternatives.

For groups without power, in communities unaware of or insensitive to their needs, the best strategy for social change is community organization. Described as an "outside the system" strategy because of its nonacceptance of status quo institutional arrangements, community organization has as its primary goal increased political power for disenfranchised groups. Two forms of community organization can be distinguished: community development strategies based upon conciliation and cooperation and social action strategies based upon power and conflict assumptions. Despite differences in tactics, advocates of both views strive for similar goals—increased citizen participation and the facilitation of community change through unified social and political action.

Both forms of community organization are hampered by factors that make it difficult to form a viable unified political constituency. Thus, community organization is difficult under conditions of extreme geographic dispersion (e.g., as in some rural areas), few shared values and traditions (as might occur among different ethnic groups), or an inadequate number of citizens for the development of an effective political voice.

Thus, each of the major intervention strategies discussed in this book requires different community conditions for optimal effectiveness. Consultation is most appropriate when there is general community concern and awareness of unmet needs; the construction of alternatives becomes a useful social change strategy when resources or access to resources are available to disenfranchised groups; and community organization can be effective when there is a sufficient base of political power.

One implication of differential effectiveness is that intervention should be preceded by careful community assessment. For the community psychologist, assessment should occur first at community and institutional levels before turning to an assessment of individuals within settings. Chapter 9 provides a framework that can guide assessment at different levels of functioning. While assessment at community levels is made more difficult by the scarcity of formal techniques, much can be learned by the judicious use of data from social indicators, surveys, and participant observation.

Finally, those adopting a community orientation should recognize the challenge inherent in working in uncharted areas. The incompleteness of knowledge about community functioning can produce threats to valid practice. Still, progress will not occur by retreat to safer, more familiar endeavors. What is needed is a willingness to grapple with unresolved problems through exploratory practice, research, and active reflection upon what has been accomplished.

References

Alinsky, S. D. *Reveille for radicals.* Chicago: University of Chicago Press, 1946.

Alinsky, S. D. *Rules for radicals.* New York: Vintage Books, Random House, 1971.

Bennett, C. C. Community psychology: Impressions of the Boston conference on the education of psychologists for community mental health. *American Psychologist,* 1965, *20,* 832–835.

Bennett, C. C., Anderson, L. S., Cooper, S., Hassol, L., Klein, D. C., & Rosenblum, G. *Community psychology: A report of the Boston conference on the education of psychologists for community mental health.* Boston: Boston University, 1966.

Bergin, A. E.   The evaluation of therapeutic outcomes. In A. E. Bergin and S. L. Garfield (Eds.), *Handbook of psychotherapy and behavior change.* New York: John Wiley & Sons, 1971, pp. 217–270.

Bloom, B. L.   The "medical model," miasma theory, and community mental health. *Community Mental Health Journal,* 1965, *1,* 333–338.

Campbell, D. T.   Methods for the experimenting society. Paper presented at the meetings of the Eastern Psychological Association, Washington, D. C., April, 1971.

Caplan, Gerald. *Principles of preventive psychiatry.* New York: Basic Books, 1964. (C) 1964 by Basic Books, Inc., Publishers, New York.

Caplan, N., & Nelson, S. D. On being useful: the nature and consequences of psychological research on social problems. *American Psychologist,* 1973, *28,* 199–211. Copyright 1973 by the American Psychological Association. Reprinted by permission.

Cook, P. E. (Ed.) *Community psychology and community mental health: Introductory readings.* San Francisco: Holden-Day, 1970.

Cowen, E. L.   Social and community intervention. *Annual Review of Psychology,* 1973, *24,* 423–472.

De Charms, R., Levy, J., & Wertheimer, M.   A note on attempted evaluations of psychotherapy. *Journal of Clinical Psychology,* 1954, *10,* 233–235.

Eysenck, H. J.   The effects of psychotherapy: An evaluation. *Journal of Consulting Psychology,* 1952, *16,* 319–324.

Eysenck, H. J.   The effects of psychotherapy. In H. J. Eysenck (Ed.), *Handbook of abnormal psychology.* New York: Basic Books, 1961, pp. 697–725.

Fixsen, D., Phillips, E., & Wolf, M.   Achievement Place: Experiments in self-government with pre-delinquents. *Journal of Applied Behavior Analysis,* 1973, *6,* 31–47.

Joint Commission on Mental Illness and Health. *Action for mental health.* New York: John Wiley & Sons, 1961.

Kelly, G. A.   Man's construction of his alternatives. In G. Lindzey (Ed.), *Assessment of human motives.* New York: Rinehart, 1958, pp. 33–64.

Kuhn, T. S.   *The structure of scientific revolutions.* Chicago: University of Chicago Press, 1962.

Levine, M., & Levine, A.   *A social history of helping services: Clinic, court, school and community.* New York: Appleton-Century-Crofts, 1970.

Luborsky, L.   A note on Eysenck's article "The effects of psychotherapy: An evaluation." *British Journal of Psychology,* 1954, *45,* 129–131.

McDonough, L., & Monahan, J.   The quality control of community care takers. *Community Mental Health Journal,* 1975, *11,* 33–43.

Price, R. H.   *Abnormal psychology: Perspectives in conflict.* New York: Holt, Rinehart & Winston, 1972.

Rappaport, J.   From Noah to Babel: Relationships between conceptions, values, analysis levels and social intervention strategies. Paper presented at a symposium: *Report of the Austin Conference: The Future of Community Psychology.* American Psychological Association, Chicago, September, 1975.

Rappaport, J., & Chinsky, J. M.   Models for delivery of service from a historical and conceptual perspective. *Professional Psychology,* 1974, 5, 42–50.

Rosenzweig, S.   A transvaluation of psychotherapy: A reply to Hans Eysenck. *Journal of Abnormal and Social Psychology,* 1954, 49, 298–304.

Shoben, E. J.   Toward a concept of the normal personality. *American Psychologist,* 1957, 12, 183–189.

Smith, M. B.   Research strategies toward a conception of positive mental health. *American Psychologist,* 1959, 14, 673–681.

Wallace, J.   An abilities conception of personality: Some implications for personality measurement. *American Psychologist,* 1966, 21, 132–138.

2

HISTORICAL TRENDS IN
MENTAL HEALTH IDEOLOGY

Emphasizing attitudes toward the retarded

WITH ROBERT M. SCHWARTZ

The value of a historical perspective: Understanding previous swings in beliefs and attitudes

UNLESS ONE ADOPTS a historical perspective, it is difficult to understand that ideology in mental health is very much influenced by social and political events. A hallmark of current community orientations is a concern for environment and its effects on behavior. Yet, there were two previous periods of concern for the effects of the environment by American mental health practitioners. The first occurred during the first part of the 19th century, with the other appearing from about 1890 to 1914. In each period, theories about psychological dysfunction and its proper remediation emphasized environmental components. In each period the theories were abandoned only to reappear again during a later era.

In their historical survey of the helping professions between 1890 and 1930, Levine and Levine (1970) develop the thesis that mental health theories emphasizing environmental determinants flourish during periods of political or social reform, while intra-psychic theories that assume the "goodness" of the environment are prominent during periods of political and social conservatism. Given the documentation of the ebb and flow of mental health ideology (Bockoven, 1963; R. Caplan, 1969; Levine & Levine, 1970), one can question

39

whether the ideas about intervention and community life reviewed in this book will be subject to the same fate—abandoned not because they are disproved but because they are no longer considered appropriate or fashionable. An example may highlight the nature of the problem.

The rise and fall of "moral treatment"

During the first half of the 19th century, "moral treatment" was the dominant influence in American psychiatry and there was great optimism concerning what could be done by changing the milieu of the mental patient. The moral therapists had great success in returning patients to productive functioning in the community. Bockoven (1963) presents data indicating that during the decade of 1833–42, the records of Worcester State Hospital claim that 78 percent of hospital patients were discharged as either "recovered" or "improved." This is a level of success that our modern-day mental hospitals would be pleased to emulate.

While the success rates claimed for treatment were quite high, the theories of psychopathology and the rationale developed for the procedures of the moral therapists were far from accurate. The insane were thought to be suffering from a physical disease that caused brain malfunction. However, the brain was thought to be extremely malleable, easily influenced by environmental stimuli. Hence, changes in environmental stimuli could affect brain functioning directly. The theory was later discredited, but in the process the therapeutic successes of the moral therapists were also discounted and their procedures fell into disuse. It would be tempting to say that the therapy did not survive because it was tied too closely to a discredited view of psychopathology. However, a much more likely reason for the decline of moral treatment was because conditions in the country were no longer favorable to its continued practice.

Moral treatment depended upon an empathic and close working relationship between doctor and patient. This type of rapport was successfully achieved during the first half of the 19th century, when the population of the United States was relatively small and homogeneous, sharing commonalities of culture and background. During the second half of the 19th century, as the United States moved from an agrarian to an industrial economy, and sharp increases in immigration led to a growth in population, swelling the cities and at the same time engulfing meager social and helping services, the psychological climate in the country changed markedly. The newcomers, speaking strange dialects, with different cultural and religious practices, often economically destitute, did not enjoy the sympathy of the native population. The economic and social stresses associated with their arrival, left them little understood or appreciated by the majority of the native populace. Even the helping professionals could not accept them. As was true of most other citizens, the psychiatrists of that period viewed foreigners as constitutionally inferior, lacking in moral fiber and unwilling to attempt self-improvement. In such a climate, moral treatment was judged a failure, but in truth, it was probably no longer appropriately attempted.

Such was the fate of moral therapy, but what about other ideas concerning psychological functioning? Have they been subjected to the same vicissitudes of social climate and changes in community life? Excellent historical reviews are available that document the extent to which psychological ideology has changed with the social climate, particularly ideas concerning the treatment of children (Levine & Levine, 1970) and changing views of mental disorder (Bockoven, 1963; R. Caplan, 1969). Each of these reviewers comes to the same conclusion—ideas about mental functioning do not thrive independent of social contexts. Since these reviews are readily available, we have gone to another less well-known area, mental retardation, for our historical documentation and have found a similar ebb and flow of psychological ideas. Some might consider retardation not particularly germane to community work. We think that such provincialism is a mistake. The historical evidence we have collected represents a fascinating story with some sobering lessons. As was true of moral therapy, the history of societal treatment of the retarded changed independent of its success or failure. What should become clear by the end of this chapter is that if we do not learn from the past we are likely to repeat mistakes. We hope that mental health professionals study more history, not less. It may be disquieting to realize that what seems new and exciting now, may have been practiced in the past only to be abandoned. The history of mental health ideology is marked by unbridled optimism, faddish swings in belief, and untested practices. Still, if we are to learn from the past we cannot turn our backs on prior mistakes, but rather we must use our knowledge of history to develop more realistic and sophisticated ideas and programs. The review that follows was written especially for this volume by Robert M. Schwartz.

Changes in the treatment and care of the retarded: Current interest in "normalization"

In recent years large institutions have been widely attacked fo creating debilitating rather than therapeutic environments. A numbe of exposés have revealed the inhuman and appalling conditions i several state institutions for the mentally retarded. From these an other developments a new consciousness about the care and treatmen of the mentally retarded has emerged, leading to a new and popula ideology and to proposals for residential alternatives to the curren form of care for the retarded. This ideology, termed "normalization," was fully articulated in the late 1960s in Scandinavia and propose that mentally retarded individuals be allowed to behave in a manne that is as close to normal as possible, given the limitations of the indi vidual. There are implications of this ideology for communit psychology, since a "normal" existence generally presupposes som kind of family life in a setting situated in or near a center of population While the advocates of this principle of "normalization" appear to b taking a new look at mental retardation, it turns out that neither th indictment of large institutions nor the ideology of normalization wit its residential implications are completely new phenomena.

Some of the recent criticisms have focused on the nontherapeuti aspects of the large state institutions, which often tend to be custodia rather than treatment- or rehabilitation-oriented. The physical an emotional atmosphere is characterized by dehumanization and lack o individual care. Overcrowding further compounds the problem, mak ing personal treatment extremely difficult. The residents are segre gated from the community, with the staff taking refuge in administra tive positions, leaving untrained and often low quality attendants t care for the patients. The general situation makes it difficult t retain high quality staff who might introduce positive reforms, factor that tends to perpetuate the status quo (Kugel, 1969; Butter field, 1969).

A more emotionally charged indictment of institutions for the re tarded comes from Blatt (1966; 1969), who took a tour of the "bac wards" of an institution that was not identified by name. Blatt was ac companied by photographer Fred Kaplan, who carried a conceale camera on his belt. They returned with a harrowing story and pictoria essay—of sickening odors, abysmal conditions, and human decay Heavy locks barricaded the doors, beds were arranged so that it wa impossible to cross the room without walking over them, and toilets were torn out or stopped up. Offenses such as breaking windows, or directing abusive language at an attendant were punished by solitary confinement for days in a 7-foot by 7-foot cell containing nothing except perhaps a blanket. The offender was forced to lie in feces since there was no toilet. At the same time, a child who had bitten off another retarded child's ear was only mildly reprimanded.

While this exposé may appear to exaggerate the abysmal side, since Blatt could no doubt have found more humane institutions, the President's Committee on Mental Retardation in its "MR 67 Report" confirmed that the situation was indeed grave. It concluded that many of our institutions are "plainly a disgrace to the nation and to the states who operate them" (Dunn, 1969, p. 214). The National Association for Retarded Children declared that "despite much talk and some improvements in recent years, the quality of care of the mentally retarded in state residential institutions remains a national disgrace" (Dunn, 1969, p. 214).

To overcome the problems of institutional care, the principle of normalization advocates the development of a comprehensive community alternative. The principle was first systematically elaborated in 1969 by Bengt Nirje, who was then the director of the Swedish Association for Retarded Children. He described it as follows: "making available to the mentally retarded patterns and conditions of everyday life which are as close as possible to the norms and patterns of the mainstream of society" (Wolfensberger, 1972, p. 27). To accomplish this goal, the person in charge of the retarded individual would elicit and maintain behaviors and appearances that are as normative as environmental circumstances and individual limitations permit. This has implications for three levels of action. First, at the person level, the attempt would be to elicit, shape, and maintain normative skills and habits in persons by means of direct physical and social interaction with them—for example, teaching a person not only to walk, but to walk with a normal gait; cutting a child's hair to minimize the facial characteristics associated with Down's Syndrome; or introducing someone as Mr. Smith, not as Joe Smith or, more condescendingly, as Joe. There are similar and more far reaching implications for action at the social and institutional levels, that involve almost every aspect of life, from the family and peer group to the laws and mores of the entire society. The ultimate goal is to redefine the role of the retarded so that he or she can function *in the community* in a way resembling a normal life-style as far as personal limitations will permit, rather than labeling the individual as "sick" and condoning removal from the mainstream of human activity by isolation at home or in a remote institution.

Previous interest in community alternatives for the retarded

One might expect that it was simply the lack of awareness of the problem until recent times that deterred us from a speedy solution. Yet if we listen to some of the recorded voices of the past, we find that the miserable condition of patients in institutions was recognized, and the negative effects of institutional care compared to the more normative effects of family life were clearly articulated. Blatt (1969) cites one reaction to an institution of 1813: "We lock these unfortunate creatures in lunatic cells, as if they were criminals. We keep them in chains in forlorn jails . . . where no sympathetic human being can ever bestow them a friendly glance, and we let them rot in their own filth" (p. 42). An anonymous writer in 1795, also quoted by Blatt (1969), sums up the ultimate effects of these institutions: "Under such terrifying conditions, it would be easier for the most rational person to become insane than for a madman to regain his sanity" (p. 42). The conditions were apparently known well enough to be described in the literature of the times, and the deleterious effect of such conditions were no secret.

In addition to humanitarian concern about the deplorable conditions in these institutions, the potential harm of even well-run large institutions was also noted. At the inauguration of a new institution for the blind in the mid 19th century, Samuel Howe, a prominent figure in the field of mental retardation, condemned this large institution in principle before it even opened its doors and had a chance to deteriorate. Howe's (1886) address will be quoted at some length because of its interesting similarity to some of the current statements advocating normalization and residential alternatives:

> All great establishments in the nature of boarding schools, where the sexes must be separated; where there must be boarding in common, and sleeping in congregate dormitories; where there must be routine, and formality, and restraint, and repression of individuality; where the charms and refining influences of the true family relation cannot be had, —all such institutions are unnatural, undesirable, and very liable to abuse. We should have as few of them as is possible, and those few should be kept as small as possible.
> The human family is the unit of society. . . . Artificial families have

been tried and found wanting. . . . Wherever there must be separation of the sexes, isolation from society, absence of true family relation, and monotony of life, there must come some evils of various kinds, which no watchfulness can prevent, and physician can cure. . . .

Such persons spring up sporadically in the community, and they should be kept diffused among sound and normal persons. Separation, and not congregation, should be the law of their treatment; for out of their infirmity or abnormality there necessarily grow some abnormal and undesirable effects, and unless these be countered by education, they disturb the harmonious developments of character. *These effects are best counteracted by bringing up the child among ordinary children, and subjecting him to ordinary social and family influences;* but, on the contrary, they are intensified by constant and close association with children who are marked by the same infirmity or peculiarity.

They [the institutions] are wrong in receiving all pupils as boarders, when they should receive those only who cannot board at home, or in private families.

Instead, then, of copying the existing institution, I think, that in organizing a new one something like the following rough plan should be adopted:—If the field were all clear, and no buildings provided, there should be built only a building for school rooms, recitation rooms, music rooms, and work shops; and these should be *in or near the center of a dense population.* For other purposes, ordinary houses would suffice." (Wolfensberger, 1969, p. 138–41, italics added)

In many respects the underlying concept of today's "principle of normalization" is contained in Howe's statement, which almost seems to be a concise summary of this "new" ideology. Howe's emphasis on the integration of the deviant, and on the importance of family and normal relations, his warnings about the inherent evils of large institutions, and his recommendations for small institutions with few buildings situated near population centers to serve only those who cannot be boarded at home, have modern overtones, which set Howe a hundred years ahead of his time.

Ideas do not exist in a vacuum: The importance of the social and political milieu

The fact that Howe was a hundred years ahead of his time implies that he was not heard by his contemporaries, or more specifically that his ideas, warnings, and suggestions were never translated into action. The recent indictment of institutions and the proposals for normalization and integration of the retarded into the community are testimony to the fact that this problem, long recognized and articulated, has not been resolved. We can learn from this brief glimpse into history that the recognition of a problem and the espousal of an ideology are not sufficient to result in the implementation of change or constructive action. As we shall see, there were many bold attempts to improve the condition of the mentally retarded through institutional development and community care, but these never fulfilled their ultimate goals. Clearly, there are forces of considerable importance that have allowed a social evil to exist through a century of incredible scientific progress.

Ideas, scientific or otherwise, do not exist in a vacuum. We must consider the larger social context in which such ideas are expounded and begin to appreciate the impact that this context can have on the degree to which ideas, suggestions, and ideologies are manifested in action. A given set of principles, regardless of inherent merit, cannot flourish unless the social, political, economic, and cultural climate of the times provides an atmosphere that will nurture those ideas. While nothing will guarantee that a given set of principles will be success-fully implemented and maintained in programs, there are a number of factors that can increase the probability of success. Advancements in the state of empirical knowledge in medicine and the social sciences provide the foundation that can anchor ideology to a factual base. But even empirically established scientific "truths" cannot, in and of themselves, insure implementation of ideas, because they are affected in crucial ways by a myriad of additional factors. The prevailing politi-cal and economic situation as well as the values embodied in current social philosophy will often prove to be a major determinant of the success or failure of a given ideology. In the current example, in order to achieve a normalization of services for the mentally retarded, it is necessary that today's advocates of this ideology examine the relevant aspects of the larger social context and understand the way in which these aspects will interact, either in a facilitating or, as is all too often the case, in an inhibiting manner.

A careful historical analysis of the relationship between the social context and the form of treatment and care for the mentally retarded can help us to achieve this understanding by revealing some of the factors that community workers will want to focus on today. What follows is an attempt to trace the development of treatment and care for the mentally retarded within a changing social context, with the hope that the lessons of history in this matter will be relevant to those today who are concerned with community change.

Attitudes toward the retarded throughout history

Ancient times to 1800

Despite a few sporadic passages in Greek and Roman literature, the Bible, Talmud, and the Koran, there is an extreme paucity of early references to the care of the mentally retarded. We know that the Spartans, in line with their social and political philosophy, used severe eugenic methods. Defective children were cast in the river or left to perish. Such practices were probably continued by the Greeks and, according to Cicero, by the Romans as well (Davies, 1930). Other early sources mention that "fools," kept as playthings of princes and the courts were recruited from persons with misshapen bodies or from the mentally retarded, thus assuming a role in society; but the majority of the mentally retarded did not fare so well. Martin Luther recommended that they be killed, because they were nothing but a "mass of flesh" with no soul, infested with the Devil (Kanner, 1967). The attitude of the layman as well as the educator before 1800 can be characterized by a quotation of Luther:

> Eight years ago, there was one at Dessau whom I, Martinus Luther, saw and grappled with. He was twelve years old, had the use of his eyes and all his senses, so that one might think that he was a normal child. But he did nothing but gorge himself as much as four peasants or threshers. He ate, defecated and drooled, and if anyone tackled him, he screamed. If things didn't go well, he wept. So I said to the Prince of Anhalt: If I were the prince, I should take this child to the Moldau River which flows near Dessau and drown him. But the Prince of Anhalt and the Prince of Saxony, who happened to be present, refused to follow my advice. Thereupon I said: Well, then the Christians shall order the Lord's Prayer to be said in church and pray that the dear Lord take the Devil away. (Kanner, 1967, p. 7)

The conception of the mentally retarded as fools or as possessed by the devil was hardly conducive to any form of treatment and care, and for this reason, before 1800, there is a notable lack of written sources that mention the mentally retarded.

The beginning of enlightened concern

Almost suddenly, in the beginning of the 19th century, interest in the retarded began to flourish, first in France and Switzerland then spreading throughout Europe and the United States. In 1799, a 12-year-old boy, Victor, was captured in the forest of Aveyron, France. Jean Itard, a physician who was working with the deaf, hoped to demonstrate that intellectual functions were not innate, but could be developed by special training (Robinson & Robinson, 1965). Although Itard failed in his ultimate goal to "civilize" Victor, he did succeed in teaching him to recognize objects, identify letters of the alphabet, comprehend the meaning of words, apply names to objects and parts of objects, make "relatively fine" sensory discriminations, and to prefer the social life of civilization to an isolated existence in the wild. Itard proved that even severely mentally retarded individuals could be improved to some extent by appropriate training (Kanner, 1967). This limited, but still astonishing success hallmarked a new attitude toward the mentally retarded that was to be carried on by Itard's pupil Séguin.

Although Itard himself was disillusioned with the prospects for curing the retarded, Séguin proceeded with enthusiasm to attempt to develop a cure using "physiological" methods, which resembled "moral treatment" (Bockoven, 1963). In practice the method was sensory motor training, but it fit the prevalent theories of the moral therapists. Séguin believed that "idiocy" was an isolation of the individual's mental life and personality due to a disease of the nervous system that removes the organs and faculties of the child from control of his own will, thus cutting him off from the moral world. By training the peripheral organs, the muscles and the senses, he believed the central nervous system would be awakened, bringing the individual into contact with the moral world and completely restoring him to health. This new philosophy of education and "medical" advance was to serve as the foundation for the efforts made by the early pioneers in the care of the mentally retarded.

Séguin's hopes and the new attitude of the 19th century toward the mentally retarded can be understood if we analyze the intellectual climate and social values of the previous century. Although the mentally retarded fared badly during the 18th century, that period is when the roots of the optimism about the educability of the retarded are to be found. The 18th century, often referred to as the Enlightenment, was characterized by intellectual activity in the cause of general education and culture that included an attempt at self-emancipation from prejudice, convention, and tradition. There was a radical criticism of everything that existed. Ideas that could not be proved by empirical, rational means were considered prejudice, superstition, or error. The conviction of the period was that all human problems could be solved through rational thinking. Reason became the main guideline of action that would allow man to achieve an ideal state of perfection. A new respect emerged for human dignity, freedom of thought, and the right of each citizen to take part in defining the society (Boesch, 1969). This was the intellectual climate that Itard and the early pioneers in the field of mental retardation had inherited. Just as the political writings of Voltaire, Diderot, and Rousseau prepared the intellectual ground upon which the French revolution could grow, so did the ideas of the Enlightenment prepare the way for the 19th-century interest in the development of the intellect of all citizens, including the mentally retarded.

Early optimism, mismanagement, and overpromise: Guggenbühl (1836–1850)

Another pioneer influenced by this intellectual heritage was Johann Jakob Guggenbühl, who established the first residence for the mentally retarded in Switzerland. A discussion with the mother of a "cretin" in a small town in Switzerland made Guggenbühl wonder if mental retardation could be ameliorated by consistent and intensive training. After studying the problem, he came to the conclusion that residential care in a suitable environment was a necessity. Since cretinism was abundant in the valleys but not known to occur at higher elevations, a site was chosen in the mountains near Interlaken. Before long the new institution was established with a large, centrally located assembly hall, residential cottages, playrooms, bathing facilities, as well as another building for training prospective attendants and teachers. Guggenbühl emphasized good mountain air, proper diet, baths, massage, and physical exercise. He tried to develop sensory perceptions, beginning with primitive excitations and progressing to increasingly more refined and complex stimuli. He hoped to awaken the "souls" of the patients through habituation to regular routine, memory exercises, and speech training. In an attempt to enliven the institution, Guggenbühl introduced two normally intelligent children of a servant, an idea not unlike the one embodied in the principle of normalization.

Guggenbühl's fame spread throughout the world, and Abendberg, as the institution was called, became the visiting place of philanthropists, physicians, and writers. Everyone praised the attempt to restore those long thought to be beyond help. The early enthusiasm is reflected in the reaction of William Twining in 1842 after returning from a visit to Adendberg:

> It is, in truth, a noble and exalted idea that, through human exertions, a mind may be awakened in what was apparently a senseless mass, and that even education may be extended to those who have been hitherto considered beyond the reach of instruction and incapable of intercourse with their fellow creatures. And what brighter and more glorious page can there be in the history of Switzerland if in a century hence it should be recorded that all Europe helped to exterminate cretinism? (Kanner, 1967, p. 26)

Notice the lofty and idealistic language used to describe this experiment, and imagine the hope that must have been engendered among those interested in the problem of cretinism and mental retardation! It was this over-optimism about the curability of cretinism, along with several other factors, that led to the rather sudden demise of this "noble and exalted idea."

Amidst the noisy encomiums there was also criticism, that was to grow increasingly louder as the initial excitement subsided. Some felt that Guggenbühl promised too much and others were irritated by his identification with the will of God. He spoke of Switzerland as the land chosen by God to shine forth as a light to other nations, and he was to be the prophet of this mission. Eventually people recognized that cretins were not "cured" by the prescribed methods and their frustration led to animosity against Guggenbühl (Kanner, 1967). The ultimate defeat came when an English minister came to visit some English patients at Abendberg. He visited in 1858, and found "the children in a most neglected condition and the whole institution (which the guide at first refused to show him) in a disgusting disorder" (Kanner, 1967, p. 28). When he asked to see the bedroom of one of the children the minister was told that "the key to the room had been misplaced." Rumors of mismanagement had been around for some time. These problems were compounded when a patient who had fallen from a precipice was not noticed missing until discovered sometime later by a peasant. Another child had died and by the time the carpenter was called to build a coffin, the body had decomposed. When the carpenter asked why he had not been summoned sooner, he was told by the personnel that they "hadn't gotten around to it." During this period Guggenbühl was on an extended trip and had been gone for approximately a year (Kanner, 1967).

A report made by the British Government in 1858 concluded the following:

1. Guggenbühl was guilty of deceiving people by calling his establishment Kretinen-Heilanstalt (treatment center for cretins), since at most one third of the inmates were cretins. The report went as far as to accuse Guggenbühl of "smuggling in" normal children to present as cured.
2. Normal children were kept from attending the public schools by housing them at Abendberg.
3. Not a single cretin had ever been cured.
4. There was no medical supervision. The director was away from four to six months each year and made no provisions for a substitute.
5. While at first well-trained instructors had been employed, Abendberg had been without a teacher for several years.
6. Heating facilities, nutrition, water supply, ventilation in dormitories, and clothing were inadequate.
7. The director never kept records of the munificent donations received.
8. No records were kept about the patients' progress.

The report characterized Guggenbühl as having begun the project out of pure and unselfish love, which soon became tainted by vanity and misconstrued martyrdom (Kanner, 1967). Guggenbühl retired in isolation, writing unpublished tirades until his death in 1863.

And so, the history of residential care for the mentally retarded was begun in this somewhat ignominious fashion. The indictment of Abendberg by the British Government sounds reminiscent of some of today's exposés. One might argue that Guggenbühl's lack of administrative and organizational skills led to the deterioration of the institution. Guggenbühl was a zealous advocate of the *idea* of the curability of cretins and retardates, but he lacked the sobriety of the practitioner who is aware of the problems encountered in actualizing such a lofty goal, and who knows how to overcome obstacles effectively. The investigation and report by the British Government clearly showed that the staff at Abendberg was out of hand, and administrative problems simply had been left unsolved. The need for careful supervision and scrutiny of staff, competent administrators, and an adequate number of trained attendants and educators as prerequisites for the success of any institution is exemplified by the unfortunate experience at Abendberg. Another important message that Guggenbühl's failure conveys is that there is danger in promising more than can be delivered. While such promises may have initially favorable results, bringing public acclaim and massive funding, it will almost inevitably lead to frustration, antipathy, and possible regressive moves when the promises cannot be met.

Despite the eventual demise of Abendberg, it was successful in stimulating the development of institutions designed to improve the intellectual functioning of mentally retarded individuals. Guggenbühl's efforts were largely responsible for helping the phenomenon of mental retardation become recognized as a social problem whose alleviation was a public responsibility. Institutions modeled in the image of Abendberg were started in Germany, Austria, Great Britain, the Netherlands, the Scandinavian countries, and the United States.

Realistic optimism: Howe (1850–1870)

The development of government-supported care for the mentally handicapped in the United States, at a time when social services for the general public were meager and privately endowed, is somewhat perplexing. Adams (1971) suggests that this can be explained in terms of the prevailing social and political philosophies in 19th-century America. Perhaps the major aspect of this philosophy is the Jeffersonian ideal that universal education is an important feature of a democracy. Somewhat less articulated, but still important, was the idea that in a young country dependent on flexibility and innovation, youth must be educated in order to maintain themselves and to contribute to national productivity. Also, it should be remembered that in America, freedom in personal and social affairs was influenced by the French Revolution and a War of Independence in which the country broke away from older, inequitable regimes. These humanistic values pervaded many aspects of human endeavor and thought: Jefferson's view of democracy, Rousseau's educational theories, and Philippe Pinel's idea of psychiatric care. Freedom was a recurring motif of the time, and it is not accidental that Howe, an innovator in the treatment of mental retardation, was involved in the Greek War of Independence and was an advocate of the emancipation of slaves; that Séguin came to America because of disillusionment with the politically regressive regime of Louis Philippe; and that in Massachusetts, where the care for the retarded was initiated, a humanitarian group led by Thoreau, Emerson, and Alcott was gaining in prominence (Adams, 1971). These values of education and freedom had a positive effect on the care of the mentally retarded. It was felt that they too should be educated like all other citizens and that through improved social and educational opportunities the retarded could be freed from the bondage of their mental deficiency.

In this positive social climate, Dr. Samuel Howe managed to convince his contemporaries that training and education of the mentally retarded was a public responsibility. In 1846, the Massachusetts House of Representatives established a committee "to consider the expediency of appointing commissioners to inquire into the condition of the idiots of the commonwealth, to ascertain their number and whether anything can be done for their relief" (Kanner, 1967, p. 41). Howe noted that Massachusetts provided the "blessing of education" to all her citizens, even the blind and deaf, but neglected the "poor idiots" who were doomed to a "dreadful fate."

Howe's efforts met with much criticism and mockery, but the Legislature was sufficiently impressed with his plan to allocate $2500 per year for three years for the teaching and training of ten retarded children. After a successful experimental period, an institution was incorporated in 1848 under the name of Massachusetts School for Idiotic and Feeble-Minded Youth. It was later moved to Waverly and is now known as the Walter E. Fernald State School. Howe can be considered the father of institutional care in the United States and the one who advocated most explicitly that acting upon the problem of mental retardation was a public responsibility (Kanner, 1967). Howe's efforts were followed by the establishment of additional training schools throughout the United States during the 1850s–1870s.

In contrast to Guggenbühl, the American pioneers in the field of mental retardation were more sober and realistic in their view of the mentally retarded individual and his or her potential. Their goals were less radical; no miracles were expected or promised. Guggenbühl was probably not so much an educator and scientist as a religious zealot, who fought for his goal of curability with idealistic fervor and blindness. The early American pioneers, however, envisioned amelioration of the condition rather than cure as the goal of residential care. They were interested in reducing intellectual impairment and increasing adaptive skills so that the retarded could at least function at some level in society. Note that both Guggenbühl and the early American pioneers had the common goal of reintegrating the patient into society. The difference between them was in the degree and level of social integration envisioned for the patients. Guggenbühl, believing in the cure of his cretins, had no reason to doubt that a full and successful integration would be possible. Howe, on the other hand, pointed out that one should not expect that each patient returning from the institution to society would be "normal"; just that he or she should be able to take a useful place in society. The leaders in the field of mental retardation in the United States were moved by more realistic expectations about what could be accomplished in their institutions. They gained legislative support with their more modest claims, while avoiding Guggenbühl's error of over-promising results.

Difficulties in coping with urban life and the shift to custodial care (1870–1890)

But even these more realistic goals were not achieved to the degree expected by their advocates and by the public. As a result, in the years following, a trend developed characterized by a change in ideology away from a developmental-educational model to a custodial model. Now the retarded were viewed as ineffectual but innocent victims of fate who should be protected from a harsh society. This change in attitude encouraged a shift away from a training institution with its goal of rehabilitation to a custodial institution with the goal of cloistering the retarded from society.

Despite the training and education many retarded individuals had received, adjustment in the community still was difficult. The industrial revolution was in full force in America, bringing with it an increasing complexity of urbanization and problems of rapid social change. A certain proportion of the residents were bound to be failures, particularly if there was a lack of community or family support upon their release. Many could find no place within the community and would end up in almshouses if left on their own or if their families died. Wolfensberger cites a statement of Walter Fernald in 1893 which makes this point clear:

> But in many cases the guardians of these children were unwilling to remove them from the institution, and begged that they might be allowed to remain there where they could be made happy and kept from harm. Many of these cases were homeless and friendless, and, if sent away from the school could only be transferred to almshouses where they became depraved and demoralized by association with adult paupers and vagrants of both sexes. . . . The placing of these feebleminded persons always proved unsatisfactory. . . . It gradually became evident

that a certain number of these higher-grade cases needed life-long care and supervision, and that there was no suitable provision for this permanent custody outside these special institutions. (Wolfensberger, 1969, p. 95)

During this period, there was no recognition of the need to educate or change the society to which the rehabilitated individual returned in order to insure greater receptivity. Howe and his contemporaries did not recognize this need. They committed the mistake of assuming that by training individuals, their reintegration into society would follow automatically as a consequence of improved social and intellectual skills. Their efforts were not misdirected by any means, but incomplete in that they failed to realize the impact of society. They did not see community forces that could counteract and vitiate the success of their training programs. This seeming failure of the institution as a school, and of some patients to adjust to the community, as well as the changes occurring in the fabric of society, led to a change in ideology between 1870 and 1890 (Wolfensberger, 1969). The developmental-educational model was replaced with a custodial model that manifested itself in changing patterns of residential care.

Now, retardates were viewed as the innocent victims of fate or parental sin, and instead of schooling they were to receive loving care and protection from society. The term "school" began to be replaced by "asylum," something Howe had explicitly warned against. Wolfensberger (1969) cites a number of quotations from the period that characterize the new perspective: "Give them an asylum, with good and kind treatment; but not a school." "A well-fed, well-cared-for idiot, is a happy creature. An idiot awakened to his condition is a miserable one." "They must be kept quietly, safely, away from the world, living like the angels in heaven, neither marrying nor given in marriage." As a result of the failure of the mentally retarded to be integrated into an increasingly complex society with little or no support, the social role perception of the retardate was changing away from one that embodied the hope of rehabilitation to one that, being based on pity, implied that one could do nothing but protect such a person from the world.

Custodial care institutions began to develop to accommodate larger numbers of retardates who were now viewed as unable to adjust to the community in any way. In 1870, New York City organized a hospital and school on Randall's Island to receive both low and high-grade cases. An institution designed especially for custodial care was established in Newark in 1878. This trend developed quickly and custodial institutions in Pennsylvania, Illinois, Massachusetts, Iowa, Minnesota, and Ontario were opened within the next three or four years (Adams, 1971). These custodial institutions bore the seeds of three dangerous trends that characterize institutions even today: isolation, enlargement, and economization. At first, isolation was viewed as protection of the deviant from the nondeviant. Institutions were removed from population centers to pastoral surroundings and writers of the time described these in rhapsodic and idyllic terms. The institution was to become a "garden of Eden" or a "happy farm." Enlargement was explained as benefiting the retardates. Small institutions were criticized as "hospitalizing" the retarded by separating them from others of their own kind. It was seen as more desirable that they be congregated in large numbers so they could be among their own type in a setting somewhat resembling a "community." Economization began with the original noble sentiment about the virtue of work for the retarded, but this soon gave way to the view that they should be working to diminish the economic burden on the public (Wolfensberger, 1969).

Indictment: Social Darwinism and the eugenic alarm (1890–1914)

The period of benevolent custodial care did not last long and soon gave way to brutalization. Beginning in the late 1880s a dramatically different view of the retardate was to dominate thinking in the field. Rather than protecting the deviant from society, society came to feel the need to protect itself from the deviant. This drastic reversal of the role perception of the retardate can be understood only by examining a number of complex social developments of the time.

Increasing urbanization brought accompanying social disorganization and growing class antagonism. Rapid changes in population, particularly through immigration to the United States, led to an increased burden on social welfare agencies, and at the same time, to fears of "national degeneracy" by foreign stocks. Even the foreigner of apparently normal intelligence, with different language and customs, was viewed with a growing distrust and dread. In addition to the apparent increase in the number of mentally retarded individuals because of population increases, there was also the "discovery" of a new class of "higher grade" retardates. This discovery was a result of increasing social complexity, which put greater demands on the in-tellectual ability of individuals; compulsory education for those who otherwise might have avoided it through self-selection; and the wide-spread use of mental tests that became a popular tool in recognizing those "retardates" who were bound to fail in school. As more retar-dates were "discovered," financial resources and adequately trained staff to deal with this growing problem could not keep pace.

This context of rapid social and economic change encouraged the development and popularization of Social Darwinism and the eugenic movement. Social Darwinists borrowed concepts from evolutionary theory such as the "struggle for existence" and "survival of the fittest" and applied them to social life. It was believed that in order to im-prove the human species, those members who were not capable of meeting the demands of existence should be left to die out according to "natural laws." In this way only the physically and mentally superior would be able to reproduce and over generations the quality of human beings would continually improve. According to Social Darwinism, retardates were no longer seen as the innocent victims of either environmental or hereditary taint, but as members of an inferior race that should be left to wither in accordance with the law of natural selection. To alleviate their burden through social assistance was viewed as misguided charity that would only perpetuate the problem that it was attempting to solve (Sarason & Doris, 1969).

A concurrent development that had implications for the care of the mentally retarded was the eugenic movement. Francis Galton, the founder of this movement, was impressed by Darwin's *The Origin of Species,* and attempted to apply key concepts of evolutionary theory to man. He advocated that since society altered the conditions of natural selection there should be conscious control of the reproduction rates of different groups in society in order to insure higher reproduction rates for individuals with positive traits than for individuals with undesir-able traits. The idea was not translated into social action until the turn of the century, yet it was preparing the intellectual climate for a vari-ety of scholars and leaders in the field of mental retardation to endorse programs of eugenic control.

The acceptance of eugenics was encouraged by "evidence" pro-vided by family studies of the time. In 1877 Robert Dugdale published the genealogical survey of the Jukes, which indicated that the majority of the offspring were of low physical and moral stature. Dugdale esti-mated that the total cost to the state resulting from the social failures of this one stock amounted to around $1,308,000 over a 75-year period (Davies, 1930). In 1891, the Reverend O. C. McCulloch presented the history of the "tribe of Ishmael," describing a highly intermarried family with a history of poverty for generations. In 1905 Joerger, a Swiss psychiatrist, assembled a family of vagrants, whom he called Zeros, as a sample of negative hereditary transmission (Kanner, 1967). Perhaps the greatest impact on bringing the eugenic scare to tremendous proportions came from H. H. Goddard's 1912 report of the Kallikak family. Martin Kallikak, a soldier of the Revolution, produced an illegitimate son with a retarded tavern girl. This son turned out to be retarded, too, and went on to produce a line of prostitutes, alcoholics, epileptics, criminals, pimps, retardates, and infant casualties. Martin himself went on to marry a respectable woman of a good family and left progeny all of which were representative of the most respectable citizens (Kanner, 1967). Jonathan Edward's family was contrasted to the Jukes and the Kallikaks, since he left 285 college graduates, of whom 65 became college professors, 13 college presidents, more than 100 lawyers, and 30 judges (Caplan, 1969). These data were interpreted at the time as conclusive evidence that mental retardation was transmitted in a simple and direct fashion according to the laws of heredity. That families share the same environment as well as the same heredity was not considered in evaluating this evidence.

It is worth noting that the amount and kind of evidence required for acceptance of a theory and the interpretation given to particular findings is in large part determined by the social philosophy and economic conditions of the times. Adams (1971) makes the interesting point that linking mental deficiency to genetic causes and therefore to a hopeless outlook, absolved the social conscience of many from attempting new measures. Accepting a genetic etiology created a situation where the problem was decried but nothing done, thus saving time and money. Most important, it diverted attention away from examining the social factors plaguing the poor, unskilled workers, and immigrants—factors that also were contributing to pathological behavior. Such an analysis of social and economic conditions would have been a fundamental challenge to the existing socioeconomic structure of the country. Considering the magnitude of the retardation problem and the lack of resources and knowledge to cope with it, the genetic explanation was no doubt an appealing, if largely incorrect, solution.

This was the social climate in which the great "indictment" of the mentally retarded grew. Far from being viewed as innocent victims to be protected from society, the mentally retarded were now associated with crime, perversions, and almost every form of "moral degeneracy." This tendency to lump deviants together has long historic roots that will not be reviewed here. However, to illustrate, we can note that the tenth (1880) U.S. census combined "defectives, dependents, and delinquents" for reporting purposes. The Public Health Service combined criminals, defectives, and delinquents as late as the 1920s. Thus, between 1875 and 1920, one of the most important human service organizations in the United States often grouped retardates with the deaf, dumb, epileptic, insane, and delinquents into one general category of "defectives." During this period, an incredible number of deviancies were claimed to be associated with retardation, including unemployment, sex offenses, and crime (Wolfensberger, 1969).

In a relatively short period of time the mentally retarded were thus transformed from objects of pity to objects of dread, from innocent victims who must be protected from society to a predatory class which was the root of almost every ill that plagued society.

Needless to say, this new role perception of the mentally retarded had vast implications for their treatment and care during this period of "Eugenic Alarm" (1890–1914). The three main alternatives for "purging from the blood of the race innately defective strains" were marriage laws, sterilization, and segregation. The laws passed against marriage were unenforceable and failed to solve the problem. It was under the influence of the same fear that in the early 1900s Dr. H. C. Sharp performed vasectomy without official sanction at the Indiana State Reformatory. In 1907, the Indiana State Legislature passed the first eugenic sterilization law providing for the prevention of the procreation of "confirmed criminals, idiots, imbeciles and rapists" (Kanner, 1967). Indiana was followed by seven other states (Washington, California, Connecticut, New Jersey, Iowa, New York, Nevada) over the next seven years. By 1936, 25 states had eugenic sterilization laws on their books, and some have remained in effect ever since. However, preventive sterilization also failed as a method of control. The line of demarcation between retarded and normal was not clear; the hereditary influence had not been quantitatively determined; the operation was dangerous; and the idea was not consonant with the thinking of part of the religious community.

The only solution left to prevent breeding was the large-scale segregation of the mentally retarded, particularly during their reproductive years. But this solution led to an increased financial burden.

Consequently, all efforts were directed at reducing the per capita costs in handling the retardates, basically by increasing the populations at the institutions and by having the higher-grade residents work to support both themselves and the lower-grade residents. In the 1880s, farm colonies came into vogue and the goals of institutions were to be self-supporting (Wolfensberger, 1969). Efforts to cut costs led to statements about introducing "simplicity" into the buildings to house the mentally retarded. Plain, substantial buildings were advocated, which soon gave way to depriving the retardate of amenities and comforts. A statement by J. T. Mastin as quoted in Wolfensberger (1969) shows how this was justified in a rather strained way:

> As a rule, mental defectives are descended from the poorer classes, and for generations their people have lived in homes having few conveniences. To expect them to be content in a great city institution with its up-to-date furnishings and equipment, and its strict routine, is unreasonable. They find little comfort in steam heat and polished floors; and the glare of electric lights too often adds to their restlessness. (p. 123)

With increasing demand for institutional space, the superintendents began to rationalize larger institutions. Some spoke about 1,000 to 1,500 inmates as being "ideal," others seriously considered 2,000 to 3,000 as reasonable numbers. These trends, which as we have seen were initiated by rather complex social factors, planted the seeds for the custodial institutions familiar to us today.

The peak of the "indictment" ended around 1914. Within the next few years most workers in the field realized that retardates were not the menace they had thought and it became apparent that the goals of segregation could not be achieved. Voices began to speak about an aversion to the idea of life-long confinement of persons who had committed no crime and who seemed to the ordinary observer not very different from many others. Even Fernald, who had advocated stern eugenic measures, began to reverse his position as illustrated in a statement cited by Wolfensberger (1969): "The average citizen is not yet convinced that he should be taxed to permanently support an individual who is capable of thirty, fifty or seventy percent of normal economic efficiency, on the *mere theory* that he is more likely than a normal individual to become a social problem" (p. 128, italics added). The "incontestable evidence" of some 10 or 20 years before, which had been used to support drastic programs of social action, was now viewed as "mere theory." A careful longitudinal study at Waverly over a period of 25 years showed that only a very small proportion of discharged male "morons" had committed crimes, married, become parents, failed to support themselves, or had become "bad" citizens (Kanner, 1967). But this and other documented facts were in and of themselves not enough to turn the tide from the indictment. Changing social attitudes that recognized the inhumanity of life-long incarceration as well as the failure of segregation to eliminate the problem were the bases for change.

The slow development of community alternatives: Post-World War I to 1950

The 1920s witnessed the establishment of a few isolated trial programs of community supervision to deal with the retarded, but despite the wealth of innovative ideas and the notable success of the few programs that were instituted, community alternatives found it difficult to survive the social and political tide that was moving against such efforts. The period after World War I was characterized by political conservatism that produced a climate not particularly conducive to social innovation.

In outlining a "modern program" for the care of the mentally defective, Davies (1930) put a heavy emphasis on community integration and supervision. Specialized training was to be done through the public schools so that intellectually subnormal children could be integrated as far as possible into community life and prevented from becoming socially incompetent. Special training in institutions was to be used only until the individual was ready to return to the community under supervision. Permanent segregation was reserved for those who absolutely could not function in the outside world. These ideas sound very modern indeed. Unfortunately they remained little more than innovative "ideas" as can be judged by the fact that New York State employed only six field workers to cover the entire state to supervise the mentally retarded in the community.

Other community-oriented programs were developed with somewhat greater apparent success. A colony plan was introduced to protect the individual from society while he was being rehabilitated in preparation for returning to society. These colonies were the prototypes of the halfway houses and sheltered workshops that are currently being introduced throughout the country. In the 1930s, a family plan was developed for those who could not be expected to benefit from the colony plan and eventually assume an independent existence in the community. It became popular to place such individuals with families who were given support by a community center that served the role of a social center for the retarded, relieved the family from responsibility for several days at a time when it became necessary, and provided medical care for problems that could not be treated in the foster home. Under the parole plan, retarded individuals were permitted to live in the community under the supervision of a social worker who took a personal interest in integrating them into society. Full discharges were given to those who could adjust. Adams (1971) makes the interesting point that if these isolated individual efforts of community care were pooled into a single program, there would have existed 25 or more years ago the continuum of care proposed for the retarded population of today. Since the ideas were there and were even implemented in successful programs on a limited scale, why did these attractive community alternatives die out, leaving us instead with sordid and overcrowded institutions?

One reason can be found in the already-cited conservative climate after the World War—it was not sympathetic to community-based programs (Levine & Levine, 1970). Also, professionals had indoctrinated the public about the menace of retardation and the unchangeability of intelligence so that a massive campaign of attitude change would have been required to promote interest in community services. General pessimism in the field led professionals to become interested in other areas of mental health, where discoveries and treatment opportunities were increasing. Perhaps the most vital blow came with the economic disaster of the Great Depression, which forced the country to curtail all but the most crucial social services. After the Depression, a period of inertia set in and World War II only served to further divert attention away from mental retardation and community services in general (Wolfensberger, 1969). Without any impetus from society, the existing bureaucracy plodded along, perpetuating services in its own image.

Renewed enthusiasm: 1950 to the present

A sudden resurgence of interest in the field of mental retardation occurred in the 1950s with the organization of parents into what was soon to become the National Association for Retarded Children. This group wielded great influence at the local and national levels and has been a prime force in developing comprehensive services for the retarded. A number of factors contributed to the movement away from the limited services and custodial care inherited from the late 19th century. Medical advances aided the survival of babies who had biological defects. Many of these children belonged to upper- and middle-class families who felt they were entitled to public assistance for their children and who were articulate in arguing their cause. Institutions fell under attack because of the low standards they maintained and because of the growing view that it was harmful to children to separate them from natural maternal care. Consequently, local groups attempted to develop community-based alternatives that would keep retarded children close to their families, such as industrial training centers, preschool programs, group activities, and smaller rehabilitative residential centers (Adams, 1971).

In October 1961, President Kennedy appointed a panel to review conditions of the retarded, and in 1962 the findings were reported in *A Proposed Program for National Action to Combat Mental Retardation.* This report contained the dismal statistics of inadequate care, personnel, and facilities provided for the retarded. In 1963, the Maternal and Child Health and Mental Retardation Planning Amendments Act was passed, a landmark piece of legislation "with the objective of assisting States and communities in preventing and combating mental retardation through expansion and improvement of the maternal and child health and crippled children's programs, through provision of prenatal, maternity and infant care for individuals with conditions associated with childbearing which may lead to mental retardation" (Adams, 1971, p. 49). The implication of this legislation was clearly to shift emphasis to preventive measures by focusing on mothers and children at risk. Furthermore, it established the role of the federal government in providing for the social welfare of its less fortunate citizens. This social philosophy of government responsibility had developed out of earlier historical events that forced the government to reexamine its relationship to individuals. It is interesting to note that while the Depression of the 1930s and World War II both diverted attention away from mental retardation and social services in general, the implications of these economic and political events for mental retardation were considerable. As Sarason and Doris (1969) point out, the Depression threatened to destroy the fabric of American society and disrupted the lives and hope of millions of people. As a consequence, the relationship between government and the individual was changed such that society began to recognize a responsibility to the individual in areas where it had previously remained aloof. World War

II forced a further examination of human resources, and it was shocking to find that 716,000 men were rejected from the armed forces on grounds of mental deficiency. Both of these events, the Depression and World War II, contributed to the increased government awareness and involvement in mental retardation. Government became more willing to help groups and individuals who for reasons beyond their control needed external assistance. Mental illness, physical disease, juvenile delinquency, and mental retardation were some of the areas where the government was allowed greater responsibility for constructive action (Sarason & Doris, 1969). In the field of mental retardation the recommendation of the President's Commission in 1963 represented an important official recognition of mental retardation as a problem of national concern after decades of relative passivity.

Reexamining the relationship between poverty and retardation

Official government concern for the problem of mental retardation stimulated public and professional interest in the field, while government funding encouraged research into the questions of intelligence, early deprivation, and education in general. Interest in how to overcome and how to prevent the effects of retardation characterize this period and continue today. The resurgence of mental retardation as a major concern was accelerated by a renewed spirit of reform that resulted in a sensitivity to social injustice and the debilitating effects of poverty. The interrelationship of minority status, education, regional-cultural factors, and mental retardation had been demonstrated a number of times (Sarason & Doris, 1969). In fact, the relationship between poverty and retardation was recognized during the "indictment" period, but then it was interpreted as retardation causing the financial problems. Now the causal relationship has been reversed, so that adverse social, economic, and cultural factors have been ascribed a major causal role, although the nature of this role has not yet been empirically determined. The report of the President's Panel on Mental Retardation (1962) reflects this attitude:

> The majority of the mentally retarded are the children of the more disadvantaged classes of our society. This extraordinarily heavy prevalence in certain deprived population groups suggests a major causative role, in some way not fully delineated, for adverse social, economic, and cultural factors. (Sarason & Doris, 1969, p. 14)

The reason that this old relationship between poverty and mental retardation now "suggests a major causative role" for adverse social and
economic factors is because of the present perceptual filters through
which this observation is made. Howe recognized that poverty was
involved in producing retardation. Today because of social and political developments, we are ready to accept Howe's position of 100 years
earlier, and choose to view poverty as a potential cause of retardation.
But as mentioned by the President's Panel this causal relationship
between poverty and mental retardation has not yet been delineated,
which is to say that it is based more on current political biases than
on empirical evidence. As long as the answers to such important questions are largely determined by the social and political climate of the
times, any kind of action based on such untested premises will be
timebound and vulnerable to new emerging environmental influences. While empirical validation of these hypotheses through careful
research cannot fully guarantee that the "truth" (e.g., regarding the
relationship between environment and mental retardation) will endure and be manifested in action, research is one way to help insulate
and protect actions taken today against the political and social vicissitudes of subsequent periods.

Conclusion: Can "normalization" survive?

The need for research is particularly evident in regard to the principle of normalization. It is important to recognize that this new ideology is a product of the unique social, cultural, and political climate of
today. The attempt to reconceptualize society's role perception of
retarded persons and to integrate them into society has grown out of an
atmosphere of greater tolerance for deviance and difference in general. Beginning with the movement for equality and power by the
black minority, other minority groups also have demanded acceptance
and a respectable place in society. This attitude, taken together with
the confidence that intelligence is malleable at least to some degree,
has created a new era of enthusiasm, monetary investment, and personal commitment to alleviating the problems of the mentally
retarded.

The new wave of optimism is reminiscent of the days of Howe and
Guggenbühl, but it would be an oversimplification to equate their
attempts with contemporary ones and thus conclude that there has

been essentially no progress. The early pioneers focused their attention on curing or training the retarded within an institution with the expectation that the gains in intellectual and behavioral functioning would allow for an automatic integration into society. This faith in the effects of training at the expense of considering larger social factors represents a naïve conception of the nature of society. It presupposes a view of society as a passive inert agent, rather than an active force that exerts a profound influence on the individual. It is in this respect that normalization can be distinguished from former attempts at integrating the retarded into society. Unlike Howe and Guggenbühl, the advocates of normalization are cognizant of the fact that the form of treatment and care of the mentally retarded is inextricably bound to the larger social context. For this reason they have explicitly incorporated interventions that focus not only on the individual but also on various societal levels, ranging from the family unit to larger social systems such as the schools, as well as general attitudes of society. For this reason, normalization is a more realistic ideology and can be considered a "step ahead," since it is a more comprehensive approach that recognizes society as a relevant and critical variable that cannot be ignored.

While the principle of normalization represents an advance, it must be remembered that it is, indeed, for the most part an ideology. Clearly, ideology should not be confused with action, which, if it occurs at all, does so more slowly. In attempting to translate the principle of normalization into specific institutional changes there are numerous problems of implementation that are involved in the creation of new settings and in program changes of any kind. While Wolfensberger, the primary advocate of normalization, distinguishes between the *process* of normalization and the *goal* of the program, which is to yield retarded individuals who lead normal lives, other adherents have merely inferred that normative procedures would automatically yield normative outcomes. However, this conclusion does not necessarily follow. For example, it is conceivable that a retarded individual could be treated according to all the techniques prescribed by the principle of normalization and still fail to be accepted as a useful member of society. It is easy to mistake the application of the procedures of normalization for the real goals, and to evaluate the program on the degree to which it has been implemented rather than on the degree to which it has successfully normalized retarded individuals. It is not enough to know that normalizing procedures have been instituted; it must also be determined whether retarded individuals have been integrated into society as predicted by the model. To avoid this critical danger, the outcomes of the normalization principle must be specified in measurable ways so that the principle can be evaluated empirically in comparison with other models, and in terms of alternative procedures within the model itself.

It should be obvious that the research implications of this perspective are vast. There are innumerable questions to answer at the person, organizational, and societal levels about which procedures are most normalizing. How can a retarded individual be presented to society so as to best enhance his or her acceptance? What types of alternative residence will lead to the most normalization and for which types of retarded individuals? What community factors must be considered in any attempt to integrate and maintain retardates in society? The innumerable questions that have to be answered in order to ensure successful implementation clearly indicate that without extensive research, normalization might well prove to be as disappointing as the noble attempts of the early pioneers.

Epilogue: The vulnerability of mental health ideology

In tracing the ebb and flow of ideas about mental retardation, it is important to keep in mind that similar swings occurred in mental health ideology generally. Ideas about the etiology of mental disorders and proper treatment methods changed with variations in the social climate. The rise and fall of moral therapy and the settlement house and child guidance movements (as documented by Bockoven, 1963; R. Caplan, 1969; and Levine & Levine, 1970) are examples of the effects of social climate on mental health theories and practices. We should also note that the purpose of our historical review is not to pinpoint "eras of reform" or of conservative backlash. Such labels function as a convenience for the historian and we need not pursue arguments that reify labels. During a particular era, more events occur than a historian may choose to abstract. For example in Chapter 9 we point out that the social ferment of the 1890s that produced reforms such as the Settlement Houses and special education classes also led to the development of more conservative "Protective Associations."

What is more crucial is to understand the reasons for the ebb and flow of mental health ideology. Ruth Caplan (1969), who documents the rise and fall of environmentally oriented ideas in 19th-century

American psychiatry, points out that the acceptance of these ideas had little to do with their intrinsic value. From her point of view, community-oriented reforms did not succeed in the past for a number of reasons, some of which are summarized below:

1. A shortage of manpower to implement programs, which in part reflects inadequate training facilities.
2. A shortage of resources associated with the low priority accorded the mentally ill by the public and their legislators.
3. Theories concerning the etiology and treatment of mental disorder favored exciting new ideas and fads. At the turn of the century, the intellectual and scientific community was buzzing with new ideas in neuropathology and psychoanalysis. Optimistic treatment modalities linking patients back to their home communities were considered unrealistic and "old-fashioned."
4. The naïveté and lack of understanding of psychiatrists about problems of community dynamics that complicated the implementation of their programs. Theories of psychic functioning cannot be formulated in a vacuum. Factors in the social, political, economic, and scientific milieu affect the manner in which theories are developed as well as the success of their implementation.
5. The tendency of psychiatrists to embrace panaceas and to hail each change as the solution to all difficulties. The system was oversold to the public and to fellow professionals. When shortcomings were revealed, there was a pendulum swing in the opposite direction with the entire system being jettisoned.
6. When public complaints about the failure of optimistic promises started to surface, psychiatrists tended to deal with such outside pressure by evasion rather than by direct confrontation. Psychiatrists retreated into their professional guild and lost touch with the realities of community life.
7. Faddish theories were entirely untested. By the time the shortcomings of expensive plans had been realized, so much propaganda and money had been spent that it was difficult to abandon or replace them.

It is sobering to recognize that these same indictments could describe problems facing the mental health professions even today. To be sure, there are reasons why these problems persist. Overselling an untested idea may lead to inevitable disappointment, but it is also a way of counteracting apathy among a citizenry for whom psychological well-being does not have a high financial priority. Preventing or ameliorating psychological distress is an extremely complex undertaking. Psychological disorder is inextricably bound to the social values and customs of society. Modifying entrenched social mores can be extremely difficult. Oversimplification is one way of making such complex problems manageable. Furthermore, when one works in an area in which the ultimate goal is so difficult to achieve, it is not surprising that practitioners, for their own professional sanity and survival, consider evaluation unnecessary, maintaining an absolute certainty in the value of their work.

Still, one cannot read the history of the recurring cycles of mental health ideology without a sense of apprehension. Are we bound to repeat the mistakes of the past? It is unlikely that new ideas about psychological well-being and community life can be developed independent of the social climate of the times. After all, those who generate such ideas develop them in response to the "Zeitgeist," or climate of opinion with which they either concur or react against. We cannot predict the future, but what we have tried to stress is that from the perspective of the past, understanding the context in which ideas are generated is crucial to the full understanding of the ideas themselves. Furthermore, we feel that an important factor in the retention of valuable ideas and practices is the availability of supporting evidence. Given the nature of our field and the stresses upon its practitioners, it may be difficult to resist the latest mental health fads. However, without taking seriously the need for analysis, evaluation, and the subsequent accumulation of verified knowledge, it will be impossible to do so. Social, political, and economic factors will always affect the fate of social innovations, regardless of their effectiveness. But today, more so than in the past, programs that can demonstrate empirical results and are based on credible scientific theories are more likely to survive the vicissitudes of history.

References

Adams, M.   *Mental retardation and its social dimensions.* New York: Columbia University Press, 1971.

Blatt, B.   Purgatory. In Robert Kugel & Wolf Wolfensberger (Eds.), *Changing patterns in residential services for the mentally retarded.* Washington, D.C.: President's Committee on Mental Retardation, 1969, pp. 35–50.

Blatt, B., & Kaplan, F.   *Christmas in purgatory.* Boston: Allyn and Bacon, 1966.

Bockoven, J.   *Moral treatment in American psychiatry.* New York: Springer, 1963.

Boesch, Joseph. *Weltgeschichte: Von der Aufklärung bis zur Gegenwart.* Zurich: Eugen Rentsch Verlag, 1969.

Butterfield, E. C.   Basic facts about public residential facilities for the mentally retarded. In Robert Kugel & Wolf Wolfensberger (Eds.), *Changing patterns in residential services for the mentally retarded.* Washington, D.C.: President's Committee on Mental Retardation, 1969, pp. 15–34.

Caplan, R. B.   *Psychiatry and the community in nineteenth century America: The recurring concern with the environment in the prevention and treatment of mental illness.* New York: Basic Books, 1969.

Davies, S. P.   *Social control of the mentally deficient.* New York: Thomas Y. Crowell Co., 1930.

Dunn, L. M.   Small special-purpose residential facilities for the retarded. In Robert Kugel & Wolf Wolfensberger (Eds.), *Changing patterns in residential services for the mentally retarded.* Washington, D.C.: President's Committee on Mental Retardation, 1969, pp. 211–226.

Kanner, L.   *A history of the care and study of the mentally retarded.* Springfield, Ill.: Charles C. Thomas, 1967.

Kugel, R.   Why innovative action? In Robert Kugel & Wolf Wolfensberger (Eds.), *Changing patterns in residential services for the mentally retarded.* Washington, D.C.: President's Committee on Mental Retardation, 1969, pp. 1–14.

Levine, M., & Levine, A.   *A social history of helping services: Clinic, court, school and community.* New York: Appleton-Century-Crofts, 1970.

President's Panel Report.   A Proposed Program for National Action to Combat Mental Retardation. Washington: D.C., Superintendent of Documents, 1962.

Robinson, H., & Robinson, N.   *The mentally retarded child: A psychological approach.* New York: McGraw-Hill, 1965.

Sarason, S., & Doris, J.   *Psychological problems in mental deficiency.* New York: Harper & Row, 1969.

Wolfensberger, W.   The origin and nature of our institutional models. In Robert Kugel & Wolf Wolfensberger (Eds.), *Changing patterns in residential services for the mentally retarded.* Washington, D.C.: President's Committee on Mental Retardation, 1969, pp. 59–172.

Wolfensberger, W.   *Normalization: The principle of normalization in human services.* Toronto, Canada: National Institute on Mental Retardation, 1972.

3

ISSUES IN COMMUNITY RESEARCH

IN THIS CHAPTER, we shall be concerned with testing hypotheses about community functioning and evaluating programs for community betterment. We have not deluded ourselves into believing that a complete treatment of the issues of community research can be accomplished in so brief a space, or, worse yet, that a "cookbook" for evaluating community programs could be proffered here. The literature on applied social research has grown voluminously in the past few years, and several gourmet cookbooks are already available for those who wish to create a program evaluation of their own. Our purpose here is more modest: we wish to place research and evaluation in perspective as tools for achieving and validating community change, and to very selectively focus on a few methodologies that we believe to be particularly relevant to community intervention.

The need for research on community change

We believe that the generation of high-quality research and first-rate evaluation is one of the most pressing needs in community psychology today. There are several reasons why empirical investigations are so central to the pursuit of community change: as a branch of behavioral science, community psychology cannot progress without an empirical knowledge base; as an applied movement for social change, community psychology will wither away and be remembered only as one of many passing fads to arise during the tumultuous 1960s if its action programs cannot verify their impact; and, there is an ethical and moral obligation on the community practitioner to be account-

71

able to those who support his or her activities. The touchstone of accountability lies in empirical evaluation.

Research as a prerequisite for scientific revolutions

The accumulation of a "body of knowledge," or a generally accepted cluster of empirically tested hypotheses, is an essential ingredient in the production of scientific progress. Kuhn (1962), in his well-known theory of "scientific revolutions," makes it clear that no revolution ever occurs unless there is an accepted body of knowledge and an accepted theoretical superstructure to incorporate that knowledge. While Kuhn's (1962) theory is sometimes used to denigrate research in favor of grand conceptualizations, a more careful reading indicates that his work is a powerful justification for empirical hypothesis-testing. Without a solid "normal science," where research facts are gradually accumulated, there is nothing to scientifically revolt *against*, and thus no springboard for scientific progress.

To be sure, Kuhn emphasizes the contribution of conceptual "paradigm shifts" in which a field "quantum jumps" from one way of viewing the world to another. It is these paradigm shifts that advance a scientific field. Research, therefore, might properly be viewed as a *prerequisite* to scientific progress—absolutely necessary, but not a sufficient condition by itself for scientific advancement. Without thorough research activity to investigate all aspects of normal science, the limits and deficiencies of accepted paradigms will never be known. In addition, research can solve many problems to which normal science does apply, and may lead to the unexpected observations that touch off scientific revolutions.

"The community movement" in psychology provides an instructive example. This new way of viewing psychological problems may be thought of as a paradigm shift. Yet it did not come about primarily through the gradual accumulation of research facts. Rather, a complex of social and conceptual forces merged to forge this new paradigm. However, without the body of research attesting to the numerous deficiencies of the traditional manner of delivering mental health service, it is doubtful that the social and conceptual impetus for the community movement would ever have arisen. And without research to evaluate current community programs and analyze current community theories, scientific advances will have difficulty emerging, regardless of whether they build upon or reject previous ideology.

Research as a way of muting cyclical swings in social policy

If research is a necessary but not sufficient condition for scientific progress in a given field, it is even more necessary for the generation of progress by a given social movement. As we described earlier, community reform often proceeds in cycles. During times of social optimism, environmental theories of human dysfunction are in favor, and the climate is good for mounting reform efforts. During periods of social conservatism, "person-blame attributions" (Caplan & Nelson, 1973) are common, and social intervention is viewed pejoratively (Levine & Levine, 1970).

While it may well be extremely difficult to launch a new community reform effort during times of social conservatism, a central question is whether community reform efforts begun in periods of social optimism can be maintained through the drought of conservatism. The answer is probably "no," *unless the reform programs have empirically demonstrated their impact.*

In periods of social optimism, ideology and rhetoric alone may suffice to initiate and continue innovative community programs. In deed, during the "New Frontier" and "Great Society" period of 1960–68, few of the new social programs had anything *but* ideology and rhetoric as their foundation. But in conservative periods the ideology and rhetoric changes, and programs without demonstrable positive impact on the community are likely to be short-lived. Faced with empirical evaluations showing that a desirable change has been achieved, however, it becomes more difficult to terminate a program.

If community programs are to escape being subjected to the prevailing political winds, they must establish independent evidence of their effectiveness, evidence that is open to scrutiny by ideological friend and foe alike. Program evaluation is the principal means of establishing such evidence.

Research as accountability

Finally, while research is a methodological necessity for the progress of a scientific discipline and a pragmatic sine qua non for the continuation of a social reform movement, it is also an ethical and moral imperative for those entrusted with the use of scarce community resources (such as funds and personnel). Those who would offer programs for social progress, and succeed in convincing the community to support their visions, have a strong obligation to report back to their supporters what the ultimate outcome of the reform effort has been. One simply cannot take the money and run. Only by actively engaging in efforts to empirically evaluate program effects can the practitioner become accountable to his or her community. Only by being presented with evaluation research can the community judge if its support has been well allocated, and continued support justified.

"Research" and "evaluation" in the community

In discussions of the scientific aspects of community psychology, one often hears "research" being contrasted with "evaluation." Two groups seem to have a psychological investment in perpetuating this distinction. The first group is composed largely of traditional academics who have reserved for themselves the title of "basic" or "pure" researchers and who disparage mere "evaluation" as an activity of their intellectual inferiors. "Evaluators are looked down on as the drones of the research fraternity, technicians drudging away on dull issues and compromising their integrity out in the corrupt world" (Weiss, 1972, p. 9). Concluding that evaluation is unworthy of scientists, this group is then free to take the high and sterile road back to their laboratory animals or laboratory students.

The second group that stresses the differences between research and evaluation is composed largely of program evaluators themselves. In this case, stressing the distinction is a "one-downsmanship" strategy to disarm potential critics. To embarrassing questions concerning methodology, they have the retort that "this is only an evaluation," and thus they cannot be held accountable for any shortcomings since too much should not be expected of them in the first place.

Despite the fact that distinguishing between research and evaluation is often an expression of academic elitism or a scientific "cop out," the distinction may at times be useful. What distinguishes evaluation from "basic" research, however, is not subject matter or methodology, but rather *intent*—the purpose for which the study is done. Weiss (1972) lists several differences in intent or purpose between program evaluation and basic research. Chief among them are *use for decision making and program-derived questions*. Basic research emphasizes the production of knowledge for its own sake and leaves its use to naturally occurring processes of dissemination and application. Evaluation *starts out* with use in mind. Evaluations are undertaken to provide information with which decision makers can make more rational decisions. Likewise, the basic researcher formulates his or her own hypotheses, while the evaluator derives questions with reference to the program and the decision maker. As Edwards, Guttentag, & Snapper (1975, p. 140) put it:

> Evaluations, we believe, exist (or perhaps only should exist) to facilitate intelligent decision-making. The scientist who conducts evaluation research, and even his sponsor, may be interested in various hypotheses about the program (or whatever it is) being evaluated out of sheer intellectual curiosity. And an evaluation research program will often satisfy curiosities. But if it does no more, if it does not improve the basis for decisions about the program and its competitors, then it loses its distinctive character as *evaluation* research and becomes simply research.*

More important than the differences between research and evaluation, however, are the similarities. The same principles of design and hypothesis testing apply to the community as well as to the laboratory. In both laboratory and community settings, methodology must be tailored to subject matter. Although some are still in the process of development, numerous research methodologies appropriate to community settings are currently available (Struening and Guttentag, 1975). The apologetic tone of so many evaluators of community programs is as unjustified as the snobbery of the field's detractors. Research and evaluation must be judged on the basis of the importance of the problem being studied as well on the elegance of methodology employed. A flawless analysis of a trivial problem can produce only a trivial result. For too long we have used methodological elephant guns to shoot problematic flies.

The primary goal of research is the same in the community as it is in the laboratory: *eliminating the plausible rival hypotheses* that can account for the findings. In casting doubt on one hypothesis, one increases the chances that another hypothesis is true. It is crucial to note that research can be of great value even if it does not eliminate all but one hypothesis. The task of the researcher is to control for as many rival hypotheses *as is realistically feasible* in a given research situation. It may be possible that a given research project could eliminate only one of a dozen rival hypotheses that explain the data. That research, however, may still be of great value. Others can then investigate the remaining 11 hypotheses, one at a time if need be, until the

---

* This, and the following excerpt, from chapter 7, "A Decision-Theoretic Approach to Evaluation Research," by Ward Edwards et al., is reprinted from Volume I, *Handbook of Evaluation Research* (E. L. Struening and M. Guttentag, Editors) © 1975, pp. 140, 144, by permission of the Publisher, Sage Publications, Inc.

correct one is identified. Edwards, Guttentag, and Snapper (1975, p. 144) provide the example of research on a community program to reduce drunk driving:

> A roadside survey finding of fewer drunk drivers after community action than before, by itself, merits little more than a "Hmmm. Interesting." If accompanied by a decrease in drunk-driving arrests (along with some reason to believe that police effort was constant before and after), the interest increases. And a finding of fewer personal-injury accidents than before would raise the interest to fever pitch, especially if other cities not participating in the program should not show such decrease. Each of these comparisons, by itself, is dubious; in none of them is the control an adequate protection against various kinds of error. Indeed, the conjunction of all of these comparisons would by no means be conclusive, given the degree to which motives other than devotion to pure science can influence the collection of social statistics at the source, and their subsequent processing. Yet the more different lines of evidence point in the same direction, the more persuaded we are likely to become.

Evaluators and researchers should always strive to climb as high on the ladder of methodological perfection as possible. It is worth the climb, however, even if one does not reach the top rung.

The politics of evaluation

Empirical techniques are being increasingly used to evaluate programs on the organizational and community level. The societal commitment to program evaluation so desired by researchers in the past is slowly becoming a reality. Program evaluation is now a major social science "industry." But evaluation researchers have paid a price for their new-found respectability. They have left the rarefied air of the ivory tower for the smoke-filled room of community politics. Kassebaum, Ward, and Wilner (1971, p. 310) point to some of the key problems of evaluation research when they discuss the implications of the massive volume of studies finding that psychological treatment is ineffective in rehabilitating prisoners:

> In more and more instances it appears that correctional agencies have begun to feel that perhaps the liberal, forward-looking, modern, scientific, and experimental stance so applauded a few years ago is ultimately repaid by sour faces and blue pencilings from legislative committees and budget analysts when negative findings are the result of program assessments. Prison administrators who once said, "Come on in and do your research, we have nothing to hide," may now be starting to feel that, after all, they do have something to hide. Because the most innovative departments have often argued their case for "treatment" funds by

appealing to the pragmatic criteria of recidivism reduction, they find it difficult to continue such urging in the light of negative results. For an organization whose output is not a tangible product, the use of systematic evaluation is a more acceptable basis on which to judge the success or failure of a program or policy than are impressions. In other words, scientific investigations are increasingly being used to justify next year's budget. This subjects the organization to cross-pressures. On the one hand, there is an intellectual commitment to the rules of science, objectivity, reliability, and comprehensiveness—but, on the other hand, there is a realistic need to use statistical material as a rationale for action and as a technique of persuasion when seeking legislative support on fiscal matters.

Evaluation research is most likely to be accepted when it is in accord with the preexisting beliefs of those in political power. The Nixon administration, for example, was most willing to tout the negative evaluations of the Johnson Great Society programs as "proof" of the ineffectiveness of spending massive funds on social programs. This politicization of evaluation research has put the evaluator, at times, in an extremely uncomfortable position. As Carol Weiss (1975, p. 23) has cogently put it:

> The evaluation researcher—now that somebody was paying attention to findings—was cast in the role of political hatchet man. Because evaluation researchers tend to be liberal, reformist, humanitarian, and advocates of the underdog, it is exceedingly uncomfortable to have evaluation findings used to justify an end to spending on domestic social programs. On the other hand, it is extremely difficult for evaluators to advocate continuation of programs they have found had no apparent results. The political dilemma is real and painful. It has led some social scientists to justify continued spending on avowedly ineffective programs to preserve the illusion that something is being done. Others have called for continued spending, whatever the outcome, so as not to lose the momentum of social progress. Others justify the programs in ways that they used to belittle in self-serving program staff: the programs serve other purposes, the evaluations are not very good, the programs need more money, they need more time. My own bent is to find some truth in each of these justifications, but they tend to be declarations based on social ideology and faith, rather than on evidence that these factors are responsible for the poor showing or that the programs are achieving other valued ends.*

Weiss (1972) had earlier discussed some of the "less legitimate" political reasons for which evaluations are undertaken:

---

* This excerpt from chapter 2, "Evaluation Research in the Political Context," by Carol H. Weiss, is reprinted from Volume I, *Handbook of Evaluation Research* (E. L. Struening and M. Guttentag, Editors) © 1975, pp. 13–26, by permission of the Publisher, Sage Publications, Inc.

1. *Postponement.* For the decision maker looking for ways to avoid making a decision, commissioning an evaluation study can be more useful than the usual ploy of appointing a committee and waiting for its report.

2. *Ducking responsibility.* Administrators may know they have to make an unpopular decision, and may call in evaluators to cloak their decision in objectivity and attribute the responsibility to the evaluators.

3. *Public relations.* Large portions of "evaluations" fall into this category. No attempt is made to collect data that could be disconfirming. A student of one of the authors, for example, wanted to evaluate a local community "rap center." The director of the center told her that he would be glad to have her evaluate his program. He walked her into a room where the staff and clients were talking and yelled, "This girl wants to evaluate our program. Do we have a good program?" They yelled back "Yes!" He turned to her and said "See, there's your evaluation!" Evaluations such as these are essentially commercials.

4. *Fulfilling grant requirements.* It is unfortunate that so many programs are evaluated only because the funding source insists on it. The role of the evaluator in this case is frustrating, because those running the program are interested only in the number of pages in the final report (thickness somehow equaling quality).

The role of the researcher in the real world of community programs can take on many forms. Is he or she the *outside expert,* with no personal investment in whether a program expands or falls? Or is he or she the *in-house evaluator,* whose job may depend upon an ability to submit glowing reports? The different roles will likely have important effects on the type of evaluation done and the analysis of the results. Note, in this connection, that the outside expert has disadvantages that can balance his or her asset of objectivity. Many programs have been destroyed by evaluators who, having no investment in the program, employ insensitive or unreliable measures of performance and conclude the program worthless when the measures do not show improvement.

The role tensions and political pressures upon a researcher or evaluator in a community setting are many. Weiss (1972) presents a concise and excellent discussion of them and suggests ways the researcher may lessen the friction inherent in his or her job—such as involving the program practitioners in the evaluation and ensuring clear role definitions and authority structures from the start. The pragmatic and political difficulties of performing valid research in community settings are not to be underestimated. But neither are they to be emphasized to the point of immobility and doing nothing. Difficulties in the practice of research are challenges for the ingenious to overcome, not quagmires to be wallowed in. We are emphatic on the point that scientific and valuable research *can* be done in the turbulent setting of social action, and must be done if action is to be guided by intelligence rather than by social whimsy.

Characteristics of community research

Price and Cherniss (in press) provide an insightful discussion of the role of research and evaluation in community work. They see dire consequences if community psychology goes the route of clinical psychology and education by emphasizing a dichotomy between research and practice, thus creating "two cultures" of community psychology, each of which is alienated from the other. They propose as an alternative "a very different role for community psychologists, one that avoids the scientist-practitioner split by developing both a new model of research and a new model of practice. It is a role that has as a basic premise the idea that the systematic gathering of information about a problem in the community or in a human service agency is the most practical thing in the world that a community psychologist could be doing." They see this new role as having several characteristics:

1. *Problem formation is stimulated by community needs.* Research is not merely an exercise in hypothesis testing or methodological development. Rather it is an attempt by community psychologists to use their knowledge and skills to deal with existing or anticipated needs of the community.

2. *Theory serves primarily as a means rather than an end.* Theory is a tool for understanding community problems. It is a guide for anticipating future events, and a framework for structuring complex situations and the nature of one's response to them.

3. *Research is a tool for social action.* Like theory, research in community psychology is a tool rather than an end in itself. Informed social action requires the systematic collection of information. "To fail to do 'research' in this sense is to fail to do justice to the problem. Although community psychologists can and should use other tools and skills, it is the utilization of research that distinguishes us from other social activists."

4. *Value issues are made explicit in professional work.* It is basic social values, along with community needs, that define the targets of community research and provide the criteria by which research is evaluated.

5. *The products of the community psychologist's research are different.* Journal articles are seldom the sole product of community research. Rather, community research should represent "a concrete embodiment of an attempt to solve a real social problem," and could include training manuals, new administrative or evaluation systems, or even new institutions.

6. *The community psychologist maintains a stance of giving rather than taking from the field setting.* Often in the past, psychologists have used agency staff and clientele time for research projects that had no demonstrable benefit to the agency or its clients. In the community research advocated by Price and Cherniss (in press), "one of the most important measures of the success of the research enterprise has to do with whether or not the product of that research actually enhances the functioning of the setting."

7. *Demonstration is not enough.* The community psychologist cannot be satisfied with demonstrating that the method or program that has been developed is preferable to the current mode of operating. Rather, he or she must plan from the beginning for the institutionalization and dissemination of the innovation.

8. *Evaluation of social action as an ethical imperative.* As we stated earlier, in addition to the scientific and pragmatic necessity for community research, there is an ethical mandate as well. One must remain accountable to the community.

We concur fully with these prescriptions. Only when research replaces rhetoric and evaluation supplants homily will community psychology assume lasting status as a discipline and a profession.

Research needs in community psychology

While for scientific, professional, and ethical reasons, research is among the most pressing needs in community psychology today, some kinds of studies are more needed than others. Almost any research on human behavior may have community implications, but these implications are more straightforward if the research is planned with community application in mind.

Table 3–1 presents a framework within which research programs of relevance to the community can be viewed. Research may first be

TABLE 3–1
Research needs in community psychology

Ecological Level	Target of analysis		
	Persons	*Environments*	*Person-environment interactions*
Individual or small group	1. Psychotherapy 2. Paraprofessionals	1. Family environments 2. Peer group influences	1. Coping styles 2. Crisis intervention
Organizational	1. Group dynamics 2. Organizational behavior	1. Organizational structure 2. Effects of architectural change	1. Effects of changes in perceived environments 2. Effects of different living environments on various groups
Community	1. Leadership formation 2. Social support networks	1. Human ecology 2. Effects of noise, air pollution	1. Behavior setting research 2. Effects of economic change on various groups

classified by virtue of its *ecological level* (see Chapter 1). Research may be at the level of *individuals*, at the level of *organizations*, or at the level of *communities*.

Equally importantly, research may have various *targets of analysis*. The three principal targets that have been stressed in recent writings in the field are *persons, environments*, and *person-environment interactions*. In the past, research has been heavily weighted toward the study of persons, and it is only in recent years that the study of environments or the interaction of people-in-environments has come into its own. Likewise, research in community psychology has strongly focused on the individual or occasionally the organizational level of analysis, rather than operating at the level of the community.

At the individual or small group level, person-oriented research studies would include those on psychotherapy and behavior change (e.g., Goldstein, Heller, & Sechrest, 1966), as well as investigations on the use of paraprofessionals as change agents (e.g., Rappaport, Chinsky, & Cowen, 1971; Dooley, 1975). More environmentally oriented studies consider the climate created in families (Moos,

1975b), or by peers. Research on the interaction of persons and environments at the individual level focuses on the coping patterns that an individual adopts in interaction with his or her environment (e.g., Todd, 1975) and would also include those forms of crisis intervention that view psychological crises as the result of temporary disequilibrium between a person's needs and the environmental supports and resources available.

At the organizational level, research on persons includes the study of group dynamics and the massive volume of research on how individuals behave in organizations (e.g., Porter, Lawler, & Hackman, 1975). The study of organizational structures, such as management hierarchies and information flow systems, as well as research on the effects of architectural modifications on behavior (Stokols, Smith, & Prostor, 1975) would be examples of environmentally oriented research at the organizational level of analysis. The interaction between organizational environments and the behavior of people in organizations can be seen in the work of Moos (1975a, 1975b) on developing scales to measure perceived organizational climate, as well as in the work of Brown (1968) studying the effects of different college living environments on the vocational choice of various kinds of students.

Finally, at the community level, research on persons would include leadership-formation studies and the investigation of networks of social support (Caplan, 1974). Environmentally oriented research is exemplified by studies in human ecology (Boughey, 1973) and by research on the effects of noise pollution on the reading ability of children (Cohen, Glass, & Singer, 1973). Person-environment interaction on the community level can be seen in the work of Barker and his colleagues studying behavior settings in two communities (Barker & Shoggen, 1973), as well as in the research of Brenner (1973) on the effects of economic change on mental hospitalization among various groups in the community.

It should be clear from Table 3–1 that many studies bridge across more than one level of analysis and more than one target area, and so classification can at times be somewhat arbitrary. We do believe, however, that this schematic represents the current research needs in community psychology.

In viewing community research in this framework, it is important to note that research in each of the nine cells is necessary for the development of a comprehensive community psychology. All three levels of analysis and all three targets of analysis refer to legitimate and needed areas of research.

It is also important to note, as mentioned above, that research in the past has emphasized certain of the nine cells more than others, and that a reordering of research needs is called for. Research on the organizational and community levels, and with environmental and interactional problems as targets, is clearly the current priority in community psychology. One factor mitigating against a shift in research priorities in community work is the fact that psychologists have traditionally been trained to study person-oriented phenomena at the individual level. Graduate education often is heavily focused on laboratory experimentation and clinical follow-up techniques. Community psychologists reared in the clinical tradition need to retool in methods more suited to studying organizational and community problems, and education in community psychology needs to emphasize community research techniques from the beginning.

Table 3–1 describes substantive content areas in which further research is needed, with the greatest areas of need occurring at the organizational and community levels. Still unanswered is the question of how best to approach research at these levels. Are there methodologies available to deal with organizational and community level problems? In the following section, we will briefly highlight two frequently overlooked research methodologies that are particularly relevant to the organizational level of analysis—management information systems and cost-effectiveness analysis—and two that seem especially suited for studying community phenomena—social indicators and epidemiology. Again, a complete treatment of these methodologies is beyond our scope, but a sensitization to new methods is necessary before the research needs of community work can be met. There are other methodologies under development with potential usefulness for organizational and community research (Kelly, Snowden, & Munoz, 1977) (e.g., participant and field observation; systems analysis, etc.), but the four to be discussed have the advantage of being clearly defined procedures whose strengths and limitations can be more readily assessed.

Research on the organizational level

Management information systems

It is impossible to run a program without producing data. Programs have a certain number of staff, they render service at a certain rate and, there are certain outcomes. Unfortunately, it is possible to run a program without *recording* data, or at least without recording it in a useful manner. Far too often, this appears to be the case with community programs. Where data are collected, it is often done grudgingly only to appease the demands of a governmental agency for an accounting of funds. Yet the ongoing basic data that a program generates can be of enormous significance to program decision makers. It can alert them to any number of discrepancies between the intent of the program and its actual functioning, and can point out areas in need of investigation and correction.

Taube (1969) and Person (1969) provide some examples of how management information systems for large-scale community programs can be implemented. Bloom (1972) describes an ongoing automated system that provides data on 12 transactions with clients (e.g., put on waiting list, discharged by mutual agreement) and takes only 15 seconds of staff time to input information. We shall describe here what is perhaps the most highly developed computerized system for the collection of ongoing mental health data—the Management Information System of the Orange County, California, Department of Mental Health, developed by J. Richard Elpers (1972; Elpers & Chapman, 1973).

The Management Information System performs five basic functions (Elpers, 1972):

1.   It defines how current resources are being allocated. The demographic characteristics of the population receiving treatment and the way each staff member allocates his or her time between direct and indirect service are capable of being assessed, as are the times when service is most used.

2.   It determines the structure of the service system. Whether people referred to another agency actually get there is ascertainable.

3.   It provides monitoring aids for program managers. Data such as the number of admissions and discharges at a given facility, or the problem characteristics of those who drop out of treatment are available.

4.   It provides data for the reporting requirements of funding agencies. This theoretically mundane aspect of the system is one of its pragmatic strong points, given that government at all levels, as well as private sources (foundations, Community Chest), demand an accounting of their funds.

5.   It generates data for use in long-range planning. For example, the identification of under-served populations can be obtained from analyzing the characteristics of those receiving treatment and this in-

formation can then be compared with similar data taken from the general population.

Five documents provide all the data necessary for the functioning of the system, and the data is analyzed within six working days after the end of every month. Administrators can obtain findings of both programmatic and clinical significance. For example, it would lead to interesting speculation if the data showed that male Therapist X saw his female neurotic patients for a mean of six months and his male neurotic patients for a mean of six weeks.

Examples of questions that have been answered through the MIS include (Elpers, 1975):

a. Utilization of services. It was found that the evening and early morning hours accounted for the majority of admissions for emergency hospitalization, that admissions during the Christmas holidays decreased but rose sharply thereafter, and that outpatient children's services decreased during summer vacation. Resource allocation decisions have been made on the basis of these findings.

b. Types of services. The Department of Mental Health had made a policy decision that there should be an 80 percent–20 percent ratio between direct and indirect (e.g., consultation) mental health services. The MIS was able to monitor this ratio and provide feedback to administrators when it was being violated.

c. Service referral. Approximately one third of the clients of the Department of Mental Health were self-referred, 14 percent were referred by other social agencies (including the local medical center), 4 percent from private practitioners, and a surprisingly large 20 percent were referred by criminal justice agencies. Liaison activities with the criminal justice system have been increased partly as a result of these findings.

d. Client and problem characteristics. The MIS confirmed that the departmental policy of emphasizing prevention services in the poorest area of the county was indeed being carried out, and that indigenous mental health workers were the most heavily involved in servicing the minority community. In several areas of the county, drug dependence was the major problem for single and divorced persons, implying an increased need for education and service programs.

Elpers (1972) correctly notes that the Management Information System, in itself, does not constitute a direct outcome measure. Rather, it is an essential *prerequisite* to performing experimental or quasi-experimental research. Evaluations augmenting the Management Information System with randomized treatment designs and thorough evaluation of selected patient samples are also being done. These evaluations, however, would not be possible without the groundwork performed by the Management Information System.

Information systems such as the one described are not without their limitations. The accumulation and hoarding of data can become a passion. One can lose sight of the fact that data are useful only if they are used to affect program decisions. Paper generates more paper, and bureaucracy feeds on nothing so much as paper.

Elpers (personal communication) provides an instructive example of how to avoid burgeoning bureaucracy in implementing his Management Information System. On-line program administrators and staff were asked what information *they* wanted about the services they were providing. The computer was programmed to answer questions in which people were actually interested. The attempt was made to have the data system *reduce* paperwork by combining old rambling forms into efficient new ones, using multiple-carbon techniques.

The technology for providing almost immediate program monitoring and feedback is currently available, and we cannot exaggerate its importance. The need to routinely collect meaningful program data is the starting point for community research.

Cost-effectiveness analysis

One form of organizational research that has gained great popularity in recent years, especially in the eyes of legislators anxious to prove to the taxpayer that tax money is being well spent, is "cost-effectiveness analysis" or "cost-benefit analysis." Cost-effectiveness refers to the relationship between what is invested in a program (the cost) and what the program produces (the effectiveness or benefit). If a dollar's worth of cost does not produce at least a dollar's worth of effectiveness, then the program is not worth continuing.

There are at least three types of costs and economic benefits that must be taken into account in analyzing community programs (Rothenberg, 1975; Levin, 1975).

Client costs.   These costs are the most obvious. Whether borne by the client or the public, the full cost of prevention or treatment services (including professional salaries, administration, capital investment in buildings, etc.) must enter the cost-effectiveness equation.

Other public costs and benefits.   Mental health programs, for example, can have an impact on many public agencies, with perhaps the welfare and criminal justice systems being the two most likely to feel the after-effects of a new community mental health program. It should be noted that a program can either increase or decrease the costs of these other public agencies. A "social rehabilitation" program that teaches severely disturbed persons the essentials of self-support might decrease welfare rolls and thus have a favorable impact on the welfare system, just as a voluntary family counseling program may divert offenders from the criminal or juvenile justice system and so reduce their costs.

Some community programs, however, may contribute more to the cost than to the effectiveness of other social agencies. The authors are aware of mental health programs that, due to governmental regulations, are open only to welfare recipients. The staff of these programs, believing them to be valuable to persons not on welfare, often work to get potential patients on the welfare rolls so that they qualify for participation. Increased welfare costs, therefore, are an unwitting side effect of the program. Likewise, closing down of state mental hospitals and return of patients to their community may result in drastic cost savings to the state mental health system while at the same time greatly increasing mental health costs at the local level. Increased work loads (and therefore, costs) for the criminal justice system have also been claimed to be a side effect of closing mental hospitals (Abramson, 1972; cf. Monahan, 1973).

Client-related costs and benefits. A change in client earnings as a result of a prevention or treatment program may also be considered part of the economic effectiveness of the program. If a community program results in getting a client off welfare and into a job, then there is economic benefit not only to the client him or herself, but also to society as a whole (increased purchasing power and tax payments, etc.).

In an era of fiscal conservatism and skepticism concerning waste in government programs, it is not surprising that cost-effectiveness analysis has gained in popularity. It gives the impression of being a hard-nosed, no-nonsense, quantitative approach to evaluation. In reality, however, it must be employed with caution and sophistication.

An initial reservation concerning the application of cost-effectiveness techniques to community programs is that such analyses are more easily written about than performed. While program costs may be computed with little difficulty, assessing the costs and benefits accruing to other public sources and to the client may be exceedingly difficult. How much is saved by diverting young offenders from the juvenile justice system to a counseling program? Unless so many are diverted that one can close down facilities and fire judges, the economic impact is unlikely to be large. If diversion from criminality is successful, should one figure in the costs that society would have incurred in terms of crimes that would have been committed, future prison costs, etc., had the counseling program not been there? This lack of agreed-upon guidelines for determining financial benefits and costs has resulted in extreme variability between different cost-effectiveness analyses of the same projects. Glennan (1969), for example, notes that three independent evaluations of the federal Job Corps program, using essentially the same data, yielded estimates of cost-benefit ratios ranging from 0.3 to 5.0. When independent analyses vary by a factor of 16, one had best be very cautious before putting faith in them.

If measuring the financial costs and benefits of a social program is difficult, measuring the nonfinancial costs and benefits often borders on the impossible. How does one price the words taught to an autistic child in a token economy program? Who will set a dollar value on a suicide prevented, an alcoholic rehabilitated, or a miserable life made more meaningful? The changes in behavior and attitudes that a community program may produce usually resist all but the most callous economic quantification. We are not opposing quantification of goals or "hard" measures of treatment success. Quite the opposite, we believe that evaluation of community programs must go far beyond loose consumer satisfaction ("Are you happier now?") measures. Goals must be expressed in observable, verifiable terms. Expressing outcome in solely *financial* terms, however, is so limiting as to be counterproductive. To ignore financial considerations in providing service is a luxury that society will no longer endure; to become obsessed with financial considerations to the extent that human factors are ignored is an equally intolerable situation.

One possible way out of the difficulty is to adopt a "fixed benefit" strategy (Weiss, 1972, p. 86), where one posits a fixed level of benefits and assumes that alternative programs are all designed to reach the same goal. To use a clinical example, if one assumes that for a given population of patients, group therapy has the same results (whatever they may be) as individual therapy, and the same therapist can see either one individual patient or eight patients in a group in a given hour, then group therapy has an 8:1 cost-benefit ratio compared with individual therapy. Or if one assumes that for a given population of patients, therapy by an indigenous paraprofessional therapist achieves the same results as therapy by a psychiatrist, and the cost of the paraprofessional's salary is only one fourth that of the psychiatrist, then the cost-benefit ratio favors the paraprofessional by 4:1. Of course, the difficulty with such a strategy is in making the initial assumption that the results to be achieved by group or individual therapy, or by the paraprofessional or the psychiatrist, are really equivalent.

A third factor to be taken into consideration in performing cost-benefit analyses is the *distribution* of costs and benefits, i.e., who is paying the costs and who is receiving the benefits? What is needed is a set of *weights* reflecting the relative value society places on increases in well-being of specific subgroups (Glennan, 1969). A benefit to one group is weighted 1.0 and to another group 1.3, for example, and similarly with costs. A program to increase the income of poor families might be considered more significant than a program that achieved the same increase with middle-class families, which, in turn, might be considered more significant than if the same gain were achieved with wealthy families. Surely a program that accomplished a 20 percent gain in income for the very poor is more valuable than one that achieved a 30 percent increase for the very rich. Consider the distribution of costs and benefits involved in closing state mental hospitals. From the perspective of the state government, the move may be immensely successful. It costs very little and saves very much. From the viewpoint of local government, which must now provide local service for those formerly under the state's care, closing the hospitals may be a cost-effective disaster. Local costs increase greatly, and the economic gain to the community is hard to find. From a third-party perspective, the move may seem to leave the cost-benefit ratio unchanged, since the total costs may be constant, and only the distribution of the providers change.

Viewed in this light, the political nature of cost-benefit analysis is evident. Different people, with different values, will weigh the distribution of costs and benefits differently. Some will weigh a benefit to minority groups heavier than a benefit to the majority, and others will reverse the ranking. Such divergence is unavoidable in a pluralistic society. What is essential is that the individual performing the cost-benefit analysis be *explicit* about weights used and not simply impose his or her own personal weights (i.e., values) as if they were "objective." There is no reason why a cost-benefit analysis could not give multiple sets of cost-benefit ratios, using multiple sets of weights. The evaluator could then say that with one set of weights the ratio is A, and with another set the ratio is B, etc., and let the choice of weights be left to the open political process, which is where it belongs.

Cost-effectiveness analyses do have the potential for making the distribution of resources more efficient. While the difficulties associated with cost-effectiveness analyses are formidable, society allocates such a small portion of its resources to genuine community programs that the thought of spending it in any but the most efficient way prompts one to make the effort.

Management information systems and cost-effectiveness analyses are two under-utilized techniques which have much to offer as research and evaluation tools at the organizational level. Two similarly underutilized techniques at the community level of analysis are social indicators and epidemiology.

Research on the community level

Social indicators

One of the boldest applications of behavioral science to the political process goes under the title "social indicators." Protagonists in the social indicator movement see it as not just guiding the development of isolated social projects, but also as playing a central feedback role in the formulation of all social policy.

The most common social indicators are published figures on rates of crime, divorce, mental hospitalization, unemployment, etc. Sheldon and Freeman (1970) point out that not all social statistics are social indicators, but rather "only measures which are employed repeatedly and at regular intervals are to be properly considered indicators; in other words, social indicators are time series that allow comparisons over an extended period and which permit one to grasp long-term trends as well as unusually sharp fluctuations in rates." Other than this identification as occurring repeatedly over time, the only other agreed-upon characteristic of social indicators is that they must be capable of being disaggregated or broken down by relevant attributes of the persons or conditions being measured (e.g., race, sex, age, etc.).

Clark (1973) distinguishes two types of indicators: descriptive and analytic. Descriptive indicators are not integrated into a theoretical model specifying their basic relationships to other dimensions of society, while analytic indicators are. Perhaps the best example of an analytic indicator is the Gross National Product (GNP), which is related in economic theory to employment, inflation, exports, etc. Clark (1973) presents four criteria for the selection of social indicators:

1. *Measurability.* In addition to choosing as indicators those variables that possess adequate reliability and validity, social indicators should not tap especially "sensitive variables". Religion, partisan political activities, and sexual practices are generally considered circumscribed from public invasion. Clark (1973) also notes the measurement problems associated with "possible strategic behavior," in that it is unrealistic to pose questions for which the respondent has an incentive to distort his or her response, and where corroborating sources are limited. To present a more virile image to interviewers, for example, males consistently report having a higher frequency of intercourse with their wives than wives report having with their husbands.

2. *Social importance and shared goals.* Useful social indicators should be directed toward questions of concern to many different sectors of society. To the extent that the goals that the indicators are approximating are generally shared goals, the indicators are much easier to collect. The federal Office of Management and Budget (OMB), for example, has begun to publish an annual compendium of social indicator data in the United States. The areas sampled "embody widely held basic objectives: Good health and long life, freedom from crime and the fear of crime, sufficient education to take part in society and make the most of the one's abilities, the opportunity to work at a job that is satisfactory and rewarding, income sufficient for the necessities of life with opportunities for improving one's income, housing that is comfortable within a congenial environment, and time and opportunity for discretionary activities" (OMB, 1973, p. xiii).

3. *Policy importance.* Other things being equal, one should use limited resources to collect social indicators that have relevance to policies that are feasible to implement. If the political climate is favorable to action on one social problem, but not another, one might consider choosing indicators that have some possibility of being acted upon. Bauer (1969, p. 67) states that "It is wisdom, not cynicism, to urge caution in extending diagnostic measures of social phenomena beyond the system's capacity to respond to the problems which are unveiled." Strong criticism of this point will be considered shortly.

4. *Integration into a model.* Where it is possible to choose as indi-

cators variables that lend themselves to integration into a theoretical model, this should be done in preference to collecting indicators that are atheoretical. Ideally, the theory could suggest those variables that would account for change in the indicator, and would tell where else to look for empirical relationships.

Sheldon and Freeman (1970) point out some of the limitations of social indicator data. Using social indicators as an aid in setting goals and evaluating effects may not result in more objective policy formation, since the very process of developing indicators is value-laden. Those not interested in providing equal service across age, ethnic, or sexual groups, for example, need only omit those items as variables in the data system and the composition of the population receiving service will remain unknown, and thus less vulnerable to criticism. Caplan and Nelson (1973) take vehement exception to making "policy importance" a criterion for the selection of social indicators. Such a position, they state, "implies that something becomes a social problem only if it is feasible to deal with it."

> As long as such attitudes prevail among the leaders of the social indicator movement, there should be no question as to whose welfare and interests—dominant political and economic interests, or the wider society—will be served by the selection and gathering of social indicators. If social scientists choose to be morally indifferent social bookkeepers and leave the selection of indicators and their use in the hands of others, then to use Biderman's (1966) term, social "vindicators" would be a better name for such measures. If our apprehensions are confirmed, these vindicators will take the form of person-blame data collected for the political management of guilt and culpability. (p. 209)

The "strategic behavior" mentioned by Clark (1973) can also be a major problem. Perhaps the most obviously reactive use of social indicator data occurs in the criminal justice system, where a change in record-keeping procedures can make it look as if there is a "crime wave" or crime decrease, while the actual number of offenses is constant. The state of New York, for example, recently enacted a drug law with extremely harsh prison sentences for drug possession. California, on the other hand, is now diverting offenders into outpatient drug treatment programs. We would not be surprised if arrest rates for drug possession (a social indicator) showed a sharp downturn in New York and an equally sharp increase in California. This would probably have nothing to do with the actual rates of drug use in either state, but would rather reflect the hesitation of New York police officers to arrest a youth for drug possession, knowing the severe penalties that await him or her, while the conscience of California law enforcement officers would be clear in the knowledge that those arrested will receive "help."

Campbell (1971) is a strong advocate for social indicators in the "experimenting society" he envisions. Yet, he notes that "the more an indicator is used, the more corruption pressures there are on it. Thus, . . . suicide statistics are least trustworthy in those religious cultures where suicide is the greatest sin" (1973, p. 13). Campbell gives a dramatic example of the moral implications of one's choice of social indicators:

> May I illustrate the problem with the following conjectural history leading up to My Lai? Initially, when we got involved in Southeast Asia, the reports of enemy casualties put out by the South Vietnamese and our own military were unbelievable. To correct this, the MacNamara Program, Planning and Budgeting Systems spirit came in and said, let's set aside those wishful estimates and get something objective. So they introduced the body count: We will only count bodies left on the field; we know that's an underestimate, but at least it will be dependable. The body count created a new military goal. In addition to, or instead of, gaining and holding territory, there was now the goal of having bodies to count. Poor Lieutenant Calley was engaged in getting bodies to count for the weekly brag sheet when he produced a lot of irrelevant bodies. But the pressure to have high productivity on body counts, combined with the fact that one couldn't limit it to bodies in uniform for guerilla warfare in which children and old men and women might be participating, created a changed military goal, one that future historians may see as intrinsically evil (1973).

The use of social indicator data to evaluate action programs must be tempered by the fact that they are often argued as a substitute for experimental evaluations (with randomized control groups), while they rarely meet the methodological requirements for drawing scientific conclusions. Decreasing rates of mental hospitalization, for example, have been used to document the success of the Community Mental Health Centers Act, while in all probability the decrease is attributable to the introduction of psychotropic medication and the escalating costs of hospitalization. The danger is not in using social indicators, but in too readily accepting their findings at face value.

Finally, Sheldon and Freeman (1970) argue that analytic social indicators, except in the field of economics, are not currently possible. A comprehensive social theory does not exist. Economic indicators are relatively easy to use since they possess a common interval measure (i.e., dollars). An analogous interval measure to use in balancing the social structure is unavailable since "adding and subtracting apples and oranges and cancers and rapes simply is not possible."

It is our position, however, that one does not need to wait for the ultimate social theory to arrive before attempting to integrate social data in analytic models. Theories abound that relate social variables and that should at least partially yield to social indicator analyses. Indeed, a comprehensive social theory may never exist unless attempts are made to approximate it by making the most of available social data. One could devise separate analytic models for distinct social problems (i.e., one set of analytic indicators for rape and another set for cancer) and then look for similarities or differences in the models, so as to expand social theory. Thus, Brenner (1973) performed a masterful analysis of the effect of economic change upon psychological disorder, using the available social indicator data on the economy and commitment rates to mental hospitals (see Chapter 5). Similar analyses with crime and disease rates could flesh out a more comprehensive theory of human behavior related to economic conditions and this, in turn, could be related to social indicators in other fields.

The use of social indicators to aid in planning and evaluating community-level programs is clearly possible and desirable. Indeed, it is absolutely necessary. One must, however, always be cautious in attributing causal directionality to correlational data, and in assuming that political planning will follow from scientific considerations. While these two caveats are applicable to all forms of social research, they seem especially relevant to the use of social indicators.

Epidemiology

Epidemiology is probably the most highly developed, yet least understood, research technique in the field of community work. While its statistical machinations may awe the uninitiated, the arithmetic basis of epidemiology is exceedingly simple: *counting*. What distinguishes the epidemiologist from other behavioral scientists is an emphasis on counting cases of disease or disorder rather than other dependent variables.

Epidemiology initially rose as a branch of medical science in relation to the study of the great epidemic diseases such as cholera, plague, and yellow fever, which, until this century, were the gravest threats to human life. In attempting to study *epidemic* rates of disease—or unusually frequent occurrences—it became obvious that one first had to have knowledge of *endemic,* or usual rates. Two epidemiological constructs evolved, which are essential to describing endemic and epidemic disease frequency in the population.

The *prevalence* of a disease is the frequency of the disease in the population at a designated point in time. The prevalence rate (sometimes called the point prevalence rate), therefore, is the proportion of the population that exhibits the disease at a specified time. It is computed as:

$$\text{Prevalence rate} = \left(\frac{\text{Number of known cases at given time}}{\text{Population at that point in time}} \right) \quad (K)$$

K being a constant, usually 1,000 or 100,000.

The *incidence* of a disease is the number of *new* cases arising within a specified period or interval of time. The incidence rate, therefore, is computed as:

$$\text{Incidence rate} =$$
$$\left(\frac{\text{Number of newly reported cases in a defined time period}}{\text{Population during that time period}} \right) \quad (K)$$

the time period usually being one year, and the constant (K) 1,000 or 100,000.

Prevalence and incidence—the two basic constructs of epidemiology—are related in the following equation:

$$\text{Prevalence rate} = \text{Incidence rate} \times \text{Average duration}$$

Crucial to acquiring knowledge about the determinants of disease frequency is the concept of causation. Epidemiological research, at best, can show a correlation between certain conditions defined as "pathological" and certain other characteristics of the affected individuals. That correlation does not necessarily imply causation is a truism in all branches of science, and probably has special relevance for epidemiology.

An illustration of an epidemiological correlation that turned out not to imply causation is found in a study that supported the hypothesis that coronary heart disease is inversely correlated with physical activity. The study found a greater frequency of heart disease among London bus drivers (who sit while working) than among bus fare collectors (who stand and move about actively), and casually attributed the heart disease to the lesser physical activity. Critics later pointed out that the drivers tended to be more obese than the fare collectors at the time of employment. In effect, biological selection had predetermined who would sit and who would stand, and the higher frequency of cardiac disease observed among the drivers may have been more related to their weight than to their relative inactivity (Fox, 1970). Note that very different preventive measures would be recommended on the basis of how one interpreted the correlation. If one attributed causality on the basis of the original correlation, preventive measures might have taken the form of a physical education program, while if the latter interpretation is accepted, emphasis might be placed on dietary restrictions.

Correlations found in an epidemiological survey then, can at best provide *clues* as to causation, which can then be tested by more experimental methods. These clues, however, may be invaluable in discovering etiological factors.

The now-famous epidemiological research, *Smoking and Health* (Surgeon General, 1964, p. 182) states the factors that have to be taken into consideration when assessing the causal significance of an obtained correlation.

> The causal significance of an association is a matter of judgment which goes beyond any statement of statistical probability. To judge or evaluate the causal significance of the association between cigarette smoking and lung cancer a number of criteria must be utilized, no one of which, by itself, is pathognomonic or a *sine qua non* for judgment. These criteria include: *(a)* the consistency of the association; *(b)* the strength of the association; *(c)* the specificity of the association; *(d)* the temporal relationship of the association; and *(e)* the coherence of the association.

By *consistency*, it is meant that diverse methods of approach to studying the correlation lead to the same basic conclusions. In the Surgeon General's report, 29 retrospective studies and 7 prospective ones all led to the same finding. By *strength* of association, the report means a high ratio of pathology rates between the groups of interest. In this case, lung cancer was nine to ten times more prevalent in smokers than in nonsmokers. *Specificity* refers to the precision with which knowledge of one component can be used to predict other components. Of the total amount of lung cancer in males, about 90 percent is associated with cigarette smoking. *Temporal relationship* means that exposure to the presumed agent must precede the disease. The early exposure to tobacco smoke and late manifestation of lung cancer fulfill this condition. *Coherence* refers to the fact that the correlation should agree with known facts about the natural history of the disease. For example, the dose-response relationship between cigarette smoking and lung cancer is in a direction supporting causality: the amount of smoking and the duration of smoking are positively correlated with the probability of cancer.

In epidemiology in general, and especially as applied to mental disorders, there is a strong principle of multiple causation, meaning that several factors may be necessary conditions for a disorder to occur, or that one condition may be necessary, but many others can have an effect on the pathological state. It is important to note that all of the causative factors do not have to be known or understood to lead to effective prevention (see Chapter 4). At the end of the 18th century, long before the microbial nature of the causative agents had been demonstrated, Edward Jenner validated a belief prevalent among rural people in parts of England that human infection with cowpox created resistance to smallpox. His "loose" epidemiological study initiated one of the most successful preventive measures of all time.

The exceedingly complex nature of psychological disorder has frustrated attempts at discovering simple etiological chains. In mental health, as in smallpox, however, it is possible to launch preventive programs without demonstrated causal knowledge. A table of *risk factors* for specific psychological disorders might be developed, based on known correlational data. This is similar to the actuarial life expectancy tables used by insurance companies. For example, a "lethality scale" for the assessment of suicide potential has been developed by the Los Angeles Suicide Prevention Center. Items, such as age, sex, medical status, and prior suicidal attempts are scored, the actuarial probability of suicide being higher if the person is over 50 years old, male, chronically ill, or has previously attempted suicide (Coleman, 1972). Ten weighted items are included. The more items scored in the positive direction, the more likely the chance of suicide. Similar tables of risk factors could be developed for alcoholism, schizophrenia, drug abuse, etc. Note that no causal assumptions are made (being male, for example, clearly does not "cause" suicide).

It is obvious that ethical considerations have to be strongly weighted before mounting intervention programs based on risk tables. Attempts to predict and prevent violent behavior by employing psychological risk variables (e.g., history of prior violence, drug abuse, psychological tests) have resulted in an extreme amount of overprediction, so that for every correct psychiatric or psychological prediction of violence there are numerous incorrect ones (see Table 4–1). Risk tables are able to predict behavioral problems at a higher level of accuracy than base rates, however, and therefore may be of use in identifying target populations for whom *voluntary* treatment resources may be available, without negative labeling effects, thus mitigating the ethical constraint against forcing treatment on those who do not need it.

Monahan (1976) also notes that characteristics of situations may be as important as characteristics of persons in preventing violence. Perhaps an epidemiological study of high-risk situations for the occurrence of violent behavior (or other types of problems) might be of significant preventive impact. Ultimately, a table of persons by situation interactions may provide a meaningful and predictive guide for intervention efforts.

Epidemiology in the field of mental health has focused heavily on the effect of socioeconomic status on psychological disorder, and on the receipt of psychological treatment. But the potential contributions of epidemiology to research at the community level of analysis are much more broadly based. Before considering the advantages of epidemiological research, however, let us briefly review three of the major problems associated with this approach.

Major problems of epidemiological research

1. *Disease Model.* The characteristic that sets epidemiology apart from other survey techniques—its emphasis on measuring frequency of disease rather than other dependent variables—also betrays the weakness of epidemiological efforts in the field of mental health. Psychiatric epidemiology has strongly allied itself with a "medical model" of psychological disorder, a model that has come under severe attack in recent years (Szasz, 1960). Fox (1970), for example, refers to "industrial accidents" as "diseases" susceptible to epidemiological analysis. The problem here cannot be dismissed as being merely a semantic one. Assumptions about the nature of "mental disease" have had profound effects upon the manner in which epidemiological studies are carried out. European epidemiologists, for example, have

used traditional psychiatric nosology to identify disease syndromes, and have searched for these syndromes in their epidemiological investigations. Many American psychiatrists, on the other hand, assume that the same etiological factors underly a wide range of "mental diseases" (Menninger, 1963). Psychiatric epidemiology in the United States, therefore, has focused on studying generalized mental disease, rather than specific syndromes (Mechanic, 1969).

Before dismissing psychiatric epidemiology because of its underpinning in the "medical model," it would be wise to distinguish between the *scientific* utility of conceptualizing abnormal behavior in disease terminology and the *social* utility of so doing (Price, 1972). "Let us research schizophrenia *as if* it were a disease" may be a legitimate scientific endeavor, while "let us behave toward schizophrenics *as if* they were diseased" may be quite objectionable. The scientific utility of the medical model depends on its ability to aid in the prediction and understanding of abnormal behavior. The social utility of the model depends more on its treatment implications and on its ramifications for how society behaves toward psychological deviants. If the medical model of abnormal behavior has any scientific utility at all, it should be reflected in the findings of psychiatric epidemiology.

2. *Reliability*. To measure the prevalence of psychological disorder in a population, one must be able to reliably recognize a case of disorder when it is encountered. An epidemiological bromide is that no study is better than its techniques of case finding. At first glance, this task may seem simple: check the records of public and private mental institutions and outpatient clinics to find rates of treated mental disorder in a defined locality. Yet such a technique of case finding would ignore all the cultural, social, economic and situational factors affecting the distribution and utilization of psychological treatment. Especially as we move from more seriously incapacitating conditions to more common forms of psychological disorder, these selective factors bringing persons to treatment are better predictors of case-finding than the psychopathology itself (Mechanic, 1969).

Only by engaging in community epidemiological surveys, like the Midtown study, is it possible to estimate *community-wide prevalence*, rather than *treated prevalence*. In the Midtown study, a random sample of 1660 individuals from midtown Manhattan (99 percent white) was obtained and each person was interviewed at home. Each of the subjects was seen for an average of two hours during which time a

65-page structured interview was administered. The subjects in this epidemiological research were questioned on many items related to psychological and physical symptoms, worries, concerns, as well as such factual items as income, education, etc. Two psychiatrists made independent ratings of each interview protocol and ventured diagnostic judgments. From the Home Interview Survey, 23 percent of the sample was rated as displaying severe, marked, and incapacitating symptoms, with another 22 percent displaying moderately severe symptoms. Yet less than 2 percent of the population of the area were being seen in a mental health facility of any kind (Lin and Stanley, 1962; Langner and Michael, 1963).

The problem of how to reliably measure psychological disorder independent of treatment status is still "the central unresolved problem of psychiatric epidemiology" (Dohrenwend and Dohrenwend, 1969). The 40 to 50 epidemiological surveys of mental disorder in the literature, for example, report prevalence rates from a low of less than 1 percent to a high of 64 percent. "There is no way to account for this great variability on substantive grounds. Rather, the differences are found to be related to differences in thoroughness of data collection and, even more, to contrasting conceptions of what constitutes a 'case.' Nor is it possible to determine which of these rates is the most valid, since none of the studies provided adequate evidence for the validity of the measures that were used" (Dohrenwend & Dohrenwend, 1969, p. 170).

The difficulties associated with subcultural differences in modes of symptom expression, mentioned earlier, is only one of the problems plaguing the measurement issue. The World Health Organization's (WHO, 1973) ten-year International Pilot Study of Schizophrenia has released its preliminary findings. The authors comment that "the two major epidemiological problems are the reliable identification of cases and the satisfactory sampling of the population at risk; the former being concerned with the accuracy of the numerator and the latter with the accuracy of the denominator in any computation of rates" (p. 29). The preliminary WHO study on the reliability of the diagnosis of schizophrenia sampled 1,202 patients in 9 countries. Using standardized procedures, the researchers generally found acceptable diagnostic reliability (r's of .77 and above) *within the same facility,* but much lower reliability between facilities in different countries (r's from .45 to .57, accounting for about one quarter of the variation in patient diagnoses). Those items with the lowest inter-judge reliability in diagnosing schizophrenia were those based on clinical observation (e.g., interview behavior, affect, and rapport) rather than on patient self-report. It is difficult to see how epidemiological research will result in breakthroughs in our understanding of psychological disorder until it has developed methods to reliably measure that disorder.

3. *Lack of control.* The countless variables operating in naturalistic social settings are largely beyond the realm of feasible or ethical control. While innovative methods for conducting truly scientific research in naturalistic situations are available, it is usually difficult to achieve the same degree of precision in analytic epidemiological research that one can obtain in more controlled—and contrived—laboratory settings. The effects of opening a day-treatment center, for example, might be better assessed by randomly assigning prospective patients to the center or to an alternate program, and later measuring the relative effect of each, than by opening the center and later conducting an epidemiological survey to see if the overall prevalence of psychological disorder in the community declined after the initiation of day treatment.

While the difficulties associated with epidemiological research are not to be underestimated, the unique potential of epidemiology for answering questions crucial to community work make it an essential tool for the community psychologist.

Advantages of epidemiological research

1. *Planning for services.* There is simply no other way to intelligently plan for mental health delivery systems than by epidemiological surveys. Only by estimating the nature and severity of psychological problems in a given locale can services be designed to meet those needs. Geriatric services are not emphasized in a "new town" composed largely of young married persons, nor does one open a day-care center in a retirement village. In addition to identifying target problems and revealing community priorities, the location of mental health facilities and staffing considerations (e.g., need for Spanish-speaking workers) may likewise be most rationally approached by having recourse to an epidemiological survey (Catalano & Monahan, 1975).

2. *Ultimate outcome measure.* While the inappropriateness of using an epidemiological survey as an outcome measure in studying a fine point of mental health technique has already been mentioned, epidemiological investigations do provide what might be called the

"ultimate test" of the effectiveness of mental health services. If the totality of services offered by a mental health center are assumed to be individually effective and have been in existence some time, one would expect the overall impact of these services to have an effect on the distribution of psychological disorder in the population. Such an effect could be revealed only in an epidemiological survey.

3. *Resolving theoretical issues in community psychology*. Despite the methodological problems confronting analytic epidemiology, it is difficult to see how any other research method could take its place. Such crucial etiological questions as the relationship between social class and psychological disorder (Dohrenwend & Dohrenwend, 1969) are amenable only to epidemiological analysis. One cannot randomly assign children to a certain social class and then raise them in a controlled "laboratory analogue" of society.

Until such naturalistic questions as "How do psychological problems develop?" and "How is mental health care utilized?" are answered, there can be no substitute for epidemiology.

We should also remember that the primary tool of psychiatric epidemiology is the *survey*, whether in the form of clinical interviews or questionnaires. Surveys, of course, have uses other than in psychiatric epidemiology. Surveys need not be restricted to measuring "mental disease" in a population. If used in other ways, they are spared the first two criticisms of epidemiological surveys mentioned above—reliance on the "medical model" and difficulties in establishing reliability of case diagnosis. There is an increasing reliance in community work upon more "public opinion"-type surveys that inquire about specific psychological problems (alcoholism, drug abuse, etc.) and priorities of the community, as well as the utilization of existing mental health facilities. While such surveys are not immune from reliability and validity problems (e.g., the self-reporting of drug use may be distorted), it is much easier to assess a person's opinion of the most urgent problems in his or her community than it is to assess whether or not the individual is "schizophrenic." Surveys can provide indispensable information for use in planning comprehensive mental health care and prevention programs. They represent an excellent form of "consumer input" into the development of psychological services. Largely because of their flexibility, surveys can retain many of the advantages of classical epidemiological research, while avoiding some of the limitations.

Conclusions

In this chapter, we have argued that substantive advances in community work are contingent upon a firm commitment to empirical investigation. The unexamined program is not worth doing, for several reasons: Kuhnian "paradigm shifts" are impossible without a research base; cyclical swings in the social "mood" will obviate any change that cannot be empirically validated; and the community has an ethical right to have those who offer programs prove their mettle.

Basic research, we believe, differs from evaluation research not in methodology or sophistication, but in intent. Evaluation is undertaken for use in decision making and for answering program-derived questions, while basic research emphasizes the production of knowledge for its own sake and has application as only a secondary consideration. The primary goal of both research and evaluation, however, is the same: eliminating the plausible rival hypotheses that can account for the obtained findings.

While the production of quality research and evaluation is among the most pressing needs in the field of community psychology, some research studies and evaluation projects are needed more than others. We have conceptualized empirical efforts as differing in terms of their ecological levels and targets of analysis. Research may take place at the level of the individual, the organization, or the community, and may have as its target the person, the environment, or person-environment interactions. Research in the past has been primarily at the individual level and with persons as targets. What is needed now is for researchers to concentrate on environmental and interactional targets at the organizational and community levels. We have discussed in detail two specific research strategies at each of these levels.

On the organizational level, management information systems can provide the kind of ongoing data base that not only makes for more informed day-to-day decision making, but provides a foundation for more controlled investigations. Cost-effectiveness analyses likewise may provide the community with valuable information for the optimal allocation of scarce resources.

On the community level, the use of social indicators has been the boldest application of behavioral science to the policy-making process. While one must always be cautious in attributing directionality to correlational data, social indicators can help both to describe the current functioning of a community and to generate interactional theories of social change. Epidemiology is another technique with descriptive and analytic functions. Simply counting the cases of problem behavior in a given community and disaggregating the data on relevant variables has led to great advances in the prevention of physical disorder and could be of similar utility in the case of other problems of human behavior.

In this chapter, we have only sampled from a myriad of research and evaluation strategies that could move empirical investigations in the mental health fields away from the preoccupation with directly studying the dispositions of individual persons and toward a critical look at the community and environmental forces impinging upon them. We have attempted to point to other methodological avenues wherever possible. In the following sections of the book we discuss the core tenets of the community approach and several perspectives on how community intervention should be conducted. In each case, the issues raised will harken back to the concerns we have just discussed and will evoke the question: How can some of the rival hypotheses be eliminated, so that we may progress in our thought and in our actions?

References

Abramson, M.   The criminalization of mentally disordered behavior. *Hospital and Community Psychiatry, 23,* 1972, 101–105.

Barker, R., & Shoggen, P.   *Qualities of community life.* San Francisco: Jossey-Bass, 1973.

Bauer, R.   Societal feedback. In B. Gross (Ed.), *Social intelligence for America's future.* Boston: Allyn and Bacon, 1969.

Biderman, A.   Social indicators and goals. In R. Bauer (Ed.), *Social indicators.* Cambridge, Mass: M.I.T. Press, 1966.

Bloom, B.   Human accountability in a community mental health center. *Community Mental Health Journal,* 1972, 8, 251–260.

Boughey, A.   *Ecology of populations.* New York: Macmillan, 1973.

Brenner, M. H.   *Mental illness and the economy.* Cambridge, Mass.: Harvard University Press, 1973.

Brown, R.   Manipulation of environmental press in a college residence hall. *Personnel and Guidance Journal,* 1968, 46, 555–560.

Campbell, D.   *Methods for the experimenting society.* Unpublished manuscript, 1971.

Campbell, D. Interview with Donald Campbell, *Evaluation,* 1973.

Caplan, G. *Support systems and community mental health.* New York: Behavioral Publications, 1974.

Caplan, N., & Nelson, S. On being useful: the nature and consequences of psychological research on social problems. *American Psychologist,* 1973, *28,* 199–211. Copyright 1973 by the American Psychological Association.

Catalano, R., & Monahan, J. The community psychologist as social planner: Designing optimal environments. *American Journal of Community Psychology,* 1975, *3,* 327–334.

Clark, T. Community social indicators: From analytic models to policy applications. *Urban Affairs Quarterly,* 1973, *9,* 3–35.

Cohen, S., Glass, D., & Singer, J. Apartment noise, auditory discrimination, and reading ability in children. *Journal of Experimental Social Psychology,* 1973, *9,* 407–422.

Coleman, J. *Abnormal psychology and modern life.* Chicago: Scott, Foresman and Co., 1972.

Dohrenwend, B., & Dohrenwend, B. *Social status and psychological disorder.* New York: John Wiley & Sons, 1969.

Dooley, D. Effect of automated reflection response training on the group assessment of interpersonal traits. *Journal of Counseling Psychology,* 1975, *22,* 535–541.

Edwards, W., Guttentag, M., & Snapper, K. A decision-theoretic approach to evaluation research. In E. Struening & M. Guttentag (Eds.), *Handbook of Evaluation Research,* Beverly Hills: Sage Publications, 1975, pp. 139–181.

Elpers, J. Management information systems: tools for integrating human services. Paper presented to the Institute on Hospital and Community Psychiatry, St. Louis, 1972.

Elpers, J. Report to the Orange County (California) Board of Supervisors, April 22, 1975.

Elpers, J., & Chapman, R. Management information for mental health services. *Administration in Mental Health,* Fall 1973, 12–25.

Fox, J. *Epidemiology: Man and disease.* New York: Macmillan, 1970.

Glennan, T. *Evaluating federal manpower programs: Notes and observations.* Santa Monica, Calif.: The Rand Corporation, 1969.

Goldstein, A., Heller, K., & Sechrest, L. *Psychotherapy and the psychology of behavior change.* New York: John Wiley & Sons, 1966.

Kassebaum, G., Ward, D., & Wilner, D. *Prison treatment and parole survival.* New York: John Wiley & Sons, 1971.

Kelly, J., Snowden, L., & Munoz, R. Social and community interventions. *Annual Review of Psychology,* 1977.

Kuhn, T. *The structure of scientific revolutions.* Chicago: University of Chicago Press, 1962.

Langner, T., & Michael, S. *Life stress and mental health,* New York: Free Press, 1963.

Levin, H.   Cost-effectiveness analysis in evaluation research. In E. Struening & M. Guttentag (Eds.), *Handbook of Evaluation Research.* Beverly Hills: Sage Publications, 1975, pp. 95–122.

Levine, M., & Levine, A.   *A social history of the helping services.* New York: Appleton-Century-Crofts, 1970.

Lin, T., & Stanley, C.   *The scope of epidemiology in psychiatry.* Geneva: World Health Organization, 1962.

Mechanic, D.   *Mental health and social policy.* Englewood Cliffs, N.J.: Prentice-Hall, 1969.

Menninger, K.   *The vital balance.* New York: Viking Press, 1963.

Monahan, J.   The psychiatrization of criminal behavior. *Hospital and Community Psychiatry,* 1973, *24,* 105–107.

Monahan, J.   The prevention of violence. In J. Monahan (Ed.), *Community mental health and the criminal justice system.* New York: Pergamon, 1976, pp. 13–34.

Moos, R.   *Evaluating correctional and community settings.* New York: John Wiley & Sons, 1975. (a)

Moos, R.   *Evaluating treatment settings.* New York: John Wiley & Sons, 1975. (b)

Office of Management and Budget.   *Social Indicators.* Washington, D.C.: Government Printing Office, 1973.

Person, P.   *A statistical information system for community mental health centers.* Washington, D.C.: Government Printing Office, 1969.

Porter, L., Lawler, E., & Hackman, J.   *Behavior in organizations.* New York: McGraw-Hill, 1975.

Price, R.   *Abnormal behavior: Perspectives in conflict.* New York: Holt, Rinehart and Winston, 1972.

Price, R., & Cherniss, C.   Training for a new profession: Research as social action. *Professional Psychology,* in press.

Rappaport, J., Chinsky, J., & Cowen, E.   *Innovations in helping chronic patients.* New York: Academic Press, 1971.

Rothenberg, J.   Cost-benefit analysis: A methodological exposition. In E. Struening & M. Guttentag (Eds.), *Handbook of Evaluation Research.* Beverly Hills: Sage Publications, 1975, pp. 55–88.

Sheldon, E., & Freeman, H.   Notes on social indicators: Promises and potential. *Policy Sciences,* 1970, *1,* 97–111.

Stokols, D., Smith, T., & Proster, J.   Partitioning and perceived crowding in a public space. *American Behavioral Scientist,* 1975, *18,* 792–814.

Struening, E., & Guttentag, M. (Eds.).   *Handbook of evaluation research.* Beverly Hills: Sage Publications, 1975 (2 volumes).

Surgeon General.   *Smoking and Health.* Washington, D.C.: Government Printing Office, 1964.

Szasz, T.   The myth of mental illness. *American Psychologist,* 1960, *15,* 113–118.

Taube, C.   *Community mental health data systems.* Washington, D.C.: Government Printing Office, 1969.

Todd, D.   Symposium on coping behavior. Presented at the American Psychological Association Convention, 1975.

Weiss, C.   *Evaluation research: Methods for assessing program effectiveness.* Englewood Cliffs, N.J.: Prentice-Hall, 1972.

Weiss, C.   Evaluation research in the political context. In E. Struening & M. Guttentag (Eds.), *Handbook of Evaluation Research.* Beverly Hills: Sage Publications, 1975, pp. 13–26.

World Health Organization.   *Report of the international pilot study of schizophrenia.* Geneva: WHO, 1973.

PART TWO

Basic concepts

4

POPULATION AND PREVENTION

A *population perspective* and a *preventive orientation* toward psychological dysfunction perhaps most sharply distinguish between community and clinical perspectives in the mental health fields. In a manner analogous to public health practice, population-oriented mental health professionals accept responsibility for the mental health of the total membership of a specific circumscribed community. As in public health work, the population and not the individual is the unit of concern; and the search becomes one of finding ways to promote the psychological well-being of populations while at the same time reducing the flow of psychological dysfunction.

In line with a population perspective, the community mental health movement is marked by a call for a preventive instead of an exclusively treatment orientation. Though difficult to implement (as we shall shortly document) the importance of prevention is not difficult to understand. In 1963, John F. Kennedy highlighted the need for prevention in a presidential message as follows:

> Our attack must be focused on three major objectives: First we must seek out the causes of mental illness and mental retardation and eradicate them. Here, more than in any other area, "an ounce of prevention is worth more than a pound of cure." For prevention is far more desirable for all concerned. It is far more economical and it is far more likely to be successful. Prevention will require both selected specific programs directed especially at known causes, and the general strengthening of our fundamental community, social welfare, and educational programs which can do much to eliminate or correct the harsh environmental conditions which often are associated with mental retardation and mental illness.

The concepts of population and prevention do not seem particularly revolutionary. It would be difficult to argue with the noble purpose

111

implicit in the presidential message stated above. Yet a population perspective and a preventive orientation do not represent the current conceptual stance of the mental health professions. As Cowen (1973) points out, a field's conceptual stance is indicated by the sum of the activities of its constituents. "If 90 percent of MH activities are in psychodiagnosis, therapy, and institutional care, then that is the field's prevailing, if implicit, conceptual bias" (Cowen, p. 429). At the present time, mental health activity primarily consists of the individual treatment of disordered behavior. This is so much the case that most mental health professionals do not have a language to adequately encompass population and prevention concepts, let alone a set of procedures that would allow them to develop practical applications.

In 1964 Hobbs decried the inadequacies in mental health training programs. He stated:

> Psychiatrists, social workers, nurses and psychologists have been trained primarily as clinicians, as intrapsychic diagnosticians, as listeners with the third ear; we are clinicians, not public health, mental health experts. Who among us knows enough about schools, courts, churches, welfare programs, recreation, effects of automation, cultural deprivation, population mobility, delinquency, family life, city planning and human ecology in general to presume to serve on the staff of a comprehensive community mental health center? The first training program we should plan should be for ourselves. We have nothing more urgent to do. (Hobbs, p. 827)

The concern that Hobbs voiced in 1964 about the inadequate training of mental health professionals in understanding the relationships between social ecology, community life, and mental health is still true today. Thus the call for the adoption of a population perspective and a preventive orientation is addressed not only to practitioners, but to the training and research centers where future practitioners are to be trained; and where the research on which practice is to be based is most likely to be generated. The call is for a change in the conceptual stance of training and research programs from which a change in practice will follow.

The developing mental health professions: Pressures for treatment and neglect of prevention

How did it happen that the mental health professions developed a treatment rather than a prevention language and technology? To begin with, one should remember that from a historical perspective, the mandate given the mental health professions was treatment or incarceration—not prevention. Communities were concerned about the troubled and deviant members in their midst. The early mental health workers, mostly medical practitioners, were asked to treat or at minimum hold in custody those who were thought to be no longer capable of caring for themselves and whose behavior was judged to be frightening and unpredictable. The doctors who worked in mental hospitals accepted this mandate. Historically, American psychiatrists were mental hospital administrators. Note that the organization now called the American Psychiatric Association had its origins in the "Association of Medical Superintendents of American Institutions for the Insane," founded in 1844 (R. Caplan, 1969). The early pioneers and heroes of the mental health professions—Janet, Charcot, Freud, Sullivan, etc.—are held in esteem primarily for their contributions to our understanding and treatment of the severe emotional disorders. Even today the status hierarchy in medicine gives highest prestige to those equipped to deal with complex and unusual disorders—though their occurrence may be relatively infrequent in the general population. General practitioners and their public health counterparts receive much less admiration from their colleagues and much less pay than more exotic specialists.

This same set of values can be seen in the status given psychiatric practitioners by their medical colleagues. Common problems in living are not considered as "real" and worthy of a great deal of expert attention. Common emotional disorders are considered malingering at worst, or as involving simple suggestibility at best. This kind of attitude would lead to a status pressure within psychiatry to de-emphasize the milder disorders and to focus upon the severe disorders that clearly would be beyond the capabilities of most medical practitioners and that the latter would be all too willing to refer to their psychiatric colleagues.

But what of clinical psychology? Why did it develop a technology that was basically treatment-oriented? It has been suggested that as clinical psychology developed, it adopted a stance toward practice that emulated the private practice mode of service dominant in the field of psychiatry. The model was that of a practitioner offering a service to those persons referred because of the intensity of the disturbance they create among their associates, who are further preselected by their ability and willingness to pay and by their acquiescence to the definition of their problems in mental health terms.

That psychiatry became the model for the practice of clinical psychology should not be too surprising. The theories dominant in the mental health professions were psychiatric in origin, academic psychology had not developed a helping technology of its own, and the facilities most interested in hiring the new fledgling psychologists were medical in orientation. One should remember that the growth of clinical psychology was accelerated after World War II, in part as a function of the government's response to the adjustment problems of returning veterans. Special grants were given to academic departments of psychology to develop clinical psychology programs, whose practicum facilities were to be the psychiatric institutions supported by the federal government through Veterans Administration and Public Health Service programs. As Albee has suggested:

> If, 25 years ago, enormously increased amounts of federal support for training in psychological intervention had been funneled through the public school system, rather than through psychiatric facilities, the present nature of clinical psychology would have been altogether different. Or, if psychological manpower had been supported and trained through the welfare system, we would be a still different field today. (Albee, 1970, p. 1073)

The practice of psychiatry in America has followed the model of the private practice of medicine. While public health concepts have always been a part of medicine, except for a concern with communicable disease and sanitation, few physicians have ever taken seriously the public health mandate of promoting general health and well-being. The House of Delegates of the American Medical Association defines public health as "the art and science of maintaining, protecting and improving the health of people through organized community efforts" (Brown, 1969). Yet, how many physicians are actively involved in or concerned with improving the health of persons outside their own specific office practice? So too for psychiatry. Hobbs (1964) has estimated that over 50 percent of the psychiatrists trained under NIMH (National Institute of Mental Health) grants (that is, whose training was subsidized by taxpayers) go into private practice.

Our chronology suggests that clinical psychology looked to psychiatry for a model of practice, while psychiatry in turn was most influenced by the prevailing private practice modes of operation dominant in general medicine. Both groups of mental health practitioners were reinforced for these views by increased status and greater financial remuneration associated with the private practice–therapy specialist model. The thinking associated with this model became so pervasive that as Cowen points out, it is as if we automatically accepted the identity: "Helping people in distress = Psychotherapy" (Cowen, 1973, p. 424).

During the late 1940s and early 1950s, this country's growing mental health problems, kept submerged during the second world war, finally became apparent. At that time, the situation was aggravated by the large numbers of war veterans who were experiencing adjustment problems upon return to civilian life. But even without this added burden, the population of the state mental hospitals had been steadily rising for decades. It was apparent to some informed observers (Hollingshead & Redlich, 1958) that the evolving system of mental health care delivery was beginning to result in the least amount of help being made available to those who needed it the most. When the government turned to the leaders of the mental health professions for a solution to the country's growing mental health problems, the answer given was to train more mental health professionals; and for the 25-year period following World War II that is exactly what the government did. Grants were given to training centers for psychiatry and clinical psychology for the purpose of increasing mental health manpower. It was assumed by the granting agencies, and by the training institutions receiving the money, that increased numbers of professionals doing the same thing (treatment) would solve the problem. One might argue that the press of cases needing treatment in those postwar years mandated a postponement in the concern for prevention. However, the press of cases is never likely to decrease. If asked to describe their current needs, clinic administrators, responding to the flood of cases to which they are constantly exposed, would still call for an expansion of treatment personnel. It is a fantasy to suppose that a community clinic, ignoring prevention activities, could ever adequately deal with local mental health problems with "just a few more" qualified therapists.

An equally important reason for the heavy emphasis on treatment in our mental health training centers since the end of World War II can be traced to the unquestioned acceptance of psychotherapy as the only way of helping people in distress. Conceptual alternatives were never seriously considered, and without a change in how one looks at a problem a change in how one deals with that problem will not occur.

What is prevention?

It is easier to say what prevention is not, than to be precise in specifying what meaning it should have. Prevention is not the extension of existing mental health treatment services to new populations formerly considered unreachable. Clearly such action, while desirable, simply extends the scope of existing services. Prevention is not training new mental health workers (paraprofessionals) to engage in remedial work that they might do more efficiently than overtaxed professionals. Again, such action serves to extend treatment facilities to new populations. Prevention is not the development of new treatment programs (e.g., community care for the mentally ill, milieu therapy, family therapy, behavior modification, etc.) no matter how sensible or in vogue such treatment programs may be. All of the above, while not prevention activities, have become associated with community work. They are important new developments that promise to make treatment more efficient. They have been readily adopted by many community mental health clinics, in part, because they are more easily understood by clinic professionals, who are most often treatment-oriented themselves.

Primary, secondary, and tertiary prevention

The most widely accepted definition of prevention is presented by Caplan's (1964) concept of "primary prevention." Caplan distinguishes between three types of prevention in the following manner:

> . . . the term preventive psychiatry refers to the body of professional knowledge, both theoretical and practical, which may be utilized to plan and carry out programs for reducing (1) the incidence of mental disorders of all types in a community (primary prevention), (2) the duration of a significant number of those disorders which do occur (secondary prevention), and (3) the impairment which may result from those disorders (tertiary prevention). (Caplan, 1964, pp. 16–17)

Bolman amplifies on this definition as follows:

> Primary prevention attempts to prevent a disorder from occurring. Secondary prevention attempts to identify and treat at the earliest possible moment so as to reduce the length and severity of disorder. Tertiary prevention attempts to reduce to a minimum the degree of handicap or impairment that results from a disorder that has already occurred. From the standpoint of the community, these distinctions are equivalent to reducing incidence, prevalence and extent of disability respectively. (Bolman, 1969 p. 208)

Some writers believe that tertiary prevention and certain types of secondary prevention should not bear the label "prevention" at all.

Cowen (1973) suggests that it is a misnomer to think of activities that are oriented toward reducing the residual effects of existing disorders as prevention. From this point of view, "so-called tertiary prevention" should be justified on grounds other than prevention, such as the need to minimize human misery and suffering. Similarly, Cowen notes that "secondary prevention" has been used in two quite distinct ways. Its first use involves identifying incipient dysfunction in the very young and intervening to forestall further maldevelopment. A second use occurs in describing efforts to detect an acute psychotic episode very early in its development rather than after weeks or months, so that it can be handled more effectively. This latter use increases the ambiguity of the concept, and we shall accept Cowen's (1973) point of view that a crisper conceptual alternative is presented if prevention is redefined to include only primary and early secondary activities.

Types of prevention programs: Community-wide, milestone, and high-risk strategies

Bloom (1968) describes a typology of preventive efforts that distinguishes more clearly among types of intervention. Bloom describes prevention as involving either *community-wide, milestone,* or *high-risk* programs. In the first, all the residents of a community are the recipients of the program. Examples might be water purification to eliminate typhoid fever and cholera, swamp drainage to reduce the risk of malaria, or supervision of food and water processing. Mental health analogues might include community development programs in disorganized slum communities, or programs aimed at initiating community-wide support for better jobs, housing, education, or child development services. In the milestone approach, citizens are exposed to the program at specified periods in their lives. "Residents of a specified area march as it were, past the program. Prior to reaching it they are not protected" (Bloom, 1968, p. 118). When they reach the program, they are exposed to its effects. An example of this type of program might be smallpox vaccination required upon admission to school. Psychological "milestones" might include critical developmental periods such as birth of a sibling, initial school attendance, entry into adolescence, first semester away from home at college, first year of marriage, birth of the first child, job change, menopause, death of a spouse, and retirement. These nodal developmental events are chosen because they have the potential for being situations of high psychological risk. While the focus in the milestone approach is on situations or events, in Bloom's third type of prevention program—the high-risk program, the focus is on vulnerable populations. Groups vulnerable to specific disorders are identified and are subject to special programs designed to reduce or prevent the incidence of dysfunction. An example might be a program in a school system to provide a special supportive relationship to children identified as showing incipient signs of emotional disorder. Other examples of high-risk populations might include: the children of alcoholics, drug addicts, or mental patients; children who experience death of a parent at an early age; children with physical handicaps, or those about to experience major surgery; and survivors of natural or man-made disasters such as earthquakes, floods, plane crashes, and wars.

Each of the three types of prevention programs described by Bloom has both strengths and liabilities. High-risk programs can be the most focused, with the intervention designed to fit the specific suspected vulnerability. However, as we shall discuss more fully, the early identification of high-risk groups poses some ethical dangers. The prediction of later disability from early signs of vulnerability is usually accompanied by an overprediction bias. More cases are tagged as needing remediation than eventually would become disabled if left alone. Furthermore, the identification of incipient disability can bring with it problems of stigma if the labeling of vulnerable cases is not done with sensitivity and tact.

Community-wide and milestone interventions avoid the problems of labeling particular groups since no one is singled out as particularly needy. The intervention is provided for everyone. The disadvantages of these approaches involve the potential for greater cost. Many more people get the program than would actually need it. A second possibility is that those who would benefit most from community-wide intervention are the most competent—who need it the least. One of the current controversies concerning the TV program "Sesame Street" concerns this very issue. The program was designed for the educationally disadvantaged, but critics have charged that children from educationally advanced homes are more likely to watch the program regularly than children from deprived homes (Cook et al., 1975).

There are no easy answers to the issues raised above. Any intervention has both costs and benefits and both must be realistically assessed in any decision involving program implementation. It is hoped that programs can be designed to minimize financial and psychological costs; but this cannot be done without full awareness of potential program liabilities.

Do prevention activities require prior knowledge of etiology?

Caplan's definition of primary prevention as reducing the incidence of mental disorders in a community, while a worthwhile goal, says nothing about how that goal should be achieved. Part of the reason for this omission is that the causes of psychic dysfunction are still obscure. How can one mount prevention programs when etiology is unknown? Some would downgrade prevention attempts for this reason. However, prevention cannot be dismissed so easily for the same might be said of treatment activities. How can one expect to successfully treat mental disorders of uncertain etiology? Yet treatment activities flourish with little apparent concern for the ambiguities of causation.

Caplan takes the position that while full knowledge of etiology would be helpful, much can be done in both prevention and treatment with less than perfect knowledge. Pointing to the history of public health activities, Caplan cites examples of successful programs of primary prevention that were instituted before valid knowledge was available concerning their etiology. Caplan describes these examples as follows:

> Some of the most successful programs of primary prevention were instituted before we had valid etiologies of the illnesses which were prevented. The prevention of smallpox by vaccination and the prevention of scurvy by eating limes and fresh vegetables preceded by many years our knowledge of the causes of these illnesses. In fact, the major advances in the control of epidemics or infectious diseases in our cities in the latter part of the 19th century predated the germ theory and the discovery of the microbial agents responsible for disease. The sanitary programs were based on the belief of the hygienic reformers that dirt, squalor, and congestion were "unnatural" and "unhealthy" and by a desire to introduce the "pure" conditions of country life into the towns.
>
> Even the history-making preventive action of Snow in removing the handle of the Broad Street pump to halt the London epidemic of cholera in the 19th century was not based on knowledge of the existence of the cholera organism in the polluted water or of the significance of this microorganism in the etiology of the epidemic.
>
> The public health practitioners in these and many other instances did not wait until they had etiological knowledge before instituting their preventive programs. They relied on the best current judgments of factors which seemed to be associated with the presence or absence of

illnesses in various segments of the population. In each instance, the proponents of a preventive program based themselves on personal observation or popular impressions. Jenner was struck by the absence of smallpox in those members of a population who had previously contracted cowpox. The British Admiralty was impressed by the stories that sailors on ships well stocked with citrus fruits and fresh vegetables did not suffer scurvy. The 19th century hygienic reformers made the general observation that epidemics occurred in the big cities and not in rural areas. And Snow carefully listed the addresses of persons contracting cholera and demonstrated that they all drew their water from the Broad Street pump, whereas those who obtained water from some other source were not infected. (Caplan, 1964, pp. 29–30)

An implication of this position is that while partial knowledge can lead to actions that might later prove to be wrong, more is to be gained by taking action based on incomplete causal information than by doing nothing. It is in this spirit that many preventive intervention programs are initiated. Even ineffective programs can lead to useful information if they are conducted in such a way that their results can be reliably assessed and reasons for lack of success can be determined.

Still, a basic problem remains. Views of the etiology of mental disorder are marked by considerable controversy. One element of the argument concerns the relative importance of biological versus social determinants of dysfunctional behavior. This aspect of the controversy has some importance since, as Price (1974) points out, assumptions about etiology do strongly influence our notions of appropriate intervention. Another element of the problem can be seen in the distinction in the prevention literature between systems-centered and person-oriented approaches (Cowen, 1973). A systems focus assumes that human development is primarily shaped by a small number of key social institutions and settings and that prevention should be oriented toward institutional or setting change. Person-oriented interventions assume that the focus of prevention should be on early childhood intervention with the key individuals who shape the child's development (e.g., parents, teachers, and other primary care-givers). The focus is on people who inhabit settings, not on the settings themselves. Thus the unanswered questions that influence prevention activities can be summarized as follows: Is the cause of dysfunctional behavior to be seen as residing within the individual or in the environment; and if in the environment, should the focus be on persons within the environment or upon environmental variables themselves. Clearly our present state of knowledge does not allow us to answer these questions, but we can suggest a direction that we believe future conceptualizations of the problem should take.

A multiple-risk-factor orientation to etiology: Implications for prevention

Epidemiologists are moving away from a conception of disease that implies a simple unitary cause. Even for medical disorders in which etiology would seem clearcut, such as tuberculosis, the appearance of the actual illness can be related to psychological stress factors (Lemkau, 1969). Price (1974) makes the same point with regard to schizophrenia. Even for disorders whose predisposing etiology may have a strong genetic loading, social factors in the form of psychosocial stresses may still determine whether disordered behavior actually occurs.

What this means is that we should now think in terms of "multifactorial causation" (Price, 1974), or "risk factors", instead of simple causation. The best analogy from physical medicine might be how we currently view the risk factors associated with the likelihood of heart disorders. We know that the risk factors associated with the appearance of heart attacks include genetic and constitutional factors, e.g., the extent to which there is a history of heart attacks in the family, age of onset, weight, and cholesterol level; but also include life-style variables such as diet, amount of smoking and exercise, pace of life, and type of reaction to stress. There is no *one* "cause" of heart disorders but anyone demonstrating a large number of the above risk factors is statistically more vulnerable to the appearance of heart disorder than is an individual with a low risk loading. Similarly an individual can reduce the likelihood of a heart attack by reducing as many of the risk factors as possible—e.g., cut down on smoking, increase exercise, control diet, etc.

Adopting a multiple-risk factor orientation to the etiology of mental disorders means that one would not expect that a *single* causative agent would ever be found that would be *the* cause of psychic dysfunction. The best strategy would be to develop risk equations for the different disorders or behavioral problems. The loadings might not be the same for each disorder, although the factors (genetic, constitutional, developmental, environmental) would surely be similar. The new orientation would also imply that intervention to reduce the incidence of dysfunctional behavior could occur at a number of levels.

Prevention efforts might be oriented toward reducing the impact of environmental stress at community, institutional, or familial levels; or intervention programs might be aimed at strengthening the capacity of vulnerable populations to deal with that stress. The issue becomes one of empirical benefit. What types of interventions produce the best results at the least financial, societal, and psychic cost?

The differential effects of intervention targeted at several levels simultaneously can be seen in an example provided by Maccoby (1975) concerning a community-wide attempt to reduce the incidence of heart disorder. Maccoby and his associates at the Stanford Heart Disease Prevention Program launched prevention-oriented media campaigns in two matched towns and compared the results with data from a matched control town in which no media efforts were undertaken. Both "experimental" towns received messages oriented toward increasing awareness of the dangers of smoking and obesity, providing information about "heart-healthy" recipes and cooking hints, and stressing the usefulness of moderate exercise. In addition, a subsample of high-risk subjects in one of the two experimental towns was singled out for more intensive individual effort to change life-style habits with regard to eating and smoking. For example: specific guidance was provided in food shopping, menu planning, and food preparation; group support and spouse encouragement were elicited during weekly weigh-ins; and a program of behavior management oriented toward a gradual decrease in cigarette smoking was initiated.

While significant changes in attitude and information occurred through the use of mass media alone, the more intensive behavioral management and group reinforcement program produced superior effects that were more likely to be carried over into daily behavior. As Maccoby noted, while increments in knowledge and useful attitude change did occur as a result of the media campaign, there were a number of people who already knew the risks associated with smoking and obesity, but who were unable to change chronic habits on their own.

The difficulty of deciding on prevention priorities

Decisions concerning the allocation of mental health resources are constantly occurring, even in the absence of completed risk equations for the different psychological disorders. Thus, when the original Joint Commission on Mental Illness recommended that the profound mental illnesses were the major unfinished business of the mental health field, they were making a priority statement about the allocation of mental health resources. Cowen (1973) disagrees with this priority. He argues that our thinking is too much shaped by an "end-state mentality" and that we are too concerned with rooted dysfunction. He argues further that concentration on profound disorders at the expense of the many who are less severely disturbed mocks the concept of "a democratic-humanitarian ethic." Cowen's point here is that the mental health professions have to make some difficult decisions concerning resource allocation; that is, they must decide whether to help the many who are subject to milder disorders or whether to concentrate on the much smaller percentage with more entrenched disorders.

While Cowen is correct that some basic decisions concerning the allocation of resources must be made, note that the feasibility of preventing disorders with different causative risk equations remains unresolved. To what extent can the incidence of different disorders be reduced? Would all disorders respond to the same type of social or community intervention, or are environmentally oriented preventive programs meant only for the milder types of dysfunction? Cowen argues that various disorders such as the neuroses and psychoses (which he labels as "adverse end-states") have common or at least overlapping roots. This would mean that prevention programs would not have to be focused on specific etiological factors for each disorder, but that social and community intervention could reduce the flow of many different types of behavior disorders simultaneously. The optimistic implication here is that community intervention though not focused on a specific disorder could reduce the incidence of all, by lowering the risk factors that the different disorders share in common. Still the basic question remains. Would all disorders respond to the same type of intervention or are environmentally oriented prevention programs meant only for the milder disorders?

As a working hypothesis, Caplan (1964) suggests that it would be impractical to provide preventive mental health programs for all; some would never need such efforts, while others live in such unfortunate circumstances that they would be unlikely to benefit from many available programs. Caplan would aim at the middle group between these extremes—those in need but not experiencing insurmountable handicaps. In Caplan's words:

> Certain individuals may have so fortunate a position or privileged a background that even apart from our program they would not become ill. Other individuals may have had the dice so loaded against them by their idiosyncratic situation and experience that no amelioration of the general

community picture would be sufficient to prevent their falling sick. The target of a community program of primary prevention is the large intermediate group, consisting of individuals in whom the balance of forces is not clearly loaded in one direction or another and who would be enabled to find a healthy way of solving life's problems if the latter are somewhat reduced or if they get a little extra help. (Caplan, 1964, p. 30)

Caplan might be willing to forego preventive intervention with groups whose behavior is likely to become severely dysfunctional. However, from the point of view of the present authors, it is probably too early to abandon primary preventive efforts for potentially severely disturbed populations, especially since there is no evidence that such programs have yet been seriously attempted.

The difficulty of defining and counting cases of disorder

Another problem with the definition of prevention as reducing the incidence and prevalence of mental disorders in a community involves the methodological difficulties in counting cases of disorder. Studies of the prevalence of mental disorders produce rates that vary by as much as 60 percent within given geographic areas (Dohrenwend & Dohrenwend, 1974a). The Dohrenwends conclude from a review of these studies that:

> . . . the main sources of the variability between studies have to do far less with substantive factors than with methodological factors such as thoroughness of data collection procedures and contrasting conceptions of what constitutes a case. (Dohrenwend & Dohrenwend, 1974a, p. 422)

There are a number of factors contributing to methodological error in epidemiological studies. How a case is counted can vary with the data collection procedures of the investigator, e.g., whether he or she analyzes written reports or interviews participants directly. According to Dohrenwend and Dohrenwend (1974a) the evidence is that clinicians making diagnostic judgments tend to be overimpressed by pathology when working from written records alone. The types of questions asked and the response bias of the target group are also important. Studies that define disorder as the admission of psychophysiological symptoms find that among certain ethnic groups (e.g., Puerto Ricans) the admission of such symptoms are more acceptable and occur with greater frequency regardless of the presence of other signs of disorder.

It should be clear that prevention studies that rely on the reduction of community-wide rates of disorder to demonstrate their effectiveness will be confronted with these very same substantive methodological problems. Global rates of disorder are probably not sensitive to many types of interventions and their use could obscure the effectiveness of prevention attempts. From the information about psychological intervention that we have accumulated thus far, it would seem that intervention, to be effective, should be keyed to specific behaviors, though not necessarily to specific etiological factors. For example, in the field of psychotherapy, the last few years have seen a de-emphasis on global psychotherapy systems. In its place is a growing body of research indicating success for therapeutic programs designed to alleviate specific target behaviors (Goldstein, Heller, & Sechrest, 1966; Strupp, 1971). We do not yet have similar information in the field of prevention, but would expect to find specificity of effects here also.

Examples of prevention programs

The available research on prevention, particularly the research on primary and early secondary prevention, is well summarized elsewhere (Cowen, 1973; Kessler & Albee, 1975; Levine & Graziano, 1972; Zax & Specter, 1974) and will not be repeated here. Instead we will review specific examples of prevention research to highlight what we see as some basic problems in the field. We will conclude with our view of some recommended directions for future prevention research.

Anticipating the stress of surgery

The effects of preparing patients for unavoidable surgical operations is well documented in the prevention literature. Compared to other areas of primary prevention, the research is relatively unambiguous. The stressor involved is clearly defined—a surgical procedure; and the effects of the operation on both the medical and psychological state of the patient are not too difficult to assess. The stress is unavoidable in that psychological intervention cannot prevent the necessity for the operation, so intervention must be geared toward improving the patient's ability to cope with the anticipated stress.

Egbert, Battit, Welch, and Bartlett (1964) prepared a group of patients for the stress of surgery by providing them with information regarding the impending operation and their possible reactions and experiences during recovery. The group of 97 patients were all to receive abdominal operations. They were all visited the night before the operation by the anesthetist who described the anesthesia, the time and duration of the operation, and told the patients that they would wake up in the recovery room. The control group (51 patients) received no further information. The 46 experimental group patients received further instruction concerning postoperative pain. They were told about its severity and duration and were instructed in simple exercises that would help relax their abdominal muscles. Finally, they were encouraged to request medication should they find it difficult to achieve a reasonable level of comfort. The results of the study revealed that patients who received the special preparation, including permission to request medication, used *less* medication and were discharged earlier than patients in the control group who received contact from the anesthetist but no instruction in pain anticipation and control.

The Egbert et al. (1964) study did not separate the effects of anticipatory guidance from those of practice in muscle relaxation and related behavioral techniques. A clearer test of the influence of information per se on the recovery of surgery patients was conducted by Andrew (1970). Subjects in a Veterans Administration hospital about to undergo hernia surgery were classified according to coping style and then presented with taped information about the operation they were about to receive. Results indicated that the midgroup on the coping style variable, those classified as "nonspecific defenders" improved most, recovering in less time and with least medication when instructed than when not instructed. Patients whose personality style was to avoid or deny threatening emotions required *more* pain-killing medication when instructed than when not, while those subjects who were sensitive to and readily acknowledged threatening feelings showed no effect for instruction. Andrew suggests that this latter group of "sensitizers" had already prepared themselves for the operation so that the taped information did not provide them with incentive for additional preparation.

These two studies when taken together (as well as other research reviewed by Averill, 1973) indicate that while preparation for stress can generally be expected to produce more effective coping, positive results will not be obtained for all; some will not need the preparation, while others will be emotionally unprepared to use the information they receive. Preparation should be less effective for either personality extreme.

Another interesting surgery study indicates the need to think of prevention in terms of *specificity of effects* as well as in terms of *specificity of intervention targets,* as would be implied from the studies just reviewed. Cassell (1965) provided preparation for cardiac catheterization through the use of puppet theatre to children between the ages of 3 and 11 who were about to undergo this diagnostic procedure. The operating room procedure that the child actually would see was acted out in puppet play, starting with changing the puppet into a hospital gown through the application of the EKG electrodes and anesthetic. After the initial enactment, role reversal occurred with the child playing the part of the doctor, and the therapist the role of a frightened child eliciting reassurance from the patient-"doctor." At the end of the session, the therapist put on a surgical mask, encouraged the child to guess whether she was happy or angry and allowed the child to take the mask back to his room. Questions and discussion were encouraged throughout the puppet sessions.

The results of the study demonstrate the specificity of effects that should be expected from intervention studies. Compared with a control group who did not receive the puppet intervention, children who received anticipatory guidance through puppet play showed less emotional upset during the catheterization procedure. Experimental group subjects also expressed a greater willingness to return to the hospital for further treatment. However, there were no differences between groups in general emotional disturbance following the procedure while they were in the hospital, or in post-hospitalization adjustment at home as rated by parents. In other words, the patients in the experimental group were not distressed by the catheterization, and were willing to return to the hospital, but their general adjustment in other areas of functioning was not affected.

Dealing with the stresses of college life

Adjustment to a college community presents some clearly definable problems. The student is subject to difficult and competitive academic demands, is pressed to finalize an occupational choice that may shape the nature of his or her life for years to come and is exposed to an intense level of social and sexual demands. For many students, the college experience represents the first extended separation from a home community and the social support systems developed therein.

Even though the stressors associated with college life may be known, it is not the case that their occurrence is easily amenable to change. It would be difficult to convince college professors that they should abandon examinations because there was clear documentation that examinations raise anxiety levels to a significant degree. It is equally unlikely that one could convince college students that they should plan a moratorium on their dating behavior because of possible sexual conflicts that would ensue with predictable frequency. The preferred preventive strategy is to reduce those stressors that are amenable to change (e.g., encourage the development of examinations that are evaluatively discriminating but are less ambiguous and can be prepared for more easily) and to offer anticipatory guidance to reduce the deleterious consequences of unavoidable stress.

The early studies of prevention in college communities did not follow the above strategy, but instead offered global, friendly, "helping" relationships as their primary intervention. Zax and Specter (1974) report two studies in which volunteers were invited to participate in discussion sessions focused on interpersonal relations. The discussions were broad ranging and nonspecific and were aimed at encouraging socialization and friendship rather than alleviating the effects of specific stressors. As might be expected, in neither study (one conducted at the Massachusetts Institute of Technology and one at the University of Rochester) did the intervention significantly affect the academic performance of participants. But in both studies, the frequency with which group members sought individual counseling at the student health service was found to be unusually low. Since participants in both studies were volunteers, they may have been less needful of psychological services. Another possibility, supported more strongly by the MIT study, was that the group meetings reduced the demand for individual counseling.

In contrast, Bloom (1971) conducted a study at the University of Colorado that was more sharply focused on the stresses confronting university freshmen. Bloom suggests that college freshmen constitute a specific high-risk group. Not only are freshmen over-represented among patients of university mental health clinics, but there is additional evidence to suggest that dropping out of school is most frequent in the freshman year. While the problem focus is clear, the difficulty is that of designing a low-cost program that potentially could reach a large segment of this vulnerable population.

The method developed by Bloom in a pilot project was to periodically administer a series of questionnaires about problems of adjustment to a group of freshmen and then to provide them written feedback about their entire group in terms of the percentages of males and females responding to the different questionnaire items. The students were thus able to compare their reaction to that of the entire group. In addition, occasional articles were distributed dealing with such topics as mental health on the college campus and human sexuality in college-age persons. Students also were invited to visit with the principal investigator, but only a few students chose this option.

Reactions to the project among participating students seemed quite favorable. Of those who responded to questionnaires at the start of their sophomore year 94 percent said they enjoyed reading the articles that were distributed, 80 percent felt they had learned things about themselves by completing the questionnaires, 99 percent indicated a willingness to continue filling out questionnaires, and 96 percent wanted to continue to receive articles and progress reports.

Enrollment data for the sophomore year indicate that while "survival rates" were generally quite high for freshmen in general, they still favored the experimental group. 85 percent of that group re-enrolled at the University, compared to 77 percent of a comparison group not in the program. What is more interesting is the fate of the non-enrollees. The difference between the groups does not represent a differential dropout rate from college. Eleven percent of the experimentals and 12 percent of the comparison group dropped out of school, a nonsignificant difference. However, only 3 percent of the experimentals transferred to another school, while 10 percent of the comparison group transferred. In other words, the program was successful in maintaining more students at the University of Colorado by affecting the transfer rate, not the dropout rate. Students who dropped out of school did so primarily because of academic difficulties or because of poor emotional adjustment. The program did not provide academic help and apparently was too minimal an intervention to help those with serious adjustment problems. Students who transferred did so because they felt the university was too large and impersonal, professors too distant, and they felt socially isolated. These were the feelings that Bloom's program was effective in counteracting.

What we should learn from the three studies cited above concerns the specificity of intervention effects. Friendly discussion with peers increases one's ability to get along with them and reduces the need to talk to professionals. Getting feedback about the problems others are having that are similar to one's own increases feeling of kinship with those others, reduces feelings of loneliness and estrangement, normalizes problems of adjustment, and increases feelings of competency. The interventions reviewed in this section did not affect general levels of adjustment, and as we shall see shortly the expectation of a generalized positive effect for preventive interventions may be unrealistic.

Factors associated with resistance to stress

In their review of the literature, Dohrenwend and Dohrenwend (1974b) conclude that there is sufficient evidence to support the hypothesis that stressful life events play a role in the etiology of various somatic and psychiatric disorders. In general, the research on stressful life events seems to demonstrate a consistent relationship between the number of reported events and physiological and psychological symptoms. In different investigations, the risk of disorder has been found to be associated with the number of stressful life events reported, their seriousness and the extent to which they represent "loss" events. For example, Paykel (1974) found that suicide attempters reported a higher frequency of stressful events and more undesirable events than did subjects from the general population. Although to a less extreme degree, suicide attempters also reported more events than did depressive subjects, and reported a marked peaking of events in the month preceding the attempt.

Perhaps the major unresolved substantive issue is that research demonstrates fairly consistently that in some cases, stress does *not* lead to disorder. For example, there have been known environmental disasters that have produced a mobilized population, with the development of pathological responses held in check (e.g., the experiences of the Israeli population preceding and during their brief 1967 war, Antonovsky, 1974). Also, there are many people who face stress in their daily lives with no apparent adverse effects. What seems to be of crucial importance in these instances are the resources available for resistance to stress and the coping ability that healthy individuals seem able to mobilize. Resources for resistance may be summarized as follows:

a. Physiological predisposition. It appears reasonable to assume that physiological processes mediate an individual's response to stressful life events. For example, reviewing his work on antecedents to heart disease, Hinkle concludes that coronary heart disease rarely occurs in individuals not predisposed. In his words:

Acute events of coronary heart disease and sudden death often occur in a setting of hard work, difficult interpersonal relations, and fatigue. They often are precipitated by activities such as arguments or emotional upsets, unexpected exertion, or sexual intercourse. These activities do appear to precipitate acute events of myocardial infarction in people with preexisting metabolic abnormalities, arteriosclerosis, hypertension, or heart disease, and they seem to precipitate fatal events in people with preexisting serious heart disease: but when people are without evidence of predisposing factors or cardiovascular disease, such activities seem to have no untoward consequences. (Hinkle, 1974, p. 38)

b. A nonreactive emotional predisposition. This factor is more speculative and is not based on a large amount of empirical evidence. However, there may be some degree of emotional insulation provided by a psychological set that allows one to avoid getting upset about issues that are out of one's personal control. In studying people exposed to dramatic shifts in their social environment (e.g., Chinese stranded in this country when the communists gained control of China), Hinkle and his associates reported an emotional insulation that was "almost sociopathic" (Hinkle, 1974, p. 41). The healthiest persons seemed to show little reaction to loss or isolation; were able to shift attachments and relationships to others when necessary; and seemed unwilling to accept overwhelming responsibilities, such as trying to rescue a relative trapped abroad.

c. Availability of opportunities for direct action. Lazarus, Averill, and Opton (1974) suggest that it is useful to divide coping into two modes of expression—direct action and intra-psychic processes. Lazarus et al. posit that the excessive use of intra-psychic defenses (eventually leading to symptom formation) occurs when more direct forms of coping are blocked.

When avenues leading to direct action on the self and the environment are closed, the only thing left for the individual to do is fall back on intra-psychic processes for coping, even though these do not succeed in changing the objective circumstances. (Lazarus et al., 1974, p. 202)

Unfortunately, once entrenched, intra-psychic defenses serve to reduce stress and hence also reduce the motivation to continue searching for relief through direct action. When successful, intra-psychic forms of coping may limit active efforts at mastery of the environment. There is an interesting role for helping behavior, such as psychotherapy, that flows from this conceptualization. If the inhibitions to direct action can be removed, the patient can learn to develop better methods of coping and stress mastery. Such a goal would be appropriate except in those instances in which stress is unresolvable and beyond the patient's personal control. In these latter situations, the availability of support networks becomes crucial. When faced with unavoidable stress, it is much better for the individual to attribute his difficulties to their actual environmental causes than to his own personal dispositions. For example, it is better to attribute unemployment to true economic and social conditions than to internalize the problems as one of personal failure and inadequacy.

   d. Availability of supportive social structures.   Often, so much emphasis is placed on individual predispositions and capacities that the social context is neglected. To be sure, successful coping depends upon individual capacities and motivation. But as Mechanic points out, an individual's abilities to cope also depend upon "the efficacy of the solutions his culture provides" (Mechanic, 1974, p. 33). Coping skills, motivation, and psychological comfort all depend upon the incentives and social supports provided by the environment. Not only does culture shape the form that adaptation will take, but more basically, whether coping behavior appears at all also depends on societal practices. Thus, for example, sufficient social organization and cooperation are necessary for the development of mastery through reciprocal help-giving relationships.

   In general, the evidence is sparse concerning the ability of supportive social structures to moderate the impact of stressful life events. Self-help groups and other natural helpers tend not to keep records. Studies of individuals under stress receiving social support from others tend to be rarely undertaken. One exception is the studies reported earlier in this chapter concerned with mitigating the stress associated with surgery. Another exception is the studies of work-related stresses by Caplan, Cobb, French, Harrison, and Pinneau (1976). These investigators report that depression and somatic complaints were related to perceived low levels of social support from supervisors and from others at work.

   If the availability of supportive social structures can moderate the impact of stressful life events, the implications for professional helping services can be profound. In their survey of mental health attitudes and practices, Gurin, Veroff, and Feld (1960) reported that less than a third of the persons who sought help for a personal problem contacted a mental health professional. One strategy to increase mental health utilization might be to increase awareness of mental health resources; and indeed, the Gurin et al. survey reported higher utilization for those with increased education. Still, an alternative strategy that has much to recommend it would be to encourage the formation of natural helping networks. According to Gurin et al. most people who sought help with a personal problem wanted comfort, reassurance, and advice; they did not seek a change in themselves. We need not perpetuate a mental health system that requires introspection and self-examination by all applicants when only a minority are prepared for such a task. Clearly there are other ways of enhancing coping skills and environmental mastery such as the stimulation of helping networks in communities. It is possible for helping functions to be adopted by groups in the community without an excessive reliance on professional intervention. Indeed, in one interesting study of the marginal occupants of low-cost rooming houses and dilapidated hotels in New York City, it was found that clusters of support groups did exist. Within such groups, reciprocal kinlike obligations developed that supported and protected the otherwise isolated derelicts (Shapiro, 1966). Social support seems to play a key role in mitigating the effects of stress. How support operates, or how its beneficial effects can be optimized is a matter for future research. But the matter is of some importance. If the Gurin et al. (1960) survey results hold true today, approximately one quarter to one third of the population is likely to have no active outlet for handling periods of unhappiness or personal worries.

Examples of secondary prevention: The issues raised by early identification and intervention

Several studies have demonstrated the feasibility of early identification of children with emotional problems (much of this research is summarized by Zax and Specter, 1974, pp. 173–201). There is evidence that children so identified are more poorly adjusted years later, particularly if no intervention has been attempted. As Zax and Specter note, the available research suggests that the emotional problems of children are not ephemeral—something that the child will outgrow— but that they tend to endure. The best evidence for this point comes from the Rochester Primary Mental Health Project under the direction of Emory Cowen.

In a series of studies beginning in 1963, Cowen and his associates (Cowen, Izzo, Miles, Telschow, Trost, & Zax, 1963) screened youngsters for early signs of emotional disturbance soon after entry into the first grade. A "Red Tag" was applied to the folders of all children who on the basis of data obtained from the mother, teachers' reports, or direct observation displayed signs of maladjustment; or in whom there was considered to be a high probability that such pathology was incipient. In various studies, the number of children so tagged was slightly over 30 percent of the total group.

By the end of the third grade, red-tagged youngsters were doing significantly less well than non-tagged children on a variety of behavioral, educational, and adjustive indexes (Cowen, Zax, Izzo, & Trost, 1966). They performed less well in school, obtained lower achievement test scores, showed greater indication of maladjustment on personality tests, and were rated less positively by their peers. Four years later, in the 7th grade, red-tagged children continued to be distinguishable from the others, scoring in a more negative direction on these same measures (Zax, Cowen, Rappaport, Beach, & Laird, 1968). In a further follow-up, these same early detected vulnerable children were found to have significantly higher appearances in a community-wide psychiatric case register, which is an index of use of psychiatric facilities (Cowen, Pederson, Babigian, Izzo, & Trost, 1973).[1]

While emotionally vulnerable youngsters can be identified at an early age, should such identification take place? Are the effects of special attention harmful to the children involved? It is not just that children labeled as "disturbed" may be treated badly by teachers and peers, but some psychologists believe that children labeled as disturbed encounter a "hands off" phenomenon (Sarason, Levine, Goldenberg, Cherlin, & Bennett, 1966). These observers note that labeled children are avoided by teachers, resulting in increased social distance and less frequent interaction with the very persons from whom they might otherwise encounter corrective social experiences. In other words, the early labeling of emotionally disturbed children can result in a decreased opportunity to learn pro-social adaptive behaviors. In

---

[1] Even so, it must be pointed out that only 19 percent of the red-tagged children appeared in the register. While red-tagged children were more likely to appear in the register than non-red-tagged children, the majority of the early identified children do not appear. In other words, red-tagging overpredicted later severe dysfunction. The same type of overprediction can be seen in a simpler but controversial example. The majority of heroin addicts are likely to have smoked marihuana earlier in their drug careers, but it would be gross overprediction to assume that the majority of marihuana users will become heroin addicts. Problems associated with overprediction in secondary prevention projects are discussed in the next section.

the previously mentioned research by Cowen et al. (1973) it was found that even without formal labeling, sociometric peer ratings in the third grade are successful predictors of appearance years later in a psychiatric case register. Young children identify troubled peers early and view them more negatively. If teachers and peers both adopt a "hands off" policy toward troubled youngsters, it is not difficult to imagine the resultant social isolation that such youngsters must learn to deal with in addition to their already manifest problems.

The issue is whether corrective intervention can reverse this negative trend so that early identification would be justified. Practitioners of secondary prevention believe that it can, but the evidence is far from conclusive. For example, Cowen et al. (1966) found that in a school provided with a comprehensive mental health program that included social work interviews with mothers, consultation to teachers, an after-school activity program, and parent-teacher discussion groups, children showed more positive scores on measures of behavior, achievement, and adjustment than did children in a matched control school that did not receive the program. Yet red-tagged children in this same experimental school still were distinguishable from non-red-tagged children as described in the previous paragraphs. How can we account for the improved adjustment found in the experimental school if the poorly adjusted red-tagged children still score significantly lower on adjustment measures? Several explanations are possible.

Levine and Graziano (1972) suggest that the red-tagged children might have done better if they were not the subjects of special attention. While the red-tag designation was known only to the research project staff, teachers could not help but know which of their children were being singled out for help by teacher aides employed by the project to provide special tutoring to identified children. Lorion, Cowen, and Kraus (1974) report that children seen *least* frequently by project staff improved the most. Children assigned to once-a-week sessions showed more improvement than those seen twice a week, yet there were no differences between these groups in initial ratings of psychopathology. It may be that teachers assumed that children chosen by the project staff for twice-a-week contact were the more serious cases and were more likely to adopt a "hands off" policy toward these children.

Another possibility is that the more positive scores of experimental children were contributed by positive changes in the least maladjusted children. In other words, those who benefited most from the school-wide intervention program may have been the non-red-tagged, normal children. This is a possibility that any community-wide intervention program must face. If special benefit is provided to all members of a group (so as not to single out any individuals as needing special attention), those initially most able and adjusted may be in the best position to take advantage of the special benefits being provided. For example, it has become part of the folk wisdom of psychotherapy that clients showing the least severe initial psychopathology are likely to show the greatest improvements in therapy.

A third possibility, and the one favored by Cowen and his colleagues, is that all children in the experimental school benefited from the mental health program, including the red-tagged children, but that the latter would have become even worse without the intervention. Cowen argues that intervention slowed a worsening adjustment for the red-tagged children. The evidence in favor of this position is that children who received special individual tutoring by nonprofessional teacher aides were rated by their parents (Cowen, Dorr, Trost, & Izzo, 1972) and by their teachers (Cowen, 1968) as showing improved adjustment. Those who knew the children receiving special attention thought that the program was helping them. Teachers increased their referrals to the nonprofessional aides to such a point that waiting lists became necessary and the school system in which the program had originated decided to hire additional teacher aides with its own funds (Zax & Specter, 1974).

The Rochester Primary Mental Health Project is perhaps the best example of secondary prevention available in the literature, yet even for this highly sophisticated research effort the evidence for the effectiveness of the program is not clear cut. The ambiguity is not in the success of the early case finding (Lorion, Cowen, & Caldwell, 1975) but in the potential of preventive intervention to reverse already identified adjustive disability.

Secondary prevention and the problem of overprediction

Secondary prevention programs are based upon early case identification in which individuals with incipient problem behaviors are predicted to develop later psychopathology. How accurate are such predictions? Will those predicted to develop a problem in fact develop one if intervention is not undertaken?

Consider the case of preventing violence in the community. Community psychologists and psychiatrists are frequently called upon to predict when a person is "dangerous" to others as the result of mental disorder, and many thousands of persons are involuntarily civilly committed each year on the basis of those predictions. Yet, if one examines the available data on the validity of psychological and psychiatric predictions of violence, presented in Table 4–1, it appears that

TABLE 4–1
The prediction of violence

Study	% true positives	% false positives	N predicted violent	Follow-up years
Wenk et al. (1972) Study 1	14.0	86.0	?	?
Wenk et al. (1972) Study 2	0.3	99.7	1630	1
Wenk et al. (1972) Study 3	6.2	93.8	104	1
Steadman (1973)	20.0	80.0	967	4
Kozol et al. (1972)	34.7	65.3	49	5
State of Maryland (1973)	46.0	54.0	221	3
Thornberry & Jacoby (1974)	14.0	86.0	438	4

Reprinted from J. Monahan, *Community Mental Health and the Criminal Justice System* (New York: Pergamon Press, 1976).

mental health professionals are extremely inaccurate predictors. In each of the studies, the percentage of "false positives," people predicted to be violent who are actually nonviolent when released into the community, exceeds the percentage of "true positives," people accurately predicted to be violent. This finding remains regardless of who is doing the predicting (psychologists, psychiatrists, computers) or what variables are used in making the predictions (tests, diagnoses, interviews, case histories). Indeed, most studies find several false positives for each accurate prediction, and the studies that report the highest percentages of true positives are generally those with the weakest methodologies. There are many reasons for this great amount of overprediction. The primary one may be simply that it is exceedingly difficult to accurately predict an event with a low base rate. As Livermore, Malmquist, and Meehl (1968) put it:

> Assume also that an exceptionally accurate test is created which differentiates with 95 percent effectiveness those who will kill from those who will not. If 100,000 people were tested, out of the 100 who would kill, 95

would be isolated. Unfortunately, out of the 99,900 who would not kill, 4,995 people would also be isolated as potential killers. In these circumstances, it is clear that we could not justify incarcerating all 5,090 people. If, in the criminal law, it is better that 10 guilty men go free than that 1 innocent man suffer, how can we say in the civil commitment area that it is better that 54 harmless people be incarcerated lest 1 dangerous man be free? (p. 84)

Unfortunately, this situation with regard to the poor ability of mental health professionals to predict behavior is not restricted to violence to others. The statistics on the prediction of suicide (Beck, Resnik, & Lettieri, 1974), delinquency (Glueck & Glueck, 1972), alcoholism (Plaut, 1972), and child abuse (Steinmetz & Straus, 1974), are not much better than that for violence. Two empirical conclusions emerge from research in this area.

1.   Mental health professionals, using psychological and demographic data, *can* predict a wide range of behavior at a level of accuracy higher than the base rates for the phenomenon.

2.   Current methods result in more people being incorrectly predicted as future cases of problem behavior than are accurately predicted to be such. "No matter how much information about the individual one adds to the predictive equation, one cannot bring the correlation coefficient between individual characteristics and prediction criteria much above about .40" (Arthur, 1971, p. 544).

For the prevention program built on the assumption that problem cases can be identified before the problems are manifested, the data we have reviewed have sobering effects. Assuming, for the moment, that an effective preventive intervention was available for those correctly predicted to be at high risk of maladaptation, the issue raised by the data concerns the psychological and legal implications for the individual incorrectly predicted to be in need of intervention. Let us take an extreme example. Numerous studies have found alcoholism to be substantially more prevalent among Irish-Americans than among other ethnic minorities (Plaut, 1972). If one took admission of Irish ancestry as a predictor of alcoholism, and then began alcoholism prevention programs with this population, one *would* be isolating a higher-than-base rate proportion of future alcoholics, and to the extent the program was effective, the prevalence of alcoholism would be reduced at least marginally. The problem with such a strategy, of course, is that the vast majority of Irish-Americans would not become alcoholics but would nevertheless be identified in the sample, and the psychological effects of being identified and treated as "pre-alcoholic" could be severe.

Consider a different example. It is standard operating procedure to place drops of silver nitrate into the eyes of newborn infants. This is to avoid blindness in the child as a result of maternal gonorrhea. This condition, however, affects only one in several thousand babies. Statistically, therefore, the case here is similar to that for alcoholism and Irish-Americans: for each correctly predicted case of disorder, there are vast numbers of incorrect predictions. Why, then, would we support the overprediction of blindness in infants and oppose the overprediction of alcoholism in Irish-Americans?

The answer is that overprediction *per se* is not necessarily bad, but becomes so only to the extent that it has negative effects on those who are overpredicted. In the alcoholism example, the negative effects can be extreme (labeling, self-fulfilling prophecy, etc.), while in the blindness example, the effects of overprediction are negligible (the silver nitrate does not injure the overpredicted infants). The precise nature of the negative effects of overprediction, of course, is sometimes controversial.

During the summer of 1973, there was a series of unprovoked attacks in San Francisco by a man who came to be known as the "Zebra Killer" after his police code name. All that was known of the individual was that he was a black male between 5 feet, 8 inches, and 6 feet tall. The mayor of San Francisco, seeking to prevent future attacks by identifying the assailant, ordered police to stop and question any young black male within the given height range. This, of course, resulted in thousands of "false positives"—law-abiding citizens—being stopped and questioned. The mayor, who was not a black male between 5 feet, 8 inches, and 6 feet, did not consider the stop-and-question procedure to be an undue imposition. The overpredicted black males, however, took great offense at what they considered a gross violation of their rights. The courts quickly agreed with them and ordered the practice stopped. In this example, both groups—the mayor's office and the black male population—were in agreement that violence was being overpredicted, but each group placed a different weight on the effects of that overprediction.

In community psychology, the weights to be assigned the effects of overprediction likewise vary according to who is attacking the weights. In many instances, the result of overprediction can be unnecessary hospitalization (e.g., of those overpredicted to be violent to others or suicidal). Some see this as a gross deprivation of rights, with serious labeling effects; others see it as unfortunate but hardly catastrophic.

We would suggest that prevention programs based on the early identification of problem cases should pass through four stages of evaluation.

Stage one: The precise "end-state" that one wishes to prevent must be defined. What cannot be defined cannot be predicted.

Stage Two: The reliability of case identification, and the validity of the predictive scheme being used must be assessed. Can different people agree that this is a potential problem case? If they can agree, does their common prediction have any basis in fact (i.e., without intervention, will the "early identified" case turn into a "full fledged" case later)?

Stage Three: Is an effective intervention program available for those people correctly predicted to be problem cases? Do those people who receive the prevention program in fact have lower rates of the problem during their lives than people who do not participate in the program?

Stage Four: What effect does the prevention program (or merely the screening process) have on those people incorrectly identified as future problem cases?

Only when the issues raised in these four stages are answered can one begin the complex ethical weighing that leads to a decision as to whether to undertake a secondary prevention program.

There are prevention programs that do not rely on screening high-risk cases. Community-wide intervention and milestone programs avoid some of the ethical quandaries of early identification. Their chief disadvantage can be expense, since everyone gets the program even though only a minority of the population need it. However, if the program in question can be delivered inexpensively, community-wide intervention has much to recommend it. One does not have to be concerned about the damaging effects of selective labeling. The "Bernard St. Bernard" series of television spots is a case in point. The Ohio Department of Mental Health and Mental Retardation developed a series of 60-second spot announcements aimed at children under six. These are currently being shown in Ohio cities. Based on principles of anticipatory guidance, the spot announcements focus on six stressful situations of childhood and upon how these situations can be resolved. The situations concern the arrival of a new baby brother or sister, a mother's pregnancy, starting school, a death in the family, hospitalization, and family arguments. Bernard is a puppet created by well-known puppeteer Bill Baird. The segment addressed to the prevention of school phobia goes as follows:

STARTING SCHOOL

Bernard: Hi . . . My name's Bernard. You might have seen me before . . . I'm on TV sometimes. Well, so you know what happened the other day? I was standing right here ready to be on TV when all of a sudden there was a baby bird sitting on my roof . . . and that baby bird wanted to ask me about a problem and no sooner than I could say "What problem?" another baby bird was sitting on my roof . . . and she wanted to ask me about a problem too. And then a third baby bird landed on my roof. I began to feel very funny with all those baby birds on my roof, but what was even funnier was that they all had the same problem.

Baby birds: We all have the same problem . . . we're afraid about going to school.

Bernard: So I asked them if their parents had told them that they would meet all sorts of new friends and learn all sorts of new things at school. And they said . . .

Baby birds: Yes, but that didn't help.

Bernard: I asked them if their parents had told them that almost everyone went to school and had all sorts of fun. And they said . . .

Baby birds: Yes, but we're still afraid about going to school.

Bernard: Goodness, I said . . . do you know a lot of children are afraid about going to school at first but the more they go the more they get used to it. Doesn't that make sense? I guess they understood because they smiled. (Television as a tool in primary prevention, 1973, p. 692)

Some criticisms of prevention research

Reviews of the available research in primary and secondary prevention have generally indicated disappointing results. While some might be tempted to conclude from this literature that prevention is not effective, our own analysis of these studies would lead to a different conclusion. It appears to us that prevention research resembles some of the early research on psychotherapy that also led to premature reports of ineffectiveness. As was true for psychotherapy research, the difficulties, both conceptual and methodological, must be understood before tests of prevention effectiveness can be successfully mounted.

The specification of target behaviors

The target of intervention attempts needs precise definition. It is not sufficient to expect "better mental health" or "improved adjustment" to result from an intervention. These concepts are themselves so global and undifferentiated that their use might lead to reports of ineffective intervention when in fact specific effects might have been demonstrated. For example, the Cassell (1965) study cited earlier, found that preparation for surgery through the use of puppet theatre did not affect overall post-operative adjustment but did reduce fear of the operation and increased willingness to return to the hospital. Bloom's (1971) program with college freshmen affected the transfer rate from the University of Colorado, but not the dropout rate. Cowen's intervention with red-tagged children did not alter adjustment as measured by psychological tests, but did influence the levels of disruptive behavior noted by teachers and parents.

The problem is further compounded because measures of change across different methods of measurement tend to be unrelated. For example, measures of overt behavior are frequently poorly related to self-report measures of adjustment such as questionnaires and inventories. Thus not only are personality test measures of change unlikely to be affected by specific interventions, because they tap a construct (maladjustment) that is itself too global, but there is also reason to believe that they are insensitive measures of change in overt behavior—the target of many prevention studies.

Rather than rely on such measures because they are available and seem to have some measure of "face validity," future work in prevention should more carefully spell out the specific effects expected from preventive interventions and then develop precise, specific measures of these behavioral targets.

The increased precision of preventive interventions

Parallel to the need for precision in measuring outcome is the need to more clearly define the intervention itself. Many interventions reported in the literature seem psychotherapy-like in nature. They qualify as prevention attempts only because the intervention is provided before official client status has been reached by the high-risk target group. Studies of this type assume that a corrective interpersonal relationship is all that is necessary to reverse the start of a deviant career.

The Cambridge-Somerville Youth study, initiated in the 1930s was one of the first formal prevention studies to test the efficacy of a friendly interpersonal relationship. In this research, predelinquent boys, first identified in school as troublesome by their teachers, were further screened by a team that included a home visitor, psychologist, and physician. Subjects were randomly assigned to treatment or control groups with treatment consisting of a friendly, big-brother relationship with one of the ten adult counselors. The "big brother" was expected to be a masculine ideal for the boy and a person to whom the boy or his family could turn for help in working out problems. The counselor could take the boy on trips, give tutorial help in school subjects, help the boy or members of his family obtain jobs; but he was prohibited from intervening in the child's environment. He could not develop neighborhood groups or clubs nor initiate community projects of any kind. His help was restricted to an individual helping relationship.

The evaluation of the project produced disappointing results. During the period of time between 1939 and 1945 a total of 325 boys had been seen for an average duration of over four years each. Despite this length of contact, differences between treated and untreated boys were either nonsignificant, or in a few cases favored the control group.

The Cambridge-Somerville Youth study can be contrasted with a similar but more precise recent study in which youngsters referred for behavior and academic problems were assigned to adult "buddies." In this study (Fo and O'Donnell, 1974) unconditional friendship and companionship offered by the buddy were compared with the contingent use of social and material reinforcements. Forty-two juveniles referred for behavior and academic problems were randomly assigned to an adult companion who attempted to influence their youngsters in one of three ways: through the development of friendship; through the use of friendship plus social approval contingent on the performance of desired behavior; or through the use of friendship, contingent social reinforcement, and contingent monetary rewards. A noncontingent positive relationship (ordinary friendship) was no more effective in producing change than a no-therapy control. However, contingent social approval and contingent social and material rewards were equally effective in increasing school attendance. In addition the social-material contingency condition was effective in decreasing problem behaviors such as fighting, returning home late, not doing home chores, etc.

In another interesting study, Chandler (1973) found that delinquents were deficient in role-taking skills, that is, the ability to see a situation from another's point of view. He then designed an intervention to correct this deficit. Subjects were invited to a video-film-making workshop held in a neighborhood storefront. During these sessions, participants were encouraged to develop, portray, and record brief skits dealing with real-life situations of persons their own age (i.e., not TV or movie characters). Each skit was rerun until each participant had occupied every role in the plot. This was the role-taking manipulation and each video "take" was viewed and discussed at the end of the day with the participants. A second "placebo" control group also participated in a film workshop and received the same amount of attention from workshop staff, but did not receive training in role-taking skills and did not see themselves on TV in the different roles. The placebo group produced animated cartoons and documentary-style films about their neighborhood, using 8-millimeter color-film equipment.

After the ten-week program, experimental subjects scored higher on a role-taking test than did the placebo group subjects. In an 18-month follow-up they were also found to have fewer delinquent offenses, as determined by police and court records.

What we should learn from these studies is that for an intervention to succeed, it must be specifically designed for the targeted behavior in question. A positive relationship with a supportive adult should increase one's ability to get along with similar adults in the future but should have no impact on peer relationships, conduct disturbances in other settings, or general adjustment levels.

There was a period of time when relationship therapy was a popular approach to psychotherapy. Much was claimed for the beneficial effects of an unconditionally accepting relationship (Rogers, 1961). More recently, these claims have been called into question and there is now a substantial number of psychotherapy researchers who believe that a positive relationship may be a necessary precondition for effective therapy but that by no means is a positive relationship by itself sufficient to produce behavior change in a majority of cases. It is our belief that it is time for prevention researchers to benefit from the accumulating knowledge of intervention methodology.

In summary, our criticisms of prevention research have focused on several interrelated areas: the need for precision in defining an intervention, the need for increased specification of target behaviors to be changed, and the need to link interventions to target populations for whom the interventions were designed. This same call for specificity has occurred among psychotherapy researchers as well. Strupp (1971) states the quest for specificity as follows:

. . . the traditional question, "Is psychotherapy effective?" is no longer fruitful or appropriate. . . . the question of the goal of psychotherapy research . . . should be reformulated as follows: What specific therapeutic interventions produce specific changes in specific patients under specific conditions? (pp. 110–111)

Summary of prevention assumptions

1. *Early social and community intervention* can influence the appearance of psychic dysfunction by reducing its frequency, intensity, and/or duration.

The etiology of most mental and emotional disorders can be described best in terms of multifactorial causation (Price, 1974). What this means is that for each disorder, a set of risk factors can be specified, so that groups demonstrating a large number of such factors would be more vulnerable to the appearance of dysfunctional behavior than those with low-risk loadings. The probability of the appearance of symptomatology can be lowered by reducing the level of any of the contributing factors.

If we move away from a concern for "causes" of disorder, and focus instead on contributing factors, there is ample evidence that ecological and environmental stress contribute to the appearance of dysfunctional behavior. (See the following chapter, "The Psychology of Social Settings.")

The evidence that psychological or social intervention can reverse the deleterious effects of environmental variables is less clear cut. In many ways, prevention research is still in its infancy, with many methodological problems to solve before research results can be accepted with any degree of confidence. At the present time, our own reading of the literature is that the more specific and targeted the intervention, the more likely it is to succeed. It is clear that we can produce interventions that mitigate the effects of specific environmental stressors. Ultimately whether such cumulative efforts would reduce the incidence of all forms of mental disorder, even the most severe cases, is another matter. However, even for cases of severe mental disorder that may have high genetic loadings, environmental intervention may have a significant role in reducing the frequency of onset, the severity, and the duration of overt symptomatology.

2. *Certain stressors in society* are more easily preventable than others, requiring only changes in environmental design or human ser-

vice programs. Other stressors may require a change in social, political, and economic conditions that are beyond the direct influence and control of mental health practitioners. Whichever the situation, the prevention-oriented researcher and practitioner does what is feasible—reducing the deleterious consequences of those stressors that are modifiable, educating the public about those not under his or her control, and helping affected populations cope better with those that are truly unavoidable.

3. *The goal of preventive efforts* need not be a completely stress-free environment. Not only would such a goal be impossible to achieve, but a society without some challenge and adversity could be a dull place indeed.

Over the years there have been many attempts to find utopian communities that could be described as "Heavens on Earth" (Holloway, 1966), where the stresses and strains of modern society have not developed. If such communities could be found the expectation was that surely they would be devoid of psychological disturbance.

Dohrenwend and Dohrenwend (1974a) review a number of studies of ethnic enclaves that have successfully preserved their traditions while the world was changing about them. None of these studies provide evidence that a simple and relatively uncomplicated way of life provides immunity from mental disorders. The Hutterites can serve as an illustrative example. They are a religiously oriented, self-sufficient communal society with a stable agrarian economy, who care for and support their own members. The Dohrenwends report that no Hutterite was allowed to become a public charge as long as he or she remained a member of the community. Only one divorce and four separations are reported in the history of the group. Yet the rates of psychosis among the Hutterites are relatively high and cannot be differentiated from the rates reported in more urban societies.

What is different about the Hutterites is the type of disorder reported. Whereas most communities report higher rates of schizophrenia than manic-depressive psychosis, the reverse is true for the Hutterites. In their society cases of manic-depression far outnumber cases of schizophrenic reactions. In addition, persistent and severe antisocial behavior and personality disorders are close to being absent among the Hutterites. This last outcome, which implies a relatively crime-free society, would be the envy of most more "advanced" urban communities.

Symptomatology expressive of social withdrawal or antisocial behavior are at low frequency and may be discouraged by the Hutterite way of life. However, the Hutterite society does not provide immunity from mental disorders for its members. It is highly possible that what may appear to be a simple society from the viewpoint of an outsider may not be stress-free. The society may be economically stable but other stresses and strains may exist. For example, the strain may not be cultural or economic but may be religious, involving existential dilemmas. We doubt that a truly stress-free society can be found. What does seem clear from the evidence provided by the Dohrenwends is that the form, intensity, and duration of symptomatology differs among contrasting cultural settings. Thus we are returned once again to the position that if stressors can be removed, or their effects reduced, such action would be the preferred prevention strategy. When the environment cannot be changed, valid preventive interventions can be mounted that provide improved "immunization" against the anticipated stress.

Some remaining ethical and moral issues

Our discussion of improving mental health and psychological well-being in communities would not be complete without attention to some important and persistent criticisms of prevention and population perspectives. In some cases, the criticisms point to real dangers but involve a misreading of the community orientation. In others, the concerns expressed are more basic, involving ethical choices for mental health professionals and highlighting needed societal safeguards against professional abuse.

The community as a mental health "patient"

One frequently heard argument is that mental health resources are too scarce already and that attempts to deal with problems of the entire community will spread mental health personnel so thinly that their efforts will be virtually useless. A related concern is expressed by those who believe that a community orientation runs the danger of turning entire populations into "patients." Critics from this view believe that mental health professionals should limit their concern to those with more narrowly defined psychiatric problems. Both views see the community approach as a potentially imperialistic movement that is out to "psychologize" the world. The frequently heard cry during the French revolution of a previous century, "To the guillotine," now becomes, "To the couch!"

As we see it, this charge represents a misreading of the community orientation. The point is to prevent the buildup of disordered behavior so as to reduce the numbers of persons achieving client status. To the extent that this goal can be achieved, the number of persons needing treatment should go down, not up. Note, for example, the findings of the MIT and Rochester research cited earlier (Webster & Harris, 1958; Wolff, 1969). Providing a minimal support group to college students reduces the frequency with which group members seek professional help.

Turning the entire population into psychiatric patients is not feasible, nor is it desirable. It is not the case that a mental health solution to society's problems is more valid than one provided by an economic, political, or social perspective. As we shall describe shortly, to protect individual liberties, society will have to establish a system of checks to prevent the domination of *any* powerful interest group. However, adopting a population perspective to mental health does clearly imply that both social and individual problems have a psychological component. To ignore this component until an individual develops a severe disability that requires treatment, for us, represents an ethically unacceptable alternative.

Does society need its deviants?

Some writers are of the opinion that prevention is not taken seriously because society needs its deviant members. According to this view, societies develop rules of conduct and social organizations to prevent the chaos that would result if everyone acted strictly according to personal desires. Rules and norms are developed to define what is permissible. Deviance from these rules is destructive of social organization since it makes it difficult to predict the behavior of others. Deviance destroys one's confidence that others will "play by the rules." As Cohen notes:

> After all, each participant to a collective enterprise has committed some resources, foregone some alternatives, made an investment in the future. He has done this on the assumption that, if he plays by the rules, so will others. His effort, whether it be chasing a ball in a baseball game, doing his homework assignment, or showing up on time to an appointment, makes sense only if complemented by appropriate and expected behav-

ior on the part of others. Distrust, even if it is unfounded, weakens organization by undermining motivation; to distrust others is to see one's own effort as pointless, wasted, and foolish, and the future as hazardous and uncertain. One is then inclined to "pull out of the game" if he can, and to invest his resources with those whom he can trust, because deviance, quite apart from its other effects, destroys faith in future performance. Of course, we may be willing to forgive; our sense of injustice may be satisfied by punishing the offender—but deviance may still leave a destructive legacy of distrust. (1966, p. 5)

In punishing the deviant, society reaffirms that playing by the rules is just and necessary.

While threatening the social order, deviance also plays an important part in keeping the social order intact by defining the boundaries of acceptable behavior. Kai Erikson makes this point as follows:

Each time the community censures some act of deviance, it sharpens the authority of the violated norm and re-establishes the boundaries of the group. (1962, p. 310)

By noting when, and to what degree deviation is punished, people learn how far they would be allowed to deviate in similar circumstances. It is in this sense that deviance in controlled quantities may be an important condition for preserving stability.

If society needs deviance to define and preserve the social order, then there might be resistance to the complete elimination of deviance, as, for example, might occur through successful rehabilitation programs for criminals or for mental patients. Furthermore, the possibility also exists that society may promote deviance by some kind of active recruitment process. Noting that many institutions built to inhibit deviance (e.g., prisons, mental hospitals) operate in such a way as to perpetuate it, Erikson offers the observation that

the institutions devised by human society for guarding against deviance sometimes seem so poorly equipped for this task that we might well ask why this is considered their "real" function at all. (1962, p. 311)

On the face of it, the implications of this view for psychological action seem rather pessimistic. For example, it might mean that prevention efforts would be increasingly resisted, the more successful they appeared. Further, if one accepted this view one would be hard put to explain the millions spent for corrections and mental health over the years. Were these projects meant only to keep us aware of the problems in these areas, to punish offenders, but not to achieve successful rehabilitation? As a society could we so successfully delude ourselves?

Does society punish its deviants in order to preserve the social order? Perhaps, but it should be clear that the establishment of social norms based upon fear of punishment is by itself a weak foundation indeed. A mother who says to her young child, "Eat your spinach or Daddy will spank you when he gets home"; or when walking down the street says, "Stop pulling at my arm or I'll tell the policeman over there," may produce temporary compliance. She is certainly not helping her child develop an effective rationale for the adoption of desired behavior, one that can be internalized and used even when the punishing stimulus is no longer to be feared. The effective establishment of social norms involves more than the suppression of unwanted behavior. Of greater importance is the encouragement and reinforcement of clearly understood and agreed-upon pro-social standards. A society that can only rely upon the fear of punishment to preserve the social order soon becomes an armed camp.

Still, the fact that society treats its deviants badly does caution us concerning the difficulties that programs in preventive intervention will encounter. Mental health activities are frightening to many people. It is much more comforting to think that mental health problems only concern some undifferentiated "other" person than to recognize psychological difficulties in oneself. It is much easier to preserve the fiction that normal adjustment means a problem-free existence than to accept as "normal" the problems in living and development that all must face with varying degrees of skill and readiness. The sociological view of deviance reminds us how narrow the margin of acceptable behavior sometimes is, how poorly we treat those who deviate from these rules, and how fearful we are lest we ourselves suddenly are perceived as belonging to some socially unacceptable stigmatized group. Preventive programs will have to deal constructively with the fear of facing psychological concerns— the fear that if one does so he will become a stigmatized "outsider" (Becker, 1963).

Sarbin and Mancuso (1970) suggest that dealing with psychological problems will be resisted as long as they are conceptualized in terms of mental health and illness. Noting the failure of mental health education campaigns and the difficulties involved in attempting to change attitudes toward "mental illness," these authors suggest that the problem with such attempts is that they may offer nothing more than the adoption of mental health metaphors to explain problems in living. As they put it, "most of the general public agree that their problems in living—their sources of unhappiness—are not made more understandable by using mental health metaphors" (Sarbin & Mancuso, 1970, p. 168). When individuals seek help with problems, they go to others—teachers, ministers, physicians, but not to mental health specialists. There is a lesson to be learned here. In developing prevention programs, the viewpoint of the average person will have to be considered. If other community care-givers are considered the front-line workers to be consulted about problems in living, mental health professionals will have to find ways to work with these new colleagues. The mental health professions will find that they can ill afford to continue what has been a traditional isolation and withdrawal from interaction with other community care-givers and from community life more generally (R. Caplan, 1969).

Civil liberties and the right to privacy

Perhaps the most serious problem that prevention programs face is that planned intervention in the lives of others *before* they are clearly in need of help violates a cultural norm of privacy, "the right and privilege of each person, and family, in a free society to mind his own business and have others mind theirs" (Bower, 1969, p. 233). Intervention is allowed when individuals are in danger of threatening the health and safety of others or when they may endanger their own lives. But in these instances, one can "become one's brother's keeper only when 'brother' is in pretty sad shape" (Bower, p. 233). Yet if preventive intervention is to be meaningful, it must occur before an individual becomes so clearly in need of special help.

The fear is that the community movement will be co-opted by the forces of social control to make people "uncomplainingly submissive to the will of the elites" (Szasz, 1970, p. 224), and that mental health technology will be used for political repression not for psychological growth and enhancement. For Szasz (1970), community mental health was spawned by the Roosevelt and Kennedy policies of "modern interventionist liberalism" (p. 32). Its purpose "seems to be the dissemination of a collectivistic mental health ethic as a kind of secular religion" (p. 33). The values of community psychiatry are clear to Szasz: "collectivism and social tranquility" (p. 224).

These charges are strong; and they are disturbing to those who see their community work as *enhancing,* rather than *destroying* human autonomy. However, the dangers are real; thus we believe that safeguards for the protection of individual liberties can and must be established. We further believe that the prevention of disability and misery is so serious a concern that the long-run benefits of prevention research must be explored. When the data are in, society will be in a better position to know the potential benefits and how the costs to individual liberty can be minimized.

The following example has been chosen to dramatically draw out the issues involved in the potential conflict between prevention and individual liberties. Consider the following: Would we ever be in the position to require a license from the state before we allow couples to have children?[2]

Anyone who observes conferences in the juvenile court soon becomes aware of the danger to children that can be perpetrated by rejecting and neglectful parents. The children who are labeled "delinquent" because of some antisocial act on their part are often the product of problem parents who claim the children as victims. After following case after case of parental neglect, drunkenness, rejection, or incest it would not be surprising if the court observer would fantasize how much simpler the life of children would be if "bad parents" were prohibited from having children.

How could such a fantasy be implemented? Suppose we were able to identify the skills necessary for good parenting. We might then be able to develop a test to measure these skills. The test might include some basic knowledge of child development, the role of emotional expression in daily life and basic principles of human communication. Such a test might include a performance task in which the ability to relate to children was tested in a standardized role-play situation. The model is similar to the way the state now licenses its automobile drivers. The purpose of the test is not to pass only those with "super" ability but to screen out those who cannot reach some minimal level of acceptable understanding and skill. Through its licensing powers, the state now restricts the civil liberties of individual drivers in the name of the common good. As a group, we are convinced that the harm to the potential victims of dangerous drivers who will not conform to society's standards is so great that we willingly accept this restriction of our freedom. Should we apply similar standards in the home? If we

---

[2] Our thanks to Richard H. Price who suggested this example.

require minimal standards to insure physical safety on the road, should we not require similar standards for psychological safety in the home?

The possibility of restricting individual freedom in the manner described should raise the hackles of any civil libertarian. Who is to decide what is acceptable parenting behavior? Will the test discriminate against minority groups whose norms for parenting behavior might be different from those of the major culture? Will the test be used by those in power to prevent citizens with unpopular ideas from multiplying? How will the test be enforced: Will couples who defy the order and have children without a license have their children taken from them, be put in jail, or both? Will mandatory sterilization be required of chronic offenders?

We have purposely chosen a "hot" example for discussion. Milder examples of how prevention might threaten individual freedom might lull us into believing that solutions are easy. The solution of complex social problems is never easy. In the example presented above, we might start by asking whether the knowledge exists to identify good parenting skills. If not, this is where the research must begin. If parenting skills can be identified, we must be sure that the knowledge and skills involved can be adequately taught. There would be little point to identifying a standard of behavior to which we should strive if we cannot help all citizens achieve this goal. If community-wide education programs available and acceptable to all could not be mounted, the prevention program would be discriminatory from its inception. Once developed, the program could be offered in the public schools before parent status is achieved, minimizing the threat to later freedom of choice. For those with special difficulty in mastering the content, extra work or special tutors might be provided. Implemented in this way, society must decide whether such an educational program is of value for its children and whether it should be supported, an easier decision than whether to prevent parents from having children.

A community-wide education program in the high schools reduces the intensity of the moral dilemma but does not remove it entirely. The possibility exists that some small minority might refuse to allow their children to participate in the program, or that even with participation and repetition of the program they might achieve such low scores that it is clear that they cannot master its content. If properly pursued, the solution to this problem should involve a balance between the rights of individuals and the rights of society as a collective to develop laws for the common good that will govern the behavior of its citizens. In the example cited perhaps no further action need be taken. A substantial majority are participating and the minority not in compliance represent so small a portion of the population that efforts to punish noncompliance may be more costly and damaging than the good that might ensue from forced compliance.

We introduced this example by posing the question: Would we ever require a license from the state before allowing couples to have children? Our answer to that question by now should be clear. We are *not* advocating the mandatory licensing of parents. Not only would such a law be impossible to enforce, but by comparison with early intervention in the schools, it would accomplish little and at great cost. Prevention programs can be designed with community input to minimize the element of coercion.

There are some who have advocated a retreat from the community, on the grounds that community intervention is too susceptible to abuse by powerful mental health professional groups. The course of action they advocate is for professionals who are working on community problems to return to their offices and wait for the voluntary patient to knock. Though such a plan would resolve the civil libertarian dilemmas, that may be its only virtue. We would be back to the traditional service delivery model, seeing only intelligent, middle-class patients and ignoring the social forces precipitating psychological disorder. In our haste to flee from the moral evil of "totalitarianism," we would be returning to a laissez-faire capitalistic system of distributing mental health service. To us, this is an equally obnoxious moral position. The alternative to community intervention "of having private practitioners see one voluntary client at a time is even more dismal and even less responsible" (Denner & Price, 1973, p. 13).

This example and its discussion should alert the reader to the issues involved, in that it highlights the tenuous *balance* between social pressures and individual rights that is constantly tested in a free society. With the development of our specialized and highly technical way of life, the balance must also include the professional as an independent force. All three forces push for dominance but we doubt that as a community we would be happy if any one force were in permanent control. A society in which individual predilections are given free reign could soon result in anarchy. The opposite, in which individual wishes were always suppressed in favor of a communal goal, would develop excesses of control and conformity. A society exclusively controlled by professional technocrats with no feedback from citizens would also be an unhappy place. In other words, the balance which we should seek is one of dynamic equilibrium, with mechanisms developed to prevent the exclusive domination of any one group. With regard to the prevention of mental disorders, the same dynamic balance should be involved. Professionals should be encouraged to do the research that will result in a prevention technology. They should be encouraged to field test their work in small demonstration projects. Once these data are in, citizen boards should decide if and when particular projects will be implemented. Those who are the recipients of prevention programs should have the right of periodic review and if appropriate should be encouraged to develop alternative programs that might better suit their needs. The abuses that occur, and which Szasz so eloquently highlights, are abuses of exclusive power that occur in a passive and unthinking society. As prevention programs are implemented, the mental health professional can take the lead in suggesting how safeguards against abuse can be developed simultaneously. The implementation of safeguards can itself provide a vehicle for activating a passive community. This too should be a task to which the community specialist contributes.

Conclusion

Prevention is a relatively new word in our psychological vocabulary, thus it should not be too surprising that it still appears foreign to many psychological practitioners. As used in public health medicine, primary prevention refers to activities aimed at reducing the incidence of new cases of disease. Transferring the concept to the psychological sphere forces a confrontation with some difficult definitional and methodological problems. Can psychological dysfunction be prevented? Is enough known about etiology to mount effective prevention programs? How can the effects of preventive intervention be assessed when there is still controversy about how cases of disorder are to be defined and counted? These and other conceptual issues have been discussed in this chapter.

Generally, we have concluded that the best approach to the etiology of mental disorders is to adopt a *multiple-risk-factor* orientation. Research and practice should not become too preoccupied with single causal factors. From this perspective, intervention programs can be mounted to reduce the effects of environmental stress at community, institutional, or familial levels; or they may be aimed at strengthening the capacity of vulnerable populations. Strengthening coping skills fits the current interest in competency building, and need not be restricted to populations at risk. Greater attention should be placed on *community-wide* programs for enhancing coping skills and environmental mastery—particularly since the identification of high-risk groups is subject to an overprediction bias.

Good research studies evaluating prevention attempts are difficult to find. Just as prevention represents a new concept, research on prevention programs also is in a rudimentary stage. Prevention researchers need to sharpen their methods and learn to ask more specific, answerable questions. The yield from prevention studies will be greater if: more precision is used in defining an intervention; there is increased specification of target behaviors to be changed; and, interventions are linked to target populations for whom the interventions were designed. The key to obtaining useful knowledge in intervention research is the adoption of more modest and specific questions, coupled with crisper experimental designs.

Even after valid prevention technologies have been developed and empirical effects demonstrated, ethical and value issues should be decided before programs are implemented on a massive scale. Questions will arise as to who determines the goals of prevention programs, and what provisions will be made for those who choose not to participate. How much authority over the lives of others should be given to any one group—even the seemingly benign "helping professions"? Our own bias leads us to favor a system of checks and balances similar to that found at the federal level of government. This would imply that while professionals should be encouraged to do prevention research, the decision to implement findings in the community does not rest with professionals alone. Citizen groups should be empaneled for periodic review of program goals and accomplishments. Similarly, legal safeguards to protect individual rights must be built into all prevention programs. The tenuous balance between individual rights, communal regulation, and professional responsibility is capable of achievement, but requires constant awareness, attention, and vigilance. It is our position that while community intervention could be used in a repressive fashion, there is no necessity that this be the case. We believe that psychological intervention in the community, free of professional obfuscation, with community input in shaping and evaluating programs, and coexisting with a strong catalog of individual safeguards is more than morally acceptable: it is a moral imperative.

References

Albee, G. W. The uncertain future of clinical psychology. *American Psychologist*, 1970, *25*, 1071–1080.

Andrew, J. M. Recovery from surgery, with and without preparatory instruction, for three coping styles. *Journal of Personality and Social Psychology*, 1970, *15*, 223–226.

Antonovsky, A. Conceptual and methodological problems in the study of resistance resources and stressful life events. In B. S. Dohrenwend & B. P. Dohrenwend (Eds.), *Stressful life events: Their nature and effects*. New York: John Wiley & Sons, 1974, pp. 245–258.

Arthur, R. Success is predictable. *Military Medicine*, 1971, *136*, 539–545.

Averill, J. R. Personal control over aversive stimuli and its relationship to stress. *Psychological Bulletin*, 1973, *80*, 286–303.

Beck, A., Resnik, H., & Lettieri, D. *The prediction of suicide*. Bowie, Md.: Charles, 1974.

Becker, H. S. *Outsiders: Studies in the sociology of deviance*. Glencoe, Ill.: Free Press, 1963.

Bloom, B. L. The evaluation of primary prevention programs. In L. M. Roberts, N. S. Greenfield, & M. H. Miller (Eds.), *Comprehensive mental health: The challenge of evaluation*. Madison: University of Wisconsin Press, 1968, pp. 117–135.

Bloom, B. L. A university freshman preventive intervention program: Report of a pilot project. *Journal of Consulting and Clinical Psychology*, 1971, *37*, 235–242.

Bolman, W. M. Toward realizing the prevention of mental illness. In L. Bellak & H. H. Barten (Eds.), *Progress in community mental health, Vol. 1*. New York: Grune & Stratton, 1969, pp. 203–231.

Bower, E. M. Primary prevention of mental and emotional disorders: A conceptual framework and action possibilities. In A. J. Bindman & A. D. Spiegel (Eds.), *Perspectives in community mental health*. Chicago: Aldine, 1969, pp. 231–249.

Brown, B. S. Philosophy and scope of extended clinic activities. In A. J. Bindman and A. D. Spiegel (Eds.) *Perspectives in community mental health*. Chicago: Aldine, 1969, pp. 41–53.

Caplan, G. *Principles of preventive psychiatry*. New York: Basic Books, 1964, pp. 16–17, 29–30. © 1964 by Basic Books, Inc., Publishers, New York.

Caplan, R. B. *Psychiatry and the community in nineteenth century America: The recurring concern with the environment in the prevention and treatment of mental illness*. New York: Basic Books, 1969.

Caplan, R. D., Cobb, S., French, J. R. P., Jr., Harrison, R. V., & Pinneau, S. R., Jr. *Job demands and worker health*. Unpublished manuscript, 1976.

Cassell, S. Effect of brief puppet therapy upon the emotional responses of children undergoing cardiac catheterization. *Journal of Consulting Psychology*, 1965, *29*, 1–8.

Chandler, M. J.   Egocentrism and antisocial behavior: The assessment and training of social perspective-taking skills. *Developmental Psychology,* 1973, *9,* 326–332.

Cohen, A. K.   *Deviance and control.* Englewood Cliffs, N.J.: Prentice-Hall, 1966.

Cook, T., Appleton, H., Connor, R., Shaffer, A., Tamkin, G., & Weber, S. *Sesame Street revisited.* New York: Russell Sage, 1975.

Cowen, E. L.   The effectiveness of secondary prevention programs using nonprofessionals in the school setting. *Proceedings of the 76th Annual Convention of the American Psychological Association,* 1968, *2,* 705–706.

Cowen, E. L.   Social and community intervention. *Annual Review of Psychology* 1973, *24,* 423–472.

Cowen, E. L., Dorr, D. A., Trost, M. A., & Izzo, L. D.   Follow-up study of maladapting school children seen by nonprofessionals. *Journal of Consulting and Clinical Psychology,* 1972, *39,* 235–238.

Cowen, E. L., Izzo, L. D., Miles, H., Telschow, E. F., Trost, M. A., & Zax, M.   A preventive mental health program in the school setting: Description and evaluation. *Journal of Psychology,* 1963, *56,* 307–356.

Cowen, E. L., Pederson, A., Babigian, H., Izzo, L. D., & Trost, M. A.   Long-term follow-up of early detected vulnerable children. *Journal of Consulting and Clincial Psychology,* 1973, *41,* 438–446.

Cowen, E. L., Zax, M., Izzo, L. D., & Trost, M. A.   Prevention of emotional disorders in the school setting: A further investigation. *Journal of Consulting Psychology,* 1966, *30,* 381–387.

Denner, B., & Price, R. H. (Eds.).   *Community mental health: Social action and reaction.* New York: Holt, Rinehart and Winston, 1973.

Dohrenwend, B. P., & Dohrenwend, B. S.   Social and cultural influences on psychopathology. *Annual Review of Psychology,* 1974, *25,* 417–452. (a)

Dohrenwend, B. S., & Dohrenwend, B. P. (Eds.).   *Stressful life events: Their nature and effects.* New York: John Wiley & Sons, 1974. (b)

Egbert, L. D., Battit, G. E., Welch, C. E., & Bartlett, M. K.   Reduction of postoperative pain by encouragement and instruction of patients. *New England Journal of Medicine,* 1964, *270,* 825–827.

Erikson, K. T.   Notes on the sociology of deviance. *Social Problems,* 1962, *9,* 307–314.

Fo, W. S. O., & O'Donnell, C. R.   The buddy system: Relationship and contingency conditions in a community intervention program for youth with professionals as behavior change agents. *Journal of Consulting and Clinical Psychology,* 1974, *42,* 163–169.

Glueck, S., & Glueck, E.   *Identifying predelinquents.* New York: Intercontinental Medical Book Corporation, 1972.

Goldstein, A. P., Heller, K., & Sechrest, L. B.   *Psychotherapy and the psychology of behavior change.* New York: John Wiley & Sons, 1966.

Gurin, G., Veroff, J., & Feld, S.   *Americans view their mental health: A nationwide survey.* New York: Basic Books, 1960.

Hinkle, L. E., Jr.   The effect of exposure to culture change, social change and changes in interpersonal relationships on health. In B. S. Dohrenwend and B. P. Dohrenwend (Eds.), *Stressful life events: Their nature and effects*. New York: John Wiley & Sons, 1974, pp. 9–44.

Hobbs, N.   Mental health's third revoltuion. *American Journal of Orthopsychiatry*, 1964, *34*, 822–833. Copyright© 1964 the American Orthopsychiatric Association, Inc. Reproduced by permission.

Hollingshead, A. G., & Redlich, F. C.   *Social class and mental illness: A community study*. New York: John Wiley & Sons, 1958.

Holloway, M.   *Heavens on earth: Utopian communities in America, 1680–1880* (2nd ed.). New York: Dover Publications, 1966.

Kessler, M., & Albee, G. W.   Primary prevention. *Annual Review of Psychology*, 1975, *26*, 557–591.

Lazarus, R. S., Averill, J. R., & Opton, E. M., Jr.   The psychology of coping: Issues of research and assessment. In G. V. Coelho, D. A. Hamburg, & J. E. Adams (Eds.), *Coping and adaptation*. New York: Basic Books, 1974, pp. 249–315.

Lemkau, P. V.   Prevention of psychiatric illnesses. In A. J. Bindman & A. D. Spiegel (Eds.), *Perspectives in community mental health*. Chicago: Aldine, 1969, pp. 223–230.

Levine, M., & Graziano, A. M.   Intervention programs in elementary schools. In S. E. Golann & C. Eisdorfer (Eds.), *Handbook of community mental health*. New York: Appleton-Century-Crofts, 1972, pp. 541–573.

Livermore, J., Malmquist, C., & Meehl, P.   On the justification for civil commitment. *University of Pennsylvania Law Review*, 1968, *117*, 75–96.

Lorion, R. P., Cowen, E. L., & Caldwell, R. A.   Normative and parametric analyses of school maladjustment. *American Journal of Community Psychology*, 1975, *3*, 291–301.

Lorion, R. P., Cowen, E. L., & Kraus, R. M.   Some hidden "regularities" in a school mental health program and their relation to intended outcomes. *Journal of Consulting and Clinical Psychology*, 1974, *42*, 346–352.

Maccoby, N.   Achieving behavior change via mass media and interpersonal communication. Paper presented at the meetings of the American Association for the Advancement of Science, New York City, 1975.

Mechanić, D.   Social structure and personal adaptation: Some neglected dimensions. In G. V. Coelho, D. A. Hamburg, & J. E. Adams (Eds.), *Coping and adaptation*. New York: Basic Books, 1974, pp. 32–44.

Monahan, J. (Ed).   *Community mental health and the criminal justice system*. New York: Pergamon Press, 1976.

Paykel, E. S.   Life stress and psychiatric disorder: Applications of the clinical approach. In B. S. Dohrenwend and B. P. Dohrenwend (Eds.), *Stressful life events: Their nature and effects*. New York: John Wiley & Sons, 1974, pp. 135–139.

Plaud, T.   The prevention of alcoholism. In S. Golann & C. Eisdorfer (Eds.), *Handbook of community mental health*. New York: Appleton Century Crofts, 1972, pp. 421–438.

Price, R. H.   Etiology, the social environment, and the prevention of psychological disorders. In P. Insel & R. H. Moos (Eds.), *Health and the social environment*. Lexington, Mass.: D. C. Heath, 1974, pp. 287–300.

Rogers, C. R.   *On becoming a person: A therapist's view of psychotherapy*. Boston: Houghton Mifflin, 1961.

Sarason, S. B., Levine, M., Goldenberg, I. I., Cherlin, D. L., & Bennett, E. M. *Psychology in community settings: Clinical, educational, vocational, social aspects*. New York: John Wiley & Sons, 1966.

Sarbin, T. R., & Mancuso, J. C.   Failure of a moral enterprise: Attitudes of the public toward mental illness. *Journal of Consulting and Clinical Psychology*, 1970, *35*, 159–173.

Shapiro, J. H.   Single room occupancy: Community of the alone. *Social Work*, 1966, *11*, 24–34.

Steinmetz, S., & Straus, M. (Eds.).   *Violence in the family*. New York: Dodd, Mead, 1974.

Strupp, H. H.   *Psychotherapy and the modification of abnormal behavior*. New York: McGraw-Hill, 1971.

Szasz, T.   *The manufacture of madness*. New York: Harper & Row, 1970.

Television as a tool in primary prevention.   *Hospital and Community Psychiatry*, 1973, *24*, 691–694.

Webster, T., & Harris, H.   Modified group psychotherapy, an experiment in group psychodynamics for college freshmen. *Group Psychotherapy*, 1958, *11*, 283–298.

Wolff, T.   *Community mental health on campus: Evaluating group discussions led by dormitory advisors and graduate students*. Unpublished doctoral dissertation, University of Rochester, 1969.

Zax, M., Cowen, E. L., Rappaport, J., Beach, D. R., & Laird, J. D.   Follow-up study of children identified early as emotionally disturbed. *Journal of Consulting and Clinical Psychology*, 1968, *32*, 369–374.

Zax, M., & Specter, G. A.   *An introduction to community psychology*.   New York: John Wiley & Sons, 1974.

5

THE PSYCHOLOGY OF SOCIAL SETTINGS

THERE has never been a lack of analogies and metaphors to guide the study of behavior disorder and behavior change on the clinical level. Price (1972) superbly demonstrates how differing theoretical perspectives, guided by such basic analogies as intra-psychic conflict, social learning, and personal growth, look at similar data in very different ways, and choose highly divergent methods of therapeutic intervention.

Since most current practitioners in the field of community psychology come from a background in clinical work, it is not surprising that they would use their clinical perspectives to guide the development of theory and intervention on the community level. There is a noticeable tendency in the literature for formerly psychoanalytic therapists to assess community problems in terms of the dynamics of unconscious conflicts. Others, when they leave the clinic for the community, find aversive stimuli lurking on street corners or quickly come to believe that the community is as much in need of "growth" as is the individual client.

The search for new analogies to guide community work

While analogies derived from the clinical study of individuals or small groups may have much to offer community work, there is virtue in searching for new analogies that have more direct relevance to community functioning. Such analogies could open community practice to new schemata of analyses and interventions otherwise concealed by reliance upon insights gleaned from the study of the individual.

161

In this chapter we would like to review and promote a prime candidate for a basic metaphor to guide community work—the concept of ecology. While the recent surge of interest in the ecological point of view is undoubtedly related to the environmental and conservationist *Zeitgeist* (air and water pollution, energy crises, overpopulation, etc.), the conceptual and empirical roots of ecological analysis are anything but faddish, having been an active field of inquiry for over a century (Bruhn, 1974).

The terms "ecological psychology," "environmental psychology," "behavioral ecology," and "social ecology" all connote somewhat different emphases in the study of person-environment relationships, but all share common roots and assumptions. We will briefly examine the origins of the ecological or environmental perspective as they are found in biological ecology, discuss their general relevance to community work, and focus on what we believe to be the three most promising research areas in the field: the physical, economic, and psychosocial environments.

Biological ecology

Ecology is the science of the relations of organisms to their environment (Bruhn, 1974). When humans are taken as the organisms of interest, it is referred to as human or social ecology. The axioms of social ecology are derived from analogizing human communities to plant "biomes". "Biome" is a biological term referring to a geographic area dominated by definable groups of plant and animal species (Catalano, in press). A biome has "abiotic" elements such as soil, moisture, and temperature, which determine the type and spatial array of the plants and animals, or the "biotic" elements, found there. Geological and atmospheric forces shift and change local abiotic elements, and these, in turn, rearrange or eradicate existing biotic species or make the appearance of new species possible. It is an ecological principle that while a change in abiotic elements may immediately affect only one species, eventually all species in the biome will be affected.

Robert Park founded the study of human ecology at the University of Chicago in 1915. He saw human ecology as a method for studying how people's relationships were affected by their habitat (Park, 1925). For Park, the biome of the human community was the city and its surrounding area. While its abiotic elements included climate and other natural conditions, the most important abiotic element in a metropolis was seen as its economic base. The city's economic base was held to largely determine the characteristics of its biotic elements (i.e., its citizens) (Catalano, in press). "Chicago School" human ecologists applied this ecological model to several facets of human behavior. Shaw et al. (1929) found that, as the model would predict, crime was most prevalent in those areas where the economic base had concentrated individuals experiencing "environmental stress." Faris and Dunham (1939), in their classic epidemiological study, confirmed that schizophrenia also followed the pattern predicted by the ecological model. More recent work by Brenner (1973) substantiates the ecologists' claim that stress precipitated by economic change and attendant demographic shifts strongly influence the incidence of psychological disorder.

James Kelly (1966, 1968, 1971, 1975, in press; Mills & Kelly, 1972; Trickett, Kelly, & Todd, 1972) has been a prolific pioneer in the application of concepts derived from biological and human ecology to the area of community intervention. For Kelly, the ecological perspective "provides a dynamic frame of reference which analyzes changes in terms of the particular setting in which they occur" (Mills & Kelly, 1972). An ecological approach to community intervention is seen as consisting of "assessing a natural setting and then redesigning the context surrounding a social problem so that a specific community problem is altered as the host environment is changed" (Kelly, 1971, p. 897). He proposes four principles, derived from biological ecology, as a guide to the planning of community interventions:

1. Interdependence. Whenever any component of a natural biome (or "ecosystem") is changed, there are alterations between all other components of the biome as well. Intervention in one community problem, or with one community agency, invariably will have an effect (for better or worse) on other community problems or agencies. Changes in the mental health system (e.g., closing state hospitals) have ramifications that will be felt by law enforcement and welfare agencies, and vice versa. This principle suggests that a narrow attention to traditional "mental health" problems—without viewing them in relation to other problems and other problems in relation to them— is a doomed effort. The notion of interdependence implies that we must take the community as our unit of concern (Kelly, 1966) and intervene at multiple levels and in roles not traditionally identified with the mental health professions.

2. The cycling of resources.   A traditional research activity in biological ecology is the measurement of energy as it is transferred from the sun to plants, and from plants to animals. Trickett, Kelly, and Todd (1972) suggest that the transfer of community resources ("energy") is an important aspect of community functioning. An analysis of the existing definition and utilization of community resources is considered to be an essential prerequisite to devising any intervention that will modify the way in which resources are distributed. "The administration of community mental health programs has indicated that prevention services that reduce the incidence of maladaptive behavior require changes in the social structure of the local population. Before recommendations for change can be considered, knowledge of the current ineffective social structure is essential" (Kelly, 1966).

3. Adaptation.   For an organism to survive over time, it must be able to cope effectively with environmental changes. Those organisms that have a wide range of tolerance for environmental influences (i.e., those with a wide *niche breadth*) will be widely distributed in diverse settings. Those organisms that cannot adapt to environmental change (e.g., dinosaurs) become extinct. "A primary method of inducing change in the direction of development is to provide the community with a greater variety of niches, or functional roles, while not directly threatening the status of those roles already legitimate in the community" (Mills & Kelly, 1972, p. 169). Existing community resources should be strengthened so that those in transition—those in the process of adapting to new roles and new environments—will find the necessary supports (Kelly, 1966).

4. Succession.   Odum (cited in Trickett et al., 1972) defines the concept of succession in terms of three parameters: "(1) It is the orderly process of community changes; these are directional, and, therefore, predictable; (2) It results from the modification of the physical environment by the community; (3) It culminates in the establishment of as stable an ecosystem as is biologically possible on the site in question." Trickett et al. (1972, p. 386) give the example of a grassland community. As the grassland persists, the annual die-off of grasses produces more mulch than can be completely decomposed during the following year. The site eventually becomes more moist due to the increased water-holding capacity of the humus, and produces an area less favorable to the continued growth of grasses and more favorable to the growth of certain flowers. "The most immediate implication of this principle is to emphasize the value of having a time perspective, a long-range view, for our efforts at the prevention of maladaptions" (p. 386). The principle of succession also suggests that the direction in which a community is *already* changing must be taken into account in the planning of new intervention strategies. In planning for mental health services for children, for example, the principle of succession suggests that rather than simply obtaining an estimate of the number of children currently in need of service, an estimate of the *rate of change* in the need for service would be needed. Given the same number of children currently in need of service, it would make a great deal of difference in planning for service, if this number were 50 percent higher or 50 percent lower than the previous year.

In a more colloquial vein, Barry Commoner (1968) proposes that the four "laws of ecology" are:

1. Everything is connected to everything else.
2. Everything must go somewhere.
3. Nature knows best.
4. There is no such thing as a free lunch.

Commoner's first law is clearly the same as Kelly's principle of "interdependence." That everything must go somewhere reminds us that if a problem is simply *moved,* it is not thereby solved. The assertion that nature knows best leads one to exercise caution whenever a "planned intervention" is attempted. The absence of free lunches likewise alerts the intervener to the possible unintended and hidden costs of intervention.

An example: The ecological interdependence of the mental health and criminal justice systems

An example of the usefulness of the ecological perspective in community work could be found in the case of "mentally disordered offenders," persons accused of breaking a law who are diagnosed as psychologically disordered.

At the present time, such persons are handled by both the criminal justice and the mental health systems. They are either prosecuted without regard to their psychological problems (except in extremely rare "insanity defense" cases) and, if convicted, placed in a prison (usually without treatment); or, the charges are dropped and they are committed to a mental hospital, often without trial or legal protection.

Two forms of intervention "in behalf of" mentally disordered offenders have become common in recent years. One approach is to
claim that they really do not belong in a prison, due to their psychological disorder, and to try to divert them to treatment programs in
mental hospitals. The other approach is to claim that their legal rights
are being abused in the mental hospital, and that they would be better
off in a prison. Each group disparages the approach of the other. Those
who shunt mentally disordered offenders into the criminal justice system are accused of "criminalizing mentally disordered behavior."
Those who suggest that they be sent to the mental health system are
charged with "psychiatrizing criminal behavior." The mentally disordered offender is the "hot potato" who is tossed back and forth as
each side alternates its victories.

An ecological orientation to the problem of mentally disordered
offenders would pay heed to Commoner's (1968) "law" that everything must go somewhere. It would suggest that what the person is
labeled (prisoner or mental patient) may be less important than what is
actually done—what services are provided and what rights assured.
An ecological approach would indicate that restricting civil commitment only to have prison rosters swell, or "decriminalizing" behavior only to cause transfers from the prison to the mental hospital
(referred to in the field as "bus therapy") will not resolve the underlying problems of either the inmate/patient or of society. What is called
for are strategies that pay more attention to the content of the intervention than to its administrative structure (Monahan & Hood, 1976;
Monahan, 1977). Other examples of ecologically based interventions
are presented in the pages that follow.

Some cautions regarding intervention

While the ecological perspective provides a wealth of implications
and hypotheses for community intervention, it also suggests a basic
caution concerning any intervention at all. Willems (1977) has cogently stated the ecological case for erring on the side of
nonintervention:

> This widening awareness—the ecological perspective—suggests that
> many things that *can* be done either should not be done or should be
> done most judiciously and that more technology will not provide solu-
> tions to many technologically—induced problems (Dubos, 1968; 1970–
> 71). Before we can be truly effective at designing and affecting human
> living conditions and alleviating human suffering, we must know much

more about the principles that characterize and govern the systems into which such designs and alleviating efforts must, of necessity, intrude. Seeking that knowledge raises a host of theoretical, metatheoretical, and methodological problems.

This line of argument may well lead to a conservatism with regard to intervention in behavior-environment systems and the clear hint that the most adaptative form of action may sometimes be *in*action. The problem is that we know little as yet about the circumstances under which the price for a particular action outweighs the price of inaction and vice versa. We need a great deal more basic research and theoretical understanding that takes account of the ecological, system-like principles that permeate the phenomena of behavior and environment. There is immediate need for a systematic, scientific basis to plan environmental designs, behavioral interventions, and technologies in such a way that they will not produce unanticipated negative costs in behavior-environment systems.

Willems' cautions are well founded. The ecological perspective alerts us to the complexities of community change and thereby reminds us of our lack of knowledge on which to base such change. Our own response to these caveats, however, is not to retreat from intervention. When confronted with a social problem in need of remediation, we cannot shy away from dealing with it due to fear that we may make things worse. A major source of the data on community change that Willems rightfully desires can come only from the empirical evaluation of attempted change. When the change attempt is successful and without adverse side effects, we can assess those variables responsible for it. When the change attempt is not successful or when negative side effects are great, we can attempt to isolate the factors contributing to this state of affairs and minimize them the next time round. The ecological approach suggests caution, not immobility. We will, indeed, never know if we can solve a problem until we have tried.

Environmental psychology

The psychological study of environments, while very compatible with the field of social or human ecology, did not derive directly from it. "Environmental psychology" is of much more recent origin, the first book in the field having been written in 1970 (Proshansky, Ittelson, & Rivlin, 1970). But the assumptions of biological ecology and environmental psychology are so similar that they have come to coalesce into the interdisciplinary field of "person-environment relations."

Lingering dissatisfactions with trait conceptions of personality—with theories that held that psychological characteristics (aggression, honesty, etc.) exist solely "within" individuals—were brought to a boil by Mischel (1968), and provided the intellectual impetus for the development of environmental psychology. Mischel masterfully summarized hundreds of studies that attempted to measure those traits of persons that manifested themselves across different situations and over time. On the basis of his review, he claimed that virtually no personality characteristics were stable or generalizable. Thus, if people behave differently in different situations and at different times, it seems fruitless to conceptualize individual behavior solely in terms of generalized personal traits. Human behavior appears to be determined as much by the environment in which one is placed as by one's personal characteristics, and is, undoubtedly, most often an interaction of the two.

While the position that behavior is a joint function of the person and the environment is not new—Lewin's field theory and Murray's environmental "press" theory being perhaps the earliest systematic presentations—until recently situational (i.e., environmental) variables were de-emphasized and attention paid only to the classification of person variables. While scores of books exist on how to conceptualize and measure individual differences, it has only been in this decade that the conceptualization and measurement of environmental differences have come to the fore. With Mischel's (1968) work and the work of Endler and Hunt (1968), showing that more of the variance of human behavior is accounted for by interactions between the person and the environment than by either person or environmental variables alone, the study of environmental variables could no longer be neglected.

The literature on the effects of the environment on human functioning has accelerated at a logarithmic rate. Several works attempt to summarize it (Ittelson, Proskansky, Rivlin, & Winkel, 1974; Heimstra & McFarling, 1974; Altman, 1975; Stokols, 1977). We shall here focus on what we believe to be the three areas of environmental psychology of most relevance to community work.

The physical environment

"Tell me the landscape in which you live and I will tell you who you are," claimed Ortega y Gassett. "We shape our buildings, and afterwards our buildings shape us," echoed Winston Churchill. One need not endorse physical determinism, however, to agree that aspects of the physical environment, both natural and man-made, can have a powerful influence upon behavior.

It is an ancient hypothesis that meteorological variables affect humans. Both the Old and New Testament of the Bible mention the moon in connection with psychological disorder. "Lunacy" itself derives from the Latin word for moon (luna).

Climate has been long associated with human emotions. It is a tritely common novelistic technique to associate mood with weather (e.g., happiness and sunshine, sadness and clouds). Extremes of temperature are widely held to inhibit efficiency and one of the arguments for industrial air conditioning is that by eliminating extreme heat, workers' efficiency is improved (Moos, 1973). Police calls increase in warm weather and the "long, hot summer" and urban discontent do not appear to mix well. In 9 of 18 ghetto riots, the day-time temperature was 90 degrees or above, and 80 or above in 8 others (National Advisory Commission, 1968). Baron and Lawton (1972) have suggested that this heat-riot correlation may be due to the heat's facilitating the aggression-eliciting influence of aggressive models. On a larger scale, Berke and Wilson (1951) have found that most major political uprisings, rebellions, and revolutions begin during the hot months. These data must be interpreted with caution, however, in light of the large number of potentially confounding variables (e.g., students being on vacation during the summer).

Noise

Among the impressive research programs on the effects of the physical environment on human functioning is that of Glass and Singer (1972). They studied the effects of noise on tolerance for frustration and task performance and found greater stressful aftereffects for unpredictable than for predictable noise. Further research has led Glass, Singer and Pennebaker (1977) to postulate that uncontrollability plays a key role in mediating the adverse effects of stressful noise.

Long-term effects of noise were studied by Cohen, Glass, and Singer (1973) using elementary school children whose apartment complex was subjected to heavy traffic noise. They found that auditory discrimination was related to reading ability, and that the noisiness of the home environment was related to the ability to make auditory discriminations. Children living on the higher—and, therefore, more quiet—floors of a 32-story building had higher reading scores than children on the lower floors. The researchers hypothesized that those on the lower floors were unable to make the kind of auditory discriminations necessary for learning verbal skills. This result stood up even when social and economic class variables were partialled out. Length of residence in the building also affected the findings: children who lived in the building less than four years showed much less reading impairment than those who had lived there more than four years.

It should be noted, too, that humans can become habituated to noise and its absence can then cause discomfort. The razing of the Third Avenue El (Elevated Railroad) in New York City in 1955 is said to have resulted in the decision of some local residents to move to the vicinity of other Els still standing (Ittelson et al., 1974, p. 266). The economic implications of Edwards Air Force Base for nearby Boron, California, outweigh any negative effects of the airport noise in the opinion of the residents. As Murray (1972) reports, "despite the fact that, on the average, some 400 flights a day take off from Edwards, and it is not unusual for the town to be rocked by 20 to 30 sonic booms between dawn and dusk, almost no one objects. On the contrary, the town makes a virtue of its affliction. 'Air progress and history are made daily in the Boron area' proclaims a brochure put out by the Chamber of Commerce. Boron, it continues, ought to be called 'The Boom Capital of the World' " (p. 89).

Architecture

The architectural or built environment has likewise been the subject of much recent research. The last few years have seen the beginnings of two journals dedicated to the interface of social science and design—*Man-Environment Systems,* and *Environment and Behavior*—as well as a large number of special degree programs.

In a classic early study of the effects of architectural variables on social group formation, Festinger, Schacter, and Back (1950) found that the two major factors affecting the development of friendships in a housing project were: (a) sheer distance between houses and (b) the direction in which a house faced. Friendships developed most frequently between next-door neighbors and as the distance between houses increased, friendship fell off so rapidly that it was rare to find a friendship among persons separated by four or five houses. People also tended to make friends with those whose houses faced their own. Residents in those houses that did not face a common courtyard reported having less than half as many friends in the housing project as did residents whose houses faced the courtyard. In apartments, Festinger et al. (1950) also found that slight architectural features had important effects on the social life of the inhabitants. The position of stairways or mailboxes near an apartment, e.g., raised the level of social interaction for those residents.

In a related study, Merton (1947) considered families who lived on opposite sides of a street. He found corner locations to be the most focal. Those residents whose doors faced the street were much more likely to make contact with their neighbors across the street than residents whose doors faced elsewhere, by a 75 to 4 percent margin.

In the same vein, Blake, Rhead, Wedge, and Menton (1956) found that in long, open barracks, recruits knew the names of more people than they did in partitioned barracks, but they had more "buddies" in the partitioned arrangement. In office areas, Gullahorn (1952) noted the same effect: those in open offices had more aquaintances but fewer friends than those in partitioned offices. Proximity, however, is clearly not a sufficient condition for friendship, as anyone who has ever disliked a neighbor can testify. Gans (1962) holds that on a community level life-style and social status are more powerful correlates of friendship than is physical proximity. Athanasiou and Yoshioka (1973) found that propinquity plays a part in establishing friendships, but for friendships to be maintained over distance (i.e., when someone has moved), similarity in social class is essential.

Proshansky (1971) posits three factors that influence whether meaningful social contacts will emerge within an area. One is the amount of time spent in the area. If the time is brief, as in walking through a lobby, meaningful contact is inhibited. The second factor is the frequency with which an occupant uses an area; the more frequent, the more chance for interaction. The final factor is facilitation, e.g., the adequacy of the space for the use intended, or whether the seating arrangements promote or discourage face-to-face contact.

Many architectural factors other than propinquity have been linked with human behavior. A study by Fanning (cited in Michelson, 1970, p. 161) compared the families of British occupation forces in Germany following World War II who were randomly assigned to live in separate houses with those assigned to live in high-rise apartments. The rates of physical illness were 57 percent higher in the apartment buildings. Psychological disorders were also higher in the apartment buildings, and within these buildings, rates of neuroses varied directly with the distance from the ground floor. These findings occurred despite the fact that all families were of approximately the same military rank, and all units had similar interiors. One possible contributor to this stress is the difficulty of supervising small children at play outside the buildings when their mother cannot see them from a high apartment (Michelson, 1970).

In his book *Defensible Space*, Newman (1972) surveys the literature relating social behavior to the design of public housing, with special reference to crime. He found that the taller the building, the higher the crime rate and lower the tenant satisfaction. Four reasons were hypothesized to account for this effect: *(a)* low-rise tenants have a greater *territorial* sense because they are adjacent to one another rather than "piled up"; *(b)* easy visibility of all sections of the project leads to an increase in *surveillance* of intruders; *(c)* the *image* of the more humanly scaled low-rise project creates an environment more conducive to personal involvement than the more regimented and massive buildings; *(d)* and finally, the *milieu* of a project, how it relates to its surrounding neighborhood, appears superior in low-rise buildings. Newman favors scattering small low-rise projects throughout the community rather than concentrating them in one area.

Attempts to improve upon concepts of public housing are currently being made. In San Francisco, a low-cost project, occupied primarily by blacks, consists of two-story, two-family "town houses". The homes emphasize privacy for individual families while they foster social contact by the use of gardens and other semipublic places. "A unique feature of this development was participation by prospective tenants in the design and decor of the houses. Construction was preceded by a series of 'encounter sessions' in which the architects sensitized themselves to the needs and desires of a racial group about whose life-style they knew little. At the same time, tenants were made aware of the practical and economic problems involved in low-cost housing" (Ittelson et al., 1974, p. 271).

Planned intervention in the architectural environment does not always work out for the best, however. To cut down on noise from the hallway in a new residence hall at Indiana State University, Terre Haute, a divider containing mechanical equipment was installed where a center corridor would otherwise have been run. "This solution, however, produced a new problem of a behavioral or sociological nature; friendship formation was severely curtailed in the new arrangement" (Wheeler, 1967). Creative design should provide solutions that allow for both quiet and camaraderie.

Kasl and Harburg's (1972) large-scale survey of neighborhoods in Detroit pointed up a variable often overlooked or minimized by architects and planners—safety. People will tolerate any number of inadequacies in their surroundings if they feel that they are at least safe. Crime was the most frequently cited reason for disliking one's neighborhood. The Office of Management and the Budget (1973) has released a nationwide survey showing that 42 percent of the population (22 percent of the males and 61 percent of the females) is afraid to walk home alone at night. In addition to women, the poor, the black, the aged, and those from large cities are disproportionately fearful.

More directly related to traditional mental health concerns, Spivack (1967) analyzed the architecture of a Veterans Administration hospital and found it conducive to many sensory distortions. One corridor was so straight and long (1,160 feet) that it was impossible to get a sense of progress in traversing it. All surfaces of another corridor—floors, walls, and ceiling—were painted in a mirror-like gloss creating numerous optical illusions. "Weirdly echoing spaces" abounded in the facility, so that distant echoes evoked "other-worldly" sounds. In one long room, a person could, in the course of a normal conversation, sound the resonant frequency of the room and the subsequent "booming" effect would last a full eight seconds. "For the mentally ill, communication is frequently difficult enough without handicaps produced by a dysfunctional environment" (p. 25). One wonders how much of the hallucinatory behavior encountered in mental patients has its genesis in the patient's pathology or in the "pathology" of the hospital environment. Spivack (1966) also notes that the design of mental health facilities provides important clues to patients about how the staff expects them to behave. The fact that in many hospital wards all finishing materials (furniture, lighting fixtures, etc.) are as indestructible and immovable as possible may give patients the message that they are potentially too violent and destructive to be trusted, and the patients may behave in a manner to fulfill the prophesy of the ward's designer.

Density

Related to issues of architectural design are concerns with density and crowding. There is a growing substantive body of research on this issue, much of which has been summarized elsewhere (Stokols, 1977). At this point we will review only selected studies, those most germane to community intervention.

Correlational surveys using census tract data have typically correlated various measures of population density with indices of social pathology. Galle, Gove, and McPherson (1972), for example, performed an ecological analysis of the city of Chicago. Employing a large number of indices of density, they found that one index—the number of persons per room in a residential dwelling—was positively related to rates of mortality, fertility, public assistance, juvenile delinquency, and admission to mental hospitals. The relationship held up even after ethnicity and social class were statistically partialled out. The authors speculate that as the number of persons in a room increases, so does the number of social obligations and demands, as well as the frustration associated with the need to inhibit individual desires.

Direct experimental manipulation is the most recent approach to the subject of crowding. One set of studies, which defined crowding in terms of group size, found that members of larger groups were more aggressive and asocial than members of smaller ones (e.g., Ittelson, Proshansky, and Rivlin, 1970). A second set of studies, keeping group size constant, but varying room size, found that the perception of crowding did not automatically translate into negative behavioral effects (Stokols, Rall, Pinner, and Schopler, 1973). A host of variables appeared to mediate the effects of crowding. Males, for example, experienced more stress in crowded than in uncrowded conditions, rated themselves as more aggressive, and manifested greater deindividuation (i.e., lack of personal identity). Females, on the other hand, appeared more comfortable in the small room than the large, and rated it more "cozy" and "quiet." For both males and females, a competitive task induced greater perceptions of crowding than a cooperative one (Stokols et al., 1973).

In addition to sex differences, a large number of personality variables have been related to the perception of crowding. Subjects who perceived themselves to be attitudinally similar to their partners gave lower self-ratings of crowding in a dyadic interaction setting than did those who perceived themselves to be dissimilar (Fisher, 1973). Schopler and Walton (1974) found that "internals" on Rotter's internal-external control scale felt less crowded than "externals" in a small group situation. Cultural traditions, in addition to personality factors, also seem to mediate the density-pathology relationship. Schmitt (1963), for example, observed that in Hong Kong density is not necessarily associated with social disorganization.

One of the principle explanatory models to account for the effects of crowding phenomena stresses the notion of stimulus overload (Stokols, 1976). Thus Milgram (1970) examined the relationship between the overload resulting from structural features of large cities and the psychological coping processes of individual city residents. Milgram defined overload as a situation in which the amount and rate of environmental inputs impinging on a person exceed his or her capacity to cope with them. Milgram hypothesized that the overloaded individual in an urban environment must enact specific behavioral adaptations to survive. Disregard of low-priority inputs, allocation of less time to each input, and the development of an aloof posture toward strangers are examples of the insulative strategies that one can adopt as a protection against sensory overload (Stokols, 1976). There is a growing body of support for viewing crowding phenomena in terms of overload. Baum, Reiss, and O'Hara (1974) found that subjects walking through a building corridor were more likely to stop and drink at screened rather than unscreened water fountains, when a confederate stranger was standing near the fountain. Baum and Valins (1973) found that students rated corridor-design dorms as more crowded than suite-designed dorms. In both cases, it was hypothesized that people wanted shielding from unwanted social interaction. Bickman, Teger, Gabriele, McLaughlin, Berger, and Sunaday (1973) found that residents of high-density dorms were less likely to return a "lost letter" than members of low-density dorms, implying a decreased involvement with others as a·means of avoiding excessive stimulation. Finally, Saegert (1973), positing that informational complexity of high-density situations impairs environmental perception, reported that Manhattan department store customers shopping for shoes were less able to recall details concerning the merchandise and layout of the department under high-versus low-density conditions.

Stokols (1973) notes two basic continuities reflected in recent analyses of density and crowding phenomena. One is an emphasis on non-spatial factors that interact with physical density to produce the experience of crowding. A conceptual distinction is made between the physical condition (density), and the subjective experience (crowding) (Stokols, 1972a, 1972b). While physical density may contribute to the experience of crowding, what appears to be necessary for crowding to occur is some form of disruption in an individual's social relations with others occupying the immediate area.

The second continuity in recent studies is the conceptualization of crowding as a subjective syndrome of stress that is experienced by the individual over time. Stokols (1973) has proposed a model of human response to crowding stress that involves a series of sequential stages: "(a) exposure of the individual to certain environmental conditions (e.g., physical density, social interference); (b) the experience of psychological and physiological stress; and (c) the enactment of behavioral, cognitive, and perceptual responses aimed at alleviating the experience of stress" (p. 142). The stress-generating nature of crowding is especially relevant to mental health concerns, given the central role hypothesized for stress in the genesis of conditions such as schizophrenia (Gottesman & Shields, 1972).

Implications for community intervention

Stokols (1973) speculates on the implications of crowding research for community functioning:

> Thus, extrapolating from psychological perspectives on density and crowding, it would appear that whole communities might minimize the macro manifestations of crowding (e.g., congestion, information overload) through the implementation of social planning and urban design interventions which would reduce social interference at the societal level. Examples of such would be the improvement of communication and transportation systems so as to diminish the frictions (e.g., traffic jams) of moving through space, and offset the occurrence of information overload. Moreover, the incorporation of mixed primary functions within city districts would reduce congestion and promote a more efficient and continuous use of space over time by attracting a variety of people (residents, consumers, recreationists) to an area during different periods of the day (p. 143; references omitted).

The research findings on the effects of architectural environments on human behavior similarly are of relevance to community work. If community tension and aggressive potential peak during the hot summer months, perhaps community mental health professionals could take the lead in prodding the political establishment to provide constructive organized activities so that the community could literally "let off steam." An obvious danger in such strategy is that it could be serving a repressive function: people may be living in unbearable conditions during the year, and when they are most ready to express their resentment the government brings in harmless diversions to distract the populace from redressing their legitimate grievances. In this regard, the Baltimore Chief of Police has recommended that all new public housing be air-conditioned to reduce the incidence of civil disorder during the summer (Rossi & Williams, 1972, p. 21).

While the possibility that such simple remedies are basically repressive is a viable one—"small reforms," Lord Morley said, "are the enemies of large ones"—the authors have great difficulty with the radical thesis that one should let things get as miserable as they can so that the populace will be motivated to revolt and thus install a new and more just political system. Such a negativistic and at times inhumane strategy does not appear to have a significant possibility of success, as the lack of basic changes in ghetto areas after the riots of the late 1960s bears witness.

It would appear that many factors account for the incidence of civil disorder during the summer. Both an underlying powerlessness *and* an uncomfortably hot environment appear to account for a portion of the variance. A meaningful community approach would address itself to the full range of responsible variables, and while it should not unduly emphasize one variable (especially a "safe" variable for the established power structure, such as the weather) neither should any be excluded on a priori grounds.

Another dramatic example of the relationship between the physical environment and psychological functioning can be found in those mental health facilities in Southern California that had a surge of acutely fearful child patients after the 1971 earthquake. If an ecological analysis reveals that the San Andreas fault lies within one's catchment area, one had best be prepared to deal with the psychological after-shocks of an earthquake. Better yet, one could educate parents—perhaps through newspaper articles—on how to deal with their children's emotions concerning earthquakes.

The research on the effects of noise on frustration and reading ability is likewise laden with potential preventive applications. Rather than dealing with the psychological casualties for whom unpredictable noise has been the stressor that broke the camel's back, or rather than trying clinically to repair the psychological damage that can coincide with poor reading ability, community mental health professionals might attempt to affect the source of stress—the noise itself. Armed with the data on the effect of excessive noise on reading ability, the community worker could make a strong case for well-insulated residences. In the case of apartment complexes that have one section for adults only and one section for families with children, the argument could be made that the children's section should be kept as far as possible from sources of highway noise.

The finding that architectural arrangements can have such a profound impact on friendship patterns should have important implications for the assessment and treatment of individual patients. One might be inclined to inquire about the housing situation of a client who complained of loneliness, before attributing the complaint solely to dispositional inadequacies. Likewise, should one wish a withdrawn client to have increased opportunity to interact with others, efforts could be made to have the client spend more of his or her waking hours in nodal areas that encourage the presence of others. Clearly, such tactics are not panaceas, and "architecture therapy," if taken to the extreme, is obviously simplistic. However, to the extent that a potentially predisposing environmental stressor can be diminished, the intensity of ensuing disorder likewise might be reduced.

On a broader level, the notion of architecturally designing facilities to consciously maximize their potential for preventing psychological stress and for enhancing human functioning appears to be precisely what community psychology should be about. Consulting with an architect to design a community facility conducive to meaningful human interaction may be a much more efficient use of professional time than later dealing with the stresses created by maladaptive environments. At the very least, the pathogenic construction noted by Spivack (1967) must come to an end. A mental health consultant who becomes conversant with architectural concepts could be an invaluable asset in designing various types of primary care facilities in the community.

On an even broader level, Catalano and Monahan (1975) have discussed the participation of community psychologists in the "environmental impact assessment" process now mandated by the federal government and by many state governments. According to these recently enacted laws, nearly all proposed private and public projects with the potential to affect the physical or human environment (including residential construction) must be accompanied by an "environmental impact statement" when submitted to a governmental agency for approval. At several points in the process by which the project is approved, disapproved, or modified, the community psychologist has the opportunity to input his or her perspective. The contribution that the community psychologist could make is of two kinds: (1) designing the project for the prevention of psychological disorder, as just discussed, and (2) predicting the change in demand for mental health services that will occur as a result of the project. The development of a retirement village in one's community has very different implications for the types of service demanded than does the growth of a community with young children. Other projects may imply an increased need for minority or Spanish-speaking professionals. Catalano and Monahan (1975) note one recent survey of an apartment complex in Irvine, California, that revealed that 65 percent of the residents were divorced women with small children. This is a staggering figure, even by Southern California standards. The implications of this finding for the design of similar projects, in terms of architectural considerations (e.g., playgrounds, with easy visual access to the mothers) as well as the provision of prevention and treatment services (e.g., consultation to day-care centers on the premises) are immense.

The economic environment

Economics has long been known as the "dismal science," and has traditionally vied with mental health for the dubious distinction of being the field in which the "experts" most disagree with one another. On one point, however, most economists do appear to be in agreement, and that is on the importance of the economic system to the physical and emotional well-being of the populace. The "free enterprise" system has been claimed to provide the incentives necessary to motivate human achievement and to generate a high standard of living. Others see only the seeds of human degradation sold in the open marketplace, and hold that the sole hope for mankind lies in the common ownership of means of production (Marx and Engels, 1848). Indeed, the primary point of international contention ever since the Russian Revolution has been a fundamental disagreement over which system of allocating economic rewards results in the greatest overall benefit to society. Billions of dollars are annually spent defending capitalist countries from encroaching communism, and vice versa.

The actual psychological effects of different economic systems upon the people who are involved are difficult to assess. Rhetoric replaces data in international debate. There is, however, a substantial body of information on the effects of one's individual economic situation on psychological functioning, and a growing sensitivity to the effects of economic change on mental health variables. The study of the "economic environment" and its effect upon the behavior of the populace has no doubt been spurred by the recession of the mid 1970s, but it promises to make a lasting contribution to the ecology of psychological disorder.

Behavior and the personal economy

The most well-known research on the effects of an individual's personal economic situation on psychological variables is the "Midtown Manhattan" study (Langner & Michael, 1963). Interviewing a random sample of 1,660 people from midtown Manhattan, the research concluded that 13 percent of the lower socioeconomic class but only 4 percent of the upper classes showed traits that psychiatrists regarded as psychotic. Neurotic traits were also almost twice as prevalent (20 percent) in the lower than in the upper classes (11 percent). Fifteen percent of the lower classes, and 5 percent of the upper classes were found to have "personality defects." Anxiety was manifested in 75 percent of all cases in the sampled population. The degree of psychological disturbance also varied significantly with class standing: 28 percent of the lower classes, 18 percent of the middle classes, and 9 percent of the upper classes were judged to be severely disturbed (Lin & Stanley, 1962, p. 26).

The relationship between social status and psychological disorder was reversed, however, with regard to the proportion of the severely disturbed receiving some form of psychotherapy: 1 percent from the lower classes, 4 percent from the middle, but 20 percent from the upper classes. The authors found that the "treated ill" were in many respects different from the "untreated ill" in their survey. Those receiving treatment were wealthier, of later generations, better educated, had more positive attitudes toward psychiatrists and seemed to be of a much different diagnostic composition (Langner & Michael, 1963, p. 82). The authors of the Midtown study commented on the implications of these findings:

> It is clearly paradoxical when the day laborer gets arrested and is sent to the emergency ward of a city hospital because he acted out his problems by punching his foreman in the nose, while his wealthier, but not necessarily healthier, counterpart is encouraged during his psycho-

analysis to conquer his neurosis and understand or even express his repressed feelings toward the vice-president in charge of sales. One man's "character disorder" may be another man's therapeutic goal! (Langner & Michael, 1963, p. 82).

Much additional research supports these contentions. Beginning in 1856 when Jarvis reported that the "pauper class" in Massachusetts furnished proportionately 64 times as many cases of "insanity" as the "independent class" (Dohrenwend & Dohrenwend, 1969), and continuing through the Midtown study already described, one of the few consistent findings across various studies of the epidemiology of mental disorder is that the highest rate of psychological disorder is found in the lowest social class. Twenty of the 25 epidemiological studies with relevant data bear out this relationship (Dohrenwend & Dohrenwend, 1969). The crucial question for analytic epidemiology concerns the causal directionality of this relationship. Is low social class a cause or a consequence of psychological disorder? Do the stresses associated with living in poverty precipitate psychological breakdowns? Or are the lower social classes populated with a larger number of persons who are genetically predisposed to psychological disorder and thus unable to rise in class? The relative importance of social *causation* versus social *selection* factors in producing this class difference in rates of psychopathology is not only a basic scientific question, it is an issue of relevance to society in general. A great deal of creative research (Dohrenwend & Dohrenwend, 1969) has been expended in trying to untie this causal knot, but without success. It appears that the expression of the symptoms of psychological disorder is so tied to social class factors that the variables may be hopelessly intertwined. Other studies (e.g., Hollingshead & Redlich, 1958) suggest that when mental health service is provided, the type of service is significantly affected by the patients' economic situation, with the poor receiving physical treatment, such as medication, and the wealthy receiving introspective treatment modalities, such as psychoanalysis.

Traditional psychological research strategies have fairly well demonstrated that a person's economic status is (*a*) negatively related to his or her probability of being diagnosed as psychologically disordered; (*b*) positively related to the probability of receiving treatment if there is a diagnosis, and (*c*) positively related to the probability of receiving "preferred" treatments if treatment is given. A new line of inquiry, of more direct relevance to community work, is focusing on the effects of *society's* economic level on the psychological functioning of individual citizens.

Behavior and the societal economy

The proposition that economic change in a society affects the behavior of the population has been offered by social scientists for some time (Burgess, 1926; Durkheim, 1951). Only in the past decade, however, has this observation been subject to empirical test. Pierce (1967) hypothesized that economic fluctuation, both up and down, reduced social cohesion and led to an increased suicide rate. Using a time-series design, he compared the white-male suicide rate for the peacetime years 1919–40 with an index of change in common stock prices. Lagging the suicide data one year behind his economic change measure, Pierce found a positive correlation of .74. Likewise, in a recent longitudinal survey, Catalano and Dooley (in press) found depressed mood to vary substantially with the regional unemployment rate.

The most important research on the relationship between economic change and abnormal behavior is Brenner's (1973) retrospective analysis of admissions to public mental hospitals in New York State. Brenner found a striking inverse relationship between first admissions to mental hospitals and economic prosperity. Rates of mental hospitalization generally increased during economic downturns and decreased during economic upturns. A similar pattern held for readmissions, emergency admissions, and admissions to hospitals for the "criminally insane." The relationship obtains for the entire 127-year period for which data are available, and significantly, has become stronger in the past 30 years.

Brenner (1973, p. 227) concludes that "psychiatry is an arm of the social system which has been called upon largely to assist in patching up ruptures resulting from poor economic and social integration." He hypothesizes that economic downturns increase both the prevalence of psychiatric symptoms and the social intolerance for psychological disorder. These two factors, in concert, account for the increases in mental hospitalization. The stress created by economic downturns may not act independently in increasing hospitalizations, but may rather be a "last straw" factor, aggravating other life stresses. Inflation, for example, will most severely affect retired persons who live on fixed pensions, and make them more susceptible to being hospitalized, whereas, if the economy was stable or in an upturn they might be able to fend for themselves.

Many other social factors act in conjunction with economic stress in producing the pattern found by Brenner. The breakdown of ethnic extended families in this culture, for example, affects the willingness of a family to accept the burden of keeping a disordered person in the home when in an economically difficult period.

Especially supportive of the community mental health position that hospitalization is to be avoided if at all possible and that clients should remain tied to social support systems, Brenner (1973, p. 228) notes that "hospitalization is not only a psychiatrically inappropriate response to economic stress, it actually compounds the social impact of economic stress enormously. Under conditions of economic stress, mental hospitalization represents the culmination of a process of disruption and disintegration of family and other close relations."

If we accept Brenner's hypothesis that "the person who becomes psychiatrically hospitalized is reacting to social changes affecting not only his own immediate style of life, but those of many other people as well," then we are led to his conclusion that "the needs of such persons probably encompass far more than has been traditionally considered the province of psychiatric care" (p. 228). A more meaningful argument for a "community" approach to mental health care could not be found.

The most straightforward implication of Brenner's work for the prevention of psychological disorder is to keep the national economy continually on an even keel. Obviously, such a solution is beyond the capabilities of mental health personnel. Judging from the tremendous inflationary spiral around the world in the mid 1970s, it may also be beyond the capabilities of economists and politicians.

But there are many other things mental health personnel *can* do in the face of stress-inducing economic change. Where a social stressor is preventable (as, for example, in the case of noise or maladaptive architectural design) we would urge mental health personnel to try to prevent it. But where a social stressor (economic downturns, for example) cannot be prevented, the role of mental health personnel lies in *mitigating the adverse effects* of social stress.

If an economic downturn were forecast for a given area, for example, the community mental health system could begin preparing the population for how to deal with the psychological ramifications of the downturn. Relying upon anticipatory guidance (Bloom, 1971) through the mass media, one could attempt to persuade the about-to-be-unemployed that their situation, while very unfortunate, is not of their own doing. They did not cause their unemployment and should not feel personally responsible for it or guilty about it. Neither should their families view them as failures. Consultation with unemployment agencies to encourage treating clients with respect rather than condescension would also be advised.

That such efforts at a preventive "attribution therapy" (Davison & Valins, 1969), where one attempts to mitigate the psychological effects of unemployment by attributing it, *correctly,* to societal rather than personal inadequacies—might be of some success is suggested by Brenner's data. During the depression of the 1930s, the increase in mental hospitalization was not as great as would have been expected from the enormity of the economic decline. "The reason for this curious finding," Brenner speculates, "may be that a very large number of persons lost income and employment at about the same time, particularly within similar industries and occupations. It may be generally true, then, that the more an individual feels he is among a minority of the economically disadvantaged, or the closer he comes to feeling singled out by economic loss, the more likely he is to see economic failure as a personal failure, one due to his own incompetence" (1973, p. 236).

Attributing psychological difficulties to their actual social causes rather than to clients' personal dispositions is the direct opposite of the traditional treatment approach that deals with many clients as if their difficulties sprang from characterological flaws rather than from a constellation of social forces (e.g., social intolerance of homosexuals or social limitations on the roles deemed "appropriate" for women). Such a change in orientation may be demanded for psychological (as well as moral) reasons if the stresses induced by social forces are to be attenuated. Lest passivity ensue from portraying the individual as a helpless victim of economic and social circumstances beyond his or her control, it may be important to separate responsibility for the development or *etiology* of a problem from responsibility for the *resolution* of the problem. While the individual should not feel personally responsible for being unemployed (or guilty if a homosexual, or anomic if a housewife), he or she should be encouraged to actively take responsibility for resolving the underlying problems (e.g., finding another job, campaigning for the repeal of anti-homosexuality laws, or beginning a new career, to mention only a few of the many options available).

Future research needs in behavior and the economy

Dooley and Catalano (in press) cogently propose four factors that future research in this area must address in order to disentangle the factors intervening between economic change and behavioral outcomes, thus sharpening the implications of the economic environment for community intervention.

1. *Economic changes and behavioral outcomes should be monitored prospectively.* Retrospective analyses such as that of Pierce (1967) on suicide and Brenner (1973) on mental hospital admissions rely on historical data that were not originally collected for the purpose of testing hypotheses concerning psychological disorder. The prospective and longitudinal collection of data especially relevant to the effects of economic change on human behavior is a prerequisite to progress in this area.

2. *Economically rather than politically defined communities should be used as the units of analysis.* Pierce and Brenner, due to the retrospective designs of their investigations, were forced to use national and state data to measure the relationship between fluctuations and behavioral outcomes. Neither national nor state data, however, measure the kinds of discrete regional economic systems that most directly affect the lives of people. The unemployment rate of New York State, for example, may be 9.5 percent, a summary statistic that could mask the fact that the unemployment rate of Rochester was only 2 percent while the unemployment rate of New York City may be 11 percent. The Bureau of the Census has long employed the Standard Metropolitan Statistical Area (SMSA) as its unit of analysis. This unit is based on economic considerations (cash flow, commuter movement, etc.) rather than political ones and would appear to be a much more sensitive index of the economic environment than state or national data (Catalano, 1975).

3. *Behavioral outcomes less catastrophic than suicide or institutionalization should be measured.* Suicide and mental hospitalization are extreme examples of maladaptation that are not typical of the experiences of most people affected by economic change. Future research should prospectively monitor a sample of families for subclini-

cal and untreated clinical problems, as well as gather actuarial data on suicide, mental hospitalization, and crime rates. Families, as well as individuals, should be studied, since there is some data (Brenner, 1973) indicating that while the breadwinner might lose or change jobs, the attendant stress is sometimes manifested by other family members.

4. *Coping strategies should be observed to clarify intervening variables and facilitate remedial interventions.* Future studies should examine the processes that lead to successful as well as unsuccessful adaptation to economically precipitated stress. Such an emphasis could answer questions such as "Does an economic downturn lead to more abnormal behavior? Does it reduce the tolerance of behavior previously accepted? Or does it force families to commit members they can no longer afford to care for at home? . . . Why do economic changes affect different sex and educational groups differently?" (Dooley & Catalano, in press).

Implications for community intervention

Research on the interactions between persons and their economic environment is one of the most recent but most exciting areas of inquiry relevant to community psychology. It is an area with which many psychologists are unfamiliar, and for which much conceptual and methodological retooling is necessary. Collaboration with economists would appear to be almost a necessity. But the potential gains from pursuing this task appear to outweigh the costs involved.

According to Dooley and Catalano (in press) economic data tied to behavioral outcomes "could provide lead time for the development of primary prevention programs in schools, factories, and unions in communities where economic change is anticipated or occurring. Predictive models could also help improve secondary intervention with clients who might be expected to suffer from economically generated stress. A better understanding of economically generated stress would be of help in the allocation of resources among mental and other health and treatment services at the state and national level."

The psychosocial environment

The third development in current ecological research is in many ways the one most directly relevant to community work. The "psychosocial environment" has been the object of scholarly attention for some time, but has only come into the limelight in the very recent past. While the origins of the study of the psychosocial environment are often traced to the versatile Kurt Lewin (1951), it is Roger Barker (1960, 1968; Barker & Shoggen, 1973) who forged the field into its currently vibrant state. Barker did so by coining the term "behavior setting," and embarking on a program of research described below.

Behavior settings

Barker (1968) defines behavior settings as having two components: (a) behavior, e.g., reciting, discussing, sitting, etc., and (b) non-psychological objects with which behavior is transacted, e.g., chairs, books, basketballs, etc. The essence of behavior settings is not just people nor just objects, but rather a complex network of *relationships* between individual psychological processes and setting components. The reason for studying behavior settings is that these settings are held to exert a great degree of influence over the behavior that occurs within them.

One of the most extensive bodies of research derived from behavior setting theory concerns the effects of the size of behavior settings on the attitudes and behaviors of the participants in those settings. Barker (1960) studied all the behavior settings in two small towns: "Midwest" Kansas and "Yoredale," Yorkshire, England. He found that Midwest, although it had only half as many residents as Yoredale, had 1.2 times as many behavior settings, and the average resident of Midwest served as a performer (rather than as an observer) in behavior settings three times as often as the average resident of Yoredale. Barker (1960) viewed the behavior settings in Midwest as *undermanned* relative to those in Yoredale. He hypothesized that participants in undermanned settings would be required to accept more positions of responsibility, and to participate in a wider variety of settings, than participants in more optimally manned settings.

The findings of Barker and Gump (1964) provide substantial support for Barker's (1960) original speculations. Assuming small schools to be undermanned compared to large ones, they compared the behavior settings of small versus large high schools. Compared to students from large schools, students from small schools participated in a much wider range of behavior settings, were active performers twice as frequently, and received direct rather than vicarious satisfaction from their personal competencies. Wicker (1969) compared behavior settings in small versus large churches and found that members of a small church contributed more money, attended Sunday worship service more frequently, spent more time in church behavior settings, and were more approving of high levels of support for church activities. In studying the effects of a merger of two churches, one large and one small, Wicker and Kauma (1974) found that members from the smaller church showed a greater decline in participation and reported feeling less close to the church as a result of the merger than did members of the larger church.

Research on the manning of behavior settings can have important implications for the study of overpopulation. Zlutnick and Altman (1972) suggest that how one defines excess population determines how he or she will seek to deal with it. Conceptualizing population in terms of density (e.g., number of people per acre) leads one to suggest two types of solutions: (1) reduce the number of people, or (2) increase the amount of space. Conceptualizing overpopulation in terms of *over-manned* behavior settings, however, leads to a broader range of strategies. Wicker (1973) gives the example of an overmanned high school play where more students sought to be in the cast than there were acting parts available. One solution suggested by behavior setting theory would be to set up an additional cast ("double casting") to perform on a different night so that twice as many people could serve as actors. Likewise, an overmanned chamber music group can reorganize to become an orchestra. In both examples, overpopulation is dealt with not by reducing the number of people, but rather by changing the nature of the behavior setting.

Of special relevance to community work, research on the manning of behavior settings has important implications for how social systems handle psychological deviants or marginal members. Barker (1968) suggests that in optimally manned settings, occupants who perform at a substandard level are dealt with by "vetoing mechanisms," i.e., by removing them from the setting. This is because the costs involved in replacing deviant persons are generally less than the costs of modifying the deviant behavior. In undermanned settings, however, the cost of replacing deviants, or of maintaining the behavior settings without them, is generally greater than the cost of modifying their behavior. Undermanned settings, therefore, are more likely to accept (albeit try to change) deviants, while optimally manned settings will reject them in favor of someone more qualified. Willems (1967) presents data to support this relationship between manning and marginal persons. He gave students from large and small high schools a list of extracurricular behavior settings (dances, plays, basketball games, etc.) and asked them to report any external pressures for attending these activities. Subjects had been selected on the basis of their being "regular" or "marginal" students. Regular students had average or better IQs and grades and were from middle-class families. Marginal students had below-average IQs and grades and were from lower-class families. Willems found that students from the small schools reported twice as many pressures to participate as did students from the large schools. More importantly, in the small schools, the pressure on marginal students to participate was nearly as great as the pressure on regular students. In the large schools, however, marginal students reported only one-fourth as many pressures as regular students, strongly confirming Barker's original hypothesis.

Willems' work suggests that under- and overmanned settings may have their greatest impact on marginal individuals. "It is these people who could most benefit by the adaptive skills potentially provided by optimally manned settings and who could also perhaps most benefit by the motivational forces generated by undermanned settings" (Price, 1974).

While the direct community application of behavior setting theory appears to be in the future, some groundwork has been laid. Price and Blashfield (1974) classified the entire population of behavior settings (N = 455) identified by Barker in a small Midwestern town by means of factor and cluster analyses. They found that the 455 settings yielded 12 distinct clusters or types, such as Youth Performance Settings, Religious Settings, and Men's and Women's Organizations. If knowledge of the structural characteristics of an area, in terms of behavior settings, could be related to different types of coping skills or degrees of social competence, the opportunities for intelligent preventive intervention would be great.

Peer-induced climates

The character of an environment depends at least in part upon the typical characteristics of the members of that environment. Since a major part of the social environment is transmitted through other people, factors related to those people, such as age, socioeconomic and educational level, etc., may be considered situational variables (Sells, 1963; Moos, 1973).

Astin (1968) has devised an Inventory of College Activities to characterize the average personal characteristics of the college environment. Great diversity was found among the hundreds of colleges and universities studied in terms of student answers to questions concerning college activities (e.g., changed a major, got married, participated in a demonstration), distribution of time (e.g., studying, watching television, sleeping), and campus organizations joined (e.g., fraternities or sororities, bands, athletic teams). Since the proportion of students who engaged in any given activity varied from no students in some colleges to almost all students in others, Astin (1968) concluded that this diversity in environment could greatly influence the behavior of the individual student.

He found, for example, that when university environments were compared with the environments of liberal arts colleges, teachers colleges, and technological institutions, the university environments were perceived as much more competitive, with much less personal involvement with faculty and much less concern for the individual student. Grading was more severe in the university, and discipline more lenient. Students at the typical university drank more, and used the library less, than students in the other types of institutions. If one makes the very plausible assumption that the type of social environment one resides in can affect individual behavior, then this research approach appears to be an exceptionally fruitful one.

In an interesting study of how the environmental "press" created by one's peers can affect individual behavior, Brown (1968) randomly assigned freshman students majoring in the humanities or the sciences to floors in a college residence hall. Two floors had 44 science students and 11 humanities students, and two floors had the ratio reversed. The students majoring in fields similar to the majority of the other students on their floor were designated the "Majority" group, and the students majoring in fields dissimilar to the majority of students on their floor were labeled the "Minority" group.

At the end of the academic year, a significantly greater portion of the Minority group changed their majors to fields similar to those of the Majority group on their floor. Of those who did not change their major, significantly more of the Minority group became less certain of their vocational goal during the school year. Thus, the social environment created by fellow inhabitants of an individual's living situation appears to have had a substantial impact on vocational choice.

Assessing the characteristics of those who compose the personal

environment of a community program could have important implica
tions for selecting the inhabitants of that environment. One might predict that the "fit" between an environment composed of middle-aged
teetotalers and a teen-aged drug addict would be less than perfect.
If one could classify alternate treatment modalities by virtue of their
current inhabitants (e.g., straight, "establishment" type; young, "coun-
terculture" type, etc.), assignment to treatment modality might be
facilitated.

Psychosocial climates

Rudolf Moos and his associates have carried on an extensive research program to measure the perceived *psychosocial climate* of
several environments. Environments studied included psychiatric
wards, community mental health programs, correctional institutions,
military communities, university student residences, high school classrooms, social groups, work milieus and families (Moos, 1973; Moos
and Insel, 1973; Moos, 1975a, 1975b). As Moos has stated:

> The social climate perspective assumes that environments have
> unique "personalities," just like people. Personality tests assess person-
> ality traits or needs and provide information about the characteristic
> ways in which people behave. Social environments can be similarly
> portrayed with a great deal of accuracy and detail. Some people are more
> supportive than others. Likewise, some social environments are more
> supportive than others. Some people feel a strong need to control others.
> Similarly, some social environments are extremely rigid, autocratic, and
> controlling. (Moos, 1975a)

Moos conceptualized three basic types of dimensions that characterize and discriminate the various environments as they are perceived by their inhabitants:

1. Relationship dimensions—assessing the extent to which individuals are involved in the environment and help and support each
   other.
2. Personal development dimensions—assessing the directions along
   which personal development and self-enhancement occur.
3. System maintenance and system change dimensions—assessing
   such variables as order, organization, clarity, and control.

Moos and Houts (Moos, 1975b), for example, have developed a Ward
Atmosphere Scale that differentiates between the social atmospheres
of different psychiatric inpatient wards. The Scale contains 12 true-false

subscales measuring variables such as Autonomy (e.g., "Patients can leave the ward without saying where they are going,"), Aggression ("On this ward staff think it's a healthy thing to argue"), and Clarity ("If a patient breaks a rule, he knows what will happen to him"). They have shown direct relationships between the psychosocial climate of the ward, patient satisfaction, and types of patient-initiated behaviors.

Social atmospheres conducive to Insight and Autonomy are associated with greater patient liking of the staff, while environments perceived to be high on Support are related to patient submissiveness to the staff. Moos (1975b) has shown the Ward Atmosphere Scales to be related to objective indices of treatment outcome. For example, wards with high release rates were perceived by patients as high in Practical Orientation and Staff Control. Wards that kept released patients in the community the longest were perceived to be high in Staff Control by both patients and staff. Wards with high dropout rates (i.e., either patient "eloping" or being released against staff advice) were associated with perceived environments low in Practical Orientation, Order, and Organization.

In the case of correctional institutions, those programs associated with a high "community tenure rate" (i.e., with success at keeping people out of prison in the future), as compared with programs associated with a low community tenure rate, "are characterized by a moderate degree of staff control, moderate interpersonal communication, resident-staff openness, and staff support, and moderate emphasis on involvement. There is an emphasis on staff control, but it is not rigid and strict enough to discourage openness and expressiveness." (Moos, 1975b, p. 327)

Moos notes that those programs showing maximum "in house" improvement of residents' morale and behavior may not be the same programs that achieve maximum results in the community, and vice versa.

Of special relevance is the fact that Moos has developed a variant of the Ward Atmosphere Scale called the Community-Oriented Programs Environment Scale (COPES) to systematically assess the environment of community treatment programs, such as halfway houses, day-care centers, and community care homes (Moos, 1975a). Since the scales are similar to the Ward Atmosphere Scale, it is possible to directly compare the perceived environmental characteristics of in-hospital and out-of-hospital programs.

Implications for community intervention

An example of the use of environmental assessment to facilitate community intervention is presented by Moos and Otto (Moos, 1975b). They report a four-stage model for the facilitation and evaluation of social change:

1. The systematic assessment of the social environment.
2. Individualized feedback to members of the environment.
3. Concrete planning of specific methods by which change might occur.
4. Reassessment of the social environment in order to monitor change.

In one study, two forms of COPES were given to the staff and residents of an adolescent residential center. On one form participants were told to describe the program as it really was, and on another form, told to describe the program as they would ideally like it to be. The initial assessment of the environment showed that, although the staff and residents agreed on the environment they would ideally like to have, they disagreed strongly about the characteristics of the environment as it actually existed. The staff, for example, saw the environment as much more supportive than the residents did. The experimenters presented the staff and patients with detailed feedback on their COPES scores. This stimulated and focused discussion on the discrepancies between the real and ideal environments, and specific changes were initiated to rectify them, e.g., formation of a resident government to increase resident autonomy. Six months after the initial environmental assessment, the real and ideal COPES forms were again administered. Significant movement of the real environment towards the ideal environment was noted for both staff and residents, with the residents perceiving the environment as much more supportive than they originally did (Moos, 1975b).

COPES and the other social climate scales are subject to some of the same problems that have afflicted paper-and-pencil measures of individual personality, such as response biases, social desirability, defensiveness, etc. It is a reasonable assumption, however, that people are less "ego invested" in their environment than they are in themselves, and so they may be less likely to distort the reporting of the perceived environment than they would be when reporting characteristics of their personalities.

Techniques for assessing the psychosocial environment would seem to have great potential for community programs, both in evaluation and facilitation of environmental change. Assessing the environments of various treatment alternatives could lead to the differential assignment of clients' on the basis of which environment best fit the individual's needs. If one could assess a given client's needs as well as what a number of environments had to offer (either in terms of behavior settings, peer influences, or COPES scales), then "person-environment fit" (Wicker, 1972) could be maximized. In this manner, one would not have to change either the person or the environment, but rather simply match one to the other. For example, a child in need of increased order and setting clarity to help control his or her behavior might be assigned to a school scoring highly on those variables, whereas another child, in need of increased autonomy, might be placed accordingly. Besides its obvious economic benefits, such an approach might be substantially more effective than trying to change the individual who is a "misfit" to his or her environment, or the environment that is misfit to the individual.

Conclusions

We have examined the biological roots of the ecological analogy and focused upon what we believe to be the three most exciting developments in the field of environmental psychology, the study of the physical, economic, and psychosocial environments. A decade ago, Goldstein, Heller, and Sechrest (1966) argued that clinical work would benefit from an openness to gathering hypotheses from the various experimental fields of psychology. We would echo this dictum in regard to community work, and suggest that environmental psychology is an excellent starting point.

However, in psychology, as in religion, there is no fervor like that of a convert. Former trait theorists have become rigid environmental determinists and there is danger that the "person" will become lost in the new-found environment. Mischel (1973) has objected to those who have misinterpreted his work as indicating that no stability exists in behavior, and that environmental situations are all that matter. "No one suggests that the organism approaches every new situation with an empty head. . . ." (Mischel, 1973, p. 262). In fact, the relationship between environmental and personal variables is likely to be exceedingly complicated, to the point of being idiosyncratic for each individual. "It would," Mischel notes, "be wasteful to create pseudocontroversies that pit person against situation in order to see which is more important. The answer must always depend on the particular situations and persons sampled. . . ." (1973, p. 256). The study of environments provides a balance to—and not a replacement of—the study of individuals (Bem & Allen, 1974). Michelson (1970), in this regard, has posited an "intersystems congruence theory," that suggests that physical settings in themselves do not determine behavior, but if the settings are congruent with the goals of those who occupy them, they will provide support for the behaviors necessary to realize those goals. We must study how people choose environments, as well as how environments affect people (Wicker, 1972).

We might parenthetically note that in addition to using environmental theory to solve psychological problems, it is also possible to use psychological theory to solve environmental problems. Mental health professionals have become active in research on overpopulation (Crawford, 1973), water pollution (Ibsen & Ballwea, 1969), air pollution (Swan, 1972), and energy conservation (Winett & Nietzel, 1975). It would seem that the mental health and environmental disciplines have much to offer one another.

References

Astin, A. *The college environment.* Washington, D.C.: American Council on Education, 1968.

Altman, I. *The environment and social behavior.* Monterey, Calif.: Brooks/Cole, 1975.

Athanasiou, R., & Yoshioka, G. The spatial character of friendship formation. *Environment and Behavior,* 1973, 5, 43–65.

Barker, R. Ecology and motivation. In M. Jones (Ed.), *Nebraska symposium on motivation.* Lincoln, Nebr.: University of Nebraska Press, 1960, 1–49.

Barker, R. *Ecological psychology.* Stanford, Calif.: Stanford University Press, 1968.

Barker, R., & Gump, P. *Big school, small school.* Stanford, Calif.: Stanford University Press, 1964.

Barker, R., & Shoggen, P. *Qualities of community life.* San Francisco: Jossey-Bass, 1973.

Baron, R., & Lawton, S. Environmental influences on aggression: The facilitation of modeling effects by high ambient temperatures. *Psychonomic Science,* 1972, 26, 80–82.

Baum, A., Reiss, M., & O'Hara, J.   Architectural variants of reaction to spatial invasion. *Environment and Behavior,* 1974, *6,* 91–100.

Baum, A., & Valins, S.   Residential environments, group size, and crowding. *Proceedings of the American Psychological Association Convention,* 1973, 211–212.

Bem, D., & Allen, A.   On predicting some of the people some of the time: The search for cross-situational consistencies in behavior. *Psychological Review,* 1974, *81,* 506–520.

Berke, J., & Wilson, V.   *Watch out for the weather.* Toronto: Macmillan, 1951.

Bickman, L., Teger, A., Gabriele, T., McLaughlin, C., Berger, M., & Sunaday, E.   Dormitory density and helping behavior. *Environment and Behavior,* 1973, *5,* 464–491.

Blake, R., Rhead, C., Wedge, B., & Menton, J.   Housing, architecture, and social interaction. *Sociometry,* 1956, *19,* 133–139.

Bloom, B.   Strategies for the prevention of mental disorders. In American Psychological Association (Ed.), *Issues in community psychology and preventive mental health.* New York: Behavioral Publications, 1971, pp. 1–20.

Brenner, J.   *Mental illness and the economy.* Cambridge, Mass: Harvard University Press, 1973.

Brown, R. Manipulation of environmental press in a college residence hall. *Personnel and Guidance Journal,* 1968, *46,* 555–560.

Bruhn, J.   Human ecology: A unifying science? *Human Ecology,* 1974, *2,* 105–125.

Burgess, E. (Ed.).   *The urban community.* Chicago: University of Chicago Press, 1926.

Catalano, R.   Community stress: A preliminary conceptualization. *Man-Environment Systems,* 1975, *5,* 307–310.

Catalano, R.   *Health, behavior and the community: An ecological perspective.* Lexington, Mass: D. C. Heath, in press.

Catalano, R., & Dooley, D.   Economic predictors of depressed mood and stressful life events. *Journal of Health and Social Behavior,* in press.

Catalano, R., & Monahan, J.   The community psychologist as social planner: Designing optimal environments. *American Journal of Community Psychology,* 1975, *3,* 327–334.

Cohen, S., Glass, D., & Singer, J.   Apartment noise, auditory discrimination and reading ability in children. *Journal of Experimental Social Psychology,* 1973, *9,* 407–422.

Commoner, B.   *The closing circle.* New York: Basic Books, 1968.

Crawford, T.   Beliefs about birth control: A consistency theory analysis. *Representative Research in Social Psychology,* 1973, *4,* 53–65.

Davison, G., & Valins, S.   Self-attribution and the maintenance of behavior change. *Journal of Personality and Social Psychology,* 1969, *11,* 25–33.

Dohrenwend, B. S., & Dohrenwend, B. P.   *Social status and psychological disorder*. New York: John Wiley & Sons, 1969.

Dooley, D., & Catalano, R.   Money and mental disorder: Toward behavioral cost accounting for primary prevention. *American Journal of Community Psychology*, in press.

Dubos, R.   *So human an animal*. New York: Charles Scribner's Sons, 1968.

Dubos, R.   The despairing optimist. *American Scholar*, 1970–71, *40*, 16–20.

Durkheim, E.   *Suicide*. Glencoe, Ill: Free Press, 1951.

Endler, N., & Hunt, J.   S-R inventories of hostility and comparisons of the proportion of variance from persons, responses, and situations for hostility and anxiousness. *Journal of Personality and Social Psychology*, 1968, 9, 309–315.

Faris, R., & Dunham, H.   *Mental disorders in urban areas*, Chicago: University of Chicago Press, 1939.

Festinger, L., Schacter, S., & Back, K.   *Social pressures in informal groups*. Stanford, Calif.: Stanford University Press, 1950.

Fisher, J.   Situation-specific variables as determinants of perceived environmental aesthetic quality and perceived crowdedness. *Journal of Research in Personality*, in press.

Galle, O., Gove, W., & McPherson, J.   Population density and pathology: What are the relations for man? *Science*, 1972, *176*, 23–30.

Gans, H.   *The urban villagers*. New York: Free Press, 1962.

Glass, D., & Singer, J.   *Urban stress*. New York: Academic Press, 1972.

Glass, D., Singer, J., & Pennebaker, J.   Behavioral effects of uncontrollable environmental events. In D. Stokols (Ed.), *Psychological perspectives on environment and behavior: conceptual and empirical trends*. New York: Plenum, 1977.

Goldstein, A., Heller, K., & Sechrest, L.   *Psychotherapy and the psychology of behavior change*. New York: John Wiley & Sons, 1966.

Gottesman, I., & Shields, J.   *Schizophrenia and genetics: A twin study vantage point*. New York: Academic Press, 1972.

Gullahorn, J.   Distance and friendship as factors in the gross interaction matrix. *Sociometry*, 1952, *15*, 123–134.

Heimstra, N., & McFarling, L.   *Environmental psychology*. Monterey, Calif.: Brooks/Cole, 1974.

Hollingshead, A., & Redlich, F.   *Social class and mental illness*. New York: John Wiley & Sons, 1958.

Ibsen, C., & Ballwea, J.   *Public perception of water resources problems*. Blacksburg, Va.: Virginia Polytechnic Institute, 1969.

Ittelson, W., Proshansky, H., & Rivlin, L.   The environmental psychology of the psychiatric ward. In H. Proshansky, W. Ittelson, & L. Rivlin (Eds.), *Environmental psychology: Man and his physical setting*. New York: Holt, Rinehart & Winston, 1970, pp. 419–439.

Ittelson, W., Proshansky, H., Rivlin, L., & Winkel, G. *An Introduction to environmental psychology.* New York: Holt, Rinehart and Winston, 1974.

Kasl, S., & Harburg, E. Perceptions of the neighborhood and the desire to move out. *Journal of the American Institute of Planners,* 1972, *38,* 318–324.

Kelly, J. Ecological constraints on mental health services. *American Psychologist,* 1966, *21,* 535–539.

Kelly, J. Toward an ecological conception of preventive interventions. In J. Carter (Ed.), *Research contributions from psychology to community mental health.* New York: Behavioral Publications, 1968, pp. 75–99.

Kelly, J. Qualities for the community psychologist. *American Psychologist,* 1971, *26,* 897–903.

Kelly, J. The ecological analogy and community work. Paper presented to the International Society for the Study of Behavioral Development Biennial Conference, University of Surrey, England, 1975.

Kelly, J. *The High School: Students and social contexts in two Midwestern communities.* New York: Human Sciences Press, in press.

Langner, T., & Michael, S. *Life stress and mental health.* New York: Free Press, 1963.

Lewin, K. *Field theory in social science.* New York: Harper & Row, 1951.

Lin, T., & Stanley, C. *The scope of epidemiology in psychiatry.* Geneva: World Health Organization, 1962.

Marx, K., & Engels, F. *The Communist manifesto.* New York: Russell & Russell, 1963 (originally published 1848).

Merton, R. The social psychology of housing. In W. Dennis (Ed.), *Current trends in social psychology.* Pittsburgh, Pa: University of Pittsburgh Press, 1947, pp. 163–217.

Michelson, W. *Man and his urban environment: A sociological approach.* Reading, Mass.: Addison-Wesley, 1970.

Milgram, S. The experience of living in cities. *Science,* 1970, *167,* 1461–1468.

Mills, R., & Kelly, J. Cultural and social adaptations to change: A case example and critique. In S. Golann & C. Eisdorfer, *Handbook of community mental health.* New York: Appleton-Century-Crofts, 1972, pp. 157–205.

Mischel, W. *Personality and assessment.* New York: John Wiley & Sons, 1968.

Mischel, W. Towards a cognitive social learning reconceptualization of personality. *Psychological Review,* 1973, *80,* 252–283.

Monahan, J. Social accountability: Preface to an integrated theory of criminal and mental health sanctions. In B. Sales (Ed.), *Perspectives in law and psychology: The criminal justice system.* New York: Spectrum Books, 1977.

Monahan, J., & Hood, G. Psychologically disordered and criminal offenders. *Criminal Justice and Behavior,* 1976, *2,* 123–134.

Moos, R. Conceptualizations of human environments. *American Psychologist,* 1973, *28,* 652–665.

Moos, R. *Evaluating correctional and community environments.* New York: John Wiley & Sons, 1975(a).

Moos, R. *Evaluating treatment environments.* New York: John Wiley & Sons, 1975(b).

Moos, R., & Insel, P. (Eds.) *Issues in social ecology: Human milieus.* Palo Alto, Calif: National Press Books, 1973.

Murray, W. The sound of the future. *The New Yorker,* September 16, 1972, pp. 85–93.

National Advisory Commission on Civil Disorders. *The Kerner Report.* New York: Bantam, 1968.

Newman, O. *Defensible space.* New York: Macmillan, 1972.

Park, R. *Human communities.* Chicago: University of Chicago Press, 1952.

Pierce, A. The economic cycle and the social suicide rate. *American Sociological Review,* 1967, *32,* 457–462.

Price, R. *Abnormal psychology: Perspectives in conflict.* New York: Holt, Rinehart and Winston, 1972.

Price, R. Etiology, the social environment and the prevention of psychological dysfunction. In P. Insel & R. Moos (Eds.), *Health and the social environment.* Lexington, Mass.: D. C. Heath, 1974, pp. 287–300.

Price, R., & Blashfield, R. Explorations in the taxonomy of behavior settings: Analysis of dimensions and classification of settings. *American Journal of Community Psychology,* 1975, *3,* 335–351.

Proshansky, H. Visual and spatial aspects of social interaction and group process. Paper presented to Society for Human Factors, New York, 1971.

Proshansky, H., Ittelson, W., & Rivlin, L. (Eds.). *Environmental psychology.* New York: Holt, Rinehart and Winston, 1970.

Rossi, P., & Williams, W. (Eds.). *Evaluating social programs: theory, practice, and politics.* New York: Seminar Press, 1972.

Saegert, S. Crowding: Cognitive overload and behavioral constraint. In W. Preiser (Ed.), *Environmental design research* (Vol. 2). Stroudsburg, Pa.: Dowden, Hutchinson & Ross, 1973.

Schmitt, R. Implications of density in Hong Kong. *Journal of the American Institute of Planners,* 1963, *24,* 210–217.

Schopler, J., & Walton, J. The effects of expected structure, expected enjoyment, and participants' internality-externality upon feelings of being crowded. Unpublished manuscript, 1974.

Sells, S. An interactionist looks at the environment. *American Psychologist,* 1963, *18,* 696–702.

Shaw, C., Zorbaugh, F., McKay, J., & Cottrell, L. *Delinquency areas.* Chicago: University of Chicago Press, 1929.

Spivack, M. Sensory distortions in tunnels and corridors. *Hospital and Community Psychiatry,* 1967, *18,* 24–30.

Stokols, D.   On the distinction between density and crowding: Some implications for future research. *Psychological Review*, 1972, 79, 275–277(a).

Stokols, D.   A social-psychological model of human crowding phenomena. *Journal of the American Institute of Planners,* 1972,38, 72–83(b). Reprinted by permission of the *Journal of the American Institute of Planners*.

Stokols, D.   The relationship between micro and macro crowding phenomena: Some implications for environmental research and design. *Man-Environment Systems*, 1973, 3, 139–149.

Stokols, D.   The experience of crowding in primary and secondary environments. *Environment and Behavior*, 1976, 8, 49–86.

Stokols, D. (Ed.).   *Psychological perspectives on environment and behavior: Conceptual and empirical trends.* New York: Plenum Press, 1977.

Stokols, D., Rall, M., Pinner, B., & Schopler, J.   Physical, social and personal determinants of the perception of crowding *Environment and Behavior*, 1973, 5, 87–115.

Swan. J.   Public response to air pollution. In J. Wohlwill & D. Carson (Eds.), *Environment and Social Sciences*. Washington, D.C., American Psychological Association, 1972, pp. 66–74.

Trickett, E., Kelly, J., & Todd, D.   The social environment of the high school. In S. Golann & C. Eisdorfer (Eds.), *Handbook of community mental health.* New York: Appleton-Century-Crofts, 1972, pp. 331–406.

Wheeler, L.   *Behavioral research for architectural planning and design.* Terre Haute, Ind.: Ewing Miller Associates, 1967.

Wicker, A.   Size of church membership and members' support of church behavior settings. *Journal of Personality and Social Psychology*, 1969, 13, 278–288.

Wicker, A.   Processes which mediate behavior-environment congruence. *Behavioral Science*, 1972, 17, 265–277.

Wicker, A.   Undermanning theory and research: Implications for the study of psychological and behavioral effects of excess populations. *Representative Research in Social Psychology*, 1973, 4, 185–206.

Wicker, A., & Kauma, C.   Effects of a merger of a small and a large organization on members' behavior and experiences. *Journal of Applied Psychology*, 1974, 59, 24–30.

Willems, E.   Sense of obligation to high school activities as related to school size and marginality of student. *Child Development*, 1967, 38, 1247–1260.

Willems, E.   Behavioral ecology. In D. Stokols (Ed.), *Psychological perspectives on environment and behavior.* New York: Plenum Press, 1977.

Winett, R., & Nietzel, M.   Behavioral ecology: Contingency management of consumer energy use. *American Journal of Community Psychology*, 1975, 3, 123–133.

Zlutnick, S., & Altman, I.   Crowding and human behavior. In J. Wohlwill & D. Carson (Eds.), *Environment and the social sciences: Perspectives and applications.* Washington, D.C., American Psychological Association, 1972, pp. 44–58.

PART THREE

Perspectives in community change

6

CONSULTATION

Psychodynamic, behavioral, and organization development perspectives

CONSULTATION refers to an approach to community change through improvement of existing social institutions. As such it represents a group of "within systems" strategies aimed at modification, renewal, and improvement—not overthrow or replacement. There is an optimism among consultants about the possibilities for social change, the responsiveness of institutions, and the desire of workers for increased job competencies. Within-systems consultants assume that institutional personnel will be responsive to attempts to help them improve their job functioning and that improved delivery of service from existing social institutions will improve community life generally. It is not surprising then to find Beisser (1972) referring to consultation as a "conservative" and "quiet" method in a time when confrontation and tumult abound.

> It [consultation] seeks to heal or prevent man/organization splits without the disruption characteristic of so many of the other methods of social change. Its purpose is to help people cope with social systems as they are *now*. Although it seeks changes from the inside, it is a lubricant to whatever outside forces may require an organization to change. (Beisser, 1972, pp. 5–6)

While the stance described above is shared by most consultation theorists, there are major differences among consultants as well. Consultants vary considerably in their theories concerned with behavioral development and change and in the techniques derived from these different conceptual perspectives (Rappaport & Chinsky, 1974).

Among psychological consultants, the major conceptual perspectives can be described as mental health, behavioral, and organization development. Each orientation arose from a different historical mission and developed goals and methods tied to that mission. For example, the mental health orientation to consultation grew among clinicians with traditional psychodynamic and psychoanalytic training who moved to work settings in rural or underdeveloped areas with few mental health professionals to share the burden of large case loads. The mandate given to the available mental health personnel was clear—the treatment and prevention of mental disorder. Yet, how could that mandate be carried out with insufficient personnel? There needed to be a way to utilize existing community resources and personnel, even though indigenous community care-givers did not have mental health training. Consultation to community care-givers became the method utilized.

Behavioral consultation arose as a natural extension of laboratory experimentation. Behavior modification in the laboratory generated impressive results, but in many cases gains achieved did not carry over into real-life settings. Laboratory experimenters did not control the reinforcement contingencies to which their subjects were exposed in real life, and significant progress could be undone by others whose dispensement of reinforcement was maintaining inappropriate behavior. For some behaviorists, the focus of their work changed from modifying deviant individuals to modifying the dispensers of reinforcement who were maintaining deviant behavior in the natural environment. Patterson (1971) refers to behavioral consultants as "dispenser modifiers."

> One might . . . label the group of investigators who work in the classroom and in the home as "dispenser modifiers" in that they introduce procedures which alter the behavior of the peer, the teacher, the parent and the sibling.
>
> In its broad outlines such an approach constitutes an, as yet, inchoate rapprochement between reinforcement theory on the one hand, and social psychology on the other. There is as yet no articulated theory; rather, it is more the case that each investigator shares the implicit assumption that intervention should occur in the environment in which the child lives, and then sets about devising his own means of bringing this about. (Patterson, 1971, p. 752.)

Organization development specialists originated as consultants to industry. Over the years, it had become clear that in the name of production efficiency, manpower practices had neglected to provide for worker morale and satisfaction. Although production gains could be realized by streamlined assembly lines, one could not ignore the attitudes, feelings, and desires of workers without efficiency suffering. Absenteeism, slipshod work, industrial sabotage, alcoholism on the job, etc. became real threats that could negate previous gains in efficiency. Basic human factors related to work could no longer be ignored.

In helping industrial organizations improve efficiency, it became clear that a major focus would have to be on management practices and the *processes* by which decisions were made and carried out. The overarching value was that of optimizing human potential in work settings. This value can be seen in the following goals for organization development provided by Bennis:

1. To create an open, problem-solving climate throughout an organization.
2. To supplement the authority associated with role or status with the authority of knowledge and competence.
3. To locate decision-making and problem-solving responsibilities as close to the information sources as possible.
4. To build trust among persons and groups throughout an organization.
5. To make competition more relevant to work goals and to maximize collaborative efforts.
6. To develop a reward system which recognizes both the achievement of the organization's goals (profits or service) and development of people.
7. To increase the sense of "ownership" of organization objectives throughout the work force.
8. To help managers to manage according to relevant objectives rather than according to "past practices" or according to objectives which do not make sense for one's area of responsibility.
9. To increase self-control and self-direction for people within the organization. (Bennis, 1969, pp. 36–37)

Our intent in the remainder of this chapter is to describe the three orientations in greater detail, in each instance highlighting major assumptions and limitations. We will then conclude with a description and critique of the assumptions and techniques that the consultation perspectives share in common.

Mental health consultation

Mental health consultation originated in a context of scarce mental health resources; most often in isolated, rural, or undeveloped areas with few mental health professionals. In these settings, it was impossible to recommend costly professional treatment, such as psychotherapy, as long as there was a chronically insufficient supply of personnel to administer such programs. On the other hand, regardless of how rural, almost all communities provide for the health, welfare, and socialization of their citizens through networks of primary care-givers and agents of social control (teachers, ministers, welfare workers, police, physicians, etc.). Since there are very few problems in real life that are exclusively psychological in nature why not encourage existing personnel to continue to deal with these problems, providing extra help with the psychological component as needed?

Gerald Caplan, perhaps the one individual most influential in the field of mental health consultation, defines the process of consultation in the following way:

> . . . consultation is used in a quite restricted sense to denote a process of interaction between two professional persons—the consultant, who is a specialist, and the consultee, who invokes the consultant's help in regard to a current work problem with which he is having some difficulty and which he has decided is within the other's area of competence. The work problem involves the management or treatment of one or more clients of the consultee, or the planning or implementation of a program to cater to such clients. (Caplan, 1970, p. 19)

The consultee referred to in the above definition is a professional with a human service specialty, who in requesting consultation, hopes to expand personal competencies by sharing in the particular mental health expertise of the consultant. As a primary, front-line community worker, it is not intended that the consultee be trained as a junior psychiatrist or psychologist. Such training would be inappropriate; little is to be gained by casting complex social problems in psychological terms implying an exclusive mental health solution. It would seem more parsimonious and economical to support natural care-giving systems in the community. This point of view, developed initially as a matter of simple economics as there was little possibility of expanding the pool of available mental health manpower, was soon reinforced by the growing view that it would be best to avoid the anticipated deleterious effects of mental patient status whenever possible.

Kiesler (1973) provides an example of a mental health consultation program established in a rural area with scarce mental health resources. When Kiesler came to northern Minnesota, he began working in a three-county area the size of the state of Massachusetts, but with only 68,000 residents. The population was relatively isolated and thinly dispersed. There were no mental health specialists in the entire area; yet the three counties had a professional manpower pool of over 300 persons who were in the business of helping troubled individuals. These helping professionals included physicians, lawyers, clergymen, court personnel, school administrators and counselors, welfare workers, and public health and school nurses.

Budget limitations made it clear that the area could support only three mental health professionals. What could one psychiatrist, one psychologist, and one psychiatric social worker do to meet the mental health needs of the area?

Each of the indigenous professional groups wanted to use the mental health specialists in the only way that was really familiar to them—by making referrals to a traditional psychiatric clinic. The family doctors wanted to turn over their most troublesome patients to the psychiatrist. The school administrators wanted the psychologist to do IQ testing. The juvenile court hoped that treatment by the social worker would somehow "turn around" their youthful offenders. The sheriffs wanted to know whether prisoners in jail were "mentally ill" or just "acting up." In general, there was a tendency to want to label immature, misbehaving, and troublesome people as "mentally ill" so that the responsibility for their care could be turned over to someone else—the mental health specialist.

The three mental health professionals began their work with the decision that none of the existing community care-givers should be allowed to abdicate responsibility for mental-health-related problems.

> We were convinced that, if the community were to meet its clinical task, firing-line professionals would not only have to continue to take responsibility for mental health problems, but they also would have to increase their proficiency in doing so. (Kiesler, 1973, p. 103)

The method of operation to implement this goal was as follows. Whenever a referral was made, it was accepted; but rather than scheduling an appointment to see the client, the mental health specialists scheduled an appointment with the referring agent instead—even if distance mandated that the contact be by telephone and not in person. During this contact, the case would be discussed and the referring agent would describe what was being done already. Sometimes, little more could be accomplished by mental health intervention, and when appropriate this was pointed out. The care-giving professionals were supported and given confidence to do what they already were doing. There were times when suggestions for alternative strategies were discussed; but only infrequently was the client seen directly. Direct clinical contact and service to clients were provided to only about 20 percent of the families about whom consultations were made.

> The fact that more than eight of every ten families about whom we consult are never seen by us does not mean that we have set up family doctors, clergymen, sheriffs, social workers, and a host of others in an imitation of psychiatric practice. These people are not interested in stepping into other professional roles than those they already have. Our experience shows that most troubled people in our area obtain no better results with our help than they do with local professional help. One of our working hypotheses is that the earlier the problems of adaptation can be defined by firing-line professionals, the better the results that can be obtained from relatively simple straightforward corrective approaches. (Kiesler, 1973, pp. 105–106)

Not all indigenous professionals were happy with the arrangement. There were some difficult problems that evoked feelings of professional inadequacy and fed the myth that "the specialist" could do a better job. However, this is rarely the case for most problems in living that confront community agencies. Over time, the indigenous care-givers in this example learned to value the consultation experience and the fresh insights provided by the opportunity to share one's work with a colleague with a different perspective. Requests for consultation rose, and requests to see patients directly, declined. This provided a considerable saving, as Kiesler was able to determine that per unit of mental health time his team was able to influence nine times as many families through consultation as would have been the case for direct clinical service.

Types of mental health consultation

Consultation theorists typically distinguish between client-centered, consultee-centered, and program-centered consultation (Mannino & Shore, 1972). In other words, consultation can focus on an agency's clients, staff, or program. Throughout, the emphasis is on work problems, improving on-the-job performance so that the agency can deliver more responsive service. It is expected that as the work problems of staff become resolved, their ability to relate to problem clients in a psychologically meaningful way will also increase. The assumption is that primary care-givers can develop more effective and psychologically sound programs and can learn to understand and deal with the social and emotional components of the problems with which their clients confront them.

A significant caution: Consultation is not psychotherapy. Note that the content focus of consultation is on work problems, not personal problems (Altrocchi, 1972). This hallmark of mental health consultation was developed for several important reasons. Most basically, mental health consultants respect the professional and personal competencies of their consultees. They assume that consultees are motivated and interested in serving their clients better and that they usually possess an adequate level of professional skill to utilize the new insights gained from consultation. Furthermore, consultation contracts rarely sanction psychotherapy for agency staff. Attempts to impose a therapeutic relationship once consultation has commenced would be an invasion of the consultee's privacy and would be a breech of professional ethics.

Problems can arise when clinically experienced mental health professionals practice consultation without training in its principles. Without recognition of the dangers involved, it is not that difficult for the minimally trained to unwittingly slide into therapeutic or quasi-therapeutic relationships. For the experienced clinician without consultation training, it may be the only professional role with which he or she is familiar. To complicate the problem even further, some consultees seem to be asking for a therapeutic relationship. These individuals may be quick to see personal inadequacies in themselves; and, it is sometimes easier to retreat to the relative safety of a therapeutic relationship with a kind clinician than to assume personal responsibility for corrective action in the face of difficulty. Thus, an untrained consultant can be pulled into a therapeutic alliance where both parties erroneously assume that what is transpiring between them is a form of mental health consultation.

In the pages that follow, we shall describe the three main types of mental health consultation, giving examples of each. *Client-centered* consultation is most frequently practiced and is most familiar to specialists in all fields. *Consultee-centered* consultation has greater potential for changing attitudes and behavior but can raise ethical issues if not practiced with the full awareness and consent of consultees. *Program-centered* consultation has the greatest potential for affecting community change. Unfortunately it is also the most difficult form of consultation, requiring the greatest understanding of community functioning.

Client-centered consultation: A frequent entry point

Client-centered consultation is the most traditional form of consultation. It occurs when a consultee, having difficulty in the management of a particular case, or group of cases, calls for a mental health specialist to make an expert assessment of the client's problem and suggest ways for the case to be handled. The focus is on how the client can best be helped, but in the process it is expected that the consultees will use this opportunity to improve their knowledge and skill so that in the future they will be better able to handle comparable problems in this case or similar ones on their own.

The first request for help from an agency is most often of this type, as client-centered consultation is most clearly understood. While in general, defensiveness may be high among potential consultees who fear criticism from the consultant, it is the least in this form of consultation since the focus is on the agency's clients, not on staff or program. Thus it represents an entry point that consultants willingly accept.

Spielberger (1967) presents a case-seminar method of consultation developed in collaboration with two colleagues (Altrocchi, Spielberger, & Eisdorfer, 1965) that provides a useful example of client-centered consultation. The project took place in a small city along the coast of North Carolina, with few mental health professionals. A case seminar with groups of indigenous community care-givers was developed as the principal consultation procedure. Groups were formed for key personnel such as public health nurses, ministers, welfare workers, elementary school teachers, and high school guidance counselors. The public health nurses, for example, worked in a variety of settings in the community; some in maternity and well-baby clinics, some as school nurses, with still others receiving home visit assignments to check on possible cases of communicable disease. Very often, the nurse, in dealing with an apparently clear-cut health problem, would find that there was a psychological component to the problem that was equally important and that prevented the achievement of restored health. The work of the seminar was to develop an understanding of the case so that an effective plan of action could be formulated.

One of the present authors (KH) provided a similar form of case consultation to public health nurses in a large eastern city and can draw upon that experience to provide a specific case example. The problem brought before the group was that of a 50-year-old man with tuberculosis. The TB had been brought under control; but the man was a heavy drinker, and this in turn was leading to a deteriorated physical condition. The drinking had also led to family conflicts; his wife and family had left him; he was lonely; he no longer worked; and seemed unmotivated to change his habits.

The group discussed the problem of a lonely man who no longer felt useful, who felt that no one cared about him, and who was sliding into alcoholism. This discussion proved illuminating to the nurse. Adopting a fresh perspective, the nurse remembered that the client still had one tie to his family. He was visited occasionally by a 19-year-old son whom he greatly admired. The group suggested to the nurse that she contact the son to see if he would be willing to develop a closer relationship with his father—who in turn might develop some motivation to deal with his drinking problem if he felt important to someone once again.

Note that the plan developed for this case did not include psychotherapy for the nurse's client. Not only was this option unavailable, but it is extremely doubtful that this form of treatment would have been acceptable to the client. We planned an intervention that was within the role prescriptions and duties of a public health nurse. She felt perfectly comfortable talking to a son about spending more time with his sick father. Eventually, if the father's motivation could be increased, Alcoholics Anonymous might be suggested. But at this point, the focus was on how to prevent a lonely man who felt useless and unwanted from sliding further into a debilitated condition.

Consultee-centered consultation

In consultee-centered consultation, the presenting problem may involve a particular case, but the focus of consultation is on the consultee's difficulties with the case. The shift in focus may not be noticed by the consultee since the content of the discussion may remain centered about a case, but the consultant is using the medium of the case to improve a deficiency assumed to be present in the consultee. As described by Caplan (1970), the focus of consultation moves to the consultee when the problem is due to a lack of knowledge or skill, a temporary loss in self-confidence, or a lapse in professional objectivity.

When a problem is due to a lack of knowledge or skill, consultants often vary as to how they deal with these deficiencies. Some offer direct training themselves in the problem areas; others refrain from direct intervention, believing that deficiencies in knowledge and skill are more appropriately dealt with through the normal channels of agency supervision. The consultant may possess specialized knowledge not available to other professions (e.g., knowledge of behavior modification principles of benefit to classroom teachers; skill in developing and motivating self-help groups for welfare mothers) and may decide that the simplest route would be to provide the missing knowledge and skill directly. In organizations where supervision is diffuse or nonexistent (e.g., as may occur in many school situations where teachers are expected to function relatively independently in the classroom) there should be little conflict between consultation and supervision. However, in agencies where line workers are closely and actively supervised (e.g., as in a welfare department) the danger exists that direct training would be resented by agency supervisors who would see the consultant's work as infringing on their duties and undermining their authority. Caplan (1970) advises that in agencies with good supervisory networks, deficiencies in knowledge or skill among line workers should not be dealt with directly by the consultant. Instead, consideration should be given to moving the point of intervention to the supervisors. Training the supervisors can increase their competence and importance in the agency, does not disturb the traditional lines of authority within the agency, and has the added advantage of potentially making the consultant's knowledge more relevant to the organization. If accomplished effectively, the supervisory group can translate the consultant's ideas into procedures that would be accepted more readily in the organization. Consultants might be tempted to bypass the supervisors, believing themselves to be more effective teachers who could present their own ideas more clearly. In addition, middle-line supervisors might be found to be most resistant to innovation, a frequent occurrence in bureaucratic organizations. Still, attempting to bypass a powerful supervisory group could easily doom the intervention program—if not immediately, then by slow erosion as the supervisors, uncommitted to the program, slowly drift back to previous procedures.

Work problems due to lapses in professional objectivity can be difficult to handle. If the consultee is aware of personal involvement with the case, this topic can be approached directly in consultation. Personal feelings of anger, frustration, or disappointment can be dis-

cussed and viewed as natural responses to difficult work circumstances. A frequently occurring myth in human service organizations
is that "true" professionals must not allow themselves to develop
personal feelings toward their clients. Thus when natural feelings of
frustration and anger arise, there is no organizational vehicle established to help work through these feelings. They are suppressed, to
avoid the label of being "foolish," "soft," or "unprofessional." The
consultant can perform an important service by helping consultees
accept and constructively use their personal feelings that develop in
the normal course of their work. If these feelings can be dealt with
in a group setting, so much the better, for the consultees then could
build their own support group that could function independently
after the consultant terminates his or her services.

Knoblock and Goldstein (1971) discuss workshops with teachers in
which the participants are encouraged to talk about the personal satis-
factions and frustrations in their particular work settings. They describe one such group as follows:

> . . . Our teachers wanted to communicate that they could represent
> themselves as complex individuals. To be sure, they also felt they had
> good ideas about what could happen in schools with children and
> teachers. Even more importantly, they believed they had many skills
> and talents other than teaching skills. Many are talented and creative
> people who outside of the school pursue many avocations but within the
> school are asked to turn those off and run the ship as usual.
>
> In a summer workshop dealing with interpersonal competence, a
> group of teachers began to discuss poetry. One of the participants began
> to bring her poems to class, some of them inspired by the workshop and
> its participants. Two things were startling about this experience. One
> was the very fact that such creative people and behavior were neither
> acknowledged nor provided for in their school jobs. The other was that
> their degree of animation over such "avocational interests" was far more
> intense and involving than their teaching activities in the classroom.
>
> It would seem from what our group and other teachers report that it is
> not sufficient to develop a personal and professional life which focuses
> exclusively on children. Teachers are equally concerned with respond-
> ing to other adults and in turn being responded to by their colleagues.
>
> In short, teachers would like very much to function as resources
> within the schools. How paradoxical it is that so many teachers do not
> see themselves as resources within their own classrooms, but rather as
> keepers of the peace, curriculum and school tradition. (Knoblock and
> Goldstein, 1971, pp. 13–14)

The function of the workshops in the Knoblock and Goldstein
example was to provide a vehicle for teachers to share their feelings

about their personal involvement in their work as one way of combating professional loneliness. As long as no one is talking about job frustrations it is very easy to erroneously assume that "everyone is satisfied so I must be the odd-ball." The realization that dissatisfaction is shared can be a spark for corrective action to improve the work climate. But even if improvement is not likely, recognizing that satisfaction may have to come from "avocational interests" would still be a valuable lesson that would probably improve overall life satisfaction.

How open should the consultant be in confronting consultee feelings and conflicts? When consultees are not aware of personal involvement in their work, the dilemma for the consultant is whether to bring these feelings into conscious awareness or to deal with them more indirectly by discussing the relevant conflict-arousing issues through the medium of the case, that is, by focusing on the behavior of the consultee's client. This indirect approach is recommended by Caplan who has developed techniques of dealing with personal conflicts in consultees through displacement (see Caplan, 1970, pp. 125–222). As Caplan sees it, in his method the personality defenses of the consultee are not disturbed since he or she is never required to confront or examine personal feelings or the reasons for overinvolvement with the case. Only the client's personality and reactions are discussed. The problem may be the consultee's, but it is discussed as if it is the client's problem exclusively.

Caplan describes the displacement technique in his description of consultation with an elementary school teacher (Caplan, 1970, pp. 140–142). The girl in question (Jean) had become a disciplinary problem, although her behavior had been trouble-free during the first half of the semester. Description of the onset of the problem by the teacher revealed that the change had occurred about the time of the first parent conference when the teacher had discovered that Jean was the younger sister of a girl she had taught three years earlier. After the vacation following the parent conference, Jean's behavior began to deteriorate rapidly. The consultant remembered that this teacher had consulted him earlier in the year about another girl in the class who was said to be suffering from a learning disorder and who also was described as someone else's younger sister.

> The consultant did not know anything about the teacher's personal life, but he hazarded a guess to himself that she probably had a younger sister with whom she had been involved in unresolved conflicts similar in pattern to those she was now imposing on the case of Jean. In this regard it appeared particularly significant that Jean became a problem to

the teacher only after she discovered that she was "a younger sister." It also seemed that Jean's poor behavior occurred only in class with that teacher and was apparently a reaction to the teacher's method of handling her. (Caplan, 1970, p. 141)

The consultant did not begin a discussion of the teacher's personal life to find the suspected unresolved conflict. Instead, he discussed the problem as if it were Jean's—that Jean was worried about being a younger sister and was afraid that the teacher would constantly compare her with her successful older sister.

He pointed out that her behavior had regressed following the teacher's interview with her mother before Christmas, during which they had discussed her older sister. He put forward the hypothesis that after this interview the mother had told Jean that the teacher had been very fond of the older sister and remembered her quite vividly, and had possibly told her that the teacher hoped Jean would be as successful a student. The consultant then involved the teacher in a discussion of what this might have meant to Jean, and the nature of the conflict that might have been set up in her mind, so that she now might imagine that the teacher was continually comparing her with her older sister. The teacher, in this discussion, began to identify with the consultant, reversing roles and empathically imagining how Jean felt as a younger sister . . . The consultant then posed the management problem as being for the teacher to work out ways of convincing Jean that her teacher was not a representative of her family constellation, and that Jean was a person in her own right and not just a "younger sister."

During the second consultation session, the teacher quite suddenly made a switch in her patterned perceptions of Jean and began to talk about her as a child struggling to overcome in the classroom her misperceptions of her teacher. She then began to plan various alternative ways of dealing with her . . .

During the remainder of the school year this teacher asked for consultation about two other cases, neither one of which was a "younger sister." She gave follow-up reports on Jean, whose behavior disorder had apparently completely resolved within three to four weeks following the second consultation discussion about her problems. (Caplan, 1970, p. 142)

Caplan's displacement approach has the advantage of reducing defensiveness in that consultees may become suspicious and anxious and may avoid future contacts if the consultant approaches emotional issues directly. The fear that mental health professionals are "out to psychoanalyze you" becomes confirmed if consultees are led into emotional confrontation without warning. Even forewarned, discussions that move into personal reactions can be seen as a violation of the consultation contract by potential consultees. On the other hand, direct discussion of personal involvement can be supported by the argument that bringing feelings into awareness can be an aid to learning and that learning without awareness is not very effective. In this sense, indirect methods may be too subtle. The main point of the consultant's message may never be received if it is made by analogy, conveyed in a parable, or presented by other similar indirect means.

The problem can be summarized as follows. Dealing with the personal involvement of the consultee in a work problem by helping to encourage its conscious recognition should lead to a more effective resolution as the consultee learns to accept and deal with the emotions engendered by the work situation. However, not all consultees are ready for emotional learning experiences and they may become anxious or attempt to flee consultation if it becomes apparent that this is the consultant's goal. Indirect methods of consultation that deal with personal involvement but never bring it to awareness would seem better suited to these instances. However, here, too, there are drawbacks. The effectiveness of learning without awareness can be questioned. An ethical question can also be raised concerning indirect methods in that consultants are forced to work under false pretenses. The focus is on change in the consultees but they must take great pains to keep this intent secret, and must steadfastly maintain that they are only talking about the consultees' cases.

There is no completely satisfactory resolution to the difficulties raised above. It is our own personal belief that direct methods of consultation for consultee-centered problems are to be preferred when they can be utilized. In organizations marked by a lack of openness and a high degree of defensiveness among line staff, the consultant must seriously consider the options available. One possibility is to deal with problems involving a lapse in professional objectivity only with those who are open to change and willing to examine their own contribution to their work problems. It could be argued that consultation should be offered only when receptivity is high. The problem is that it is difficult to ignore lapses in professional objectivity if they occur in more defensive care-givers who occupy important positions in the socialization and care-giving network of a community. For example, one could not expect to have a major impact on the lives of children if their teachers were ignored as being too resistant to change. It is for these special instances when the need for intervention is particularly acute that we believe that indirect methods of consultee-centered consultation have some value.

A special case of consultee-centered consultation: Theme interference reduction. We have already seen that Caplan advocates dealing with personal problems of consultees through displacement of the problem onto case material. As a psychoanalyst, Caplan believes that such indirection is even more important for personal problems associated with "repressed impulses." For such "unconscious" problems that represent an interfering theme in the client's work, Caplan has devised a special technique that he has labeled "theme interference reduction." The technique will be described at this point because of its prominence and because, as we shall explain shortly, we believe it has some value in dealing with untested stereotypes that can affect worker performance. We are not analysts, but will present the analytic rationale so that the procedures may be properly understood.

Caplan posits that a lack of professional objectivity in an otherwise competent consultee can be caused by the sudden emergence of a heretofore successfully repressed impulse. The original repression occurred because, in his or her own psychological development, the consultee was led to expect severe punishment if the impulse in question was expressed. Now years later, the consultee comes across a case with a similar theme. The case disturbs the defensive equilibrium that the consultee has established, raises considerable tension in the consultee, and leads to the lapse in professional objectivity. The consultee is upset because only an unfortunate consequence can be seen as the outcome to this particular case. The case is "doomed" because it represents the sense of doom the consultee anticipates personally, should unacceptable impulses emerge.

Caplan's technique is to demonstrate to the consultee that the case that represents the prohibited theme can possibly escape the doomed outcome. By indirection, the message to the consultee is that those with similar problems (including the consultee) need not be doomed. However, this message cannot be stated directly. Doing so would be to confront the consultee with the repressed prohibited theme, an upsetting personal experience that in addition would probably be ineffective. Confronted with unconscious material, the consultee would most likely not recognize the theme, deny its personal relevance, become anxious and then angry at the consultant. Helping the consultee become aware of the interfering theme more gradually is also not recommended. This more gradual procedure would not be traumatic to the consultee, but it would bring the consultation relationship closer to psychotherapy—which is rarely sanctioned in consultation and would represent an inefficient use of time. Except for the displaced problem, the consultee is assumed to be functioning adequately. Becoming involved in psychotherapy would further restrict the range of other problems to which the consultant could be exposed. There is simply no time to develop a long-term therapeutic relationship with one consultee.

The technique of theme interference reduction is designed to reduce the psychological interference produced by the problem case without the consultee becoming aware that the difficulty in the case is a result of his or her own unresolved conflict. The consultant keeps the discussion constantly on the case and in this sense deals with the unconscious conflicts of the consultee by displacing them onto the case. The technique involves finding the interfering theme or themes in the case material by monitoring the consultee's interview behavior for signs of increasing anxiety, overinvolvement, confusion, or any other unusual professional conduct. The anxiety-arousing material is never dealt with directly. Once it is discovered, the consultant moves away from the "hot" topic only to return to it later to discover the full extent of the theme. In Caplanian language, the consultant is attempting to "identify a syllogistic theme with its definable Initial Category and Inevitable Outcome" (Caplan, 1970, p. 154) so as to break the link between the two.

The "Initial Category" refers to the stereotyped view of the case that the consultee maintains because it reflects his or her own unacceptable impulses. Hence the consultee cannot think about the case clearly, without anxiety. The "Inevitable Outcome" refers to the sense of foreboding about the case's outcome the consultee feels because it relates to the unrecognized belief that all persons with similar unacceptable impulses (including himself or herself) are also "doomed."

According to Caplan, theme interference can be reduced in two ways. The first approach, called "unlinking," attempts to change the consultee's perception of the client so as to remove the client from the Initial Category—or in other words, unlinking the client from the consultee's theme. For example, if the Initial Category was "All people who masturbate excessively," unlinking would involve convincing the consultee that the level of masturbation exhibited by the client was not excessive for a boy of his age. Unlinking is said to be "a cardinal error" in consultation technique, for even though the consultee may gain temporary relief from anxiety, the unconscious theme is left intact at full strength.

A more lasting benefit is claimed for the second consultation approach. The consultant agrees with the categorization of the client as fitting the Initial Category but then proceeds to reexamine the evidence for the Inevitable Outcome. If the consultant can open the consultee's perception to the recognition that other more beneficial outcomes are not only possible but perhaps more likely, again consultee tension lessens, but this time because the effects of the interfering theme are being reduced. In Caplan's words:

> Because the theme applies also to him, the invalidation of the syllogism for his client also has an effect of significantly reducing the consultee's tension regarding his own underlying conflict (Caplan, 1970, p. 149).

Reinterpreting theme-interference reduction as a procedure for dealing with stereotyped attitudes. There are several questions that can be put to this approach. First, do unconscious conflicts exist, and if so are they capable of interfering with the work capacity of a consultee in so circumscribed a manner? Remember that the assumption is that the psychological adjustment of the consultee is adequate; the effects of unconscious conflict are seen only by its displacement on the case. If the conflict is strong, why does it not show in other behaviors of the consultee? If it is weak, why does it produce so pronounced an effect with this *one* case, and why do the otherwise intact defenses of the consultee not help in providing a successful resolution without the necessity of consultation intervention?

A second line of questions concerns the avoidance of consultee awareness. Not only is the consultee unaware that personal conflicts are the subject of consultation, but the consultant also does not know the full, detailed content of these conflicts, and is prohibited by the technique from finding out. Their content is known only in a general way by noting the topics that produce the most consultee tension and anxiety. Consultation moves along without either party knowing the content of the conflicts to which it is addressed. That it is moving on the right track can be determined only from the drop in tension level exhibited by the consultee. Considering the wide array of factors that can produce tension reduction in the consultee (e.g., increased rapport with and trust of the consultant; "unlinking"; a new cognitive grasp of the case, having nothing to do with unconscious conflict) it is difficult to see how the presence of an unconscious conflict can ever be truly determined. By avoiding consultee awareness, other issues are also raised. Is it ethical to work on another's conflicts without explicit permission? And, once it becomes generally known that consultants are looking for unconscious conflicts in consultees, this latter group, also becoming aware of the consultants' intent are no longer proper subjects for theme interference reduction. Finally, the coordinate relationship of two professionals, consultant and consultee, working on a common problem together is destroyed when one of them is all the while secretly tampering with the psyche of the other.

If it is removed from its psychoanalytic underpinning, there may be some usefulness to Caplan's technique. Consider the possibility that a consultee may at times be suffering from an overgeneralized stereotype. The stereotype might be a reflection of cultural attitudes learned in early socialization, e.g., stereotypes such as "blacks are sexually promiscuous"; "men who don't work are lazy"; "masturbation leads to insanity"; "women who have extramarital affairs can't be good mothers"; etc. Or, the stereotyped attitude could result from an unfortunate personal experience that has been blown up out of proportion and is now the source of an inappropriately overgeneralized negative attitude.

Regardless of their origins, stereotyped views are rarely accessible to change through direct attack or challenge. We agree with Caplan that excluding one individual from a stereotype can change an attitude toward that individual but the stereotype still may be left intact. The process Caplan calls "unlinking" involves removing a case from the consultee's general stereotype and we would agree that it is less preferred as a method of influencing stereotyped attitudes. A much better possibility would be to expand the consultee's perceptual field by broadening the view of members of the stereotyped group. This can be done by demonstrating that one member of the stereotyped group whom the consultee knows well (the case) has unrecognized assets. This is essentially what Caplan does when he demonstrates that an unfortunate or "doomed" outcome is not inevitable.

In summary, we feel that Caplan's procedures are enmeshed in a psychoanalytic rationale that hides their more general utility. We doubt that many consultees are bothered by unconscious conflicts that operate in the circumscribed way that Caplan's method requires. However, this does not invalidate the technique, only the theory. Caplan's procedure is one way of dealing with overgeneralized, and untested stereotyped attitudes. In the name of reducing interfering themes, Caplan and his co-workers may be obtaining consultee affective relief and movement on a case because the consultee is no longer trapped by perception of restricted alternatives available to the client. Expanding these alternatives can serve to broaden one's picture of the entire situation. This is essentially what Levy refers to as psychological interpretation, "a redefining or restructuring of the situation through the presentation of an alternate description of some behavior datum" (Levy, 1963, p. 5). Theme interference reduction seems to be just such a process.

Program-centered consultation

Program-centered consultation offers the greatest potential for significant and enduring changes in an organizational system. Changes in programs and policies have a far reaching, radiating effect throughout the entire organization and can have a greater potential effect than can be obtained from consultation at the case level or by improving the work performance of individual staff members. Ultimately the goal of program-centered consultation is to insure that the psychological component of that agency's mission is being handled in the most competent manner. Whether the system is a school, welfare department, or police precinct, consultants align themselves with those policies that allow the agency involved to perform its primary mission (e.g., education, aid to indigents, peace-keeping, etc.) in a manner that articulates best with current knowledge of psychological development and well-being. The assumption is that since primary care-givers constantly deal with human behavior and its problems, the more they know about psychological development and behavior dynamics, and how to implement this knowledge, the more likely will it be that agency programs will reflect psychologically sound and humane policies.

Mann (1971) provides an interesting example of consultation with a police department that became more program-centered over time. During the period of consultation, the consultant was thrust into a police department crisis—how to handle an illegal massive anti-war demonstration (Mann & Iscoe, 1971). That the planned demonstration was prevented from becoming a riot was to some degree a reflection of the success of the anticipatory guidance and planning provided by the consultant.

The initial contact between the consultant and the police was made with the chief of police, inviting him to send departmental representatives to a project whose goal was the coordination of resources within a particular high-risk neighborhood. Police representatives attended a series of biweekly meetings of agency workers oriented toward specific neighborhood problems. The meetings were led by the consultant and other staff of the mental health center, giving the police an opportunity to observe and become familiar with the individuals involved. At the same time, with the approval of the Chief, the consultant accompanied policemen on their rounds, riding in various patrol cars to familiarize himself with police operations.

After this initial period of relationship building, the consultant began to receive calls from the police involving crisis intervention activities, in which help was requested in handling particularly difficult emotionally disturbed persons. Initially, the consultant went to the police station and interviewed the person with the referring officer sitting in on the interview. This allowed the consultant to serve as a model for the policemen in interview procedures. Later, the officers were encouraged to handle these cases on their own, discussing their work with the consultant as necessary.

As a consequence of these activities, the consultant was asked to participate in training new recruits, and then later in training command-level officers. Work toward program modification occurred as the consultant encouraged the police to use other helping resources in the community. Standard operating procedures were changed to allow for greater referral to social service agencies.

During the period of this growing relationship with the consultant, the police suddenly were faced with a crisis situation. Students at the local university, aroused by the deaths at Kent State University, planned a massive anti-war demonstration. Violence already had erupted in a smaller demonstration the day before, and the City Council, fearing the worst, denied a parade permit to the anti-war groups. The protesters decided to appeal the council ruling in court, but made plans to march regardless of the outcome of their appeal.

The consultant had access to both sides in the conflict, the police and the anti-war groups. As tension mounted, he discussed potential provocations with individuals from both groups, counseling restraint and suggesting ways to avoid over-reaction. Most of the participants on both sides wanted to prevent violence but had felt powerless to avoid it. The consultant was impressed with how easy it was for reasonable persons to become caught up in an escalating situation and noted: "It is a chilling experience to observe both parties to a confrontation preparing for combat, each hoping and wishing that its preparations will prove unnecessary" (Mann & Iscoe, 1971, p. 111).

Luckily, the parade permit was granted although at the very last minute. Six thousand students and citizens marched without incident in a "legal" parade. As the parade concluded its peaceful course, one policeman turned to the consultant, shook his hand and said: "At times like these, I'm glad there are people like you around who I can talk to and trust" (Mann & Iscoe, 1971, p. 111).

Despite its great potential in affecting system-wide changes, it is surprising how little literature exists describing program-centered mental health consultation. Mannino and Shore (1972) reviewed 16 studies of consultation outcome appearing in the literature between 1958 and 1969. Half of the studies had control groups, and of these eight, five reported positive outcomes—a success rate of 63 percent, similar to the reports of the success achieved in psychotherapy. Of special significance to the discussion at this point, is that only 1 of the 16 studies was concerned with program-centered consultation, and this study was not within the mental health sphere because it involved consultation to a hospital dietary service. The remainder of the studies dealt exclusively with consultee-centered or client-centered consultation.

Problems associated with program-centered consultation.   There are a number of difficulties involved in implementing program-centered consultation. To begin with, it is not easy to obtain entrée into an organization. Agencies rarely call for outside consultation when contemplating program changes, and in all probability would be reluctant to trust an outsider who volunteered his or her services. Program changes are most often made internally; it is the rare organization that calls for an outside point of view in the formulation of new policies. What is a more frequent occurrence is for outside pressures to force an organization to review its practices, for example, as might occur when dissatisfied parents demand change in school programs, or blue-ribbon commissions are set up to investigate prison abuses, etc. In these instances, an organization under stress may seek an outside consultant, not because it wishes a true examination and eventual reform of its policies and procedures, but because it hopes to create the appearance of flexibility and cooperation—at least until the pressure is off. Program-centered consultation to organizations experiencing outside pressure can be successful if the consultant avoids proposals that would reduce outside pressure for reform before organizational practices contributing to the problem are thoroughly examined. For example, an elementary school in a low-income area might be experiencing considerable pressure from parents concerned about the chronic low levels of reading skills demonstrated by their children. The school principal may have contemplated adding a part-time remedial reading teacher to the staff, and in initiating consultation hopes that the consultant would lend formal endorsement to the proposal, which in turn would lead to greater parental acceptance. Instead, the consultant might do well to call for a review of the reading curriculum at all levels and convince the principal that a more lasting solution might be obtained if the teachers were to become involved in curriculum improvement themselves, perhaps through a series of reading workshops with a reading specialist. This latter course, while more time-consuming, attacks the problems where they originate, in the classroom, and has the potential of demonstrating a problem-solving approach that the school itself can adopt as curriculum modifications are needed in the future.

A second difficulty in implementing program-centered consultation involves a resistance to and fear of innovation, even among seemingly cooperative administrators. It is not unusual to find that some administrators are quite willing to give the consultant a free hand to work with their subordinates. It may become clear only after some time that this freedom of operation applies to subordinates but not to the administrator. Administrators sometimes show the all-too-human quality of being in favor of change in others, but fearing that self-examination will reveal "weakness" in themselves. The consultant must know how to deal with fear of exposure and censure once it becomes manifest, by demonstrating to the administrator that consultation does not involve evaluative "blame-casting." However, there are also realistic reasons for administrators to fear change. In most agencies, it is the administrator, not the staff or the consultant, who bears the total responsibility for the actions of the agency, including its mistakes. An administrator has more to lose by an idea gone wrong than anybody else. Administrators know this and are necessarily cautious. Those that are honest may tell the consultant that they do not lack for good ideas, and that they know where they would like to take their organization to make it a model agency. The constraints in carrying out their ideas involve the limitations imposed by community sentiments, budget, and staff competencies. The administrator may report feeling "trapped." He may feel that good ideas cannot be implemented because they would be opposed by a more conservative community, or the necessary budget is lacking, or the staff does not have the required competencies to carry out the ideas. These are realistic constraints, but they are not as insurmountable as administrators usually believe. Often there is room for change and for administrators to show leadership in revitalizing their organizations and in bringing new ideas to the community. There are risks, but administrators of human service organizations are in positions where they are expected to show leadership in solving human problems. To avoid these issues is to subject themselves and their communities to greater pressure in the future as unmet minor issues fester and become major problems.

A final difficulty in carrying out program-centered consultation is that many consultants lack skills in this area. Most consultants who come to community work through clinical training are experts in personality dynamics and interpersonal behavior, skills that are well suited to work at case and consultee levels. Program-centered consultation requires some knowledge of organizational theory and practice, planning, and fiscal and personnel management (Caplan, 1970). In addition, the consultant must be fully aware of community sentiments that impinge upon organizations and must be experienced in the practical politics of agency survival. Programs cannot change in one agency without affecting the entire community network of care-giving responsibilities. Mental health consultants without the necessary training and experience will be exposed to considerable frustration and may withdraw to safer case-centered and consultee-centered work.

In summary, we feel that program-centered consultation has the greatest potential for effecting enduring organizational change. However, it is the most difficult form of consultation as it thrusts the consultant into the vortex of competing community forces.

Behavioral consultation

The behavioral perspective comes to community psychology by way of clinical psychology, where it has come to assume a position of prominence. Sparked by a growing dissatisfaction with dynamically oriented approaches and a reemphasis on environmental concerns, clinical psychologists in the 1960s became concerned with helping people improve their everyday functioning. The traditional goals of psychotherapy—understanding, inner contentment, and acceptance of self were no longer considered sufficient if they were not accompanied by changes that helped people become more effective in their daily lives (Ford & Urban, 1967). The behaviorists met a receptive audience among clinical psychologists who were grasping for procedures that would allow them to be helpful in dealing with the kinds of changes for which their clients seemed to be asking—symptom removal and increased interpersonal effectiveness.

The behavioral approach was an extension of ideas that originated in the learning laboratory, and this provided its second source of appeal. The academic training of American clinical psychologists was research-oriented, covering a number of areas within general psychology. With this basic training, the clinical psychologist was well-versed in fields such as child development, social psychology, and learning. However, when it came to issues in his or her own field, clinical psychology, the theories were mostly psychiatric in origin—heavily influenced by introspective reflection and observation of individual cases rather than empirically acquired knowledge. The behaviorists provided the clinician with a link back to general psychology; it was their influence that opened the possibility of deriving clinical techniques from a new source—the psychological laboratory.

Behavior modification can be understood best as a special form of behavior influence. It is based upon the general principle that people are influenced by the consequences of their behavior (Stolz, Wienckowski, & Brown, 1975). Some behaviorists went further in asserting that clinical phenomena were to be explained exclusively by the same principles that governed normal psychological development. Thus, in a major text in abnormal psychology, Ullmann and Krasner described their major premise as follows:

> The central idea of this book is that the behaviors traditionally called abnormal are no different, either quantitatively or qualitatively, in their development and maintenance from other learned behaviors. (Ullmann & Krasner, 1969, p. 1)

The same argument is presented by Tharp and Wetzel as follows:

> . . . the laws of learning, like the rains, fall upon us all. There are no separate principles for abnormal behavior and for normal, and the "mentally ill" are no longer supposed to behave, or to learn, by different rules than their brothers. (Tharp & Wetzel, 1969, p. 5)

Besides asserting the generality and applicability of learning to all behaviors, abnormal as well as normal, the authors quoted above also propose that learning principles can explain two issues. The *acquisition* or development of dysfunctional behavior; and the *maintenance* of inappropriate behavior once established. Most of the controversy surrounding the behavioral position involve their assertions concerning the former—that the laws of learning are sufficient to account for behavioral acquisition. Critics have pointed out that this position systematically ignores genetic and constitutional predispositions as well as more molar environmental and social system variables. Also, the "laws of learning" generally alluded to are based almost exclusively upon classical and operant conditioning; only recently have attempts been made to develop procedures based upon more complex learning and higher-order thought processes.

At this point, we shall go no further in the debate concerning learning and the acquisition of behavior, but refer the interested reader elsewhere (Breger & McGaugh, 1965; Buchwald & Young, 1969; Heller & Marlatt, 1969). In this chapter we are less concerned with problems of etiology, and are more interested in factors associated with behavior maintenance and change.

Etiology and behavior change are independent issues; evidence for one does not necessarily provide support for the other. Arguments about etiology are not solved by research demonstrating the efficacy of behavioral techniques producing change. As Buchwald and Young (1969) note, the demonstration that behavior can be changed by specific techniques says nothing about how that behavior originated in the first place. For example, that a brain-damaged patient can be taught to speak again by psychological means does not negate the physiological trauma that may have been received. Or, that a mute schizophrenic can be taught to speak again by shaping and reinforcement does not imply that speech was originally "lost due to the operation of reinforcing factors in his social environment" (Buchwald & Young, 1969, p. 618).

In general, the available research evidence does support the efficacy of behavioral techniques in producing behavior change. An effective behavioral technology does exist. However, can it be applied to problems of community psychology?

Behavior modification in the natural environment

Much of the early work of behaviorally oriented psychologists was in restricted therapy settings (see Ullmann & Krasner, 1965, for a good cross-sectional sample of this work). However, it did not take long for behaviorists to recognize that they did not control the major sources of reinforcement in their patient's lives. Regardless of how much practice in correct responding the patient received in therapy, a punishing environment could undo much of this work (Heller & Marlatt, 1969).

The patient could be well prepared in new coping procedures, but without environmental reinforcement for the new behaviors, they would soon extinguish. There was a need for methods to achieve better stimulus control of behavior in natural environments. The basic behavior modification techniques were known; the problem was how to transfer them to real-life settings. It seemed natural to turn to those in the patient's environment who controlled the dispensement of reinforcement, and if they were willing, work through them to shape pro-social behavior. The behaviorally oriented psychologist thus became a consultant to key environmental figures who controlled real-life reinforcement contingencies. Since teachers and parents are key reinforcers in the lives of most individuals during their formative years, behavioral psychologists became consultants to these important reinforcement dispensers.

There are a number of examples of the successful application of behavior modification programs in natural environments (Tharp & Wetzel, 1969; Wetzel, 1966). Much of this literature is case-centered; helping environmental agents deal with individual instances of problem behavior. In contrast, a more recent form of behavioral consultation involves attempts at designing cultures and shaping environments so that desired behaviors are reinforced in open community settings. The focus is on increasing the base rates of low-frequency but desired community behaviors. For example, Everett, Hayward, and Meyers (1974) used a token system to increase bus ridership. All persons boarding a clearly marked bus were given tokens as they paid their fares. The tokens were wallet-sized cards that could be accumulated and redeemed in local stores for merchandise such as ice cream, beer, pizza, cigarettes, records, etc., or for free bus rides. The procedure increased bus ridership by 150 percent over baseline level with the majority (53 percent) of the tokens being redeemed for free bus rides. Thus, besides accomplishing its stated goal, program cost was relatively inexpensive. Similar procedures have been used to: reduce littering in parks and movie theaters; encourage the return of deposit bottles; reduce noise levels in college dormitories; and promote racial integration in classrooms (Meyers, Craighead, & Meyers, 1974).

Steps in establishing a behavioral program in a natural setting

The basic behavioral strategy is simple; its most prominent feature involves strengthening desirable behavior through reward, while at the same time making sure not to reward undesirable behavior. O'Leary and O'Leary (1972) present a detailed compendium of articles to describe how behavioral techniques can be applied to problems of classroom management. O'Leary and Drabman (1971) point out that the idea of rewarding good behavior has been known and practiced for centuries. They describe one example in which prizes such as nuts, figs, and honey were used in the 12th century to reward academic achievement in Torah reading; and in another example, describe a 16th-century advocate of cherries and cakes as rewards for learning Latin and Greek—instead of the more common practice of the day of punishing mistakes by the use of the cane. It may seem surprising that a good, centuries-old idea has taken so long to achieve widespread social acceptance, but such has been the case. For example, the *systematic* application of reinforcement principles to classroom learning is only a recent phenomenon (O'Leary & Drabman, 1971). We shall discuss shortly possible reasons why the behavioral approach has not achieved more widespread adoption. However at this point, we will first summarize the basic ingredients of a behavioral program so that we can achieve a common understanding of the procedures involved.

The components in a typical behavior modification program have been described in detail by Tharp and Wetzel (1969, pp. 190–200). Our discussion is based upon their presentation.

1. Establish a clear definition of the problem in behavioral terms.

A clear behavioral description is crucial. The tendency to use evaluative labels (immoral, crazy, incorrigible, etc.) or descriptions that refer to internal states (unmotivated, a poor attitude, defiant, lazy, etc.) are to be avoided. Reducing the frequency of problem behavior by establishing reinforcement contingencies requires that reward be paired with clear behavioral referents. The following example illustrates the need for describing problems in behavioral terms:

> In a sheltered workshop for recent patients of a state mental hospital, the supervisor complained of 22-year-old Emily's recent "regressive tendencies"; the supervisor feared that Emily would have to be returned to the hospital. In a staff conference, the consultant psychiatrist persisted in questioning the supervisor for a behavioral specification of the "regression." It was soon apparent that Emily had been taking off her shoes with increasing frequency. This was against the rules, and was certainly inappropriate in a work-training setting. The psychiatrist suggested that prior to rehospitalization a simple contingency might be tried; Emily

was advised that she could remain in the workshop if she kept her shoes on, but that she could not if she continued removing them. Emily was grateful for this information, since she had perceived vaguely that the staff was worried about something. She kept her shoes on, and proceeded through the workshop training. (Tharp & Wetzel, 1969, p. 190)

2.   Provide for accurate observation and recording of behavior.

Once the problem behaviors have been conceptualized in observable units, baseline recording of their frequency can begin. At the same time, prosocial behaviors should not be neglected, particularly if they are to be increased, so recording of their frequency also should take place. The recorder should be the person who can perform the recording task most reliably and economically; often this may mean that a parent, teacher, or work supervisor becomes involved at this point. Sometimes the choice narrows sharply, depending upon who is present when the problem behavior occurs.

A rehabilitation counselor, though pleased with the trade-school progress made by her 27-year-old paranoid client, was concerned that the client's parents might petition for his recommitment. The client, Clarence, reported that his parents thought he was going crazy again, and threatened every night to return him to the hospital. After careful inquiry of Clarence, the counselor could appreciate the parents' views; while the old couple watched television at night, Clarence would intrude himself between them and the screen, grasp his throat, and gurgle and gasp, thus communicating that he believed (delusionally) that his throat was cancerous. Clarence regretted this behavior to the counselor, but reported that sometimes he was doing it before he knew it. Thus, the client himself was inappropriate as a recorder of gurgling-and-gasping behavior, and the choice was immediately only the mother or the father. (Tharp & Wetzel, 1969, pp. 190–191)

3.   Select an appropriate reinforcement and find an individual (reinforcement mediator) who can maintain the necessary reinforcement contingencies.

Since consultants do not control the major reinforcements in the subject's life, they must work through those who do. The mediator selected must possess the necessary reinforcements and must be able and willing to dispense them according to an established contingency contract.

A dormitory supervisor, for a boarding school of the Bureau of Indian Affairs, determined that there were two potentially satisfactory reinforcers available in managing the case of a 13-year-old lazy and belligerent boy. The first was probably the most powerful: time with the dormitory-owned electric guitar and amplifier. The mediator for the guitar would be a night-shift dorm aide, Walter. The other potential reinforcer was the mediator, Billy, the stationwagon driver. The supervisor knew that Walter was a capricious man, whose bad moods sometimes led him to lock up all the entertainment-center equipment: guitars, the stereo, and the pool cues. Billy was a steady young man, interested in "wayward youth," but not at all comfortable with the proposed intervention plan, which seemed to him like bribery. The supervisor believed, nevertheless, that he could influence Billy to dispense rides-to-town on contingency, whether or not there was philosophical agreement. Walter, on the other hand, would require supervision during hours when the interventionist was often out of the building. The mediator of choice was Billy. This eliminated the guitar from consideration, and the plan moved to the second-ranked reinforcer, town-passes. (Tharp & Wetzel, 1969, p. 193)

4.   Establish and maintain *systematic* contingencies between desirable behavior and reinforcement.

Rewards and punishments are constantly used in everyday life. What is being added by the behavioral approach is their consistent use. Note that a reinforcement schedule can be intermittent, varying according to some particular ratio of reinforcement to response, but even here, once the schedule has been established, it must be maintained. Reppucci and Saunders (1974) point out that insisting on program maintenance can give the impression of a consultant as a "hard ass." There are a variety of circumstances in natural environments that threaten to compromise a behavior modification program, yet the consultant must champion staying with the contingency. Consider the following examples that Reppucci and Saunders provide from their experience at a state training school.

> Last summer, the academic school department announced that it had received a grant for a special summer program and requested that all residents be allowed to participate. The program involved a weekly trip off campus and four days of study related to the trip. The trips included a Broadway play; an old whaling village at Mystic, Connecticut; and the historic Freedom Trail in Boston. The Yale consultants pointed out that behaviorally these trips were rewarding as well as educational and, as such, should be subject to the token economy rules relating to off-grounds privileges. Moreover, we reminded staff that, according to the rules of the token economy, residents were required to work their way through three levels of achievement and that this progression was associated with increasing access to community-based rewards and eventually led to community placement. We argued that we should continue

to deny residents in the bottom level of achievement the off-campus rewards such as the school trips because they could be used to motivate residents to earn their way into the higher levels and eventually back into the community. The school department argued that the trips were not rewarding; that there was no distinction between the four days of classroom study and the trip on the fifth day, as it was all educational. The assistant principal of the school even argued that, since it was all educational, no resident in the bottom level of achievement could participate in the study classes if he did not go on the trip. The whole week was educational and the trips were mandatory . . . In the end, a major exception was made to the token economy rule that boys in the bottom level of achievement cannot go off campus.

. . . by Christmas time it came to the attention of the Yale consultants that the amendment was being violated . . . two members of the school department were taking a group of residents, many of whom were in the bottom level of achievement, off campus on caroling trips. When confronted on this issue, one of the staff involved said that the caroling was being done under the guidance of a music teacher at the school and, as such, was educational. He had not thought much about it, but he assumed that any educational trip off campus was permissible. At about this same point in time, the recreation department was requesting that staff vote on a further amendment, which would allow residents in the bottom level of achievement to compete off campus in basketball games. Naturally, the rationale here was that it was recreational. The convergence of these new threats to the integrity of the token economy elicited a defensive posture on the part of the Yale consultants. Sensing this, and feeling that he might lose where the school department had won, the head of the recreation department called one of the consultants a "hard ass." Although this was a minority opinion, spoken half in jest, it describes well the inflexible attitude behavior modifiers are often seen as assuming in the natural environment. (Reppucci & Saunders, 1974, pp. 656–657)

Problems in implementing behavioral programs in natural environments

The behavioral technology outlined above is not difficult to understand in that its principles are fairly straightforward and uncomplicated. However, this simplicity is misleading. Behavior modification techniques are precise, and their implementation often requires the behavior modifier to have substantial resources and control over the environment. It is not the case that a determined behavior modifier "armed with a knowledge of learning theory and a stiff upper lip" can manipulate contingencies in the natural environment as is done in the laboratory (Reppucci & Saunders, 1974).

Tharp and Wetzel (1969) and Reppucci and Saunders (1974) present excellent discussions of the constraints encountered in attempts to implement behavior modification programs in natural settings. The problems encountered can be summarized as follows:

1. Mediator problems. Behavior modification programs require the active cooperation of others who control the reinforcement contingencies to which target subjects are exposed. There are a number of reasons why obtaining the cooperation of these program mediators may be difficult. To begin with, the mediator may be personally disorganized and unable to follow a systematic schedule. For example, a mother who is hallucinating may be unable to distinguish the reality of her child's behavior from responses that she thinks she sees. While one does not need a superior level of mental health to follow simple behavioral instructions (there are many examples in the behavioral literature of successful contingencies administered by psychologically disturbed mediators, e.g., Whalen & Henker, 1969) there is a minimal level of consistent contact with reality required for successful program implementation.

The mediator's motivation and willingness to participate is a crucial variable. There are times when mediators are so angry at the target subject that they simply refuse to follow instructions, or sabotage the intervention plan in other ways. Tharp and Wetzel present two dramatic examples of attempts to undermine behavioral programs that succeeded in doing so. The first example illustrates an uncooperative mediator in the home.

> Case #63. A very seriously predelinquent adolescent boy had repeatedly engaged in fist-fights with his stepfather. The stepfather had hated the child for years. After 4 weeks of a closely proctored intervention plan, the boy's misbehavior was rapidly decreasing. The father, fearful that the boy might stay in the home if he reformed, disobeyed every instruction which our staff gave him. The case disintegrated; the boy ran away. It was very clear that the boy's continued presence in the home was so punishing to the father that the rewards our staff offered him—praise, encouragement, attention—were swamped. (Tharp & Wetzel, 1969, pp. 131–132)

In a similar manner, teachers, motivated by frustration and anger, can also undermine an effective program, ultimately to the detriment of the target child.

> Case #30. Benny was a low-achieving ninth-grader who felt he was getting an unfair deal from his home environment as well as his school environment. He had struggled through two very inconsistent step-

fathers and a number of nonmotivating teachers. The only thing that kept him in school and out of the grasp of the police was his devotion to his mother.

After overcoming a number of crises at the school, and establishing a concrete reinforcer at home, we intervened into Benny's intermittent work habits in the classroom. He began to work quite diligently in all his classes except math, where he had had the greatest teacher friction. The math teacher had been opposed to Benny and to the intervention all along. Two weeks after the intervention plan was started, Benny was suspended from math, on the slim pretext that on that day he didn't bring his book to class. The teacher accused him of stealing the book he had, and told him the homework he had been turning in was not up to par. He was called a "no-good bum" and told he would be better off out of school, and certainly out of math class. For Benny this was the last straw. He feared that the same thing would eventually happen in all his classes. He stopped coming to school. His mother, whom we had almost convinced that the school was finally giving her son a new opportunity, sympathized with Benny and did not demand that he return. She allowed Benny to get a job. Benny was a drop-out (or "push-out"); the case was terminated. (Tharp & Wetzel, 1969, pp. 132–133)

We have stated previously that the behavioral consultant does not control the real-life reinforcement contingencies for target subjects, but must work through mediators. A major problem in gaining the cooperation of mediators is that the consultant also does not control the major sources of reinforcement to mediators either. The contingencies that influence the behavior of staff in most settings are variables such as salaries, promotions, and job security. Even if he or she wanted to control these ultimate rewards in the name of efficient program management, it is doubtful that society would or should allow the consultant to have such extensive power. From a practical point of view, it is unlikely that the consultant could circumvent civil service merit systems, tenure policies, or union practices that control the potent rewards to mediators in the real world. The behavior modifier must use more indirect and voluntary methods to gain the cooperation of mediators. Persuasion and in-service training are the methods which must be used.

The need to persuade or to "sell" one's program to mediators takes on a special meaning for behavioral consultants because of the attitudes toward behavior modification principles that exist among some people. For some, there is a rejection of determinism that is implicit in the behavioral perspective. Others consider reinforcement as akin to bribery. In the words of one school principal, "I will not reward a child for doing his moral duty" (Tharp & Wetzel, 1969, p. 128). Others prefer aversive control, in the belief that "the rod will prevent spoiling the child" (Tharp & Wetzel, 1969, p. 129). Another attitudinal resistance to behavior modification can be seen in the belief that "all children should be treated alike." From this point of view, altering environmental contingencies for one child is seen as "favoritism." While each of these arguments can be countered (e.g., children are rarely treated alike despite the intent), the fact remains that it is still the mediator who is the key person in determining the success of a behavioral program. The consultant's conviction as to the validity of his or her perspective is not sufficient if the mediator is not equally convinced and cooperative.

Of course, the problem of gaining the cooperation of mediators is not unique to the behavioral perspective. All forms of consultation require the active participation of consultees for program effectiveness. Consultation is a voluntary, not a coercive, method. At this point, the issue under discussion is whether the behavioral perspective imposes special conditions that may be impediments to cooperation. Our estimate is that the number of such limiting conditions is not greater than would apply to other forms of consultation. However, their nature is different. Behavioral techniques require a more careful and systematic application. Ultimately, they also require a willingness to adopt a value system that undergirds the technology.

2. Institutional and agency problems. At times, institutional practices can conflict with procedures necessary for the proper execution of behavioral programs. Originally set up for the convenience of administration and staff, these procedures can be extremely resistant to change, as they regulate what can be complex organizational patterns. Still, from the point of view of behavioral programming, they may make no sense at all. Consider the problem of staff communication patterns. Behavioral programs often require follow-through and cooperation by all members of an institution. Staff may be interested and well-meaning, but may not possess the communication channels necessary to carry through on agreed-upon procedures. The problem is well illustrated in the following example:

> Case #11. An intervention plan was proposed to a school in which Case #11 would be allowed to participate in the after-school football program as a daily reinforcer for his good behavior in the morning section of his elementary school. The school administration objected to this on two grounds. First, they did not believe they could make after-school foot-

ball contingent for this one child, when it was a noncontingent opportunity for all the other children. Second, and undoubtedly most important, the school had no way of forwarding information from the morning teacher to the coach of the afternoon activity. Since no communication channel existed, the school pronounced the plan impossible. Nowhere in the school was there an individual whose normal role included carrying such a message. Both the teacher and the coach would have considered it a violation of their job descriptions to seek out the other. It was necessary in this instance, as in many others, to have the BA (behavior analyst) fill in the interstices in the organization and become the communication channel himself. The BA either called or came by in the morning to verify criterion performance with the teacher and delivered the report to the coach.

It should be reported that the administration of Case #11's school was not at all opposed to continuation of behavior modification programming for the child once they had some concrete demonstration of its efficacy. The behavior engineer cannot ask for more open-mindedness or opportunity than that; but even with the philosophical support of the principal, still the organizational structure did not allow for these two positions—teacher and coach—to regularly and directly communicate over an individual child. This difficulty was entirely independent of the personalities or values of these two mediators; both were reliable, cooperative, and interested professionals. There was simply no time, no moment of spatial proximity, and no habit which would allow for the transmission of information. (Tharp & Wetzel, 1969, pp. 141–142)

Note that in the problem just described, the behavioral consultant provided the resources (in the person of an assistant—the BA) to overcome the communication impediment. The BA carried the message from the teacher to the coach. In the real world, resources to carry out behavioral programs can be in short supply. Limited manpower and finances are more likely to be the norm that the behavioral consultant must expect in daily practice (Reppucci & Saunders, 1974). For example, measuring behavior to establish a baseline may seem like a simple step. Yet many staff consider recording to be an unnecessary burden, which can be overwhelming if they are already taxed by their regular duties.

How should behavioral consultants deal with the problem of limited resources? On the one hand, as in the previous example from Tharp and Wetzel, they can provide the necessary resources themselves. This may be a reasonable alternative if there is an external source of funds (e.g., a research grant) or an available supply of manpower (e.g., students eager to participate in return for academic credit or relevant work experience). However, if the program ultimately is to be adopted by the community, it cannot depend upon external support indefinitely. The institution receiving consultation will have to decide whether it has sufficient funds and whether it is willing to divert some of its resources to support the program.

There are two special situations in which it may be advisable for consultants to provide their own program resources: (1) Initially, an agency may be unconvinced of the potential value of the program and may need to be shown definite accomplishments before it will invest its own resources. (2) Another special circumstance occurs when dealing with severe behavioral deficiencies. In this situation, mediators may be unable or unwilling to do all of the complex shaping necessary to establish initial behavioral control, but may be quite willing to *maintain* appropriate behavior once it has been established in a special training program. Complex, or long-standing behavioral deficiencies may require much more intensive effort than may be available in a typical community agency. For example, Wolf, Phillips, and Fixsen (1972) present a program for the community treatment of delinquent behavior. The main ingredient in their program is a group home for six to ten youngsters supervised by an adult couple who serve as "teaching-parents." The home is designed and run according to behavior modification principles. Each day, the boys earn tokens that can be cashed in for privileges and rewards.

Wolf et al. found that the behavior of the boys was often so disruptive that in their usual environments parents and teachers had great difficulty in gaining behavioral control. Teachers often were no longer willing to "apply positive social reinforcements for small approximations to appropriate behavior" (Wolf, Phillips, & Fixsen, 1972, p. 55). On the other hand, once behavioral control was established in the group home, teachers could maintain that improvement in class by filling out and signing a special daily report card. The child was required to carry the report card and return it to the group home in order to earn his points and privileges there.

Another example of institutional constraints on effective behavioral programming can be seen in typical school policies concerning grades. On first view, it should seem that grades can be powerful rewards. The problem is that usually they are not administered contingent with behavior. A typical grading period of six weeks presents too long a latency between performance and consequences to effectively shape the academic behavior of many children. They are summed evaluations of the teacher's total response to the child, both the social and the academic behavior. Often the grade reflects the attitude of the teacher as well as the behavior of the child. From the point of view of behavior modification, "because the grade is a reaction to everything, it is not a reaction to anything" (Tharp & Wetzel, 1969, p. 139). To be useful in a behavioral program, "grades" must be provided daily, hourly, or in terms of instantaneous comments.

3.   Community problems.   Behavioral consultants soon come to recognize that some of the problems that are called to their attention defy intervention at individual or institutional levels because concern comes from a confused mandate in the community at large. It makes no sense to work for the elimination of behavioral deviance if, at the same time, the community is implicitly reinforcing the very same behaviors. Consider the following two examples:

> In one city which the BRP staff has consulted, gambling is legal. Virtually the entire economy—jobs, institutions, social services—is dependent upon the prosperity of the gambling and entertainment industry. The city is alight from dusk to dawn with fantastic and effective stimuli; an electric and human circus exists which is impressively engineered to evoke staying-out-late behavior. The most frequent "predelinquent" complaints in this city are curfew violations.
>
> BRP case consultation was performed in a northern coast town whose principal product is canned seafood. After a typical escalating conflict between the school and the target, a 15-year-old girl, she dropped out and began to work part-time at the cannery. The income was valued by the family, but the court was determined that she return to school. In investigating the possibilities of making part-time cannery employment contingent on school attendance, we were confronted with the discovery that several adolescent drop-outs, school "withdrawals," and flunk-outs were part of the cannery peak-season work force. The reason given for this pattern was that such "kids like to make the money." Only as we began to explore alternatives for the cannery–school arrangement did it become clear that the community could not, with impunity, change things very much. There was a critical labor shortage during the brief peak-season. (Tharp & Wetzel, 1969, pp. 145–146.)

Problems such as these are really beyond the scope of behavioral technology. Despite the sometimes grandiose rhetoric, behavior modification was never intended to provide a basis for describing, understanding, or changing natural settings (Reppucci & Saunders, 1974). Behavioral consultants will need to borrow from other perspectives in order to find techniques to help communities confront and constructively resolve confused mandates based upon conflicting values. There are group and organizational methods derived from other consultation perspectives that are applicable to these problems. However, considering these techniques will make sense to behaviorists only if they expand the scope of their theoretical interests to develop a better understanding of the social psychology of complex organizations and communities.

The effectiveness of behavioral techniques: The problems of generalization across settings and persistence over time

It seems to us that there is good evidence to support the effectiveness of behavioral techniques in shaping and controlling individual behavior. It is to their credit that the behaviorists have been willing to tackle difficult problem behaviors. Behavior therapy seems to have achieved notable success in relieving psychological problems that previously have been immune to other methods of intervention (Davison & Stuart, 1975). For example, the success of *traditional* psychotherapy with "conduct disorders" (e.g., delinquency, sexual aberrations, alcohol habituation, etc.) tends to be low and many psychotherapists refuse to work with such populations. Behavioral approaches have had greater success in modifying these undesirable behaviors. Established behavioral programs can now be found for delinquency (Alexander & Parsons, 1973; Binder, Monahan, & Newkirk, 1976; Cohen & Filipczak, 1971; Davidson & Seidman, 1974; Wolf, Phillips, & Fixsen, 1972), sexual disorders (Callahan & Leitenberg, 1973), and alcohol habituation (Davidson, 1974; Lloyd & Salzberg, 1975; Marlatt, 1975).

Despite these successes, a thorny problem remaining for behaviorists concerns the permanence and extent of generalization of improvement. It would not be much help if improved behavior did not persist over time or in new situations different from the one in which the original contingencies were established. This is a difficult problem for behaviorists because their theory should lead them to expect that generalization would *not* occur in situations in which the reinforcement contingencies were not maintained. Behaviorally oriented psychologists generally reject notions of personality "traits" that the individual carries to different situations. Behavior is thought of as situation specific so that when the situation changes so does the behavior. The typical designs used in behavioral experiments are variants of *ABA* designs with a period of baseline observation, a treatment period, and a final period in which previously established reinforcement contingencies are removed. The expectation is that without reinforcement, extinction should occur.

The empirical findings support this expectation in that most studies have reported that newly reinforced behaviors often do not persist with the removal of reinforcement contingencies. Generalization tends to be difficult to achieve. Thus, from a practical point of view, if generalization is desired it should be specifically included as part of the behavioral program. This can be accomplished in two ways. First, an attempt can be made to increase the similarity between the setting in which the new responses are initially acquired and other settings in the individual's environment (Goldstein, Heller, & Sechrest, 1966). It is probably easier to make the original reinforcement setting a close analogue to real life than it is to manipulate real-life contingencies directly. Environmental manipulation outside of closed institutional settings is possible (e.g., at home or in school) but is often limited to only one or two cooperating settings.

The second method to maximize generalization involves moving from extrinsic reinforcement (money, tokens, candy etc.) to intrinsic motivation. Improvement is carried forward because the individual is now motivated to learn techniques for self-regulation and self-control. There is a growing body of literature on cognitive approaches to behavior modification that emphasizes self-control techniques (Kanfer & Goldstein, 1975; Mahoney, 1974). One excellent example is provided by Novaco (1975) who built an anger control program for subjects with chronic problems of anger management. Still we must remember that self-control programs require motivation for improvement and active cooperation by participants (e.g., all of Novaco's subjects were persons who wanted to learn how to control their anger). Hence we must stress that behavioral programs are least effective as devices for "automatic conditioning." It is the programs that rely exclusively on extrinsic motivation that have the most difficulty in demonstrating generalization and persistence of new behaviors once the extrinsic rewards are removed.

Behavioral consultation: A technology in need of values and goals

Viewed simply as an effective technology, behavior modification techniques can be used for moral or immoral purposes. As Skinner has noted, the technology "is ethically neutral. It can be used by villain or saint" (Stolz, Wienckowski, & Brown, 1975). However, there is some concern that despite this disclaimer the work of behavior modifiers has not been used in a neutral and value-free manner. Winett & Winkler (1972) claim that behavior modifiers have allowed their work to be used to maintain the status quo by reinforcing conformity and adherence to routine. After all, what behaviors should be deemed as inappropriate and in need of modification? How does one decide? Winett and Winkler charge that in their review of the literature on the uses of behavior modification in the classroom, "inappropriate" behaviors have included: getting out of seat, walking around, rattling papers, crying, singing, laughing, or simply doing something different from that which the child has been directed to do.

> Taken as a fairly accurate indicator of what public schools deemed as the "model" child, these studies described this pupil as one who stays glued to his seat and desk all day, continually looks at his teacher or his text/workbook, does not talk to or in fact look at other children, does not talk unless asked to by his teacher, hopefully does not laugh or sing (or at the wrong time), and assuredly passes silently in halls. (Winett & Winkler, 1972, p. 501)

Winett and Winkler believe that behavior modifiers accepted the school's apparent desire for conformity and order. Their primary goal was to demonstrate that their techniques worked and that behavior control in the classroom could be achieved. "The nature of the behavior being controlled was a secondary consideration" (Winett & Winkler, 1972, p. 501) and they did not consider the value impact of their work.

In a subsequent rejoinder defending behavior modification in the classroom, O'Leary (1972) accepted the *potential* danger of misuse, but denied that behavior modifiers or teachers would ever want the extreme level of docility suggested by Winett and Winkler.

It would seem that in the final analysis the problem cannot be resolved without value considerations. Reducing disruptiveness can be important if classroom learning is to move forward. The disruptive child impedes his or her own academic performance and has a similar effect on the progress of other class members. Still, when does reducing classroom disruption become fostering docility? The danger is greatest in those settings in which obedience and order are valued much more highly than learning and creativity. If there already exists a preoccupation with order and control, there is a high likelihood that behavior modification techniques will be abused. These concerns cannot be avoided by the behavioral consultant and should become part of the initial assessment. Ultimately O'Leary also agrees:

> . . . if the behavior modifier is to have maximal impact . . . he must seriously question whether the behavior he is being asked to change should really be changed. . . . the behavior modification approach provides a set of rather well-defined procedures to change behavior, but the procedures do not spell out the goals or the behaviors which *ought* to be taught or changed (O'Leary, 1972, p. 509)

Behavioral modification programs in prisons and mental hospitals present some special ethical problems (Davison & Stuart, 1975; Stolz, Wienckowski, & Brown, 1975). In both types of institutions, residents are incarcerated against their will. The usual caveat applicable to outpatient programs—that participation is voluntary—is a less meaningful protection of individual rights. Prisoners and mental patients may be told that nonparticipation will not be held against them, but such a statement may be hard to believe, given the ambiguity of what constitutes "rehabilitation" in many inpatient settings, particularly if tenure is indeterminate and a function of staff judgment of "readiness." It would be reasonable for an inmate to expect that participation might lead to early release. If the cost of nonparticipation cannot be assessed (e.g., will the officials really hold it against me if I don't cooperate with a "treatment" that they all insist is good for me?), why jeopardize the possibility of early release? Under these circumstances, "volunteering" does not mean a lack of coercion, however subtle the coercive pressure may be.

Some critics have suggested that behaviorists are naïve to think that their programs can remain immune to subversion by punitive institutions. It is not difficult to find evidence to substantiate this charge—instances in which prisons and mental hospitals used behavior modification programs for punishment and control, not for rehabilitation. Either alternative—attempting to improve punitive institutions or deciding they are beyond redemption—involves some human cost. For example, eliminating behavioral programs from prisons could deny the opportunity for improvement for those inmates who genuinely want to participate and who might benefit from the programs (Stolz et al., 1975). There are no easy answers to issues such as these. Our own personal values and priorities lead us to believe that when clearly punitive institutions have been identified, more is to be gained by designing alternatives than by attempting to support such institutions. However, we cannot fault psychologists who think otherwise, and who devote their professional energies to improving archaic prisons and mental hospitals. In these instances, our main concern is that of safeguards. Procedures must be developed to monitor treatment programs to insure that participation is not coercive, that consent is truly informed, and that the programs are rehabilitative and humane. Procedures such as review committees with staff, inmate, and general citizen participation can be implemented to perform this function. While the potential for abuse is more clearly recognized for behavioral programs, a system of review to protect individual liberties is crucial for all community programs.

We do not believe as do some critics that behavior modification programs will *inevitably* lead to the development of mind control techniques that will be used by an authoritarian state to manipulate and control its citizens. The potency of behavioral techniques have been grossly exaggerated in the popular press. The claims for effectiveness of the procedures described in films such as *The Manchurian Candidate* or *A Clockwork Orange* are simply untrue. Behavior modification techniques do not have the power to control thought and action as portrayed in these films; nor are they likely to develop such a power. Behavioral procedures with human subjects are most effective when they rely on the active cooperation of the participants who are willing to internalize the reinforcement contingencies and use them for self-monitoring and self-control. Despite the links in the popular press between behavior modification and brainwashing, current behavioral techniques are least effective when they are utilized simply as devices for automatic conditioning (Heller & Marlatt, 1969) and are much more effective when they involve cooperation and active cognitive participation. For example, Davidson (1974) reports that the evidence from studies of aversive conditioning as a treatment for alcoholics does not support a simple avoidance conditioning point of view. The most successful programs are those in which the motivation and cooperation of the patients are highest (Lloyd & Salzberg, 1975).

The evidence seems to indicate that behavior modification programs are most successful when the individual receiving the contingencies is responsive and cooperative. If coercion is used to administer a program, it may force cooperation for a time; but once the coercion is removed the evidence seems to suggest that program effects dissipate—that is, unless the individual voluntarily carries them forward.

We would conclude that the extreme fear of behavioral technology that exists in some quarters is generally unwarranted. Research using behavioral techniques should continue since it has already demonstrated a potential for relieving some types of distress and maladaptive behavior resistant to change by other methods of intervention. Still, once we leave the confines of the outpatient clinic in which participation is voluntary and under the control of the patient, potential for abuse becomes a real danger and safeguards are needed. Behavioral consultants should be at the forefront of those concerned with developing safeguards and should actively seek opportunities to explain their work to the public. Ultimately, without public acceptance there will be no permission to use this technology to solve real community problems.

Organization development

Organization development (OD) has functioned as a change strategy since the late 1940s, deriving largely from Kurt Lewin's theoretical conviction that human behavior could be fully understood only as an interaction between man and his natural living environment. Some of Lewin's students organized the National Training Laboratories at Bethel, Maine, in 1947, and that institution is still the mecca of organization development specialists (Benne, Bradford, & Lippett, 1964).

OD has prospered primarily within business organizations where a reaffirmation of human values served as a welcome antidote to the depersonalized, mechanistic values that often grew unchecked in bureaucratic organizations. At one time, corporation executives believed that all that was necessary was to "set the work before the men and they will do it" (Bennis, 1969, p. 45). Now, many business organizations are taking more seriously the problem of how to integrate human needs and organizational goals.

While OD is not an approach that immediately comes to mind when one thinks of community psychology or community mental health, it is one of the major behavioral science strategies in use today for inducing change at the organizational or agency level. The fact that many mental health personnel are not acquainted with OD approaches reflects the inattention that has traditionally been paid to the "work environment" by psychologists and psychiatrists. With the exception of a relatively small group of "industrial" psychologists, many of whom are engaged in human factors research such as the location of gauges in airplane cockpits, extraordinarily little attention has been devoted to the area in which most people devote the majority of their adult waking life—their job. Consultation to business organizations by mental health specialists has yet to achieve the popularity of consultation to educational, welfare, or criminal justice agencies. Yet the impact of *work* on an individual—and therefore on his or her family—is clearly a substantial one.

Organization development is defined by Friedlander and Brown (1974) in their recent review as "a method for facilitating change and development in people (e.g., styles, values, skills), in technology (e.g., greater simplicity, complexity), and in organizational processes and structures (e.g., relationships, roles). It is at once a set of personal values, a set of change technologies, and a set of processes or structures, through which the change agent relates to the organizational system" (pp. 314–316). Only by intervening at *both* the technical-structural level *and* at the personal level can meaningful change be accomplished, according to many OD proponents. The joint objectives of OD are optimizing human fulfillment and increasing organizational efficiency.

It is important to recognize that while there are specific techniques associated with OD (e.g., team building, job design, survey feedback, sensitivity training, etc.) the field is also marked by an explicit set of values. These are related to the existential view of people as reflected in concerns for openness and freedom in individual life and the manner in which these values are suppressed by environmental pressures. The values are humanistic and democratic in nature in that they emphasize: a positive view of people as "whole persons"; encouraging the effective expression of feelings; authenticity; risk; confrontation; and collaboration (Friedlander & Brown, 1974).

> The objectives of OD are obviously colored by these values. They include creating an open problem-solving climate, supplementing the authority of role and status with the authority of knowledge and competence, locating decision-making and problem-solving as close to information sources as possible, building trust and collaboration, developing a reward system which recognizes the organizational mission and the growth of people, helping managers to manage according to relevant objectives rather than past practices, and increasing self-control and self-direction for people within the organization. (Friedlander & Brown, 1974, p. 316)

A work setting can be improved by changing its structure (e.g., methods of production, how the job is carried out, etc.) or by improving relationships between job participants. Each of these, structural changes and interaction or process changes, has been a focus of OD consultation. In the next section, each will be discussed in turn.

Technical and structural approaches

Structural approaches are of several varieties. In one that Friedlander and Brown (1974) call sociotechnical systems intervention, the overall system of production is modified. Trist and Bamforth (1951), for example, found that different production systems in the British coal mining industry were associated with different levels of absenteeism, productivity, and accidents. Traditional coal mining utilized small, cohesive, and autonomous work teams, in which each worker performed a variety of roles and the work group was paid as a team. "Advances" in technology led to larger work groups that were more impersonal, that divided the labor more narrowly, and that paid on an individual, rather than a team, basis. The result was lower performance, higher absenteeism and accidents, and a general worker indifference. When the sociotechnical structure was modified to reintroduce group identification and cohesion, noted improvement on the given measures was achieved (Trist, Higgin, Murray, & Pollack, 1963). Preliminary reports on large-scale Scandinavian experiments in "industrial democracy" or "workers' control" of production also are very encouraging (Hunnius, Garson & Case, 1973).

Another example of an OD structural intervention can be seen in the study of "Flexi-Time" reported by Golembiewski, Hilles, and Kagno (1974). Flexi-Time simply means flexible work hours. In the version adopted in this research, employees could start work any time between 7:00 and 9:15 A.M. and could stop between 3:00 and 6:00 P.M.; all employees were required to be on duty every day during the core period between 9:15 A.M. and 3:00 P.M. The Flexi-Time program grew out of several years of prior OD work in which the host organization had participated in a wide range of OD activities and had already internalized OD values. Thus, in interpreting the effects of this intervention, the context in which it occurred cannot be overlooked.

The effects of the intervention were positive for groups on Flexi-Time compared with units of the company on fixed work time schedules. Flexi-Time increased worker morale and job satisfaction and increased productivity on some key measures. Absenteeism was reduced as well as the need for overtime to make up for lost man-hours. It is interesting to note that while workers were given freedom to choose arrival and departure times, little change actually occurred except for extended weekends and the summer months. The freedom to choose flexible work hours may have been more important than a flexible work schedule itself.

Job enlargement is another structural OD strategy. Here, several duties are combined in one job, rather than having different persons work on each. Marks (1954), for example, combined several tasks into one job in an industrial shop and noted improvements in output, quality, and worker attitude. When assembly line jobs are changed into independent bench work, production time decreases and quality increases (Conant & Kilbridge, 1965).

Several reviews of job enlargement programs indicate general increases in worker satisfaction and often increases in productivity. Davis (1966) hypothesizes that such improvements are the result of increased variety of tasks, self-determination and self-pacing, increased discretion and responsibility, and a sense of work completion.

Job *enrichment* differs from job *enlargement* in that the combination of tasks is vertical in the case of enrichment and horizontal in the case of enlargement. When a job is enlarged, different tasks at the same level in the organization are added. When a job is enriched, more responsibilities from higher organizational levels are added.

The studies of Ford (1969) at American Telephone and Telegraph indicate that when jobs are enriched by adding higher-level responsibilities, turnover and absenteeism are reduced, quality of service increased, and employee attitudes improved. Other studies show similar patterns of results. The notion of "increased motivation" is frequently cited as a causal factor in the observed change.

Friedlander and Brown (1974) conclude that, in general, structural improvements of the work setting do tend to increase performance and productivity, often as a result of increases in the quality of the work, lowered absenteeism, and lowered turnover. Kahn (1974) agrees that structural modifications seem to have positive and persisting effects and suggests that this may be so because the trend in industry toward job fragmentation has gone too far, and that "gains in performance and satisfaction are obtainable by reducing the fragmentation and increasing the variety of content" (Kahn, 1974, p. 495). Still, improvements from structural changes are not always forthcoming. For example, job enlargement tends to result in a more socially isolated worker, and this must be compensated for by social restructuring of the work group, i.e., building in opportunities for increased interaction. Job enrich-

ment is not always successful because some workers respond negatively to complex jobs. The evidence seems to be that the degree of
satisfaction is a function of the cognitive complexity of the employee.
Some workers respond well to challenge, variety, and complexity;
others do not. To achieve maximal benefit, technostructural modification must also pay attention to individual difference and human process variables.

Human process intervention

The distinction between structural and process techniques is
clearly arbitrary and can be misleading. Organizational structures and
processes are not independent. Both represent *interdependent* patterns, which, as they recur over time, come to represent the total organization (Kahn, 1974). Seashore and Bowers (1970) present impressive data on the durability of change in one organization (the Weldon
Company) measured five years after OD activity terminated. The authors believe that their success may have been due to the interdependence of structural changes in the work system combined with an early
legitimization of concern about organizational process. Still, the distinction between process and structure is useful, if for no other reason
than to describe more accurately the different activities of OD consultants. As it turns out, while OD is defined as including both structural
and human process approaches, in reality many OD practitioners and
writers seem to concentrate on the latter. People-oriented approaches
to organizational change seem to be much more the norm of what is
actually undertaken in the field.

Schmuck and Runkel (1972) present an interesting demonstration
of the use of organizational training by a school system. The purpose of
the demonstration was to communicate *experientially* the nature of
OD training to those with little experience in it. The demonstration
was a prelude to a two-year program of OD within the entire school
district. Attending the demonstration were the superintendent, his
cabinet, elementary and secondary school principals, and selected
teachers who were key officers in the local educational association.
Other teachers were added to this group so that there would be at least
one teacher from every school building.

> The event lasted four days, but only the superintendent's cabinet was
> present all of the time. On the evening of the first day, before others

arrived, the superintendent and his cabinet discussed ways in which communication had broken down among them, the lack of clarity of their role definitions, the ambiguous norms that existed in the cabinet, and, finally, their strengths as a group. The trainers gave structure to the discussion and kept it centered on organizational topics.

On the second day, the principals joined the cabinet in a specially designed confrontation that brought into the open organizational problems seen by each group as involving the other. First, the entire group divided into three units: cabinet, elementary principals, and secondary principals. Next, each of these units met separately to consider helpful and unhelpful work-related behaviors of the other two groups toward their own group. At the end of two hours, all perceived actions of the other groups were written in large letters on sheets of newsprint. Problems between groups brought to the surface were earmarked for future problem-solving procedures. The session ended with a brief period of training in the communicative skills of paraphrasing and behavior description.

Next, one group sat in a circle, surrounded by members of the other two groups. Participants sitting in the outer ring read aloud the descriptions they had written of the inside group. A member of the inner circle then paraphrased the description to make sure that his colleagues understood it. During this step, group members in the inner circle who were receiving descriptions of their own group were *not* allowed to defend their group against the allegations made by the others. After all items describing the inside group were read, the remaining two groups took their turns in the center circle.

After this step, the three groups again met separately to find evidence that would support the descriptions they had received; they were instructed to recall examples of their own behavior that could have given the other group its impressions. The three groups then came together once again with one group forming an inner circle. Each inner group told the others of the evidence it had recalled to verify the perceptions of the others. Once again, the inner group was discouraged from defending itself; members were asked simply to describe the behavioral events they thought supported the others' perceptions.

On the evening of the second day, teachers arrived to join the principals and cabinet, and for four hours all of the key line personnel in the Kent district were together. A modified confrontation design was continued, culminating in a meeting in which the three groups indicated the organizational problems they thought existed in the Kent district. Discussion was lively, penetrating, and constructive; most personnel had never before confronted persons in other positions so openly with their perceptions of district problems. The principals went back to their buildings the next day, leaving time for teachers and cabinet to interact with one another. On the fourth day, the cabinet met alone to schedule some dates for future problem-solving. (Schmuck & Runkel, 1972, pp. 27–28)

Types of OD process intervention

One problem that has slowed the large-scale adoption of OD human process technology has been the lack of clearly delineated operational descriptions of the methods of intervention (Schmuck & Miles, 1971). There is no generally agreed-upon set of procedures, and in addition, many OD consultants do not describe their techniques explicitly. However, there have been several attempts at synthesis and we shall focus on two of these (Schmuck & Miles, 1971; Friedlander & Brown, 1974).

Schmuck and Miles summarize the types of intervention practiced by OD consultants in the following way:

1. Training or education: procedures involving direct teaching or experience-based learning. Such technologies as lectures, exercises, simulations, and T-groups are examples.
2. Process consultation: watching and aiding ongoing processes and coaching to improve them.
3. Confrontation: bringing together units of the organization (persons, roles, or groups) which have previously been in poor communication; usually accompanied by supporting data.
4. Data feedback: systematic collection of information, which is then reported back to appropriate organizational units as a base for diagnosis, problem-solving, and planning.
5. Problem-solving: meetings essentially focusing on problem identification, diagnosis, and solution invention and implementation.
6. Plan-making: activity focused primarily on planning and goal setting to replot the organization's future.
7. OD task force establishment: setting up ad hoc problem-solving groups or internal teams of specialists to ensure that the organization solves problems and carries out plans continuously.
8. Techno-structural activity: action which has as its prime focus the alteration of the organization's structure, work-flow, and means of accomplishing tasks. (Schmuck & Miles, 1971, p. 9)*

Friedlander and Brown state that "human process intervention focuses on the human participants and the organization processes (e.g., communication, problem solving, decision making) through which they accomplish their own and the organization's goals" (Friedlander & Brown, 1974, p. 325).

Survey feedback, group, and intergroup development

The primary modes of process-oriented intervention involve combinations of three methods: survey feedback, group development, and

---

* Reprinted from Richard A. Schmuck and Matthew B. Miles (Eds.), *Organization Development in Schools*. La Jolla, Calif.: University Associates, 1971. Used with permission.

intergroup development. In survey-feedback intervention, data are systematically collected from members of an organization or agency (usually by questionnaires), summarized, and fed back to the members.
The assumption is that discrepancies between organizational ideals
and actual responses will generate motivation for change. This process
is strikingly similar to that employed by Moos (1975) (described more
fully in Chapter 5), who administered two forms of his social environment scales to the staff of an adolescent treatment center. On
one form, the staff and residents were told to describe the program
as it really was, and on the other form as it ideally should be. Discrepancies between the two assessments were fed back to the center's
members and actions were taken toward their reduction. Six months
later, movement of the real toward the ideal perceived environment
was recorded when the scales were readministered.

There is some evidence that survey feedback is one of the more
potent OD techniques, particularly in terms of attitudinal changes in
participants (Bowers, 1973). Participation in feedback can affect a,
group's perceptions and expectations, which in turn can lead to
changes in group interaction and subsequent increases in job satisfaction. The effectiveness of survey feedback is increased even further
when workers participate fully in designing the questions to be asked
and collecting the relevant data. However, improved satisfaction does
not always mean that substantive organizational changes will take
place. The active participation of supervisory personnel is also important because a resistant or antagonistic superior can undermine the
process. Furthermore, without planning for follow-up, little change
may occur after the initial glow of involvement wears off. Friedlander
and Brown conclude that the primary effects seem to be on attitudes
and perceptions and that "there is little evidence that survey feedback
alone [emphasis added] leads to changes in individual behavior or
organizational performance" (Friedlander & Brown, 1974, p. 327).

Feedback also has been a key ingredient in activities that are
oriented toward group and intergroup development. For example, in
attempting to reduce intergroup conflict, the goal has generally been
to foster a "problem solving" approach to intergroup relations. The
interventions are based on the sharing of information, confrontation of
differences, and "working through" problems to develop mutually acceptable solutions (Friedlander & Brown, 1974, p. 330). The prototyp-
ical design of Blake, Mouton, and Sloma (1965) involves each group
listing perceptions of itself, the other group, and its views of the other's

perceptions of itself (e.g., "how do you think they perceive you?"), then sharing lists for improved understanding and future cooperation.

Feedback is also a focal ingredient in group development via sensitivity training. Participants in the group must honestly inform each other as to how the other's behavior is interpreted by them, and the feelings that follow from the interpretation. In such a fashion, information that is otherwise unavailable to the individual due to the social constraints of everyday interaction is obtained. Individuals are then more aware of the effects of their behavior on others, and of the cues to which others are responding. Some persons, for example, may think that their frequent suggestions to others are motivated by their concern and helpfulness. In the T-group they may find out that others, in fact, perceive these acts as critical and hostile. Thus, having been made aware of the effects of their behavior on others, they are then in a position to either (1) modify their behavior so as to change the way others view it, or (2) introspectively examine the actual meaning of their behavior (e.g., were they really being hostile?). Whatever the outcome, the assumption is that individuals are better off with this information than without it.

Besides using feedback, group development and "team building" activities take a number of forms such as: goal setting activities in which clear team goals are established; interpersonal relations development (sensitivity training) to improve the quality of interaction among team members; and role analysis activities for increased clarity about member duties and responsibilities. However, since the major activity of OD professionals involved in group development is sensitivity training, we shall now consider this activity in some detail.

Sensitivity training

A good example of sensitivity training (T-groups) may be found in Kuriloff and Atkins (1966). They hold that the main assumption of T-groups is that "acceptance or rejection of company data [one could include any organization here] transmitted between people often depends upon the acceptance or rejection of each other as people, and upon how much the people respect, trust, and like each other." Their group consisted of 15 people in an engineering firm:*

> Jim, the young project engineer, who was formerly second-in-
> command under Rod, voiced his concern about his relationship with

---

* Reproduced by special permission from *The Journal of Applied Behavioral Science.* "T Group for a Work Team," by Arthur H. Kuriloff and Stuart Atkins. Volume 2, No. 1, pp. 63–93. Copyright 1966 NTL Institute for Applied Behavioral Science.

him. With an eager, expectant look, he turned to Rod and asked, "What's happened to us? Lately we can't seem to get anywhere on design problems."

"Strange," Rod replied, in his cool, composed way, "I've noticed it, too."

They began talking as if they were just getting to know each other. Groping to pin down this uneasiness in their relationship, they discovered the turning point. It was the time of acquisition of the company, when Jim was given a design group of his own, and Rod was made manager of custom engineering instead of chief engineer over all engineering operations—and Jim.

Jack asked Rod, "How did you feel about your loss of status?"

Smiling, Rod replied, "Of course I didn't like it." He went on in a matter-of-fact tone, "You know, the usual things happened. I sent out some resumés. But things seemed to straighten out here after a while, and good jobs weren't easy to find." Rod went on to relate that it appeared to him that now that Jim had a design group of his own, he had done a turnabout in his philosophy of working and solving engineering problems. In fact, Rod said that Jim seemed downright dishonest, that he had agreed with Rod's philosophies formerly only because Rod was the boss at the time.

Jim was puzzled and disclaimed the accusation of dishonesty. Talking across the circle, Rod and Jim became deeply enmeshed in trying to clarify this misunderstanding. Occasionally their intense exchange was interrupted by questions and opinions from other people who were acting as psychological negotiators to help them come to terms with their relationship.

At the most heated points in their exchange, Rod smiled continuously. Jack finally commented to Rod, "I've noticed you always smile when you're expressing resentment. It's difficult to tell that you're really bothered. This can confuse people. I know, I do the same thing."

At first Rod denied being resentful. Then he said he was unaware of his smiling. The group could not understand why Rod would not be resentful under the circumstances and made this very clear to him. Finally, Rod admitted his resentment. But he smiled. The group pointed this out, too. Rod found it difficult not to accept the consistent and concerted opinions of thirteen other people.

"If you had only let me know how you felt," Jim implored, "we could have straightened this out long ago."

"Well, I got the message that you didn't much care what I thought," Rod countered. "When you invited the engineering people to your house for that barbecue, you didn't invite me. I assumed you wanted the opportunity to solidify your position with your new people."

"Wait a minute!" Jim protested. "I swear that wasn't an intentional slight. Someone told me you were going on a trip and leaving that Sunday afternoon. And as for being dishonest with you about what I told you when I worked for you—well, I did mean what I said. But I never had a design group before, and we've never had a design problem like we've had on the new line. I had to change my point of view on some things."

I [the Group Facilitator] used this experience to point out the curious way untested assumptions can lead us so far from the reality of a situation and from contact and closeness with people. I stated, too, that Rod's failure to express his resentment had only made it well up inside—so much so that he had to attribute the same feelings to Jim and interpreted many things along these lines.

It is interesting to note the differences between the organization-development approach using T-groups as typified in this example and mental health consultation as practiced by Caplan. Sensitivity training, with emphasis on the cathartic venting of feelings and resentments and the freedom of group members to offer interpretations of each others' behavior is clearly more similar to traditional group psychotherapy than is Caplanian consultation. Caplan would probably hold that the confrontation fostered in T-groups would tread on unconscious themes of some members, and they would be unable to cope with the results. In addition, once "word got around" of the self-disclosing nature of the groups, other members of the organization would feel too threatened to approach the consultant with work problems, lest they open themselves to being candidates for a group.

The ethical T-group practitioner does attempt to screen out people with a more than normal burden of personal problems. Work with mental health casualties is specifically avoided in that it is assumed that T-groups are for people who are well-adjusted and psychologically healthy. Still, the fears of a Caplanian regarding T-groups do not appear to be entirely unwarranted. Some individuals might be unable to cope with negative feedback from a host of their co-workers. They could drown in a tidal wave of well-intentioned "feedback." It is surely the case that some persons in an organization, whether from a neurotic fear of revealing themselves to others or from a healthy self-actualized sense of privacy, will wish to avoid the T-group experience and the consultant who is associated with it.

The commitment to sensitivity training as a method of promoting change by OD practitioners is real, but the extent of its use remains an open question. Burke argues that "the T-group as such is simply not a major OD device" (Burke, 1973, p. 198). On the other hand, Bennis (1969) and Kahn (1974) point out that the major OD intervention discussed in the literature tends to be some form of T-group experience. Bennis feels that OD is not "simply sensitivity training," but confusion exists in people's mind because most OD cases that finally reach print focus almost exclusively on the T-group as the basic strategy of intervention.

To the extent that sensitivity training methods are relied upon, the basic assumptions of T-group practice become of prime concern. If the assumption of sensitivity training cannot be met, the work of the OD practitioner who uses these methods will be limited.

Assumptions for sensitivity training as an organizational change strategy

The major assumptions underlying sensitivity training will now be listed; then each will be discussed in turn.

1. Organizational problems are due to poor interpersonal relations among members of the organization.
2. Organization members are capable of open and sensitive interpersonal relations and willingly would assume increased involvement and responsibility.
3. Honest feedback achieved in the psychological safety of the T-group will transfer to real-life work settings.

In what situations can these assumptions be met? In studying the list above, it should be clear that the T-group approach is not universally applicable but depends on the particular problems, persons, and organizations involved. This point should be highlighted in the discussion that follows:

1. Are organizational problems due to poor interpersonal relations among members of the organization?

Organizational problems are *sometimes* due to poor interpersonal relations. Sensitivity sessions can serve the useful purpose of exposing participants to individuals they would normally avoid in daily contact, and provide an opportunity to learn something of the point of view and experience of the avoided, stereotyped other.

But what of those organizational situations where the problems are not ones of interpersonal misunderstandings, but rather concern substantive issues of organizational policy? Here the members of the organization may understand *exactly* what the underlying difficulties are, and may strenuously disagree on their resolution. A T-group involving the oppressed employees of a feudal sweat-shop and the management would more likely lead to a revolt than to the amiable resolution of "misunderstandings." In this instance, the workers need power and organization; not sensitivity training.

There are still other organizations that have managed to maintain a tenuous cohesion among their members despite basic differences on policy issues. Differences may be real and irreconcilable. In these instances one may wonder whether sensitivity training should be attempted if there is a strong likelihood that the resultant effort will not resolve differences, but simply help the participants see their differences more clearly. Bringing true dissension to the fore and treating it as if it were simply a problem in communication may serve to destroy the delicate balance that allowed for organizational continuity.

2. Are organization members capable of open and sensitive interpersonal relations and would they willingly assume increased involvement and responsibility?

Sensitivity training requires that there exist within an organization, a sufficient number of interpersonally skilled members who are willing participants and who can quickly learn to operate constructively even though initial sensitivity meetings are designed to be anxiety-arousing (Campbell & Dunnette, 1968). Unfortunately this may mean that the most needful organizations, those with few interpersonally sensitive members, or those whose repressive climate stifles interpersonal sensitivity are least likely to benefit.

Competence in job skills among members of an organization is also an asset to group development work. Leaders of organizations can take the risk of sharing their authority and decision-making power when they can be assured that their subordinates are competent and will handle their delegated power wisely. OD practitioners assume that most organizations do contain technically competent personnel whose job productivity and morale will increase if they can participate in important job decisions. But what if members of an organization are not capable of operating at high levels of job competence, or do not want increased responsibility and involvement? Interpersonal trust and sharing requires commitments from participants interested in and prepared to carry out their commitments. Group development and sensitivity training assumptions imply that these interests and capabilities already exist and need only be recognized. Lack of job competence and long standing abhorrence of increased job responsibilities present problems for the OD practitioner not readily resolved by sensitivity training. Thus, Bennis and Peter (1966) note that the organization development model was designed for modern, large-scale organizations that are very diverse and full of specialized individuals. They further note that many dependent members in organizations typically do not want more involvement and participation in decision making and that "the model is immediately useful only among those who do" (p. 313).

3. Would honest feedback achieved in the psychological safety of the T-group transfer to real-life work settings?

An early assumption of the T-group method was that a focus on individual growth and development could radiate through an organization, thereby changing it. However, it soon became apparent that a focus on individual growth was not sufficient if the ultimate goal was to produce lasting changes in institutions and organizations. The very conditions that were most conducive to T-group functioning (a group of strangers who will not meet again, coming together in an isolated environment, playing a temporary interpersonal "game") were also those least likely to produce transfer back to a participants's organizational setting (Campbell & Dunnette, 1968). To meet this problem, the basic T-group methodology was retained but groups were conducted closer to the work situation, involving people from the same organization, and incorporating particular organizational problems for discussion. These modifications reduced the possibility of building a climate of trust and safety so necessary for proper T-group functioning. To convey unpleasant information to another, even in the most constructive way, when that other is in a position to make decisions having great relevance to one's own future is at best difficult. To admit weaknesses to others who could possibly use those weaknesses to one's own disadvantage may be too much to expect. A compromise solution to this problem was developed in the use of "cousin labs." Sensitivity groups were established for individuals of similar organizational rank but from different functional work groups. Members could concentrate on similar work problems but obtain interpersonal feedback, in relative safety, from individuals with whom they had no outside contact.

Still, the problem of generalization remains. It has yet to be established that changes in self-perception will automatically lead to changes in behavior or that behavior displayed in a T-group will be sustained in day-to-day contacts. As we have already learned about change in psychotherapy, the transfer from the therapy room to real-life is not an automatic process (Goldstein, Heller, & Sechrest, 1966), and much is still to be learned about the conditions that facilitate such transfer.

OD values: A humanistic orientation versus power and profit motives

It is to their credit that the proponents of OD are explicit about the value context in which their activities take place. OD attempts to look at men and women as "whole persons," as people "in process." It encourages the expression of feelings and resentments, risk, "authenticity," and confrontation. The specific objectives of OD are heavily colored by its existential and humanistic underpinnings. OD operates on an "attitude change strategy" (Walton, 1965) based on humanistic values, rather than a "power strategy" (Gamson, 1968) based on conflict and coercion. Power considerations are more relevant to approaches such as social advocacy.

While OD is to be lauded for articulating a coherent set of social values, articulation is not the same as implementation. The joint goals of OD are to increase *both* organizational efficiency and human fulfillment. The assumption is that these values will go hand in hand: more actualized people should be more efficient workers. Everybody wins.

Given that the OD consultant is invited to the organization (and paid) by the management, however, there may be a more than trivial bias that when productivity and fulfillment are at odds—as they often can be—OD should favor the former. As Friedlander and Brown (1974, p. 335) put it: "OD as a field runs the risk of encouraging and implementing subtle but persuasive forms of exploitation, curtailment of freedom, control of personality, violation of dignity, intrusion of privacy—all in the name of science and of economic and technological efficiency." OD, they state, "may well be another organizational palliative," engaged in "making some people happier at the job of making other people richer" (Ross, 1971, p. 583).

While OD practitioners are quick to spout humanistic and existential values, they are often mute when asked to reconcile these values with the realities of the seamier side of American business. To the extent that laissez-faire capitalists outnumber existential humanists in corporate board rooms, the worker's psychological fulfillment may be fostered if *and only if* it does not interfere with profit ratios (Monahan, Novaco & Geis, in press).

Among community human service agencies, OD values are particu-larly appealing since the call for self-awareness and open communica-tion fits already firmly established humanitarian values. The assump-tion is that as members of a human service organization increase their job satisfaction and productivity, and learn to interact better with one another, they will automatically transfer this learning to their interac-tion with the organization's clients and thereby be more responsive to the needs of those clients. The problem is that even if the goals of increased self-awareness and interpersonal trust between members of an organization are achieved, constraints on effective behavioral change may still exist. The community and institutional pressures that work against the maintenance of cooperation and trust between an agency and its clients cannot be ignored. Even with the best intent, frustration between worker and client is bound to rise as they both face the real constraints to change produced by the intransigence of agency policy, the conflicting missions imposed on the agency by community sentiment, and the real-life educational and economic deficits of clients—to name but a few. Increasing the interpersonal sensitivity of already receptive agency personnel, by itself, may be the least effec-tive way to deal with these problems. Even changes that are initiated may have to be terminated not only because of their conflict with other "interface units" (Bennis, 1970) but more basically because the OD "truth-love" model "systematically avoids the problems of power and the politics of change" and "has no alternate model to guide practice under conditions of distrust, violence and conflict" (Bennis, 1969).

In approaching organizational change, the wise OD consultant does not try to "sell" a particular method of operation simply because that happens to be a favorite procedure—one that the consultant knows best. OD work begins by assessing the organization's major needs and designing interventions to meet those needs. If process interventions such as sensitivity training seem indicated, the consultant must de-termine whether the assumptions of the method can be met. The deci-sion to be made is whether to concentrate on structural and program changes or whether to focus on improvements in interpersonal pro-cesses. Both are important, but the sequence in which these activities should occur is still at issue. On the one hand, one could argue that if people overcome their misunderstandings, they will work construc-tively on program changes. Conversely, it is likely that reducing job stresses by redesigning programs and the structure of work tasks, also can provide the needed motivation for later focus on improvements in interpersonal relations. Which should be undertaken first probably depends on the specific situation at hand. The well-trained OD consultant can facilitate both types of changes. The OD approach can provide useful tools for organizations ready for self-improvement.

Summary of consultation assumptions

From our point of view, regardless of specialized content or techniques, the essential similarity among consultants of the various perspectives is that they are all oriented toward a similar goal—that is, to effect positive changes in essential human service and socialization institutions through program modification, and by increasing the psychological sophistication and work capacity of the primary care-givers within these institutions.

As applied to human service organizations, the following assumptions can be derived from the various consultation perspectives:

1. Very few problems in real life are exclusively psychological in nature. The most troubling problems are those with complex determinants, of which the psychological component, while significant, is just one among many. There is little gained when clients with difficulties in living are "taken over" by personnel in the mental health sphere. If anything, there are distinct disadvantages to labeling problems exclusively in mental health terms, not only because of the adverse consequences for the individual so labeled, or because the mental health professions could never develop the manpower needed to deal with all those who would then be thrust upon them. An even more critical disadvantage is that the mental health professions do not control the tangible real-life reinforcements necessary for changing individual or corporate behavior in our society. By themselves, they do not possess the leverage to affect social contingencies impinging upon individuals.

2. Communities have well-developed systems for providing human services. The greatest benefit can be obtained if mental health personnel use their expertise to ensure that these services are administered in such a way that they do not contribute to conditions that would increase the likelihood of producing mental health casualties. It is assumed that since primary care-givers and agents of social control constantly deal with problems of behavior, the more they know about psychological development and the principles of behavior, the more likely will it be that they will take psychologically sound, humane action.

3. Considering the great array of human service professions, consultants will realize the greatest preventive potential in their work if they affiliate with units in the community that have primary responsibility for psychological and social development and that deal with young populations still in their formative years. For example, there would be greater preventive potential in working with administrative officials who determine policy and programs with regard to school behavior or with teachers making mental health referrals than with clinics to whom such referrals are made. There would be similar advantages in working with probation or police departments rather than in correctional facilities for convicted offenders; or on an intake unit that screens disordered individuals brought to a hospital as compared with hospital wards for chronic mental patients.

4. The consultant's long-term goal is to obtain some permanent change in the consultee or the consultee's institution. There would be little economic gain if all cases with a psychological component were called to a consultant's attention. Neither would there be any particular advantage if consultants were sought out only for some particular difficulties, while over time, the nature of the problems called to their attention remained the same. Consultants hope that their efforts will go beyond the specific case material brought to their attention. It is in this sense that consultation can be thought of as a radiating process (Kelly, 1970). Improved functioning by consultees or better programs developed by consultee institutions affect the client populations who are beneficiaries of the improved service. Thus the impact of consultation is most appropriately measured, not just by changes in consultees, but by changes in those significant others who are served by the consultees.

It should be clear from the above that consultation does not denote a new profession independent of others. A consultant must have a background in some substantive content area that relates to understanding the human condition. The area of specialization need not be the traditional mental health professions—some would argue that the mental health fields represent too narrow a view of community life. But whatever the area, it must have a body of knowledge and skills that the consultant can use in orienting the direction of work. Nothing is sadder to see in the field than a consultant who has nothing to offer the host organization, and who seems to assume that his or her mere presence alone will "make things happen."

The substantive areas from which mental health consultants might draw are quite varied, including the range from urban planning, sociology, and public health nursing to the more traditional mental health "team"—psychiatry, psychology, and psychiatric social work. Caplan (1970) suggests that the consultant's particular expertise is in the mental health area. However, there are consultants who would prefer to describe their work as "psychological" or as "behavioral" rather than accept the language of health and illness. Other consultants would point out that their expertise is in "problem solving," so that the help they provide is not circumscribed by a particular type of problem. Instead they teach problem-solving skills that should be applicable to work difficulties of almost any content.

Critical comments

Not all human service workers can benefit from consultation. There are several problems confronting those attempting to develop a program of intervention based upon the above assumptions, problems that are not typically addressed by consultation theorists. To begin with, one may ask whether it is reasonable to expect non-mental health personnel to perform psychological functions. The consultant *does* ask human service workers to concern themselves with the psychological components of their work. To those who respond that their training does not equip them to "dabble in the psyche of others," the consultant replies that their normal work functions are made more difficult when attempts are not made to understand and deal with behavior patterns of clients. There is accumulating evidence to support the consultant's claim that non-mental health personnel can be trained to respond in psychologically helpful ways (Guerney, 1969). However, a problem is that not all can be so trained. Some individuals who have gravitated to community care-giving and socialization roles, still may be so deficient in interpersonal sensitivity and skill, that no amount of training will improve their functioning. These individuals would probably do less harm if they did not attempt to intervene in a psychologically meaningful manner. We are not referring to consultees who simply differ in values or interpersonal style from their consultants. Most consultants already know that they must guard themselves against the tendency to assume that all who disagree with their mission are of dubious mental health. We are referring to those individuals whose entry into a human service field was clearly in error and who are unamenable to change by a consultant despite his or her best effort.

All human service professions (including the mental health professions) contain a small minority of members whose adjustment is tenuous, and who should not be in work that requires sensitivity and responsiveness to others. Undoubtedly, the professions themselves could do better screening of those who apply to their training programs. The mental health consultant who finds these individuals in working with agencies has very few options. The point we are making here is simply that consultation should not be expected to be effective under all circumstances. There are primary care-givers who are not amenable to change. However, in working for institutional change from within organizational structures, the consultant hopes and expects that the majority will be basically competent and psychologically healthy and will be responsive to improving their work performance.

Consultation is impeded by conflicting goals between agency and consultant.   A greater constraint on the work of consultants occurs when their goals and the primary goals of consulting institutions are so antithetical that consultees are prevented from acting in a psychologically helpful manner although they have the skill and capacity to do so. It is here that the consultant encounters the greatest difficulties. Many community agencies have multifaceted missions, among which the psychological well-being of clients may not be primary. These competing goals may be unstated, but nonetheless may be important motivators of behavior supported by powerful community sanctions. For example, agencies assigned formal care-giving, socialization, or rehabilitation functions might also be responding to community sentiments such as the need to control those who disrupt the social order, economic motives (e.g., saving the taxpayer's dollar) or upholding social customs (e.g., the maintenance of racially segregated living patterns). Faced with agency goals that conflict with a psychological mission, the consultant may attempt to demonstrate that some divergent goals are not irreconcilable. For example, it may be possible to show that social control in a classroom need not be sacrificed by attending to the psychological needs of students, or that motivating welfare clients toward self-care may be more economical in the long run than demoralizing investigations followed by impersonally administered aid. However, if differences in goals are indeed irreconcilable, the consultant might find the time better spent outside the agency, for example, by working toward a change in community sentiments impinging on agency policy. The consultant and institution need not share all goals, but must be willing to work toward some meaningful common goals that are congruent with the values of both parties.

Gains from consultation can be used for oppressive purposes.   An ethical issue raised by consultation concerns the ultimate use of the new knowledge and skills provided by the consultant. Consultants assume that its use will be benevolent and that primary care-givers are sincerely interested in the welfare of their clients. However, we also know that, in varying degrees, institution members are interested in the maintenance of their institution and their role within it. What happens when values surrounding institutional maintenance and the welfare of clients conflict? How will skills, newly learned through consultation, be used? A case in point involves consultants who teach behavior modification skills that can be used oppressively in the service of social control or benevolently to ensure more effective learning. For example, a teacher who learns new techniques of behavioral management is likely to have a less disruptive classroom, which in turn increases the possibility of decreased tension and acting-out behaviors and more effective learning. But increased control in the classroom *by itself* is a poor goal and one that can lead to stultifying oppression. The point is that consultants cannot simply assume that intervention will automatically improve a situation. The effects of their work can be good or bad, and without appropriate evaluation they will never know.

Institutional rigidity limits gains from consultation.   A final problem concerns the general responsiveness of institutions to the needs of clients served. Some community institutions charged with a helping mission may be resistant to change and yet may so aggravate the conditions they are supposed to correct that no amount of internal repair initiated by a consultant can salvage effective functioning. Community agitation for more responsive institutions may be necessary. What complicates a clear assessment of the situation is that, from the point of view of the casual observer, institutions almost always appear more rigid than they are, and the danger of impatience with slow progress is ever present. Still, consultants are not magicians, and questions about feasibility of operation in unresponsive institutions must be faced, and methods for assessing the responsivity of institutions must be developed. In the words of one consultation theorist: "Resources are too limited to be dissipated in futile efforts to achieve currently unattainable ends" (Caplan, 1970, p. 41).

Conclusion: A comparison among consultation perspectives

Three approaches to consultation were highlighted in this chapter. Since each was developed from a different conceptual tradition, the assumptions and procedures of each naturally reflect these differences.

The most widely cited point of view describing mental health consultation was developed by Gerald Caplan. Hence, we selected Caplan's psychodynamic views as the starting point for our discussion. Mental health consultation, as initially developed by Caplan, was focused on the consultee, or primary care-giver. Case-centered consultation was seen as the entry point—as the way to reach the consultee to effect enduring changes in attitudes and behavior. The problems of the consultee could be deficiencies in knowledge or skill, but the problems of greatest interest to Caplan were those described as "lapses in professional objectivity." These were hypothesized to be caused by unresolved personal problems of which the consultee was probably unaware, or at least was resistant to explore. With such a clearly clinical, intra-psychic orientation there was a need to sharply distinguish consultation from formal psychotherapy. Compared to psychotherapy, consultation had a more restricted scope. The consultant was interested in the consultee's conflicts only as they might affect on-the-job performance; aspects of the consultee's personal life were off limits to investigation. Furthermore, the content of personal conflicts was never explored directly, and was dealt with only if it could be displaced onto case material. It was expected that clarifying the case and achieving an improved case outcome would help dissipate the consultee's problem also, to the extent that it was projected onto the case material.

A number of mental health consultants believe that the intra-psychic orientation outlined above is much too narrow. By concentrating on the personality of the consultee, roles within the organization as well as organizational characteristics that impinge upon individual behavior are too easily overlooked. Generally, mental health consultation has become more eclectic, borrowing from organizational theory and social and environmental psychology. Depending upon background and training, the consultant offers help at a number of organizational levels (line staff, supervisors, or administrators) and for a variety of problems (low morale, lacks of knowledge or skill, deficiencies in inter-agency linking patterns, etc.). Mental health consultation has become so diverse that it can be misleading to speak of a unitary consultation perspective.

Still, there is some agreement that by focusing primarily on work problems rather than on agency personnel, the consultant is allowed a less defensive entry. Slowly, over time, as the consultant gains the confidence of organization members, the focus of consultation may change. The greatest benefit to the organization is expected to accrue through program-centered consultation; and the consultant is more likely to be asked to work on programmatic concerns after demonstrating competence in handling other agency requests. This slow process of trust building can be contrasted with the organization development approach that requires an initial commitment to self-examination as a *prerequisite* for consultation.

Organization development (OD) developed from an orientation quite different from the intra-psychic formulation of Caplan. OD practitioners, heavily influenced by Kurt Lewin and gestalt psychology, focused on the interaction of environmental pressures and individual characteristics. An organization's "environment" consisted of both structural and psychosocial elements, the latter referring to the processes by which individuals within the setting interact. These processes proved to be the primary interest of OD specialists.

Organization development seems best suited to problems of distrust, alienation, and poor morale in organizations that are engendered by faulty interpersonal communication and interaction. Poor communication leads to a downward spiral of misunderstanding, inaccurate perception, and further misunderstanding. Getting people together in open communication in which honest feedback can be transmitted is one of the primary goals of the OD specialist. It is expected that aware and interpersonally honest personnel will lead to more humane and effective institutions and organizations. But these characteristics need to exist to a moderate degree as a prior condition, before organization development can be initiated. Basic to OD work is member motivation and commitment, and minimal organizational defensiveness. Because OD activity is more direct and confrontive more can be accomplished in a brief period of time. But in order to tolerate confrontation, consultee motivation and receptivity must be high. Honest feedback falls on deaf ears if those for whom it is intended are unwilling to receive the message.

Behavioral consultation also has its roots in clinical theory and practice. Initially, behavioral consultants worked as clinicians applying a learning-based technology to difficult management problems. This work was moved from the clinic to more real-life settings for two main reasons: the clinician did not control the important reinforcers in the patient's life and behavior change was more likely to be maintained if reinforcing stimuli could be developed in the patient's natural environment.

The initial efforts of behavioral consultation were case-centered, aimed at demonstrating that stimulus control over difficult behavior could be maintained by reinforcement "mediators" in the patient's environment. The mediator is the consultee in Caplan's typology, so translating across consultation perspectives, what was accomplished was "consultee-centered case consultation" with an emphasis on providing the consultee with new knowledge and skills. In this work, personal characteristics of consultees are not considered except as they may interfere with the successful implementation of behavioral programming. Communication patterns and relationships between members of the organization or setting also are not given primary attention. Unfortunately, these member characteristics and organizational problems can be the very issues that torpedo the successful execution of behavioral programs.

More recently, behavioral psychologists have become interested in fostering change at community levels. To the extent that *total* control of the environment will be required by these efforts, opportunities for behavioral management in the community probably will remain limited. There is a literature on the successful application of "token economies," but these programs have been undertaken primarily in closed institutions (mental hospitals, prisons, etc.) that already exert nearly complete control over their members. It is unlikely that society would allow the behavioral consultant to dictate the rules that govern behavior in other natural settings.

There is still unexplored potential in the behavioral approach that we can see if we shift the focus of discussion slightly. Rather than continuing the preoccupation with behavioral "control" and its attendant problems, we should remember that the behaviorist also is providing us with a message about *incentives*. If desired community behaviors are reinforced, their frequency of occurrence is likely to increase. We need only be clear about the desirable behaviors to be encouraged, and be willing to provide incentives for their performance. Are we willing to meaningfully and consistently reward pro-social behaviors like citizenship, participation, and responsibility? Coercion would not be required; much could be accomplished through voluntary incentives as described in the experiments aimed at reducing littering and increasing bus ridership. However, we should remember that given the present structure of society, there are realistic limits to a plan based solely on incentives. In a society in which rewards are distributed unevenly, frequently unrelated to performance, and in which there is often no relationship between wealth and desirable behavior (e.g., is the TV entertainer really more socially useful than the garbage collector?), a meaningful behavioristic society based on voluntary incentives is a long way off.

We close this chapter by returning to the basic similarity among the consultation perspectives with regard to community change. All focus on the improvement of existing social institutions. All hope to expand the programmatic scope of agencies and organizations. Community life is expected to improve as service delivery becomes more responsive and psychologically sophisticated. But what if agencies, and personnel within them, are unwilling or unable to change? These more pessimistic outcomes lead to the considerations described in the next two chapters.

References

Alexander, J. F., & Parsons, B. V.   Short-term behavioral intervention with delinquent families: Impact on family process and recidivism. *Journal of Abnormal Psychology*, 1973, *81*, 219–225.

Altrocchi, J.   Mental health consultation.   In S. E. Golann & C. Eisdorfer (Eds.), *Handbook of community mental health*. New York: Appleton-Century-Crofts, 1972, pp. 477–508.

Altrocchi, J., Spielberger, C. D. & Eisdorfer, C.   Mental health consultation with groups. *Community Mental Health Journal*, 1965, *1*, 127–134.

Beisser, A. R.   *Mental health consultation and education*. Palo Alto, Calif.: National Press Books, 1972.

Benne, K. D., Bradford, L. P., & Lippett, R.   The laboratory method. In L. P. Bradford, J. R. Gibb, & K. D. Benne (Eds.), *T-Group theory and laboratory method*. New York: John Wiley & Sons, 1964, pp. 15–44.

Bennis, W. G.   *Organization development: Its nature, origins and perspectives*. Reading, Mass.: Addison-Wesley, 1969.

Bennis, W. G.   A funny thing happened on the way to the future. *American Psychologist*, 1970, *7*, 595–608.

Bennis, W. G., & Peter, H. W.   Applying behavioral science for organizational change. In H. W. Peter (Ed.), *Comparative theories of social change*. Ann

Arbor, Mich.: Foundation for Research on Human Behavior, 1966, pp. 290–315.

Binder, A., Monahan, J., & Newkirk, M.   Diversion from the juvenile justice system and the prevention of delinquency. In J. Monahan (Ed.), *Community mental health and the criminal justice system.* New York: Pergamon Press, 1976, pp. 131–140.

Blake, R. R., Mouton, J. S., & Sloma, R. L.   The union-management intergroup laboratory: Strategy for resolving intergroup conflict. *Journal of Applied Behavioral Science,* 1965, *1,* 25–57.

Bowers, D.   OD techniques and their results in 23 organizations: The Michigan ICL study. *Journal of Applied Behavioral Science,* 1973, *9,* 21–43.

Breger, L., & McGaugh, J. L.   Critique and reformulation of "learning theory" approaches to psychotherapy and neurosis. *Psychological Bulletin,* 1965, *63,* 338–358.

Buchwald, A. M., & Young, R. D.   Some comments on the foundations of behavior therapy. In C. M. Franks (Ed.), *Behavior therapy: Appraisal and status.* New York: McGraw-Hill, 1969, pp. 607–624.

Burke, W. W.   Organization development. *Professional Psychology,* May 1973, pp. 194–200.

Callahan, E. J., & Leitenberg, H.   Aversion therapy for sexual deviation: contingent shock and covert sensitization. *Journal of Abnormal Psychology,* 1973, *81,* 60–73.

Campbell, J. P., & Dunnette, M.D.   Effectiveness of T-Group experiences in managerial training and development. *Psychological Bulletin,* 1968, *70,* 73–104.

Caplan, G.   *The theory and practice of mental health consultation.* New York: Basic Books, 1970.

Cohen, H. L. & Filipczak, J.   *A new learning environment.* San Francisco: Jossey-Bass, 1971.

Conant, E. H., & Kilbridge, M. D.   An interdisciplinary analysis of job enlargement: Technology, costs and behavioral implications. *Indiana Labor Relations Review,* 1965, *18,* 377–395.

Davidson, W. S.   Studies of aversive conditioning for alcoholics: A critical review of theory and research methodology. *Psychological Bulletin,* 1974, *81,* 571–581.

Davidson, W. S., & Seidman, E.   Studies of behavior modification and juvenile delinquency: A review, methodological critique, and social perspective. *Psychological Bulletin,* 1974, *81,* 998–1011.

Davis, L. E.   The design of jobs. *Industrial Relations,* 1966, *6,* 21–45.

Davison, G. C., & Stuart, R. B.   Behavior therapy and civil liberties. *American Psychologist,* 1975, *30,* 755–763.

Everett, P. B., Hayward, S. C., & Meyers, A. W.   The effects of a token reinforcement procedure on bus ridership. *Journal of Applied Behavior Analysis,* 1974, *7,* 1–9.

Ford, D. H., & Urban, H. B.   Psychotherapy. *Annual Review of Psychology,* 1967, *18,* 333–372.

Ford, R. N.   *Motivation through work itself.* New York: Amenaan Management Association, 1969.

Friedlander, F., & Brown, L. D.   Organization development. *Annual Review of Psychology,* 1974, *25,* 313–341.

Gamson, W. A.   *Power and discontent.* Homewood, Ill.: The Dorsey Press, 1968.

Goldstein, A. P., Heller, K., & Sechrest, L. B.   *Psychotherapy and the psychology of behavior change.* New York: John Wiley & Sons, 1966.

Golembiewski, R. T., Hilles, R., & Kagno, M. S.   A longitudinal study of flexi-time effects: Some consequences of an OD structural intervention. *Journal of Applied Behavioral Science,* 1974, *10,* 503–532.

Guerney, B. G., Jr. (Ed.).   *Psychotherapeutic agents: New roles for non-professionals, parents and teachers.* New York: Holt, Rinehart and Winston, 1969.

Heller, K., & Marlatt, G. A.   Verbal conditioning, behavior therapy, and behavior change: Some problems in extrapolation. In C. M. Franks (Ed.), *Behavior therapy: Appraisal and status.* New York: McGraw-Hill, 1969, pp. 569–588.

Hunnius, G., Garson, G., & Case, J.   *Workers' control.* New York: Random House, 1973.

Kahn, R. L.   Organization development: Some problems and proposals. *Journal of Applied Behavioral Science,* 1974, *10,* 485–502.

Kanfer, F. H., & Goldstein, A. P.   *Helping people change: A textbook of methods.* New York: Pergamon Press, 1975.

Kelly, J. G.   The quest for valid preventive interventions. In C. D. Spielberger (Ed.), *Current topics in clinical and community psychology* (Vol. 2). New York: Academic Press, 1970, pp. 183–207.

Kiesler, F.   Programming for prevention. *North Carolina Journal of Mental Health,* 1965.

Knoblock, P., & Goldstein, A. P.   *The lonely teacher.* Boston, Mass.: Allyn and Bacon, 1971.

Kuriloff, A. H., & Atkins, S.   T group for a work team. *Journal of Applied Behavioral Science,* 1966, *2,* 63–94.

Levy, L. H.   *Psychological interpretation.* New York: Holt, Rinehart and Winston, 1963.

Lloyd, R. W., Jr., & Salzberg, H. C.   Controlled social drinking: An alternative to abstinence as a treatment goal for some alcohol abusers. *Psychological Bulletin,* 1975, *82,* 815–842.

Mahoney, M. J.   *Cognition and behavior modification.* Cambridge, Mass.: Ballinger, 1974.

Mann, P. A.   Establishing a mental health consultation program with a police department. *Community Mental Health Journal,* 1971, 7, 118–126.

Mann, P. A., & Iscoe, I.   Mass behavior and community organization: Reflections on a peaceful demonstration. *American Psychologist,* 1971, 26, 108–113.

Mannino, F. V., & Shore, M. F.   Research in mental health consultation. In S. E. Golann & C. Eisdorfer (Eds.), *Handbook of community mental health.* New York: Appleton-Century-Crofts, 1972, pp. 755–777.

Marks, A. R. N.   An investigation of modifications of job design in an industrial situation and their effects on some measures of economic productivity Unpublished doctoral dissertation, University of California, Berkeley, 1954.

Marlatt, G. A.   Training responsible drinking with college students. Paper presented at the meetings of the American Psychological Association, Chicago, Ill., 1975.

Meyers, A. W., Craighead, W. E., & Meyers, H. H.   A behavioral-preventive approach to community mental health. *American Journal of Community Psychology,* 1974, 2, 275–285.

Monahan, J., Novaco, R., & Geis, G.   Corporate violence: Research strategies for community psychology. In T. Sarbin (Ed.) *Community psychology and criminal justice.* N. Y.: Human Sciences Press, in press.

Moos, R. H.   *Evaluating correctional and community settings.* New York: John Wiley & Sons, 1975.

Novaco, R. W.   *Anger control.* Lexington, Mass.: D. C. Heath, 1975.

O'Leary, K. D.   Behavior modification in the classroom: A rejoinder to Winett and Winkler. *Journal of Applied Behavior Analysis,* 1972, 5, 505–511.

O'Leary, K. D., & Drabman, R.   Token reinforcement programs in the classroom: A review. *Psychological Bulletin,* 1971, 75, 379–398.

O'Leary, K. D., & O'Leary, S. G.   *Classroom management: The successful use of behavior modification.* New York: Pergamon Press, 1972.

Patterson, G. R.   Behavioral intervention procedures in the classroom and in the home. In A. E. Bergin & S. L. Garfield (Eds.), *Handbook of psychotherapy and behavior change: An empirical analysis.* New York: John Wiley & Sons, 1971, pp. 751–775.

Rappaport, J., & Chinsky, J. M.   Models for delivery of service from a historical and conceptual perspective. *Professional Psychology,* 1974, 5, 42–50.

Reppucci, N. D., & Saunders, J. T.   Social psychology of behavior modification: Problems of implementation in natural settings. *American Psychologist,* 1974, 29, 649–660.

Ross, R.   OD for whom? *Journal of Applied Behavioral Science,* 1971, 7, 58–85.

Schmuck, R. A., & Miles, M. B. (Eds.). *Organization development in schools.* Palo Alto, Calif.: National Press Books, 1971.

Schmuck, R. A., & Runkel, P. J. *Handbook of organization development in schools.* Palo Alto, Calif.: National Press Books, 1972. By permission of Mayfield Publishing Company, formerly National Press Books. Copyright © CASEA 1972.

Seashore, S. E., & Bowers, D. G. Durability of organizational change. *American Psychologist,* 1970, *25,* 227–233.

Spielberger, C. D. A mental health consultation program in a small community with limited professional mental health resources. In E. L. Cowen, E. A. Gardner, & M. Zax (Eds.), *Emergent approaches to mental health problems.* New York: Appleton-Century-Crofts, 1967, pp. 214–236.

Stolz, S., Wienckowski, L. A., & Brown, B. S. Behavior modification: A perspective on critical issues. *American Psychologist,* 1975, *30,* 1027–1048.

Tharp, R. G., & Wetzel, R. J. *Behavior modification in the natural environment.* New York: Academic Press, 1969.

Trist, E. L., & Bamforth, R. Some social and psychological consequences of the long wall method of coal-getting. *Human Relations,* 1951, *4,* 3–38.

Trist, E. L., Higgin, G. W., Murray, H., & Pollack, A. B. *Organizational choice.* London: Tavistock, 1963.

Ullmann, L. P., & Krasner, L. *Case studies in behavior modification.* New York: Holt, Rinehart and Winston, 1965.

Ullmann, L. P., & Krasner, L. *A psychological approach to abnormal behavior.* Englewood Cliffs, N.J.: Prentice-Hall, 1969.

Walton, R. E. Two strategies of social change and their dilemmas. *Journal of Applied Behavioral Science,* 1965, *1,* 167–179.

Wetzel, R. Use of behavioral techniques in a case of compulsive stealing. *Journal of Consulting Psychology,* 1966, *30,* 367–374.

Whalen, C., & Henker, B. Creating therapeutic pyramids using mentally retarded patients. *American Journal of Mental Deficiency,* 1969, *74,* 331–337.

Winett. R. A., & Winkler, R. C. Current behavior modification in the classroom: Be still, be quiet, be docile. *Journal of Applied Behavior Analysis,* 1972, *5,* 499–504.

Wolf, M. M., Phillips, E. L., & Fixsen, D. L. The teaching family: A new model for the treatment of deviant child behavior in the community. In S. W. Bijou & E. L. Ribes-Inesta (Eds.), *Behavior modification: issues and extensions.* New York: Academic Press, 1972, pp. 51–62.

7

ALTERNATIVE INSTITUTIONS AND NEW CAREERS

The move toward the creation of new social structures

THE EMPHASIS in the 1960s on environmental factors contributing to the poor quality of life, particularly among oppressed minorities, and the full realization of the injustice of such oppression, turned the spotlight of attention on the functioning of social institutions. Educational, helping, and service agencies were indicted not only because they were seen as impotent, but because they were also seen as contributing in an insidious way to the misery, impoverishment, and helplessness they were created to remedy. Thus, Goldenberg (1971b) notes with regard to the community mental health movement that:

> . . . it was finally recognized that an inordinate amount of human misery was somehow caused, exacerbated by or connected with the functioning of a variety of social and economic institutions (e.g., schools, welfare and employment settings, etc.) which, when taken together, exercise enormous power in determining the quality of life in any given community and for any given group of people. Their inadequacies, whether by design or by accident, had as much to do with generating the conditions for mental and emotional dysfunctioning as did the unresolved problems traditionally associated with conflict-ridden psychosexual development. (p. 11)

Some of those who faulted social institutions for contributing to human misery believed that attempts at change from within would be futile, and that internal reform could only produce the appearance of innovation without basic change (Smith, 1974). For those who had lost confidence in the ability of existing social institutions to remedy the conditions with which they were initially designed to cope, there seemed little choice but to plan for the design of new, more responsive institutions; or at minimum, to work toward supplying existing institutions with new workers who by temperament, training, or general moral commitment would be more effective and dedicated.

The creation of new social institutions has been a traditional response to social change in this country. From a historical perspective, the creation of separate institutions or even separate societies by those who found existing social institutions unresponsive to their needs is not difficult to document. For some, dissatisfied with the social forces impinging on them, but who had the resources that allowed freedom of choice, little problem existed. They could choose life-styles and living arrangements consonant with their beliefs. The history of the United States is replete with examples of groups who, in rejecting dominant cultural institutions (or being rejected for their deviant views), developed separate social enclaves. This was the action taken by the first European settlers in this country and it is still the choice of others who have the personal, social, or financial resources to lead separate lives.

What is new about this point of view is that the creation of new social systems is being proposed as a solution to psychological problems, and the mental health fields are being urged to develop expertise in the construction of these systems. Training programs have been proposed to implement these views. For example, Tornatzky, Fairweather, and O'Kelly (1970) describe a training program at Michigan State University whose goals are to train a new breed of professional proficient in:

> (a) the development of alternative social models or subsystems to replace contemporary systems that have been demonstrated to be ineffective or harmful; and (b) creating the conditions for adoption by the general population of such demonstrably successful models by experimental means. (p. 886)

Do social institutions have a role in contributing to the inequities in community life?

The charge against existing institutions is that they are not innocent bystanders in the problems of community life and that they contribute to the conditions that produce psychological dysfunction. Furthermore, the claim is that abuses often are undertaken with a "malevolent intent" to subjugate the minority for the benefit of the majority. Is it the case, for example, that school policy expresses the general fear of minorities and the wish of the majority to keep minorities in their place? The charge is serious and is vigorously denied by workers within care-giving and socialization institutions who often point with pride to their own liberal political attitudes.

Protecting the public from deviant minorities

Rhodes (1972) would probably be unwilling to use the term "malevolent intent," but he does suggest that political and social service agencies serve the function of protecting the public from the threat produced by its deviant minorities. Rhodes's hypothesis is that:

> . . . the vast web of service agencies and systems tends to be diverted to the alleviation of threat anxiety in the culture-bearing majority and to the creation of protective barriers between this majority and certain minority groups whose culturally divergent behavior produces threat.
>
> . . . the minority exciter group and its behavior is frequently cut off from normal communication with the majority population and regular channels of social intercourse. Special channels of communication and societal devices are maneuvered between the rest of the community and these exciters. These devices may be community buffer zones like those that surround slums. They may also be programs of agencies and institutions that come between majority and minority groups. (Rhodes, 1972, pp. 4 and 15)

If Rhodes is correct, then one reason that social institutions may be unresponsive to the needs of their clients is that serving those needs may not be their primary function—despite the institutions' officially stated purpose. Rhodes's hypothesis would suggest that welfare departments are not set up to rehabilitate the poor but to protect the general public from the poor. Similarly, prisons and mental hospitals serve a protective function more than a rehabilitative function. And so for other social agencies as well. Schools also can be seen as serving a protective function by acculturating deviant minority members into the mores and values of the culture-bearing majority. If this acculturation process is resisted then other special institutions (reform schools, special education classes, etc.) are invoked to help reduce the threat posed by the deviant member.

Those advocating the creation of new social institutions would argue that when existing institutions no longer follow their officially designated mandates of serving their client populations as their primary goals, then the time for institutional replacement is at hand. The new institutions would be prevented from developing the same anti-minority stance because their governing bodies would have better representation of minority viewpoints. They would be at least partially controlled by, and therefore more accountable to, their clients.

Forces associated with institutional maintenance and survival

A second ingredient contributing to the general unresponsivity of existing social systems involves the forces within institutions pushing for institutional maintenance and enhancement. Institutions seem to develop a way of life and functional autonomy of their own so that, once established, institutional maintenance itself becomes a primary goal. One would be hard put to think of a social institution that declared itself disbanded because its services were no longer necessary. For example, when polio was removed as a national health hazard by successful immunization, the foundation set up to raise money specifically to combat polio did not disband despite the successful preventive outcome. Instead it broadened its mission as a fund-raising organization to fight crippling birth defects.[1]

An emphasis on institution maintenance does not necessarily imply an unresponsivity to client needs, but sometimes the two do go hand in hand. Special education classes, originally established as a true educational reform to provide more specialized and relevant education for intellectually slow children, developed a special education technology and cadres of school psychometricians to provide an adequate supply of children for these classes. Other attempts at educational reforms—for example, those aimed at keeping handicapped children integrated in the normal classroom as long as possible—were at times vigorously opposed by an organized professional group (psychometricians) who worried about losing their jobs if the reform succeeded.

The point is that racism, discrimination, or, more generally, not serving the best interests of a client population need not be motivated by a conscious and deliberate racial or political attitude. Being excessively interested in agency survival, job security, or personal power

---

[1] We are not arguing that a successful program should disband, only that it is unlikely to do so. Some would say that the successful organization continues because its leaders choose to devote their expertise to the solution of other pressing problems. An equally plausible reason is that the organization continues because institutional maintenance involves jobs and careers that are not easily changed or given up.

are sufficient to perpetuate harmful agency policies and practices. Unfortunately, these problems tend to be universal. It is difficult to conceive of any institution that over time will not develop strong forces oriented toward self-maintenance.

An important rationale for alternative institutions: Optimizing person-environment fit and promoting diversity

Thus far, the discussion has emphasized an indictment of unresponsive social institutions as a rationale for creating alternatives. But perhaps too much is expected by the critics. Institutional maintenance and job security are "facts of life" and cannot be avoided. Furthermore, it may be that no *single* social institution can be responsive to the needs of all. Innovative social institutions of a previous era (documented by Levine and Levine, 1970) may have lost their special innovative character and spirit, at least in part, because they were overwhelmed by the number and diversity of social problems confronting them. A plurality of institutional accommodations may be required to effectively deal with diversity.

Smith (1974) points out that the single institution serving a specified need in a local community (e.g., a public high school) was established in an era when communities were smaller and more homogeneous. But with increased numbers comes diversity of needs. For example, the small general store of a previous century is no longer adequate for modern communities of any significant size. Even if its inventory was unusually large, with a variety of merchandise in different price ranges, it is likely that many citizens would still choose to shop in neighboring communities for individual purchases. If communities can sustain a diversity of commercial institutions (e.g., groceries, furniture stores, hamburger and pizza establishments, etc.) and a diversity in some social institutions (e.g., churches), why should there be only one high school, one program for the poor or one mental health clinic?

Excessive cost is the most obvious deterrent to the proliferation of alternative settings. But the problem of cost is not as simple as it may first appear. For example, one high-volume furniture store could sell its goods more cheaply than each of several smaller specialty shops. Yet in some instances we are willing to pay for uniqueness, and patronize more expensive shops. As another example, we know of a small rural community (population 4,400) with only two physicians, one movie theater, and one public high school, but which supports 22 churches of varying Protestant denominations. Obviously, religious values are important in this community, and the churches serve other than strictly religious functions. Still, the community with many churches but only one high school is making a statement of priorities. It is willing to pay for diversity in one area (religion) but not in another (education). The decision may not be consciously thought out, since historically there is a tradition in this country of religious diversity and educational homogeneity (the "one room school" tradition). Nonetheless, similar decisions are being made in communities constantly. The proponents of alternatives would like to see these decisions become overt and deliberate; and would propose that communities consider diversity in areas in which it is now lacking.

The alternatives perspective emphasizes *choice*. Citizens are viewed as consumers who should have the freedom to purchase with their tax dollars services that best suit their individual predispositions. Choice is not the same as the imposition of alternatives according to some method of classification. For example, schools now have track programs that segregate "fast" learners from "slower," "vocational" students. Such labeling and tracking provides very little choice to students and their parents. Given the opportunity they might choose alternatives quite different than those provided. On the other hand, matching students to school environments according to the informed choices of those involved should help reduce discontent and misbehavior. Providing choice should reduce stress by optimizing person-environment fit. It should also reduce the number of nonfunctional school environments. A setting that is chosen by no one is not a viable alternative and can be corrected or disbanded.

Examples of alternative social institutions

Parallel institutions that perform a service already provided by the community usually are set up when a significant minority believes that its needs are not being met by existing programs. Lack of responsivity to subgroup needs might be a function of the uniqueness of those needs. Similarly, those in charge of community-wide programs might not have the skill or knowledge to cater to a group's special needs or may be unwilling to invest community-wide resources in special projects that would benefit only a few. For example, teachers generally complain that they do not have the knowledge or skill to mount special programs to meet the needs of handicapped children. Instead they advocate separate educational facilities for such groups. Similarly, schools financed by public tax funds are legally prohibited from offering separate programs for children with special needs in the religious area. Parents of such children turn to parochial schools (perhaps the most widespread example of an alternative institution) to fulfill their requirements for religious education for their children.

Alternatives as competing government bureaucracies: The welfare example

Parallel institutions are at times set up by governmental action. Special services to subgroups become institutionalized in this way, as for example, when law mandates school districts to provide separate classes for the education of mentally retarded youngsters. What is surprising is the occasional establishment of a governmental agency to perform functions parallel to those of already established governmental agencies, even when the two compete to serve the same client population. In effect, this is what happened during the War on Poverty of the 1960s. A welfare bureaucracy established to deal with the problems of the poor already existed at the state level. The setting up of a new agency with separate federal funds, the Community Action Program (CAP), was an admission that the functions performed by welfare departments were not sufficient to deal with the problems of poverty. The welfare departments were not phased out because they were ineffective; nor were they asked to change their approach and adopt new operating principles and procedures. They were allowed to continue functioning as usual. The new CAPs simply set up competing agencies with a competing philosophy—and both the CAPs and welfare departments were supported by the public tax dollar.

Since the welfare departments and the CAP programs were both supported by public funds, although at different levels of government, why was there no attempt to abolish one of these programs in favor of the other? If the welfare departments were not amenable to change, why were they not replaced by the new programs? Their nonreplacement may reflect the staying power of institutionalized programs once they have been established. It is difficult to remove from office those with tenure and seniority. It is also difficult to remove from office those with powerful friends within governmental bureaucracies. For some agencies these reasons alone might account for their survival long past their usefulness. However, they are not sufficient to explain the persistence of institutionalized structures in the welfare department example. Unlike school teachers, welfare workers do not have tenure. Furthermore, welfare departments are not particularly powerful organizations—if anything their constituents are among the least powerful citizens. We suspect that one reason the welfare departments were not abolished was because their values were more congruent with community sentiments toward the poor than were the CAP programs. The welfare emphasis on "charity" to the "deserving poor" fit the American ethic of helping the downtrodden. The CAP emphasis on rehabilitating the poor by helping the poor to help themselves (e.g., through community organization, to be discussed in the next chapter) was threatening to the American social fabric and was not accepted as an important value by many people. In the 1970s as federal funds were cut back, it was the CAP programs, not the welfare departments, that felt the major financial crunch. Many states chose not to continue the CAP programs, nor did state welfare departments change to adapt to the CAP philosophy.

There are a number of reasons for the perpetuation of the welfare system and the eclipse of CAP programs.[2] We have focused on only two aspects of the problem. It appears to us that one lesson to be learned is that alternative programs will not be sustained over time by public funds if they do not resonate with community sentiments. Another lesson concerns the peculiar bureaucratic problems that develop when government-sponsored programs are set up as alternatives to other government programs, rather than as a response to citizen petition. Competition among established bureaucracies and the enhancement of personal "empires" are a few of the problems that ensue. They are aggravated by the constraints of outmoded legislation not subject to periodic public review and evaluation. Unfortunately, when the forces of agency enhancement run counter to client needs, the latter may be subjugated; only when agency interest and client need coincide is it most likely that client need will be served.

Alternative schools

The movement toward alternative education was given impetus not only by the reform movement of the 1960s but also by the failure of

---

[2] Problems associated with CAP are analyzed in more detail in Chapter 8.

that movement to effect basic changes in public education. Few school interventionists of the 1960s recognized the complexities involved (Sarason, 1971). Change imposed from the outside, without the active involvement of within-system personnel, was slow in taking hold. Those looking for faster progress condemned the "resistance" of the schools and proceeded to develop alternatives under their own control. As V. H. Smith (1973) a proponent of alternatives in education states:

> The attempts of the 60s were all based on intervention strategies. Someone was attempting to do something to change the schools, that is, to make them better for someone else. In alternative public schools, on the other hand, students, parents, and teachers choose what is best for themselves. There is no intervention, no coercion; only voluntary choice. (Smith, V. H., 1973, p. 437)

Attempts at change from within existing school systems were abandoned by a substantial block of educational reformers who in 1969 met and "invented a movement" (Barr, 1973). But there was little unanimity as to what that movement represented. As with all revolutions, there was greater agreement as to what they all opposed, in this case traditional schools, than there was in deciding upon the essential ingredients of the new alternative education. As Barr points out, what seemed to evolve were two types of schools.

> On the one hand were the predominantly white middle- and upper-class free schools in which the coercion, regimentation, and authoritarian atmosphere of the public schools was replaced with the free learning environment of "do-your-own-thing" pedagogy. The other group of schools, usually poor, black, and inner-city, might better be described as community-control schools. Related historically to the earlier civil-rights freedom schools, these free schools typify the larger struggle of minority groups against racist institutions and have been set up by parents to liberate their children from the "indoctrination and destruction" of the public schools. These community schools are the antithesis of the "classical" free school, usually having a good deal of structure, required classes, and intensive drill in basic skills. (Barr, 1973, p. 455)

At the present time, the diversity in educational alternatives is even more pronounced. Generally, the majority of alternative public schools fit into one or several of the following groupings described by V. H. Smith (1974, pp. 16–17).

> *Open schools:* Learning activities are individualized and organized around interest centers within the classroom or building.

Schools-without-walls: Learning activities are carried on throughout the community and with much interaction between school and community.

Learning centers: Learning resources are concentrated in one location available to all the students in the community. This would include magnet schools, educational parks, career-education centers, vocational and technical high schools, and similar institutions.

Continuation schools: These schools provide for students whose education in the conventional school has been (or might be) interrupted. This would include dropout centers, reentry programs, pregnancy-maternity centers, evening and adult high schools, street academies, and the like.

Multicultural schools: These schools emphasize cultural pluralism and ethnic and racial awareness and usually serve a multicultural student body. Bilingual schools with optional enrollment would be included here.

Free schools: These schools emphasize greater freedom for students and teachers. This term is usually applied to nonpublic alternative schools, but a few are available by choice within public school systems.

Schools-within-schools: A small number of students and teachers are involved by choice in a different kind of learning program. This would include mini-schools and satellite schools. A satellite school is a school at another location which maintains administrative ties to the parent school. The schools-within-schools would usually belong to one or more of the six types described above.

Alternative schools have much in their favor. They are often staffed by the brightest and most dedicated of teachers. Their small size allows them to develop humane student-teacher relationships with fewer rules and bureaucratic constraints for pupils and teachers alike (V. H. Smith, 1973). When the emphasis on voluntary choice can be added, the school also has the advantage of pupil selectivity; only those committed to this form of education need participate.

However, alternative schools are not without their problems. To begin with there is the problem of deciding the content and goals of the educational alternative. Is the alternative to represent different educational goals or a varied approach to the same goals? In other words, should the alternative concern itself with basic skill development and college and vocational preparation—the focus of most traditional schools; or should there be a greater concern for individuality, creativity, and psychological development? Fantini (1973a) concludes with respect to public acceptance of alternative education:

Unless an alternative school can give assurance that the student will be equipped for further learning, will succeed in college, the option is doomed. (Fantini, 1973a, p. 445)

Yet for others, the emphasis on basic skill acquisition and future vocational success robs the alternative school of its unique mission—helping actualize each student as a human being, and allowing the student to take responsibility for his or her own individual learning priorities (DeTurk & Mackin, 1973). For this latter group, alternative education should provide true content alternatives and should not involve merely different and perhaps better ways of doing the same thing.

How the problem is resolved depends in part on whether the alternatives are to be privately financed or are to become part of the public education network in a community. If the latter is the case, we would agree with Fantini (1973a & b) that community sentiments would not allow schools to abandon their traditional roles of knowledge trans-. mission, the development of language and numerical skills, and the transmission of the "intellectual history of civilized man" (M. Smith, 1973).

Fantini goes further and lists the following "ground rules" for legitimizing alternatives within public school systems.

1. The alternative must be made available to students, teachers, and parents by choice. It cannot be superimposed.
2. It cannot claim the capacity to replace existing alternatives like the standard school. Premature claims of superiority, belittling the worth of other alternatives, tend to create a negative political climate. The option being advanced is just that: an option for those students, parents, and teachers who are attracted to it. The existing alternatives are just as legitimate as those being proposed.
3. It must give evidence of being geared to the attainment of a comprehensive set of educational objectives; those for which the public school is accountable and not merely selected ones. Public schools are responsible for intellectual and emotional development. They include development of basic skills such as reading, writing, speaking, and appreciating; learning-to-learn skills such as critical thinking, planning, problem solving; talent and career development; citizenship preparation; a positive feeling of self-worth; and the like.
    An alternative which emphasizes only the intellectual or only the emotional is suspect. For example, if a free school embraces only the educational objective of joy or "ecstasy" (however viable this is), it is doubtful that such an alternative could be legitimized as a public school. The other range of educational objectives must be also

guaranteed to the consumer. If such alternatives were legitimized, it is possible to have a student who is happy while in school but unable to read, write, or otherwise qualify for the economic survival needs of modern society. Public schools cannot shortchange the learner because of the limited nature of the public school alternative he may have chosen. The public must be protected from consumer fraud.

4. It is not designed to promote exclusivity—racial, religious, or socioeconomic. Equal access must be guaranteed.

5. It is not dependent on significant amounts of extra money to implement and does not increase the per-student expenditures beyond those of established options. The idea is to utilize existing resources differently—perhaps more effectively. (Fantini, 1973a, p. 445)

As one examines this list, one begins to realize that while it may be relatively easy to set up an alternative school, it is much more difficult to establish one that meets the above goals. A truly responsive public alternative school may be as difficult to achieve as helping a more traditional school change from within to begin with. And herein lies the dilemma. The ultimate value to society of alternative schools is not that they are successful in rescuing a small minority of students from the "evils" of traditional education. Compared with 50 million children in public schools, the 13,000 free-school students comprise much less than 1 percent of all school-age children (Barr, 1973). If alternative education is to provide any value to society it will be in the extent to which educational reform initiated in alternative schools can be incorporated into more traditional schools. In other words, alternative schools can provide a challenge to traditional education. They can provide a goad for change and a model of how change can take place. But in order to serve this function, collaboration and interchange between the more traditional and the alternative schools need to be developed and nurtured. This is not likely to occur in an atmosphere in which the alternative proponents act superior and isolate themselves from traditional educators, a frequent occurrence in the development of any new setting (Sarason, 1972). Nor is collaboration likely to be fruitful when the traditionalists, resentful of the "rebels," throw obstacles in their paths, or become less interested in the problems that gave rise to the need for an alternative in the first place. In other words, the presence of a new institution, such as an alternative educational program, can weaken or eliminate whatever community tendencies and pressures may have existed to accept responsibility for the original problems. It becomes too easy for a school to say in effect "we don't have to worry any longer about problems that our school is producing, since those who don't fit our program can always be handled in the alternative program." Like the special education classes that resulted from educational reforms of an earlier era, it can become easier to dump children in a special program than to face up to the need for basic educational reevaluation and modification.

Alternatives to the criminal justice and mental health systems

Separate institutions (e.g., free schools) or separate living arrangements (e.g., communes) can be solutions for those with resources; however separation as a way of meeting personal and social needs typically is not available to those without the resources to support the newly created institutions. Those in greatest need are usually those least able to change the institutional constraints impinging on them. What alternatives are available to those without the resources to create and maintain separate institutions? The advocates of the alternative institutions approach suggest helping build more responsive institutions when disenfranchised groups are unable to do so on their own. They are concerned about the possibility of person-blame attributions—that individuals who are unable or who refuse to adjust to malevolent circumstances will be faulted automatically. Their strategy is to help specific disenfranchised groups develop new institutions that would be more responsive to their needs, with the expectation that the institutions so developed would serve as examples of institution building that could be emulated by others.

Prime candidates for the role of disenfranchised social system "casualties" alluded to in the above paragraph are the clients of the mental health and criminal justice systems, the major social institutions set up to deal with those unable or unwilling to conform to the norms of "appropriate" social conduct as defined by the majority culture. The rhetoric of the alternative institutions movement leaves no doubt that it is society and not the individual which is responsible for his or her unfortunate predicament. This is a debate which we need not join to recognize that even if social institutions do not "cause" deviant behavior in the first place, they do contribute to its perpetuation. Prisons do not reduce recidivism rates (Martinson, 1974); nor are prisons rehabilitation-oriented. Shah (1972) reports that 91 percent of the personnel of correctional institutions in this country are concerned with custodial duties and service and maintenance functions. Only 9 percent are involved in education, counseling, or other treatment functions. Rehabilitating the inmate for a return to productive community life has much lower priority than punishment and incarceration.

The picture is similar for mental institutions, although perhaps not as bad. Mental hospitals receive greater support from the community than do prisons, but for these institutions as well, intensive treatment opportunities for patients are the exception rather than the rule. It is still the case that a lengthy stay in a mental hospital does not imply more prolonged or intensive treatment; the longer the period of hospitalization, the less likely it is that the patient will return to normal functioning. The point has been made many times over that mental hospitals provide insufficient training for responsible social living and instead emphasize the "good patient" role. Learning to conform to institutional life is not the same as preparing for independent living, and hospitals do the job of re-integrating the patient back into the community rather poorly.

There have been a number of alternatives developed to both the criminal justice and mental hospital systems. Despite the fact that these institutions serve different populations, the nature of the alternatives seem fairly similar. On the one hand are those that emphasize open community living, skill training, and employment, so that the individual involved makes up whatever deficits may have exacerbated the problem behavior in the first place. Problems are defined in terms of skill deficits (e.g., socialization or educational deficits) that can be remedied with proper training. Other alternatives completely de-emphasize help to the "problem person" and instead provide help to those in the social network where malfunctioning may contribute to the individual's behavior reaching problem proportions. Another possibility is to concentrate on community organization as a way of preventing the buildup of social conditions that foster deviant behavior and emotional breakdown. In other words, criminal behavior and mental breakdown need not be viewed primarily as problems of individuals but may involve community, social network, or family problems as well. Traditional institutions, at least in this country, rarely have the mandate or the flexibility to deal with these more global factors.

Most descriptions of alternative programs are published before the effects of the alternative have been properly assessed. Thus, while descriptions of alternatives are quite numerous, alternatives with demonstrable effects are more difficult to find. However, there are a few documented examples of alternative programs for both the criminal justice and mental health systems and we will use these examples as the basis for our subsequent discussion.

The residential home as an alternative for delinquency rehabilitation. In the criminal justice system, the rehabilitation of delinquents has received the greatest attention from innovators. The potential for rehabilitation is greatest among this young group. Many offenses considered acts of delinquency would not be counted as crimes by standards of adult conduct. The declaration of delinquency by a juvenile court not only implies unacceptable behavior on the part of the perpetrator, but also often means a breakdown of normal socialization and social control functions in the family and/or in the community. The adjudication of delinquency often implies an exhaustion of community resources.

Traditionally, the most frequent disposition of young persons declared delinquent has been institutionalization. Up until recent years, most communities did not have adequate resources to deal with families or youngsters in trouble. The situation improved somewhat with the federal legislation of the late 1960s. Money became available to deal with social problems in the name of delinquency and crime prevention, and various alternatives were investigated.

A most popular alternative was the residential home in the community, and indeed one state (Massachusetts) closed its institutions for juvenile offenders in favor of this alternative. The evidence evaluating this large-scale social experiment is not yet in, but some of the research on residential alternatives is now available for inspection (Ohlin, Coates & Miller, 1974).

Goldenberg (1971a) presents a detailed and well-documented description of the development of one such residential alternative in New Haven, Connecticut. The Residential Youth Center (RYC) which opened its doors in New Haven in 1966, and which was funded as an experimental demonstration project by the U.S. Department of Labor, had as some of the primary goals, the following:

> To evaluate the degree to which a neighborhood-based Residential Youth Center, developed within a manpower-oriented Community Action Program, could be utilized to facilitate the growth and rehabilitation of economically disadvantaged and/or disrupted adolescents and their families.
> To explore the clinical and vocational potential of an indigenous non-

professional staff with respect to their competence in dealing with both the psychological problems associated with poverty and a population heretofore dealt with exclusively by professional personnel. (Goldenberg, 1971a, pp. 3-4)

The Residential Youth Center described by Goldenberg was part of the massive "War on Poverty" of the late 1960s, but conceptually it was a reaction against some of the programs generated by that same federal thrust. Specifically, Goldenberg's group objected to practices of the Job Corps in which inner-city, disadvantaged minority group youth were removed to isolated rural camps, often run by staff who did not understand the problems or life-style of their trainees, and who provided training in skills often inappropriate to urban settings.

The Residential Youth Center in New Haven opened its doors to 20 urban youngsters with a full-time staff of 9, plus 6 part-time psychology student volunteers. This first group of RYC residents came from disrupted and disorganized families with long histories of unsuccessful contacts with social service agencies. Most of the families were on welfare; and all of the boys were high school dropouts, with previous records of involvement with the law. Many were failing in a job training program run by the local community action agency. During its first year of operation, the RYC dealt with 50 such youngsters and their families, with each resident and his family being assigned to a particular worker. The worker's job was to get to know his youngsters and their families and to use himself "as a therapeutic lever in their lives" (Goldenberg, 1971a, p. 150). Both the clients and the paraprofessional staff were expected to benefit from and grow psychologically as a result of their contact. The RYC was committed to the establishment of such a growth-enhancing setting while at the same time also being concerned with more formal signs of client achievement (successful employment or participation in employment training; reduction in legal offenses; helping a youngster return home or establish himself successfully in his own apartment, etc.). The program emphasized a "horizontal structure" of shared decision making involving both staff and residents, and a modified form of sensitivity training as the manner of dealing with all problems and conflicts. Close contact between workers, youngsters, and their families preceded official entry into residence and continued throughout the course of the program.

The research comparisons testing the effectiveness of the program compared the first group of 20 youth with a comparable control sample. An original sample of 50 boys were nominated by community agencies and police as their most difficult to reach "hard-core" cases. This list of "50 Most Difficult" was then ranked by members of these same agencies, and after matching for age and race, the 25 "most difficult" were placed in the RYC program while the 25 "next most difficult" were assigned to the control group.[3]

Except for one variable (work attendance) there were no significant statistical differences between experimental and control groups on any of the attitudinal or behavioral measures administered before the program began. In the case of work attendance, the control group was initially superior, attending work 86 percent of the time, compared to the work attendance record of 65 percent for the RYC-bound group. After 36 weeks of treatment, attendance records were clearly reversed. RYC youth attended work 97 percent of the time while work attendance for the control group was 56 percent. The difficulty in interpreting the data for this measure was that changes in work attendance were already occurring at the time of the initial selection of subjects, so that during the 12-week period when youngsters were being prepared for RYC residence, after selection but before official residence, significant changes in work attendance were already occurring for both groups. Contact with program personnel alone, without residence at RYC seems to have produced the most significant impact.

The drop in work attendance rates for the control group as well as their increasingly poorer scores over time on other behavioral and community adjustment measures is cause for concern. It is unclear whether their deteriorating adjustment truly reflects what would have represented a normal course of events for them. It may reflect an exacerbation of their condition—an increase in anger and/or hopelessness as a result of not being picked for this widely publicized program.

At any rate, the RYC youngsters did improve substantially. They stayed on the job longer, earned more money, got into less trouble with the law and showed some positive change in attitude both compared with the control group and compared with their own behavior before initial contact with the program. What factors produced the changes in the boys is extremely difficult to determine although the relationship between the boy and his worker is one definite possibility since changes were already evident after contact with the worker had been established, but before residence in the RYC house had begun.

---

[3] Note that while this procedure did not represent random assignment, it could have accommodated a regression-discontinuity analysis (Campbell, 1969).

A dilemma: Clinical success but modest community impact. Until now we have been discussing the clinical success of the RYC program—that is, its rehabilitative potential in intervening in the lives of boys already found to be "most difficult." The RYC was involved in the treatment and rehabilitation of known, hard-core cases, by innovative and particularly humane and responsive procedures. However, the staff of RYC also was concerned with institutional change. There was an implicit hope in the program's establishment that its success could serve as a model for other youth-serving agencies. Indeed, such may be its greatest eventual success at the national level. The RYC model has applicability not only as a treatment setting but suggests the kinds of personnel, relationships, and programs that might be attempted in community agencies with more primary care-giving functions. However in the local New Haven area, the RYC only made a limited impact in this direction. For example, the relationship between RYC staff and the schools steadily improved as RYC personnel visited the schools and participated in conferences concerning their youngsters. After some time, the schools turned to the RYC for help with special problems of their own. Assistance was requested during a period of racial disruption in the schools and then again help was requested with a project to improve the education of inner-city retarded youngsters. However, the schools were the only community institution in New Haven to respond so favorably. The impact of the RYC on other institutions (police, mental health, and social service agencies) was much more limited and was restricted to individual workers within these agencies who came into contact with RYC staff and who already were receptive to RYC philosophy and procedures.

It should be pointed out that affecting community agencies was only a tangential goal of the RYC founders. For them, the mission of creating an innovative setting was the primary concern. In the spirit of true believers they were unwilling to compromise these goals, and at times acted out in anger when their philosophy was challenged (Goldenberg, 1971a, pp. 248–251). Lack of agency change not only represented intransigent attitudes within those agencies, but uncompromising idealism among the RYC reformers as well.

The difficulty of maintaining innovation. Goldenberg's book follows the RYC for two years after its establishment. Most of the initial staff had gone on to other opportunities, and the new staff had the job of institution maintainance. The "bitter-sweet job of initial revolution was a thing of the past" (Goldenberg 1971a, p. 439), and the new staff inherited programs and concepts that were not of their making. As Goldenberg notes:

> For most of the Center's original staff, the RYC was indeed a "love affair," an undertaking which, for all its moments of panic and uncertainty, possessed the binding qualities of a revolution. We were (or at least felt ourselves to be) a little band of rebels, scornful of tradition and duly unimpressed by the accomplishments of those who had preceded us—a group of missionaries committed to the creation of a very personal and earthbound utopia. For us, such things as sensitivity training and horizontal structure were far more than concepts: they were adventures, attempts by a "special" group of people to develop new and different patterns of relating to one another and to an organization. For those who followed us, on the other hand, there could be no immediate or self-evident identity between the setting's underlying assumptions and their own experiences. For them, concepts like horizontality and sensitivity training were just that—concepts, theoretical formulations that sounded good but had no firm foundation in a shared and mutually understandable past. Having been unable to be a part of the RYC's history, they entered the setting not as its creators but as its perpetuators, not as its founders but as its heirs. Theirs would be a far more difficult task than ours ever was, for it was a situation in which fervor would have to be replaced by more formal training. (Goldenberg, 1971a, pp. 440–441)

The RYC had arrived at the point that faces all new settings—how to maintain the unique spirit of the project so that it does not drift into a routinized pattern of processing and store-housing humanity. Only time will tell whether the RYC is capable of escaping this all-too-common fate.

A community alternative for mental patients. Projects such as the group home described by Goldenberg have become popular alternatives to traditional institutionalization. Their advocacy is not restricted to delinquent or criminal populations. Whenever society has acted to protect itself from deviant members by declaring them unfit to live as free citizens in the community, the evils of institutionalization have been noted, and supervised group living in the community has been championed as a more humane and rehabilitative alternative. But in each case, public acceptance of the alternative arrangement depends less upon its rehabilitative success and more upon how well it protects the interests and safety of the community. To be accepted as a viable alternative, the threat originally posed by the deviant members, which resulted in institutionalization in the first place, must be lessened by any alternative arrangement that moves the individuals involved back into the community.

Such was the primary problem faced by Fairweather and his associates as they developed a program to bring hospitalized chronic schizophrenics back into ongoing community life. At first glance, it would appear that the problems involved in helping schizophrenic individuals achieve a community living arrangement are vastly different than those encountered in working with delinquents, but, as we shall see, despite the differences in program associated with the form of behavior involved, important similarities also exist. The problems involved are those in which deviant or marginal people attempt a community adjustment—thus forcing the larger community to deal more actively with their differences.

Fairweather's first project involved the development of a milieu therapy program on the ward of a mental hospital. In his small-group ward treatment program, patients lived in small, self-governing group units. Members were required to take care of one another and make realistic decisions about their own lives and those of other group members. They could not rely on the staff to make such decisions for them as would be the case on a more traditional mental hospital ward. Treatment staff in this experiment were expressly prohibited from doing so. Patients were expected to develop their own leaders, make sure that they and their fellow group members participated in work activities, and handle ward privileges appropriately. The entire group was rewarded for the constructive behavior of its members while rewards and privileges were withheld if appropriate member behavior was not forthcoming. Thus, the special program depended upon two main factors: increased group interaction with group norms established for cooperation and responsibility; and the encouragement of prosocial behavior and group interaction through social and monetary reinforcement. The usual effects of mental hospital living, namely dependency on staff and hospital routine, squelching of initiative, and the reinforcement of bizarre and pathological behavior were clearly discouraged in this program.

The results of the 1964 study indicate that the small-group treatment milieu had a significant impact on patient activity in the hospital. Compared with a control group who received a traditional mental hospital routine, the treatment group displayed heightened social activity in the hospital, higher morale, greater personal involvement in the adjustment of other members of their group and higher expectations for the future. The active participation of even the most chronic patients was impressive (Fairweather, 1964, p. 283). The morale of the staff also improved as they became adjusted to a routine in which they were no longer responsible for housekeeping and ward maintenance duties, and now could function as patient counselors, supervisors, and helpers.

Despite the improved functioning in the hospital, the community adjustment of the patients upon discharge continued to be a problem, although some positive effects of the program could still be found. The main problem was that of recidivism. The treatment group did not remain out of the hospital for a significantly longer period of time than did the control group. Those least able to sustain an adequate community adjustment were the chronic psychotics and the alcoholic nonpsychotics. Those with a good community adjustment were the acute psychotics who maintained a fairly good employment record and were involved in minimal problem drinking. In terms of community adjustment then, a formal diagnosis of psychosis was not particularly relevant. Both the chronic psychotics and the alcoholic nonpsychotic patients could be seen as "marginal men" (Fairweather et al., 1969) whose life-styles and methods of coping with stress have put them on the fringes of society. Buoyed up by peer group support available in the small-group ward treatment program, both of these groups became more socially responsive. With that support gone upon discharge from the hospital, both groups reverted to their prior inadequate levels of functioning and were returned to the hospital. Would taking the small-group program into the community as an alternative living arrangement for the former patients provide the needed social support to effect successful community living? This was the problem addressed by Fairweather's next large-scale project (Fairweather et al., 1969).

A community lodge for mental patients. Establishing an alternative community living arrangement for persons who would otherwise be institutionalized is not an easy task. Its most important elements involve the establishment of a social subsystem that is more tolerant of deviance than the community-at-large, while at the same time serving as a protective buffer between the community and the deviant member. Fairweather describes the essential characteristics of the new social subsystem in the following way:

> It must provide alternative nondeviant social roles in the community to the chronic patient; it must maintain sufficient social distance from the community's agents of social control so that regulation of behavior takes place within the framework of the subsociety itself; it must protect him from hostile community forces and from power confrontations which he

must inevitably lose, further destroying his confidence and self-esteem; it must reduce the visibility of the chronic deviant's rule-breaking behavior and attempt to regulate it within the normative framework of a cohesive subcommunity; it must assume control over the degree and amount of rule-breaking the subcommunity can tolerate. In general, this newly created social system must be organized in such a way that the largely ascribed social status of the chronic mental patient is displaced by an achieved social status within his own subcommunity which would depend on the individual's residual capabilities rather than on the characteristics of his psychological impairment. (Fairweather et al., 1969, p. 21)

It should be noted that many of the goals of Fairweather's community unit for chronic mental patients are not that different from what might be the goals of other residential units serving other special subpopulations. For example, a list of the necessary characteristics for a residential program serving delinquent youth might involve similar functions. Providing an opportunity for constructive social roles, the enhancement of self-esteem based on achievement, regulating social rule-breaking by decreasing its incidence or its visibility, would be necessary ingredients in any such alternative social subsystem. However, it is important to recognize the extent to which Fairweather emphasizes the need for protection of members of his subcommunity. This strong emphasis on protection "from hostile community forces and from power confrontations which he must inevitably lose" might be more a function of the special population of socially inadequate men served by this home for chronic mental patients.

The main question of interest addressed by Fairweather's project concerns the extent to which chronic mental patients who would otherwise be institutionalized are capable of productive lives in the community. It was not just a matter of discharging patients from the hospital, but the question was how to make a community adjustment "stick." Simple release from the hospital was not the answer. By 1961, it was already recognized that the movement toward high release rates and shortened hospital stays had also seen rising relapse and readmission rates (Fairweather et al., 1969, p. 13). In establishing his alternative program, Fairweather clearly understood what some seem to have forgotten in the more recent rush to empty mental hospitals. Those who have been unable to adjust to normal social living are not adequately served by returning them to similar situations, when there have not been significant changes in the patients or in the circumstances that impinge upon them. In designing an alternative living arrangement, Fairweather did not attempt to change environmental pressures in society at large, but unlike some classical therapeutic approaches that completely ignore malevolent environmental factors, he did attempt to reduce their impact in his target patients by interposing a supportive social subsystem.

The study reported in 1969 involved taking patients from the small-group ward program who volunteered for the new community program and assigning them either to the "community lodge" or to more traditional community after-care. The community-lodge society began with 15 chronic mental patients. Over the period of its existence from late 1963 to mid 1966, some 75 persons had been members of the lodge for varying periods of time with an equal number of non-lodge controls. Even in the protected environment of the lodge, adjustment was difficult for some of the patients. For example, three of the original 15 members did not survive the first week at the lodge, and were returned to the less demanding routine of the hospital.

The lodge developed its own business, a janitorial service that was first supervised by a member of the resident staff and then later by one of the ex-patient members. Some members could not adjust to a community work situation, even one that was closely supervised and fairly tolerant of differences in work rates and behavioral styles. In general, the patients were accepting of eccentric behavior within their midst but were not tolerant of those who were unable or unwilling to share in the work and in the management of the house. For the most part, patients did have successful employment records while at the lodge, indicating that in an appropriate setting, chronic mental patients could remain productively occupied in the community.

This experiment demonstrated that psychotic patients could live in the community if placed in a protected environment. When group members left the lodge however, their employment and adjustment record resembled that of the control group. That is, there was a greater likelihood for them to become unemployed, with eventual return to a hospital or institutional setting a strong possibility. The lodge provided the patients with an opportunity to participate in useful social roles in society with no danger to the larger community whatsoever. But they could not sustain these roles or attain independent community living without the interposition of the supportive social subsystem found at the lodge.

The argument for greater community tolerance of marginality

The Fairweather research raises the issue of how a community should deal with its marginal citizens who have chronic personal handicaps. The present solution seems to involve avoiding differences and ignoring handicaps as long as possible, expecting full community adjustment and participation from all. When the limits of social convention are finally breached, society no longer remains tolerant and ejects the clearly deviant member. Fairweather argues, as do others (Braginsky, Braginsky, & Ring, 1969) that other alternatives are needed. They argue that there should be a greater tolerance of differences and that means should be found to allow every person to contribute to community life regardless of how limited that contribution might initially seem. Such participation from marginal citizens could eventuate in an enrichment of society from which all could benefit. Creating alternative institutions could sanction alternative coping styles, could reduce the negative effects of psychiatric labeling and "patienthood" (Levinson & Gallagher, 1964), and could allow participation in community life from those now on the fringes of society.

Difficulties involved in gaining professional acceptance

Despite the clarity of the findings that psychotics could live more useful lives in the community with less of an economic strain on society, alternative community care facilities for mental patients have been developing very slowly. Demonstrating the potential success of a new program is not the same as changing established patterns of professional practice. For example, the hospital from which all the patients for the Fairweather study came, did not incorporate the new program as part of its own ongoing treatment programming. Prior to the termination of grant support, other federal, state, and county mental health agencies were contacted as well, with similar results. None were willing to support the continuation of the program despite their agreement in principle about the need for community treatment programs. Fairweather lists the following reasons agencies gave for their nonsupport:

    [1]   They would need additional funds for such a new program (despite the cost reduction shown in the results);

[2]   Such a unique program would not fit into the agency's practices;

[3]   Professional staffs would not accept a program which would allow more autonomy for mental patients, since granting such autonomy would require unwelcome changes in professional roles. (Fairweather et al., 1969, p. 101)[4]

Both the Goldenberg and Fairweather projects found less difficulty in gaining acceptance from community members than from human service professionals. Both projects were able to gain community sanction for returning extruded or about-to-be-extruded deviants back into their midst. In locating the residences, the experimenters had to deal with citizen fear for the safety of their families if known delinquents or mental patients were allowed to live in their neighborhoods. This problem was solved either by ensuring adequate police surveillance and protection and/or by placing the alternative home in a "less desirable" neighborhood so that the members of the home would be more desirable than the former occupants of the same premises. For example, Fairweather's lodge had been a former motel with an attached bar. The neighbors viewed the quiet ex-mental patients, who kept up the property, as more desirable residents than the previous "high living" occupants.

While both programs were able to overcome initial public apprehension, were successfully launched, and were capable of demonstrating some moderate degree of success in improving community adjustment, neither program was successful in gaining the acceptance of mental health or social service professionals in their home communities. Both programs were based on sound ideas, but the soundness of the projects did not guarantee their continued implementation. The agencies involved were unable to "shift gears" to accommodate the new programs. Their professional practices were unusually fixed by bureaucratic regulation, by restriction in training among their staff, and by accompanying defensiveness, so that on all these grounds the new program appeared completely foreign to agency personnel. What makes this problem a dilemma of major proportions is that the responsibility and discretion given to mental health, education, and social service professionals is usually so complete that inflexibility on their part can essentially doom innovation. The mental health professions have total responsibility for the care of those called mentally

---

[4] See Fairweather, Sanders, and Tornatzky (1974) for an extended discussion of the favorable conditions and organizational characteristics associated with willingness to adopt a community lodge program.

ill; the schools have total responsibility for all facets of education; while the judiciary exercises similar control of programs for delinquents and criminals. For the most part the community has abdicated its concern in these areas to the social institutions, and has usually invested in these institutions what sometimes can amount to total power over the lives of clients. Few citizens consider the fallibility or limitations of the personnel and practices of such institutions unless they are touched directly by services from them.

Implications for change

Once again we have returned to the problem of institutional change and how to achieve it. Those who develop alternative programs and parallel institutions, in publishing their results, are in effect saying to the community at large "look at us; don't you see that our approach is more effective in dealing with these problems." Yet, unless the community is aroused and convinced that existing programs are completely inadequate, such pleas usually fall on deaf ears; or are referred to existing social institutions for implementation—the very institutions that are threatened by the success of the alternative programs. In the ensuing competition for financial support, unless the alternative program has a vocal, aroused, or politically powerful constituency, it will usually lose. As Graziano (1969) has pointed out, the *implementation* of innovative ideas in mental health does not depend upon "science," or scientific documentation, but upon a broad spectrum of professional and social politics.

One route to gaining community acceptance of an alternative program is by gaining a constituency of followers. However, "selling" a project is a difficult and time-consuming endeavor, and one that some innovators shy away from for reasons of temperament. A successful innovator and "professional revolutionary" is not always personally equipped to gain converts and followers beyond the circle of immediate associates. The innovator sometimes mistakenly adopts the pose that others should see the "rightness" of the innovation as clearly as he or she does, and may be offended by the suggestion that the ideas must be "sold." Yet, establishing a powerful constituency remains an important tool for the implementation of innovation.

A second route for the establishment of an innovation is through consultation with and education of those within social institutions that have responsibilities in the areas in question. It is not the case that institutional inflexibility must remain so. The possibility exists for reducing defensiveness, overcoming deficiencies in training, and changing bureaucratic rules so that innovation and change can be adopted and become the new standard operating procedure. But here again we find that innovators of new programs often are extremely pessimistic about changing others whom they see as the "enemy" and the "entrenched bureaucracy". A basic incompatibility is seen between institutional self-interest and scientific or humanitarian integrity. For example, this point of view can be seen in the following remarks:

> . . . progress will not be initiated by or through the power structure, but will depend upon successfully changing or ignoring that structure. It does not seem possible at this point to join the structure and still maintain the integrity of both areas, that is, the essentially political power structure, and the humanitarian and scientific ideals. The two areas are incompatible; science and humanitarianism cannot be achieved through the present self-perpetuating focus of the power structure. (Graziano, 1969, p. 17)

Effecting change is difficult, no matter what the route, whether by developing a constituency that supports the new program as an independent entity, or by changing existing social institutions so that the new program becomes part of already established ongoing procedures. At this point it seems unwise to foreclose one route in favor of the other without more careful consideration of the factors facilitating the process of change.

Assumptions of the alternatives perspective

1. Social institutions can contribute to the general malaise in community life. When clients have choice among several alternatives, accountability and responsivity should increase.

Social institutions were developed to serve the needs of the majority, and in carrying out their mission, they sometimes do so at the expense of certain subgroups. If minority subgroups pose a threat to the majority, social institutions often are expected to reduce that threat. A primary interest of the majority is in upholding social order and maintaining social equilibrium. Thus, in reducing minority threat, social institutions are expected to give higher priority to reducing pressures for change than to responding to legitimate grievances.

Social institutions can be unresponsive to client needs for other reasons as well. Bureaucratic regulation, the forces operating within institutions for institutional maintenance and agency survival, and the pressure for professional enhancement and job security all can serve as barriers to social change and responsivity to client need.

From the alternatives perspective, working for social change from within social institutions will be futile. Attempts to generate change from within, most likely, would meet formidable opposition. Even if an innovator's ideas were ostensibly accepted, encouragement might be used only to give a public semblance of progressiveness, while in reality innovation had been subtly but surely nullified. As one advocate of the alternatives approach has charged, a motto for many social institutions might well be "innovation without change!" (Graziano, 1969)

2.   Alternative institutions provide the best vehicle for maximizing person-environment fit.

Given a community of heterogeneous citizens, why should it be expected that all can fit the same mold of social life? Since there already exists a great diversity of behavior, would it not be more humane and less grief-producing to fashion social institutions to accommodate to this diversity? It is extremely difficult to change established social institutions. Rather than embarking on what might be a futile effort—the creation of institutions that are responsive to *all* segments of a heterogeneous community—it might be more effective in the long run to allow the development of alternative institutions to meet the needs of specialized groups. Alternative institutions have the double advantage of neither requiring individuals to change to meet social demands to "fit in," nor requiring social institutions to change to meet specialized minority needs. Alternative institutions and alternative living arrangements by maximizing person-environment fit, allow the greatest diversity in social life with the least amount of strain.

Critical comments

Problems in maintaining the innovative character of a new program

In order to survive, reforms need to be nurtured. It is a mistake to assume that the successful launching of an innovative program is all that is necessary to insure that reform will take place. The same factors operating to maintain the unresponsivity of existing institutions can overtake new ones as well. Sustaining the purpose and enthusiasm of a new program during counter-swings in the political and social climate of the country; the difficulties involved as institutional functions become established and routinized; and maintaining a free, innovative climate as the original, spirited founders of the program are replaced by less dedicated workers—are all problems that alternative programs must eventually face.

Again, history provides us with examples of these problems as reformers of a previous era attempted to build institutions responsive to the needs of the relatively disenfranchised and powerless (Levine & Levine, 1970). For example, during the first quarter of the 20th century, the target population for the efforts of reformers were the large numbers of foreign immigrants who had settled in the major industrial cities and who were meeting with difficulty in becoming assimilated into the work force and social fabric of the country. The major social institutions of the day were not prepared to handle the large numbers of non–English-speaking, destitute families. The city public schools, for the most part, were unprepared for the large influx of children that immigration and the newly enacted compulsory school attendance laws thrust upon them. Over the years 1890–1920 the public school population increased by 70 percent, overwhelming schools that had made no provision for handling difficult children with special educational problems, compounded by poverty and differences in cultural background. Parallel forms of education were created within the formal educational structure (special education classes) and in outside organizations (settlement houses) and new careers developed by dedicated volunteers were the forerunners of new helping professions.

The first volunteer social workers of the 20th century were upper-class, college-educated women who were active social reformers. Similarly, the early settlement-house workers, visiting nurses, and probation workers also were drawn from the ranks of the young, liberal elite. However, as these fields grew, the early pioneers and "fiery radicals" (Levine & Levine, 1970, p. 251) were supplemented by those of lower socioeconomic status, who saw the new professions as an opportunity to gain economic advantage and upward social mobility. These latter groups proved less willing to jeopardize their own positions by challenging social institutions and championing social reform. By the 1920s, not only were the early social reformers displaced by more timid followers, but as the entire country moved toward a more conservative political stance, social institutions drifted toward more individually oriented, conservative forms of treatment. In agencies and clinics originally established to prevent delinquency and emotional disorders in the young, the intra-psychic orientation of psychoanalysis displaced the socially oriented perspective of the reformers. The potential for social change of the new helping professions, the clinics, and settlement houses became subverted by the change in treatment emphasis toward the better adjusted, more responsive clients of the middle and upper classes.

Sarason points out that those who create new settings "are usually 'action people' in whom the historical sense is weak or nonexistent" (Sarason, 1972, p. 37). This is especially true when it comes to problems of organization development and maintenance. Even if dimly aware of past innovations, reformers rarely concern themselves with the study of why these previous reforms from the past were not successfully maintained. Sarason gives a personal example from his own experience as follows:

> Long before I started the Yale Psycho-Educational Clinic I was aware that the first clinic in this country was started in 1896 by Professor Lightner Witmer in the department of psychology of the University of Pennsylvania. I always considered him one of the really great pioneers in the mental health field, albeit largely unrecognized today as such by others. . . . When I started the Yale clinic I very consciously identified myself as in the Witmer tradition, professionally and personally. He was one of my heroes and I wanted to be like him. The very name of our clinic as well as its emphasis reflected this identification. However, it never dawned on me to try to find out how and why his clinic was organized the way it was, the problems he encountered by virtue of being in an academic department, how he and those around him "lived together" and maintained themselves intellectually and financially, and what contributed (and when) to its decline and Witmer's role in this. (Sarason, 1972, pp. 35–36)

The need for mechanisms for problem resolution

It is a mistake to assume that a point will be reached in a new setting when all major problems will have been solved, all major goals achieved, and a conflict-free future assured. Agreement on basic values and goals and a strong motivation to succeed are important characteristics for those involved in innovation, but they are not sufficient conditions for the maintenance of a new setting even when power has finally been achieved and the new setting comes into existence. Without built-in provisions for problem resolution, what has been accomplished can slowly fragment and disintegrate. For example, what brings members together and attracts them to work for the development of a new setting is their disappointment in previous settings, not necessarily their ability to get along. Each assumes that the new setting will allow him to "do his thing" (Sarason, 1972, p. 79). Yet this individualism may be exactly what prevented members from getting along in the previous setting and may provide the seeds for later conflict and disruption. What are needed are mechanisms for conflict resolution and problem solving that do not destroy innovation and individuality. Conditions should exist within settings that allow members to experience change, growth, and diversity, in a setting where conflict can be resolved constructively. It is these very constructive maintenance procedures that cannot be ignored and must be built into innovative settings if they are to survive.

Dedication is no substitute for skill

In its early stages, the excitement surrounding the establishment of an innovative setting is a sufficiently attractive magnet to draw a highly motivated and dedicated staff. The new setting is viewed as somehow different from and superior to those that preceded it and a sense of unique mission and enthusiasm is generated (Sarason, 1972). In this initial period, those who share the common vision of a glorious future are eagerly welcomed, with little thought given to the details of how the vision will be implemented or whether the original core group has within it persons with the necessary skills for successful implementation. But once the new setting becomes reality, it also becomes responsible for the success of its program and moves from the role of critic to that of implementor. Skills are now required to build effective programs; ideology, commitment, and dedication are not enough. For example, in an educational setting, children will still need to acquire reading and arithmetic skills; in a new community agency in a poverty area, effective programs for the unemployed will still be required. Miller and Riessman (1968) make a similar point in describing the dilemmas of the Community Action Programs which suddenly found themselves with easy access to federal funding and with a power base in poor communities. Noting that "power without program can lead to little material improvement in people's lives," the authors point out the need for trained professionals as program consultants. The ideal is to find a way of using professional assistance while retaining control of the program in the hands of consumer-citizens. The authors describe their position as follows:

> The involvement of the poor is no panacea for the ills and difficulties of the social-service world. Nor is this participation a substitute for trained, professional competence as some seem to imply. Effective involvement of the poor requires effective professionals rather than the withdrawal of all professionals. But the relations of the professional will change when he defines the service users as consumers and citizens rather than as "clients." Consumers and citizens have choices and rights, visible preferences, and access to redress. There are strong tensions in this change, but we believe that this tension offers creative possibilities for the professional in his ability to make contact with those he seeks to help, and to shape agency activities so that they are more relevant to need and style. (Miller & Riessman, 1968, pp. 201–202)*

The setting that has managed to acquire dedicated staff with the necessary programmatic skills is indeed fortunate; the setting that manages to maintain the morale of its skilled and dedicated workers so that they don't drift away when the going gets rough, is blessed.

Financial strain and community avoidance of responsibility can be fostered by alternative facilities

Alternative programs compete for community dollars with ongoing programs whose services they parallel but do not replace. It is a myth to assume that community resources are unlimited (Sarason, 1972) and are capable of indefinitely supporting duplicate programs. As a matter of fact, when such overlapping programs are being simultaneously maintained, one should immediately question who is gaining the most from this arrangement.

Is it the local real estate and building contractors who profit from the proliferation of new buildings, an unfortunately frequent correlate to the establishment of new programs? Sarason refers to buildings as program "distractions" and notes that:

> in the area of human service putting up new buildings tends to perpetuate the problem of limited resources, contributes to the inadequate services they ordinarily provide, and separates the setting from the larger society. (Sarason, 1972, p. 100)

Does the benefit provided by the new program accrue to the pro-

---

* Excerpted from *Social class and social policy* by S. M. Miller and Frank Riessman, © 1968 by Basic Books, Inc., Publishers, New York.

gram staff, for whom a program of their own represents a seemingly unlimited opportunity for innovation without the "hassle" of accommodating to existing institutions and agencies? The new setting, by its very recency and isolation appears to provide an opportunity for escape from intra-agency conflict.

Perhaps the most serious problem generated by the creation of a new setting is its tendency to absolve the community of its continuing responsibility for the problems that were instrumental in the formation of the setting in the first place. Sarason states the issue as follows:

> The presence of a new institution in the community facilitates the unfortunate process whereby the community looks to the institution as the place to which all relevant problems are or should be sent, thereby weakening or eliminating whatever community tendencies may have existed to accept responsibility for these problems. (Sarason, 1972, p. 169)

By ignoring its own contribution to the problem, the community often does nothing toward its alleviation. The problem continues in force, ensuring that the new institution will never adequately resolve it. For example, it has always been the case that building new mental hospitals and clinics does not reduce the need for similar facilities a few years hence as the original programs become filled and develop waiting lists. The community has a new place to send its problem cases and does not have to examine how it may be contributing to the production of new "cases." In a similar fashion, alternative schools can delude a community into thinking that educational reform is not needed in its regular schools; while the construction of special live-in facilities for the retarded tends to reduce to zero the willingness of parents and other social agencies to share responsibility for the ongoing care and programming needs of this group (Sarason, 1972).

Factors associated with the potential contribution of alternatives

Who then benefits from the creation of a new alternative institution: the business interests of a community; the staff of the new facility; or the community that is deluded into thinking that all its problems will be solved by the new setting? In a sense all benefit to some degree as settings proliferate. Communities vie for new institutions as they would for new industry; new institutions are "good for the economy." But what about the client populations to be served by the new settings; are their interests served by the proliferation of alternative institutions? Here the answer must be more qualified. It depends on several factors: how responsive the new institution is to its clients; the extent to which the setting provides a better person-environment fit than those institutions that it replaces; the programmatic innovations presented by the new institution; and finally, but perhaps most important of all, its staying power as an innovative setting. This last point refers not just to the physical perpetuation of the setting over time, but to the staying power of its innovative character. Considering the cost of maintaining duplicate structures, we also would count an alternative program as successful if its innovative features were taken over by existing institutions, though the alternative ceased operation as a separate facility.

The New Careers movement as an alternative to existing institutional arrangements

The shortage of mental health personnel and the inability of professional schools to meet mental health manpower needs were some of the factors that gave rise to the interest in community care. The shortage of trained personnel was noticed first in mental hospitals, where it became clear that except for medication, few opportunities for therapeutic contact were made available to the overwhelming majority of patients. The first attempts to come to grips with this problem did not attempt to challenge the appropriateness of the primary mode of care delivery, namely, psychotherapy. Instead, inadequacies of clinical service were addressed in simple manpower terms. If clinical practice was not reaching all who could benefit from it, a new source of manpower was needed.

Clinical manpower: Housewives and students

The generally acknowledged hallmark research was that of Margaret Rioch in training mature housewives as mental health counselors (Rioch, 1967). Training began in 1960 and involved a total of 16 women, who were participants in two separate projects. A group of eight were trained to function as traditional therapists working with by-and-large middle-class patients. A second group of eight were trained to counsel lower-class mothers in child care practices. This second project was preventive in orientation in that it was hoped that if emotional problems could be nipped in the bud of infancy or early childhood, more severe disturbance could be avoided later.

The evaluation of the first project indicated that mental health counselors with the equivalent of one year of full-time training could do their jobs as psychotherapists quite well (Magoon, Golann, and Freeman, 1969). Counseling lower-class mothers in child care proved to be the more difficult of the two tasks in that the problems faced by the mothers were often adjustment problems exacerbated by real, socioeconomic complications such as lack of housing, employment, or education. Still, the physicians in charge of the clinics were unanimous in their positive evaluation of the services that the second group of trainees provided, and all indicated a desire for the trainees to continue on a full-time basis.

Mature women who choose not to work initially but whose primary child care responsibilities diminish as their own children spend the good share of the day at school, are a largely untapped source of mental health manpower. However, the more frequent attempts at increasing mental health manpower have involved the training and utilization of college students (Goodman, 1972; Holzberg, Knapp, & Turner, 1967; Poser, 1966; Rappaport, Chinsky, & Cowen, 1971; Sanders, 1967). Not that the skill of a young college student is greater than that of a mature housewife. Quite the contrary, there is suggestive evidence that, particularly in child care settings, older women who have themselves been mothers can provide more empathic service and are seen by agency staff as more reliable workers (Cowen, 1968; Cowen, Dorr, Trost, & Izzo, 1972). The preference for college student mental health workers may simply reflect their greater accessibility to university-based researchers, and their greater willingness to serve enthusiastically without pay.

A frequently quoted study using college student mental health volunteers is that of Poser (1966), who compared the therapeutic potential of untrained female undergraduates with that of professional therapists. The patients were all hospitalized, male, chronic schizophrenics who were seen in group sessions by either trained or untrained therapists. Sessions were conducted in whatever manner therapists chose. Some therapists used only verbal communication during therapy; others arranged group activities that included party games, dancing, painting, and public speaking.

The results of this experiment revealed that patients treated by the college student therapists did better on the test battery than those treated by professional therapists. The improved performance was not seen in terms of their hospital adjustment, nor in terms of discharge rates from the hospital, but was demonstrated on tests of psychomotor speed and verbal fluency. In other words, the patients who were being seen by the college students became more alert and responsive.

Rappaport, Chinsky, and Cowen (1971) confirmed the results of the Poser study in finding that a female student leader and male chronic patient was the best combination for improving patient motivation and responsiveness; but also like the Poser study differences in discharge rates from the hospital were not found. The most effective ingredient provided by the student volunteers was probably patient re-motivation. Supporting this view was the finding that those chronic patients who were initially more poorly adjusted, maintained the most interest in the program and showed the greatest gains.

College student volunteers as a source of mental health manpower have not been restricted to work with chronic hospitalized mental patients. College students as mental health aides have been used in elementary school settings (Cowen, Zax, & Laird, 1966); as companions for emotionally disturbed school-age children (Goodman, 1972); as client-centered play therapists for children referred by child guidance and psychological clinics (Stollak, 1969); and as behavior therapists for hospitalized emotionally disturbed children (Kreitzer, 1969). Other roles for college student nonprofessionals have been described by Gruver (1971) and by Zax and Specter (1974).

Critical comments. The use of college students and educated middle-class housewives is but one solution to mental health manpower needs. Most often their work was only intended to provide a much needed direct clinical service and involved minimal community orientation. In their second project, Rioch's housewives did engage in preventive work in offering mental health and child care counseling to high-risk, low-income mothers. The other programs described in this section involved new forms of direct service to already identified problem persons but were not oriented toward prevention.

In many cases, the patients involved benefited from the service, as did the new "therapists" themselves. The effects of the programs on the agencies and institutions involved were more difficult to assess. On the positive side, the enthusiasm generated by the new workers can infuse an entire organization with a new hopeful spurt. Personnel in institutions for patients whom society has labeled as "hopeless cases" (e.g., chronic mental patients, the mentally retarded, or the elderly) may be led to find a new motivation in their work. Similarly, by naïve questioning, students may be able to encourage agency personnel to reexamine habitual routines and procedures that have a negative effect on patient care but are continued because of inertia and discouragement.

On the other hand, except for the above, new nonprofessionals within agencies are in a weak position to effect significant institutional change. They come to the agency in a position of low levels of authority and often do not have the ear of the agency administrator. Student workers are transitory within an organization; both the students and the agency personnel know that their involvement is temporary. If students push too hard for change the agency can confidently coalesce against them; or, alternatively, give the appearance of seriously considering the students' proposals, knowing that in a short time the students will leave as the agency assignment comes to an end. In addition, students who become too disruptive can be given busy work to do or can be isolated in a special unit, thus diminishing their opportunity to learn about the entire agency operations. In other words, the reform impact of student volunteers or other temporary staff can be easily neutralized; the change potential of temporary manpower is not great.

New Careers for indigenous nonprofessionals

Until now, we have been discussing programs whose primary purpose is to broaden the scope and reach of traditional mental health institutions. The new workers—college students and educated housewives—tend to come from the same social and economic strata of society as do existing mental health professionals. But suppose the new professionals were purposely drawn from the most disadvantaged groups, those with the highest environmental risk for later maladjustment and disorder. Would the employment of a significant number of indigenous nonprofessionals in the various helping fields improve their economic condition to such an extent that the mental health of their primary group, as measured by rates of psychiatric impairment, would also respond favorably? Furthermore, if the employment of indigenous workers were in the very social institutions that currently impinge upon and exacerbate social conditions for poverty groups, would the performance of those institutions be considerably improved? These questions address themselves to the possibility that social change can be accomplished by increasing the economic employment opportunities in primary social institutions for those lowest on the socioeconomic scale. This point of view represents the guiding philosophy of the proponents of the New Careers movement.

A basic tenet of the New Careers movement is that there is nothing inherently wrong with poor people other than their poverty. It is the economic poverty of the poor that begets personal and social problems among its citizenry. Unfortunately, society only responds to these secondary effects, spawning a social service bureaucracy aimed at remedying the consequences of poverty but leaving economic conditions untouched. Proponents of the New Careers movement argue that the poor do not need psychotherapy, case work, or other remedial programs if their basic living conditions remain untouched. They dispute the claim that the employment problems of the poor can be traced to their lack of vocationally attractive personal and job skills. Unemployability is viewed as an artifact created by an inflexible society, not as a function of personal disability or individual handicap (Pearl, 1970a).

Some of the goals of the New Careers movement can be summarized as follows (Pearl & Riessman, 1965):

1. A sufficient number of jobs for all persons without work.
2. The jobs to be so defined and distributed that placements exist for the unskilled and uneducated.
3. The jobs to be permanent and provide opportunity for life-long careers.
4. An opportunity for the motivated and talented poor to advance from low-skill entry jobs to any station available to the more favored members of society.
5. The work to contribute to the well-being of society.

Points 2 and 4 above form the heart of the "career ladder" concept associated with the New Careers movement. Point 2 implies that entrance to the lowest rung of the career ladder will be made available to the unskilled and uneducated without the imposition of a credentials requirement that effectively blocks the employment of those without access to the necessary training. The slogan is "jobs first and education later" (Pearl, 1970b), which means that the lowest rung of the career ladder must be available to all who apply. Further advancement would depend on advanced education and training, but such training should be available to all those with sufficient motivation and native talent.

There are a number of social institutions in which jobs could be created that would depend primarily upon interpersonal skill and sensitivity and less upon formal training and credentials. For example, within the welfare, education, medical and mental health systems, jobs such as child care and household management tutors, teaching assistants, public health associates, or mental health technicians could be developed. In each case, technical skill might play a minor role while sensitivity and experiences in life might provide the bulk of the worker's expertise. The interpersonally skilled worker can be taught the technical requirements "on the job." Thus, a cadre of indigenous workers could be developed to meet the needs of the poor. The service to the poor would be from the poor, hopefully increasing the humane quality of that service.

TABLE 7–1
Career sequence for preparation of psychologists

Job title	Duties	Prerequisites
Psychology aide	Clerical functions, interviewing, operation of desk calculators, maintenance of records	None
Psychology assistant	Statistical treatment of data, counseling under supervision, data collection	Two years of appropriate college or work experience
Psychology associate	Supervision of lower echelon staff, research design, report writing, involvement in therapeutic process	Four years of appropriate college or work experience
Psychologist	Team manager, chief tactition in research and clerical activity	M.A. or equivalent
Doctor of psychology	Strategist and planner, staff trainer and supervisor	Ph.D. or equivalent

Reprinted from A. Pearl, The poverty of psychology—an indictment. In V. L. Allen (Ed.), *Psychological factors in poverty* (Chicago: Markham Publishing Company, 1970).

A New Careers approach to the preparation of psychologists can be seen in Table 7–1. The table, prepared by Pearl (1970a) is described by him as follows:

> The New Career idea begins with specifying the entry tasks which everyone could be expected to do—there are some clerical and record-keeping functions, and some client and subject interviewing that persons with limited skill, training, and experience can perform adequately. The entry position should be considered the bottom rung of a career ladder. The position should be permanent. The person who occupies the position has all the rights and privileges of any other staff member. He has

job security, and if he never aspires to a higher station he has at least horizontal mobility; he can receive salary increments for years of service.

If the person occupying the entry rung has talent, he should be allowed to climb as far as his talents and ambitions carry him. This is the unique feature of the New Career approach—the entry worker is not dead-ended into clerical roles, nor is the position a temporary slot for a student moving on to better things. For the ascension to be a reality, way stations must be created along the route. . . . There must be a definition of tasks that are going to be performed at each of the rungs in the career ladder. And, finally, the training and the education that New Careerists will need to function at every level must be specified. . . .

The training offered in New Careers is consistent with most theoretical approaches to learning. Practice would accompany theory: students would be allowed to put into practice what they have been taught, and the training would be a natural outgrowth of problems encountered on the job. Replacing the fragmented and often irrelevant jumble of courses that describes the university program would be coordinated, sequential development of skill and knowledge with payoffs at regularly scheduled intervals. (Pearl, 1970a, p. 360–361)

In summary, the New Careers approach provides a double-pronged focus. Direct alleviation of poverty by provision for immediate employment and eventual upward mobility; and humanizing social institutions by reducing the status differential between the service providers and the clients served.

Critical comments

Problems of selection

Programs specifically designed for one group must face the immediate problem of whether they will exclude the entry of other groups or whether they will be made available to all. Exclusive programs will be seen as discriminatory and will be resented in the larger community even though the new "discrimination" is to correct previous inequity experienced by minority groups. If the program is made available to applicants from all segments of society and if it is attractive enough, majority group members will also apply and will outnumber minority applicants. This was the experience of several districts in California when they advertised for mental health aide positions for which there were essentially no prerequisites. Majority applicants outnumbered minority applicants by over five to one with the former still being able to demonstrate more impressive formal qualifications. The only way minority group candidates could be hired was if the decision to favor their candidacy was agreed upon beforehand.

If one does not use credentials to screen applicants because of their inherent bias against minority applicants, developing selection criteria becomes difficult. A personal interview is often chosen, with the interviewer attempting to screen out those in the midst of some identifiable personal crisis. The interviewer might help eliminate those who were obviously unsuitable, but how should the choice be made among the remaining applicants? One suggestion (Riessman, 1967) is to look for characteristics such as informality, humor, earthiness, and neighborliness. Unfortunately these personal attributes sometimes are difficult to discover in an interview format. The problem is compounded by the possible presence of other characteristics in low-income populations that might interfere with an effective helper role—characteristics such as moral indignation, punitiveness, and suspicion. Some might wish to eliminate applicants with the latter traits, yet Goldenberg (1971) reports that he purposely chose applicants who were angry and dissatisfied and who might be seen as "troublemakers" in other agencies. Goldenberg wanted workers who could relate to troubled teen-agers, who would put extra effort in their work but who would not put up with injustice even if it occurred within their own agency. As Riessman (1967) points out, there are many different types of indigenous nonprofessionals: "some are earthy, some are tough, some are angry, some are surprisingly articulate, some are slick, clever wheeler-dealers, and nearly all are greatly concerned about their new roles and their relationship to professionals." What is clear is that one cannot magically expect that the status of being poor automatically confers upon the individual greater wisdom or humanitarianism. Positive personality traits are distributed among members of the poor just as they are among members of other groups. That the task of selecting indigenous workers from among the poor may be more difficult is not because there are fewer or greater numbers of individuals with positive characteristics, but because the usual methods of selecting mental health workers based on credentials reflecting levels of training, education, and experience, cannot be meaningfully applied in this situation.

One possible solution to the selection problem can be illustrated by the work of Goodman (1972) who developed a technique to measure therapeutic sensitivity. Goodman was involved in a project to select and train college student companions for emotionally disturbed boys.

The method, referred to as the GAIT (Group Assessment of Interpersonal Traits), involves setting up an assessment situation in which job performance skills can be elicited and evaluated. Since Goodman was interested in therapeutic skills, the GAIT provides an opportunity for disclosing and listening skills to be tested. Applicants meet in a group and complete the following procedure in which they are required to talk about themselves and listen to others do likewise:

1. The applicants sit in a circle and wear letter tags. Mr. A begins by reading one of his statements [a self-disclosing statement written earlier] to the group. He is designated as the discloser.

2. Any applicant can spontaneously respond to the discloser and engage him in a five-minute dialogue. The applicant who responds is called the understander. Other group members are asked to remain silent. A kitchen timer (bell-type) passed from one discloser to another can be used to time dialogues.

3. In the rare instance where no response is offered to the discloser's first statement within a minute, the discloser is asked to read his second statement.

4. Understanders are asked to avoid giving advice, making judgments, asking questions, or offering interpretations. Instead, they should reflect feelings, disclose their own relevant thoughts or immediate reactions, or simply "listen very hard" while saying nothing.

5. When the five-minute dialogue has terminated, the understander tries a brief (thirty-second) summary of the interaction.

6. The discloser then rereads his initial statement. The juxtaposition of initial statement and summary gives the group a sharper view of the understander's grasp of the situation and his success at facilitating the expansion of the problem presented.

7. Mr. B now becomes the discloser, and anyone except the person who responded to Mr. A can now respond to Mr. B. The group continues to form dyads in this manner until everyone in the circle has performed both tasks.

8. Each applicant is asked to rate the other applicant on sociometric scales describing such interpersonal traits as understanding, openness, acceptance, rigidity. The same scale is used by attending staff members to rate applicants.

9. When the scales are completed, the group is open for free discussion, with the staff answering questions. The entire procedure takes about an hour and a half. (Goodman, 1972, pp. 29–30.)

The assessment technique illustrated by the GAIT involves building a performance test that, in miniature, captures the skills necessary for effective on-the-job performance. When credentials cannot be used in selecting nonprofessionals, a performance test represents a viable alternative.

Role ambiguity and "representativeness"

Riessman (1967) astutely points out that the term "nonprofessional" describes what indigenous workers are *not*, but does not give a clear indication of what they are. They are supposed to be "representative" of the low-income community from which they come so that their ability to communicate effectively with members of their own group is maximized. Yet the longer they stay on the job, the less representative and the more professional they become, especially if employed by an agency that takes the New Careers philosophy seriously and has provided opportunities to move up the career ladder to higher professional levels. Riessman (1967) believes that the issue is not whether nonprofessionals identify with the poor but whether they remain committed to them. Even if professional status is attained, what is needed beyond identification with the poor is knowledge, commitment, and the ability to communicate.

The issue is not a simple one. The occupational role itself has built-in strains and contradictions. The worker is often forced to live in two worlds: the agency with its hierarchical professional role relationships, and the community that he or she "represents" but is also attempting to change. Yet the definition of actual job duties might be ill-defined, especially if the job and agency program are new. The worker is not a professional but may be seen as such by community members who may see *any* agency personnel as "social workers." Within the agency, role definition may also be ambiguous. Is the nonprofessional expected to operate in a traditional one-to-one helping relationship, as a spokesperson for the poor to agency personnel, as an advocate for the rights of the poor, or as a community organizer? The mission may be confused for the indigenous worker and for the agency as well, particularly if careful planning did not accompany the establishment of the New Careers program.

The problems of role ambiguity can be seen in the first-person account of Laura Hines, a 41-year-old black woman who left school at the age of 15 to help support her family, and eventually became a mental health nonprofessional. Excerpts from her moving report follow. We pick up her story after the termination of a temporary three-month job as a home and school coordinator.

> After the job terminated, I returned to the antipoverty office to see if there were any more openings. They told me that the community mental health center was going to conduct a survey of the North Philadelphia

area and that they were going to hire people to work as census takers. I applied at the center, was interviewed, and hired. On October 10, 1966, training began. Training consisted of interviewing techniques. We spent two weeks of training and then the frustration began (census taking).

I had to get used to going in and out of different neighborhoods and had to adjust myself to different kinds of personalities. Most people in the survey area were very reluctant about answering questions. They were tired of answering questions and having promises made. It was hard to tell people that you were from Temple University because of the feelings that people had about Temple. Some people thought that you were spying for other agencies. It was difficult: being polite to people when they in turn were rude, seeing people who were hungry, seeing people who were jobless, seeing family after family without a father and the mother trying to survive on her welfare grant, seeing all these things and nothing being done about them. Some people's attitudes were almost unbearable. But I worked, knowing how people felt, feeling that what we were trying to develop would be a good place for the community, hoping that some pressures would be removed. I grew a lot with the survey; I was not aware that there were starving people living only blocks away from where I have lived all my life.

In early 1967, I moved from census-taking to mental health assistant I. I had ten weeks of full-time training that consisted of seminars dealing with psychiatric and social concepts. The training consisted of lectures, reading, and paper work. It was given by professional staff from the center—psychiatrists, a psychologist, a social worker, and a nurse. . . .

Learning to become a mental health assistant was a frustrating experience for me. It was made as simple as possible, but I still had a tough time getting adjusted. There were nights that I hardly slept, thinking of tomorrow when class would resume. It was hard for me to adjust because I never liked school anyway, and I had been out of it for so long. But I was able to adjust with the help of the training director, who was nice but stern. For example, each week she insisted upon your learning to use ten words that were unfamiliar to you. I had to learn how to pronounce them, spell them correctly, and use them in a sentence (which I thought was very useless). It proved to be quite useful in work when talking with different people in other agencies about patients who were in some way connected with their agency.

The director of the program also was a very stern person but one who made every effort to make his teaching as simple as possible for all the trainees: describing symptoms, problems, medication, color of medication, effectiveness, and so on. Some days I came away from class feeling like a social worker. I had to take this learning, put it together, and make it work. . . .

Having been taught all I know about mental illness by a psychiatrist, I felt as though any psychiatrist could teach and support people with less education than they. But I learned how different psychiatrists could be when I started in our psychosocial clinic and had a psychiatrist for a supervisor. He made me feel less important and needed than I had felt from the beginning of my training. My ideas were not accepted as good ideas but as useless thoughts. He did not realize that if we worked together and worked hard, we would be able to be effective and do a great job together for the people that we serve. He should not have let differences in theories or methods prevent him from working with me. Together we could plan and maybe initiate the needed change in our area and also try to create solutions to some problems. But as I worked on, my perception of professionals changed some from my first thoughts. To some extent some professionals still relate to you on a professional-nonprofessional level and do not want to learn your ways of thinking. . . .

During the survey I was almost shocked to see how some people kept their homes and their children, and I wanted to do something about this. I brought this back to the center, and I was given the responsibility of developing a homemaking service. There are a few agencies that use the service in the needed way, but most agencies are afraid to really deal with the "nitty gritty" of the problems that exist in the poor areas. They do things that only create more problems. Rehabilitating houses and not rehabilitating people is a most unrealistic thing. They are only building more ghettos. Also there is no service available to people who are in a depressed stage or even going through a crisis, not able to take care of their family. We do not have any kind of service to keep this family together. . . .

I did not receive any help at first in developing the homemaking service. The director of the program, who has always been a busy man at the center, helped me with it and gave me all the moral support that he could. And this was all that I had to keep me going. Other people who were able to help just did not. There were people (professionals) who even told me to forget it because I would not be able to write such a proposal. There were also agency people who communicated freely with me until they found out I was a nonprofessional. And there were professional people who tried to discourage me because they had previously submitted similar proposals and had been rejected. But through the frustration and tears I have finally written a proposal that I think has very good content and value, and one that I think will work. At this point, now that they (professionals) have seen that I was not giving up, they are beginning to support me. Although most of them are late getting involved, I am still very happy to have their support. I think that my effort and desire to complete what I had been assigned to do has in some way influenced the professional people in the nonprofessional's capabilities. (Hines, 1970, pp. 1467–1472)

Competition with professionals

The excerpt from the report of Laura Hines also illustrates what is perhaps the most volatile problem confronting the New Careers movement—competition with already established professionals. Laura Hines talks about professionals being jealous of her work, discouraging her, and talking down to her. The problems between professionals and nonprofessionals also go the other way, with the nonprofessionals jealous of the power and salary differentials between themselves and the professionals. Nonprofessionals are sometimes led to believe what can be a patronizing rhetoric: the professional employer convinces them that they were hired because they had better interactive skills with low-income populations than do professionals. It is quite natural for them then to assume that once they are trained in the special skills and knowledge of the professional they will be "double smart" (Riessman, 1967) and will be even more competent than the professional. There is no way either side can win if the work is described in terms that encourage rivalry. The professionals will fear that their roles will be usurped and that nonprofessionals will do successfully what they have been unable to do alone—to rehabilitate the poor (Christmas, Wallace, and Edwards, 1970). The nonprofessionals will become overconcerned with personnel practices, grievance machinery, lines of authority, and group power-issues concerned with status enhancement and job security as opposed to innovative programs.

What can ensue from these concerns is a power struggle between the two groups. At the Lincoln Hospital Community Mental Health Center in New York, the organization and politicalization of the nonprofessional workers led to a bitter strike that eventually closed the center (Roman, 1973). Other programs have been more fortunate in that the antagonistic feelings present were either tolerated better or were resolved in terms of an increased respect for the mutual expertise and background of both professional and nonprofessional (Schiff, 1970).

The career ladder concept does exacerbate competitive striving between the two groups, for it implies that the nonprofessional can reach the same level as the professional albeit through alternative routes such as on-the-job experience and in-service training. Is this a reasonable assumption? Is it reasonable to assume that there can be enough jobs for all to continue up the rungs of the career ladder? This assumption overestimates the funds available to human service organizations and the level of potential new monies that society would be willing to give such agencies as the core of new professionals grows. It may be true that the human and social cost to society of not providing useful employment to those in poverty far outweighs the cost of a new career program. Unfortunately the alleviation of human misery is not always a universally agreed-upon humanitarian goal, particularly if it is costly to achieve and threatens to displace those with already established clear access to the professions. This then represents an important social issue—should access to the top be available for all who want to get there; and, in the name of increasing the quality of human life should society ease that access for all upwardly motivated citizens. We strongly believe so, but there are clear arguments on both sides of the question. Since so much is at stake, these important decisions should not be left in the hands of social service professionals alone. It should be clear that the decision as to how to improve the public good cannot be made without the participation of the general citizenry. The New Careers movement does have the potential for improving the condition of the poor by allowing greater access to the social service and helping professions. But the potential will be realized only if the decision is made to provide sufficient access to upper levels of the career ladder to all those with sufficient motivation who would qualify.

New Careerists as institutional change agents

There are really no longer any serious doubts as to the ability of nonprofessionals to provide useful direct service in the helping and social service fields. Their growing popularity in human service agencies attests to an increased acceptance. That their service is less costly to the agency than the employment of fully credentialed professionals is also in their favor. But does the basic mission of an agency and the manner in which it carries out that mission change as a result of the employment of a new breed of personnel who conduct the agency's affairs? Is the programmatic thrust of social institutions changed in any significant way with the establishment of New Careers programs?

Some see the change potential of the New Careers movement in terms of political power. If the poor are trained for advancement up a career ladder and if a significant percentage of them are given an opportunity to enter a profession, then the balance of political power might swing to include these otherwise disenfranchised groups. In this view, power is said to come from jobs and the economic status that new positions might command. In evaluating this claim, it is difficult to argue against any program that allows minority groups to gain entry to the professions and improve their lot economically. But economic and political power should not be confused. It is possible for an *organized* poor community to achieve greater political power than isolated and unorganized members of professional groups. Economic advancement can mean increased political power but only if those with new resources learn to participate meaningfully in the political process. Too often participation by the poor in the political process is assumed to mean organized confrontation of existing power groups to dramatize unmet needs. However, rent strikes, civil rights marches, welfare rights meetings, and other confrontation tactics represent only one approach to the political process, and do not represent the only methods available to organized groups to achieve their goals. New professionalism by itself does not guarantee automatic political power; to imply that it does is to raise false expectations among minority group members that can only lead to bitter disappointment. However, increased professionalism can be one component in community change if it is accompanied by increased community awareness, community organization, and a careful and strategic use of intervention options.

Another potential within the New Careers movement is the possibility that service by the poor to the poor will upgrade the quality of that service by making it both more humane and more relevant. Removing status barriers between those served and those providing the service, and increasing the possibility of empathy and compassion between the two, are benefits offered by the New Careers movement. Again, this process is not automatic. As indigenous lower-class workers start to take on the mantle of middle-class status through their own upward mobility, they may look with disdain upon their former neighbors who may be less motivated for self-improvement. Upward striving can decrease the workers' desire to identify with their former group. The term "white trash" was not coined by blacks, but by whites ashamed of members of their own group. Furthermore, as organizations become more bureaucratized, humane service is jeopardized regardless of who is administering that service. Thus, understanding, empathic indigenous workers can help upgrade agency service, but they alone are not sufficient to do so if larger organizational forces are operating unchecked in a counter direction.

Perhaps the main issue in considering whether new careerists can function as institutional change agents is their programmatic assignments. Clinical services might be made more effective if indigenous nonprofessionals were trained as therapists, but the community potential of an agency does not depend upon who its therapists are, but upon its programmatic thrust. Training nonprofessionals to provide better clinical service trades one group of therapists for another but does not change the nature of the service provided. In evaluating the programmatic impact of new careerists one must ask whether the agency is utilizing their different skills to provide new, more community-oriented services. Are the new careerists being utilized to increase community organization? Are they being trained to help agencies upgrade existing programs? Are new programs being developed that contain a greater preventive component? Agencies can use the skills of indigenous nonprofessionals to move closer to the communities they serve. However such changes require more than the employment of indigenous nonprofessionals. They require careful planning and commitment on the part of all staff as to the new programmatic emphasis desired. Nonprofessionals cannot push the professional staff into a more community-oriented stance if the latter do not agree to this goal. An agency in which the nonprofessionals alone do community work and the professionals do clinical work opens itself to professional-nonprofessional conflicts that ultimately will emasculate effective programs.

Summary and evaluation of New Career assumptions

1. Human service can be made more effective and humane when it is provided to the poor by the poor—without status differentials between helper and client.

There is probably no longer any question about the ability of nonprofessionals to function in direct service delivery. Formal credentials are not needed for a number of roles typically performed exclusively by professionals. In some human service fields, the only foreseeable solution to chronic manpower shortages is in the utilization of nonprofessionals. Federal legislation now exists to train and employ previously unemployed persons for jobs in public service, and the use of nonprofessionals is increasing in programs such as mental health, education, and community action.

Whether service by indigenous nonprofessionals is "better" than that provided by professionals remains an open question. There are experimental data concerning the effectiveness of nonprofessionals drawn from the ranks of college students and middle-class housewives but comparable experimental evaluations tend to be lacking for indig-

enous low-income new careerists. We would expect to find considerable variability in the effectiveness of indigenous nonprofessionals.
This is also Grosser's conclusion in his review of nine manpower development programs (Rothman, 1969). The behavior of nonprofessionals varied as a function of the tasks assigned to them.

> In one of the projects nonprofessionals assigned to a service-provision
> program demanded regularly scheduled weekly supervisory confer-
> ences; offices equipped with desks, blotters, and lamps; and appoint-
> ment books and office hours. These workers wished to avoid home visits
> to deteriorated buildings, baby-sitting, and homemaking assignments.
> However, nonprofessionals in the same agency who were assigned to
> community-organization tasks did not pursue a similar pattern. The suc-
> cess of this latter group depended on viable community ties. Thus they
> frequented the streets and the tenements, preferred storefront locations,
> dressed casually, and avoided any distinctions which would separate
> them from the neighborhood residents. (Grossser, 1969, p. 136).

Grosser points out that job assignment influences the behavior of
nonprofessionals just as it would other workers who were interested in
job security. Identification with the work role becomes one way of
achieving such security.

Variation in job performance should also depend upon personal
characteristics. For example, Goodman (1972) in his study of college
student companions to emotionally disturbed boys, found that some
workers produced more effective outcomes than others. "Outgoing"
companions produced more positive changes in their boys then did
"quiet" companions. Similarly, in the Poser study in which chronic
male schizophrenics were seen by female undergraduate students,
there was greater variability in the effects produced by the students
than for a comparison group of professionals. The nonprofessionals
produced significant changes for some patients but not for others,
while the effects for professionals were more uniform.

2. The problem of the poor is their poverty. Nonprofessional employment and upward economic mobility will lead to social change.

New careerists assume that the primary problem of the poor is that
they have been locked out of a credentialed society. Without formal
credentials based on training, there are few opportunities for advancement. With "nowhere to go" in terms of employment there is
disillusionment and poor motivation, which in turn feed poor
academic and job performance. The cycle repeats itself as the next
generation of school and job "dropouts" find upward mobility blocked

in a similar fashion. How is change to take place? Where is the cycle to be broken? The motto of the New Careers movement "Jobs now— education later" is meant to emphasize the hope and pride that can ensue from meaningful reliable employment. Jobs provide the best demonstration to the poor that they possess potentially valuable competencies that can be strengthened with further training.

The suggestion that poverty and its unfortunate concomitants will be eliminated by the employment of new careerists is appealing, but also quite misleading. A false expectation is created that the problems of poverty will be solved by allowing some representatives of the poor to enter mainstream employment. What is more likely to occur is a process of "creaming" in which only the most capable are employed, leaving the "hard core" poor unaffected. For example, in one survey of the utilization of nonprofessionals in Community Action Program (CAP) projects, it was found that most indigenous nonprofessionals were not "hard-core." Seventy-five percent of those employed possessed high school diplomas, with about 20 percent also completing some college course work (Goldberg, 1969). Furthermore, the CAP programs did not provide a "career ladder" for nonprofessionals in that only one job level was provided in the majority of programs. Job advancement was not possible. In this regard, the new nonprofessional jobs were indistinguishable from other jobs usually available to the poor—dead-end jobs with no opportunity for advancement.

Even if New Careers guidelines had been followed, the social change potential of the New Careers movement must be viewed more realistically. There is no doubt that providing increased employment and training opportunities for the poor is extremely important; but it is no panacea. If poverty is to be eliminated, greater social and economic restructuring will be required. As Grosser, Henry, and Kelly (1969, p. 6) note, what is called for are "changes in the mainstream itself, rather than attempts to immerse the poor in it."

Conclusion

Two interrelated strategies for producing community change have been reviewed, both of which involve bypassing existing institutional structures and personnel. When alternative programs are developed outside the structure of traditional agencies, or when new personnel are employed to administer already existing programs, coercive change is avoided. Voluntary program options are developed as demonstrations that can be emulated by others. Also, alternatives encourage diversity and by so doing provide a variety of programs for a more optimal fit between individuals and settings.

The role of alternatives as demonstrations of how innovation can be actualized needs emphasis. Personnel performing traditional roles can learn from those in more innovative settings, which being newer, have fewer built-in constraints. Learning how others perform similar functions can be stimulating. In ensuing discussions, program ideas can be adapted and modified as needed. But collaboration requires a willingness to engage in beneficial interchange, and a structure that encourages dialogue. Too often, these are missing elements as alternatives are developed in an atmosphere that encourages isolation and suspicion between traditional and innovative settings.

Nonprofessional personnel can serve as a similar stimulant for innovative practice if they can demonstrate beneficial results by more economical, simpler, and more straightforward procedures. This impact has already been felt in the mental health professions as nonprofessional workers have managed to produce competent results in functions previously reserved for the "properly qualified" credentialed professional. Nonprofessional competency challenges the very definition of "helping service." For example, is professionally administered psychotherapy unique, or can similar effects be produced by others regardless of the status of the helper? If nonprofessionals can provide significant help, perhaps similar effects can be produced by friends and neighbors. Social support from peers such as these, because it is constantly available, may have greater utility than help provided by a formal practitioner regardless of his professional status. Thus, a change in service provider while of less import by itself, can lead to stimulating new questions. When is the treatment of choice psychotherapy; and under what conditions does a more optimal treatment strategy involve the development of alternatives such as support networks?

As we learn more about the capabilities of nonprofessionals, we are likely to find that both groups (nonprofessionals and professionals) excel at different functions. We would expect that professionals would be uniquely suited to roles involving program planning, research and case supervision, and the interpretation of personality functioning—jobs that are difficult without advanced training. Similarly, there should be roles that are performed more adequately by nonprofessional personnel. Reaching out to others and providing friendly support and interest are prime candidates for nonprofessional speciality. The concept of differential effectiveness should not be seen as demeaning to either group since the particular situation or problem should determine the skill called for. For example, forming a supportive relationship with a client may be less valued by professionals than dynamic psychotherapy, yet at times the former may be the treatment of choice. Dreiblatt and Weatherley (1965) reported that newly admitted mental hospital patients responded much more favorably to brief, friendly contact than they did to more problem-focused discussions. The authors speculate that non-symptom-oriented friendly contacts convey a feeling of support and interest not available in more structured symptom-oriented interactions.

The main cautions associated with alternatives and new careers involves fostering the illusion of significant innovation, when in fact little social change may occur. Alternatives can be used to maintain the status quo by encouraging community avoidance of responsibility. It is seductively easy to use alternative programs to separate problem "cases" and "dissidents" under the banner of a special program while at the same time ignoring community and institutional contributions to the problem. The special program can be an excuse for inaction and for doing nothing toward problem alleviation.

Similarly, by allowing only a few of the most talented minority group members into mainstream employment, a massive social problem (poverty) may be dealt with by token measures. Priority changes to allow for increased resources to the social services would be required to initiate any large scale increases in personnel. Also required would be changes in the structure of the helping professions to allow nonprofessionals to attain upper rungs in a career ladder through alternative preparation. Little would be accomplished if the new manpower remained in low-paying, low-status, dead-end jobs.

We are not advocating the perpetuation of misery until society is ready for massive social change. However, we are counseling realism. The social change potential of alternatives and new careers is not as great as the proponents believe, nor as bleak as the detractors claim. Initially, as alternatives are developed and nurtured, it may be necessary to bypass traditional agencies and personnel. It is difficult to build a new program in a hostile and unresponsive environment. However, for maximum impact, the isolation of alternatives should not be perpetuated. We believe that more can be accomplished by seeking accommodation with existing agencies, and by using alternatives as demonstrations of innovative service that can be adopted by others. For such demonstrations to succeed, attention must be paid to conditions under which the dissemination of knowledge is most likely to be maximized. Increased opportunities for contact must be developed. Uncompromising idealism, intransigent attitudes, or smoldering resentment, on either side, become obstacles that ultimately undermine significant social change.

References

Barr, R. D. Whatever happened to the free school movement? *Phi Delta Kappan,* 1973, *54,* 454–457.

Braginsky, B. M., Braginsky, D D., & Ring, K. *Methods of madness: The mental hospital as a last resort.* New York: Holt, Rinehart and Winston, 1969.

Campbell, D. T. Reforms as experiments. *American Psychologist,* 1969, *24,* 409–429.

Christmas, J. J., Wallace, H., & Edwards, J. New careers and new mental health services: Fantasy or future? *American Journal of Psychiatry,* 1970, *127,* 1480–1486.

Cowen, E. L. The effectiveness of secondary prevention programs using nonprofessionals in the school setting. *Proceedings of the 76th Annual Convention of the American Psychological Association,* 1968, *2,* 705–706.

Cowen, E. L., Dorr, D. A., Trost, M. A., & Izzo, L. D. Follow-up study of maladapting school children seen by nonprofessionals. *Journal of Consulting and Clinical Psychology,* 1972, 39, 235–238.

Cowen, E. L., Zax, M., & Laird, J. D. A college student volunteer program in the elementary school setting. *Community Mental Health Journal,* 1966, *2,* 319–328.

DeTurk, P., & Mackin, R. Lions in the park: An alternative meaning and setting for learning. *Phi Delta Kappan,* 1973, *59,* 458–460.

Dreiblatt, I. S., & Weatherley, D. An evaluation of the efficacy of brief-contact therapy with hospitalized psychiatric patients. *Journal of Consulting Psychology,* 1965, *29,* 513–519.

Fairweather, G. W. (Ed.) *Social psychology in treating mental illness: An experimental approach.* New York: John Wiley & Sons, 1964.

Fairweather, G. W., Sanders, D. H., Maynard, H. & Cressler, D. L. *Community life for the mentally ill: An alternative to institutional care.* Chicago,: Aldine, 1969.

Fairweather, G. W., Sanders, D. H., & Tornatzky, L. G. *Creating change in mental health organizations.* New York: Pergamon Press, 1974.

Fantini, M. Alternatives within public schools. *Phi Delta Kappan,* 1973, *54,* 444–448. (a)

Fantini, M.   *Public schools of choice.* New York: Simon and Schuster, 1973. (b).

Goldberg, G. S.   Nonprofessionals in human services. In C. Grosser, W. E. Henry, and J. G. Kelly (Eds.), *Nonprofessionals in the human services.* San Francisco: Jossey-Bass, 1969, pp. 12–39.

Goldenberg, I. I.   *Build me a mountain: Youth, poverty and the creation of new settings.* Cambridge, Mass.: The MIT Press, 1971. (a)

Goldenberg, I. I.   The relationship of the university to the community: Implications for community mental health programs. Paper presented at the meetings of the American Psychological Association, Washington, D.C., 1971. (b)

Goodman, G.   *Companionship therapy: Studies in structured intimacy.* San Francisco: Jossey-Bass, 1972.

Graziano, A. M. Clinical innovation and the mental health power structure: A social case history. *American Psychologist,* 1969, *24,* 10–18.

Grosser, C.   Manpower development programs. In C. Grosser, W. E. Henry, and J. G. Kelly, (Eds.), *Nonprofessionals in the human services.* San Francisco: Jossey-Bass, 1969, pp. 116–148.

Grosser, C., Henry, W. E., & Kelly, J. G. (Eds.) *Nonprofessionals in the human services.* San Francisco: Jossey-Bass, 1969.

Gruver, G. G.   College students as therapeutic agents. *Psychological Bulletin,* 1971, *76,* 111–127.

Hines, L. A nonprofessional discusses her role in mental health. *American Journal of Psychiatry,* 1970, *126,* pp. 1467–1472. Copyright 1970, the American Psychiatric Association. Reprinted by permission.

Holzberg, J. D., Knapp, R. H., & Turner, J. L.   College students as companions to the mentally ill. In E. L. Cowen, E. A. Gardner, & M. Zax (Eds.), *Emergent approaches to mental health problems.* New York: Appleton-Century-Crofts, 1967, pp. 91–109.

Kreitzer, S. F.   College students in a behavior therapy program with hospitalized emotionally disturbed children. In B. G. Guerney, Jr. (Ed.), *Psychotherapeutic agents: New roles for nonprofessionals, parents and teachers.* New York: Holt, Rinehart and Winston, 1969, pp. 226–230.

Levine, M., & Levine, A.   *A social history of helping services: Clinic, court, school and community.* New York: Appleton-Century-Crofts, 1970.

Levinson, D. J., & Gallagher, E. B.   *Patienthood in the mental hospital.* Boston: Houghton Mifflin, 1964.

Magoon, T. M., Golann, S. E., & Freeman, R. W.   *Mental health counselors at work.* New York: Pergamon Press, 1969.

Martinson, R.   What works? Questions and answers about prison reform. *The Public Interest,* Spring 1974, 22–54.

Miller, S. M., & Riessman, F.   *Social class and social policy.* New York: Basic Books, 1968, pp. 201–202.

Ohlin, L., Coates, R., & Miller, A.   Radical correctional reform: A case study of the Massachusetts Youth Correctional System. *Harvard Educational Review,* 1974, *44,* 74–112.

Pearl, A. The poverty of psychology—an indictment. In V. L. Allen (Ed.), *Psychological factors in poverty*. Chicago: Markham Publishing Company, 1970, pp. 348–364. (a)

Pearl, A. New careers and model cities. In L. E. Sneden (Ed.), *Poverty: A psychosocial analysis*. Berkeley, Calif.: McCutchan Publishing Corp., 1970, pp. 270–289. (b)

Pearl, A., & Riessman, F. *New careers for the poor*. Glencoe, Ill.: Free Press, 1965.

Poser, E. G. The effect of therapist training on group therapeutic outcome. *Journal of Consulting Psychology*, 1966, *30*, 283–289.

Rappaport, J., Chinsky, J. M., & Cowen, E. L. *Innovations in helping chronic patients: College students in a mental institution*. New York: Academic Press, 1971.

Rhodes, W. C. *Behavioral threat and community response: A community psychology inquiry*. New York: Behavioral Publications, 1972.

Riessman, F. Strategies and suggestions for training nonprofessionals. *Community Mental Health Journal*, 1967, *3*, 103–110.

Rioch, M. J. Pilot projects in training mental health counselors. In E. L. Cowen, E. A. Gardner, & M. Zax (Eds.), *Emergent approaches to mental health problems*. New York: Appleton-Century-Crofts, 1967, pp. 110–127.

Roman, M. Community control and the community mental health center: A view from the Lincoln bridge. In B. Denner and R. H. Price (Eds.), *Community mental health: Social action and reaction*. New York: Holt, Rinehart and Winston, 1973, pp. 270–284.

Rothman, B. Social work education. In C. Grosser, W. E. Henry, & J. G. Kelly (Eds.), *Nonprofessionals in the human services*. San Francisco: Jossey-Bass, 1969, pp. 149–173.

Sanders, R. New manpower for mental hospital service. In E. L. Cowen, E. A. Gardner, & M. Zax (Eds.), *Emergent approaches to mental health problems*. New York: Appleton-Century-Crofts, 1967, pp. 128–143.

Sarason, S. B. *The culture of the school and the problem of change*. Boston: Allyn and Bacon, 1971.

Sarason, S. B. *The creation of settings and the future societies*. San Francisco: Jossey-Bass, 1972.

Schiff, S. K. Community accountability and mental health services. *Mental Hygiene*, 1970, *54*, 205–214.

Shah, S. A. The criminal justice system. In S. E. Golann & C. Eisdorfer (Eds.), *Handbook of community mental health*. New York: Appleton-Century-Crofts, 1972, pp. 73–105.

Smith, M. CBE views the alternatives. *Phi Delta Kappan*, 1973, *54*, 441–443.

Smith, V. H. Options in public education: The quiet revolution. *Phi Delta Kappan*, 1973, *54*, 434–437.

Smith, V. H. *Alternative schools: The development of options in public education*. Lincoln, Neb.: Professional Educators Publications, Inc., 1974.

Stollak, G. E.   The experimental effects of training college students as play therapists. In B. G. Guerney, Jr. (Ed.), *Psychotherapeutic agents: New roles for nonprofessionals, parents and teachers*. New York: Holt, Rinehart and Winston, 1969, pp. 510–518.

Tornatzky, L. G., Fairweather, G. W., & O'Kelly, L. I.   A Ph. D. program aimed at survival. *American Psychologist*, 1970, 25, 884–888.

Zax, M., & Specter, G. A.   *An introduction to community psychology*. New York: John Wiley & Sons, 1974.

8

COMMUNITY ORGANIZATION

Community change through the development of organized constituencies

FROM a community organization perspective, the inequities and injustices found in society can be directly attributed to a lack of political power. Thus, community organization represents a group of strategies aimed at effecting community change through unified social and political action. It does not spring from a mental health tradition and many mental health practitioners are uncomfortable in what is so clearly a political arena. Mental health specialists are likely to believe that their professional activities are politically neutral. Not so, suggests the community organization perspective: one either helps oppressed, disenfranchised groups or tacitly supports their oppression. From this point of view, mental health consultants, working for changes in social institutions from within, can still find themselves on the "wrong side of the political fence" if the effect of their work is to unwittingly help malignant social institutions survive.

Political solutions to social and psychological problems

Consider the following example: A team of mental health consultants, offering consultation to a school system in a large city, was becoming concerned about the effectiveness of their work. Over a period of several years, the city had become polarized along racial lines, and racial tensions had pervaded the schools. School officials seemed reluctant to deal with the school system's many problems and stead-

330

fastly ignored the increasing racial tensions. This was because the majority community through its school board was committed to a policy of segregation. However, since segregation in public facilities violated federal law, the issue could not be discussed openly. The consultation team discussed the dilemma among themselves and decided that their initial task was to "survive" in the system and avoid being "kicked out" of the schools. Their hope was that if firm trust and good relationships with school officials could be established, they could become an important resource for the school when open racial conflict became more severe. They embarked on a strategy of offering case consultation and skill building to teachers, knowing that they were avoiding the major source of tension in the system.

Racial confrontation was not long in coming. A group of black parents, dissatisfied with the quality of education offered their children, withdrew their children from school and organized a school boycott in black neighborhoods. The parent group used as its rallying cry "community control of the schools" and seemed to be demanding a greater voice in local school governance and more attention to the educational needs of black children.

As tensions rose, consultation team members offered themselves as mediators in the dispute and tried to bring the black parents and school officials together for negotiation sessions. Both sides agreed to negotiate but the parents rejected the consultation team as mediators. The consultants who had hoped to maintain a stance of neutrality found that both sides saw them as biased in favor of the schools. The parents held this view because they knew that the consultants were the recipients of a fairly large school consultation contract. The school personnel had already had previous meetings with the consultants concerning how to negotiate the parent demands, and perceived the consultants as allies in reducing the intensity of the conflict. The parents who had incited the conflict in the first place, however, did not share this goal. They were quite willing to escalate the conflict, at least until such time as they could see tangible improvement in the educational setting.

It is possible that given the complexity and intensity of the racial feelings in the city at large, the most that school personnel could do was to "cool out" the agitating parents. Indeed, even though this one dispute was eventually settled by negotiation, it was an early signal of a more intense battle to follow. The city and its schools became involved in a larger bitter dispute over court-ordered desegregation and busing. It was an issue that piecemeal negotiation could not solve as long as an overarching value in the community was the preservation of racial segregation in the schools. It required a political solution that could only be achieved by a group of dedicated, organized parents and concerned citizens who were willing to keep this unfortunate situation in the community's focus. Social action, not mental health consultation, was the necessary strategy.[1]

The role of the mental health professional in political action

Do mental health workers have a professional role in social action efforts? On the one hand, one could adopt the stance that social change is a citizen responsibility and should not involve the helping professions directly. Clients and professionals, as citizens, may engage in social action, but politics is not a mental health specialty, and mental health professionals should not concern themselves with political questions as part of their professional roles. Psychotherapy may free individuals from their inhibitions so that they may live more creatively, and perhaps choose to become politically involved; but the ultimate goal of clinical activity is psychological well-being, not political participation.

In contrast to the position stated in the previous paragraph is the view that mental health activity can never be politically neutral; those engaged in mental health practice cannot escape a political value choice. While the manifest goal of psychotherapy might be self-actualization, psychotherapy can also be seen as reflecting a value that conflicts between individuals and society are best dealt with by individual change. Asking individuals to adjust to society is as much a political statement as working for the improvement of social conditions to better meet human needs.

If neither stance is politically neutral, is one more correct than the other? Despite the appealing rhetoric associated with both positions, the question cannot be answered in the abstract. Existing social conditions in any given community may lead one orientation to be more appropriate than the other. In more optimal societies with minimal environmental stress, a focus on individual adjustment may be more

---

[1] A more detailed presentation of this example with comments from a different point of view can be found in Caplan (1970, pp. 359–381).

appropriate. If people are still disturbed despite optimal surroundings, the reasons for maladjustment may be more a function of internal conflicts. For example, Lemkau believes that planned communities are not likely to reduce rates of psychological depression (Zax & Specter, 1974). Depressive reactions are most frequent among responsible citizens who internalize guilt and blame—a more likely occurrence when the reasons for personal unhappiness cannot be attributed to environmental pressures. On the other hand, in oppressive societies, changing social conditions may be the more important priority. Robert Reiff (1966) has pointed out that it is meaningless to talk about programs for developing self-actualization in groups that do not have self-determination. In these instances, community organization to obtain political power and self-determination may be a prerequisite for more optimal psychological functioning. Thus, the dispute between a social and an individual focus should be answered in terms of assessing existing social conditions.

Given that a decision can be made that social action is a pressing priority and assuming that a mental health professional wants to become involved in such action, what role should he or she play in the organizational efforts? Does one adopt the role of community organizer, or leave such responsibilities to indigenous citizens while offering to act only as a technical consultant to fledgling community groups? Of course the choice will involve a personal decision concerning the extent of political involvement with which the individual will feel comfortable. But the decision is also a function of the model of community organization adopted. As we shall detail later in this chapter, there are two main forms of community organization: community development emphasizing cooperation between diverse segments of a community; and social action based upon conflict assumptions (Cox, Erlich, Rothman, & Tropman, 1974). A goal of community development strategies is to develop indigenous leadership, trained in democratic procedures, which can involve a wide spectrum of people in local decision making. Social action based on conflict strategies aims for increased political participation for disenfranchised groups achieved by whatever alliances and pressure tactics may be necessary to get the job done. In the former case, once local leadership has been identified, all subsequent actions flow through them. The professional role is defined as that of technical adviser. In the social action model this restriction does not apply. The spark for movement can come from any source including the professional organizer. It should be clear, however, that in neither case can mental health professionals assume that they can work without the involvement and sanction of indigenous community members. Community organization does not involve solo professional performance.

Community control, political power, and participatory democracy

Community control as a political force is not foreign to the American way of life. Political power in the hands of local governmental units has been and still is part of the American tradition. It operates best in the small cities and towns where elected officials represent the wishes of their constituents and where accountability is ensured by the direct access and communication channels available between citizens and their representatives.

From a historical point of view, the tradition in American government has been to apply minimal constraints to individual behavior. Under conditions of unlimited natural resources, open distance between people who could escape elsewhere when conflict became too intense, and a relatively homogeneous population in terms of values and life-styles, this form of laissez-faire democracy worked quite well. With the advent of the industrial revolution and the closing of the American frontier, new accommodations were required. Immigration brought new workers to this country with few occupational skills and with major differences in language and culture. Crowding in urban areas became commonplace and with it came a host of social problems. The "melting pot" concept was put to severe tests as the dominant American culture sought to accommodate to and assimilate these new influences.

Accommodation took place in a variety of ways: sometimes through violence, as in the labor strikes that occurred in this country from 1886–1921 when unions were struggling to gain employer recognition; sometimes through more peaceful evolution, as in the case of the assumption of political power by Catholics in Boston at the turn of the century. Sometimes accommodation was successful because new opportunities were available in an expanding job market that valued the skills of the new immigrants and their children. This factor was important to the adjustment and increased social mobility available to the descendants of the Jewish immigrants in New York, and was repeated in the case of Cuban refugees in Miami. But despite these successes, problems of accommodation, which were always more difficult to overcome in urban areas, remain. In part, the problems can be attributed to the disparity between cultures that makes assimilation difficult. Add to this the limited economic resources available to most city governments, the increased distance between government and the governed that occurs in complex societies, and the despair of industrial workers who find that they have little control over the economic forces that affect their lives, and you have disruption and conflict.

The concern for the deterioration of urban life, the unresponsiveness of governing structures and community institutions, and the accompanying alienation of citizens have been the sparks that have brought forth the call to social and political action. The deficiencies of contemporary industrial society have been described by Alinsky as follows:

> In our modern urban civilization, multitudes of our people have been condemned to urban anonymity—to living the kind of life where many of them neither know nor care about their own neighbors. They find themselves isolated from the life of their community and their nation, driven by social forces beyond their control into little individual worlds in which their own individual objectives have become paramount to the collective good. Social objectives, social welfare, the good of the nation, the democratic way of life—all these have become nebulous, meaningless, sterile phrases.
>
> This course of urban anonymity, of individual divorce from the general social life, erodes the foundations of democracy. For although we profess to be citizens of a democracy, and although we may vote once every four years, millions of our people feel deep down in their heart of hearts that there is no place for them—that they do not "count." They have no voice of their own, no organization (really their own instead of absentee) to represent them, no way in which they may lay their hand or their heart to the shaping of their own destinies. (Alinsky, 1946, pp. 67–68).

One reads this passage and sees inequity, alienation, and helplessness produced as by-products of industrial development. It is sobering to recognize that many of the problems described by Alinsky in 1946 are still with us and have not improved significantly over time. They now touch the lives of many citizens, not just the poor. As we think of solutions to these problems, we must recognize that it is not just a question of what shall be done. Also involved is the issue of who decides. For example, any number of solutions could be offered to decrease the disparity in economic gain between employer and worker. However, the message of the community organizer is that increased equity, while desirable, is not enough; alienation can be found at all socioeconomic levels. Ways must be found to increase the participation of citizens in the crucial decisions that affect their lives. The answer to the debilitating effects of alienation and powerlessness produced in complex technological societies is to make a conscious effort to increase true participatory democracy.

The distinction between laissez-faire and participatory democracy

The terms "community control" and "participatory democracy" may evoke different images. Yet, are they referring to different processes? Both imply decision making in the hands of the many, not just by the privileged few. Both require that important acts by individuals, major institutions, or interest groups conform to the common good. It is in this sense that participatory democracy or community control differs from the brand of laissez-faire democracy to which we have grown accustomed in this country. In a laissez-faire democracy, the emphasis is on freedom of action that is constrained *only* when it clearly violates the rights of others. Participatory democracy implies that a primary value should be on decisions reached by group consensus, though the group may restrict individual prerogatives for the sake of the common good.

Laissez-faire democracy can be traced to the view of capitalism and society proposed by Adam Smith in 1776 (Bernard, 1973). Free trade among nations and nonintervention by governments were its cornerstone beliefs. The economy was to be regulated by market conditions, not by bureaucrats or planners. At the level of the individual, personal initiative and achievement were important to carry the system forward. This view held that "enterprising persons, each specializing in the work he could do relatively best and exchanging his products in the market for the goods and services of others also doing their best, would indeed maximize the welfare of all" (Bernard, 1973, p. 17).

The policies of capitalism and laissez-faire government did open new possibilities compared with pre-industrial society in which a person's station in life was determined by family and place of birth. Men were no longer bound by the soil or family connections. Individuals could amass great fortunes on their own initiative if they could understand and take advantage of the new economic system. Although inequities would be produced, with some having more than others, this too was as it should be, according to the theory. In this system anyone could rise to the top if he just worked hard enough and had ability.

Over time, it became clear that the free market could also operate perversely, and increasing government control was often seen as necessary. The believers in a true laissez-faire system called this development "creeping socialism," but it was not based on socialist doctrine or on welfare-state economics (Bernard, 1973). A completely unregulated system was just not working. What was profitable for the individual entrepreneur was not always desirable for the community as a whole. Reliance on market mechanisms *alone* meant that certain essential goods and services—e.g., garbage disposal or public transportation—were not being provided because they were not profitable. Other services, such as utilities, were only profitable as a regulated monopoly and could not survive in a completely free market. In addition, some free-market decisions were actually deleterious to the public welfare. For example, leaving decisions about land and water use to the vagaries of the market was leading to disastrous results in terms of environmental pollution.

The nature of individual participation in a democratic society

If there is to be some government regulation or community control over the actions of individuals, how is the common good to be determined—by the will of powerful elites or by group consensus? Classical democratic theory holds that government should be based on the rule of the majority. The public is expected to play an active role in debating and formulating policy, while elected officials, as "servants of the people," are expected to be more passive agents, whose function is to execute the public's will. Actually, true participatory democracy is an ideal that is difficult to achieve in contemporary society. We no longer have a way of life in which town meetings can be held on all important issues. We assume that elected officials will serve our interests with veracity and are often disappointed when they do not. Levin (1960) believes that such disappointment is inevitable because classical democratic theory promises more than it can deliver. In a democracy, a citizen is supposed to be interested in political affairs, have a capacity for rational discussion, and have the ability to evaluate information necessary to make informed choices. The individual is expected to act according to the common good, not just on the basis of personal interest; and public officials are expected to show the same honesty and integrity. Levin believes that classical democratic theory demands more of individual citizens and their representatives than can be delivered.

> Most citizens do not and cannot play an active role or display the sustained interest in politics required of them by the theory. The majority do not engage in true discussion, are not well-informed or motivated, and do not vote on the basis of principles. . . . The theory also fails to account for the necessary roles of leadership and exaggerates the active role of the masses. Those who do lead are therefore regarded as potential usurpers of what rightfully belongs to the electorate. The theory also leads its followers to believe that the bargaining and compromising which is so essential to democratic politics, is necessarily evil. In short, the roles as defined by eighteenth-century democratic theory are too demanding and the political structure designed to implement them cannot be what it is supposed to be. (Levin, 1960, pp. 73–74)

Levin believes that disenchantment with the political process and feelings of alienation are inevitable as long as the classical view of democracy is maintained. The political role individuals expect to play and believe is rightfully theirs can never be realized. Pessimistically, Levin offers no solution to this dilemma, although he does believe that a more realistic view of democracy should be developed. In his view, realism would accept corruption and selfishness as part of the human condition, so that citizens should not be too disappointed when these traits are seen in public officials. Realism also suggests that bargaining and compromise be viewed not as evils but as essentials in democratic politics.

We agree that it is naïve to expect a utopia of selflessness on the part of elected officials, and we are ready to accept the realities of political life in which self-interest and the interest of one's group are primary motivating forces. The trouble is that too many citizens are disenfranchised from even this level of political participation. Having no opportunity for self-determination is quite different from having access to the political process and choosing not to participate. For some segments of our society, improved political participation is an important goal, and community organization is a significant method for achieving that goal.

Levin's point is that disenchantment with the political process occurs when people are frustrated in their desire for a more active voice in communal affairs. Citizens expect that their individual voices as voters and taxpayers should count; yet often they do not. Indeed, a characteristic of a pluralistic society is that individuals remain political outsiders unless they can organize in such a way that their individual voices receive more weight. For the very rich, a stronger voice in politics can be bought through contributions to politicians. For the less wealthy, an effective political voice can only be achieved through organization. It is the absence of organized groups that leaves citizens vulnerable to feelings of alienation. This is a lesson as important for suburbia as for the inner city resident. The realities of participatory democracy require more than *individual* interest and motivation. Effective political participation requires group organization, articulate leaders, and political pressure.

Some historical examples of groups with access to local political power: Commercial elites and party bosses

Directly after the Industrial Revolution, those in control of government in the larger cities often were the commercial elites. For example, Dahl (1970) traced the social background and occupations of the political leaders of New Haven from 1784, the year that the city was first incorporated. Before the Industrial Revolution, the mayors of New Haven came from "patrician familes." They were landed aristocracy who had been senators, congressmen, judges, and lawyers. However, from 1842–99, power passed to the "entrepreneurs" recruited from commercial and industrial firms. In 1842, a carpet manufacturer and insurance company executive, Philip Galpin, was elected, and he was followed by a succession of manufacturers and prominent businessmen.

A similar domination by the commercial elites occurred in Chicago, except that this city did not really have a pre-industrial revolution history In 1830, Chicago was only a small trading post with a population of less than 100 citizens (Bradley & Zald, 1969). When it was incorporated in 1837 business domination was already evident. From that date till 1868, the mayor of Chicago was chosen almost exclusively from the ranks of prominent businessmen.

The social welfare functions of the political machine. There is some indication that commercial elites continued to dominate civic affairs into the 20th century in many American mid-sized cities and towns. However, in the larger cities, with growing numbers of foreign immigrants, the balance of power shifted toward charismatic ethnic leaders who used the political machine as a basis for political power.

In some cities, political leaders were chosen from the predominant ethnic group. In others with a greater diversity of ethnic composition, the political machine became a vehicle for compromising the demands of various groups by distributing jobs and patronage among them. In several of its functions, the political machine served as an early form of community organization, in that social and economic services were provided members as well as help in negotiating a "hostile system." For example, ward leaders provided help in emergencies such as relocating after a tenement fire, helping husbands get jobs, and getting sons out of jail. At times, the ward leader served as a broker between the poor and official administrative agencies. The immigrant told his or her problem to the local leader who was willing to send the message through the party apparatus to various offices for appropriate action (Aiken & Mott, 1970). To be sure, these services were provided at a steep price—the toleration of corruption that benefited the politician more than his constituents. But when the poor could find help in no other quarter, there was no choice but to turn to the sympathetic machine politician.

Levine and Levine present the following quote from a Tammany Hall leader, George Plunkitt, that shows the method he used for holding the allegiance of his constituents.

There's only one way to hold a district; you must study human nature and act accordin'. You can't study human nature in books. Books is a hindrance more than anything else. If you have been to college, so much the worse for you. You'll have to unlearn all you learned before you can get right down to human nature, and unlearnin' takes a lot of time. Some men can never forget what they learned at college. Such men may get to be district leaders by a fluke, but they never last.

To learn real human nature you have to go among the people, see them and be seen. I know every man, woman and child in the Fifteenth District, except them that's been born this summer—and I know some of them too. I know what they like and what they don't like, what they are strong at and what they are weak in, and I reach them by approachin' at the right side.

For instance, here's how I gather in the young men. I hear of a young feller that's proud of his voice, that he can sing fine. I ask him to come around to Washington Hall and join our Glee Club. He comes and sings, and he's a follower of Plunkitt for life. Another young feller gains a reputation as a baseball player in a vacant lot. I bring him into our baseball club. That fixes him. You'll find him workin' for my ticket at the polls next election day. Then there's the feller that likes rowin' on the river, the young feller that makes a name as a waltzer on his block, the young feller that's handy with his dukes—I rope them all in by given' them opportunities to show themselves off. I don't trouble them with political arguments. I just study human nature and act accordin'. . . .

What tells in holdin' your grip on your district is to go right down among the poor families and help them in the different ways they need help. I've got a regular system for this. If there's a fire in Ninth, Tenth, or Eleventh Avenue, for example, any hour of the day or night, I'm usually there with some of my election district captains as soon as the fire engines. If a family is burned out I don't ask whether they are Republicans or Democrats, and I don't refer them to the Charity Organization Society, which would investigate their case in a month or two and decide they were worthy of help about the time they are dead from starvation. I just get quarters for them, buy clothes for them if their clothes were burned up, and fix them up till they get things runnin' again. It's philanthropy, but it's politics, too—mighty good politics. Who can tell how many votes one of these fires bring me? The poor are the most grateful people in the world, and, let me tell you, they have more friends in their neighborhoods than the rich have in theirs.

If there's a family in my district in want I know it before the charitable societies do, and me and my men are first on the ground. I have a special corps to look up such cases. The consequence is that the poor look up to George W. Plunkitt as a father, come to him in trouble—and don't forget him on election day.

Another thing, I can always get a job for a deservin' man. I make it a point to keep on the track of jobs, and it seldom happens that I don't have a few up my sleeve ready for use. I know every big employer in the district and in the whole city, for that matter, and they ain't in the habit of sayin' no to me when I ask them for a job.

And the children—the little roses of the district! Do I forget them? Oh no! They know me, every one of them, and they know that a sight of Uncle George and candy means the same thing. Some of them are the best kind of votegetters. I'll tell you a case. Last year a little Eleventh Avenue rosebud whose father is a Republican, caught hold of his whiskers on election day and said she wouldn't let go till he'd promise to vote for me. And she didn't. (Levine & Levine, 1970, p. 110–112. Quoted from W. L. Riordan, *Plunkitt of Tammany Hall,* New York: McClure Phillips, 1905)

If party machines provided human services to ward constituents in the larger cities, it is not surprising that at the turn of the century, political leaders felt threatened by the rise of settlement houses in their districts. Both groups provided services with the eventual goal of increased political participation. The political bosses were content to simply buy votes. The settlement workers wanted to build a more active responsible constituency through community organization. In districts in which political leaders were benevolent and honest, the settlement workers tended to cooperate with the established leadership. It was not too difficult to show these politicians that community improvement was best for their own political interest. In other districts, the settlement workers supported reform candidates who hoped to overthrow the party machine. This tended to be a dangerous undertaking because the political boss sometimes had enough power to close the settlement house (e.g., through zoning violations) or make it difficult for its members to find employment. Moreover, if the reform candidate won, the people who supported him still expected him to provide them political favors—as the previous ward leader had done. As Levine and Levine note, the settlement house workers discovered that the system of political favors served important functions in the newly expanded cities—"functions which impartially administered laws could not provide for the people" (Levine & Levine, 1970, p. 114).

The changing role of commercial elites in local politics.   In cities without large ethnic blocs and accompanying political machines, commercial elites seemed to dominate politics for a longer period of this country's history; but even in these cities, business families started to withdraw from active political involvement over time. Initially, political participation was an important civic responsibility for the well-to-do. Over time, political participation became less important and social prestige was no longer attached to office holding. Political scientists generally agree in noting the withdrawal of commercial elites from political participation (Aiken & Mott, 1970); however there is still some dispute concerning the reasons for the withdrawal.

One possibility cited is that as industrial firms grew, they developed a national character and local plants of the national firm became absentee-owned. Executives of the absentee-owned businesses were less likely to become involved in local community decision making. If they were upwardly mobile, their ties were to advancement within the organization, not necessarily to their local community. Economic conditions that determined company policy were more likely to involve national and international considerations and were less likely to involve strictly local matters. Finally, some companies may have felt that an unpopular local political stance could "hurt business" by alienating customers. In sum, the gains from local political participation by business became less important compared with the possible cost of such involvement.

There is some controversy as to whether commercial elites ever played the large role in community affairs ascribed to them in some community studies. For example, extrapolating from their study of "Middletown, USA" (Muncie, Indiana), Robert and Helen Lynd concluded that an upper-class power elite ruled most American cities. However, subsequent studies revealed that finding elites tended to be associated with the method of the investigator. If "the reputational approach" was used, i.e., asking citizens to list influential individuals or groups in the community, elites were more likely to be found than if the actual political decision-making process was studied. The reputational method studies *beliefs* about power distribution, not the *behavior* of political leaders vis-à-vis community groups. In reviewing more recent studies of community power, Aiken and Mott (1970) concluded that communities actually are more pluralistic than the early studies of elites seemed to indicate. In their words:

> The field of community power structure has matured considerably; it has lost its elite obsession. The older penchant to ferret out an elite composed of business leaders, who singlemindedly preserved in their own image the institutions of the community, has given way to a more complex and pluralistic view of communities. All manner and shapes of power structures are now known to exist. Therefore, the most generalized model of community views it as composed of a number of centers of power varying in the amount of power they possess and how they are related to one another. (Aiken & Mott, 1970, p. 361)

Access to power in a pluralistic society

An implication of the view described by Aiken and Mott is that while decision making may be limited to small groups of individuals, on different issues the composition of the decision makers may shift. Depending on the nature of the problem, the individuals entrusted with decision-making responsibility may vary considerably. Sayre and Polsby (1965) agree and note further that while routine decisions are often ignored by community members, important decisions go unchallenged only if the decision-making group has achieved some special legitimacy for the issue in question. On the important issues, the decision makers must have the consent of other important groups (other elites) or of the general citizenry. Citizens can block the action of leaders by: (1) withholding their support at critical stages of the

decision-making process, e.g., by failing to support a necessary refer-
endum; (2) by creating independent sources of power, e.g., union
members running their own candidate for office; or (3) by forming
coalitions with other groups to achieve some common goal. In other
words, in a pluralistic society there is a fair amount of leeway for
citizen input. But citizens will be heard only if they know enough
about decision making in their community to articulate their views to
the right group at the right time. Community organization can be an
important method for achieving these goals.

Community development and social action: Two strategies for community organization

When it comes to developing community control, two major strategies have been put forth, each resting on differing assumptions. Self-
determination can be viewed from either a community development
or a social-action-oriented approach to community growth. Development strategies assume that different segments of a community have
common interests and that differences between groups are reconcilable. Active citizen participation, indigenous leadership, self-help
projects and locally sponsored programs are emphasized. There is an
effort to get a wide range of citizens involved in determining their
needs and solving their problems in a spirit of cooperation.

Social action approaches based upon conflict assumptions view resources as finite. Participants from this point of view believe that those
in power obtain an inordinate share of these resources at the expense
of others. Differences between groups are not easily reconcilable because the powerful have a vested interest in preventing equal access
to and sharing of community resources. It is frequently implied that all
gains for the "have-nots" must be achieved at the expense of the "haves"
(Miller & Riessman, 1968). Conflict strategies emphasize organizing
mass action to bring pressure on selected targets as if to say, "Let's
organize to destroy our oppressor" (Rothman, 1968).

Table 8–1 (adapted from Rothman, 1968 and 1974) summarizes the
essential characteristics of each of the models. The discussion that follows will examine each model in turn, with examples to provide an
understanding of the approach in action. We will conclude with a
discussion of the strengths and weaknesses of each approach and an
examination of the conditions under which each might be most
appropriate.

TABLE 8-1
Models of community organization (adapted from Rothman, 1968 and 1974)

		Community development	*Social action*
1.	Goals	Self-help; increases in community capacity	Shifting of power relationships and resources; basic institutional change
2.	Assumptions concerning community structure and problem conditions	Community eclipsed, anomie; lack of democratic problem-solving opportunities	Disadvantaged populations, social injustice, deprivation, inequity
3.	Basic change strategy	Broad cross section of people involved in determining and solving their own problems	Crystallization of issues and organization of people to take action against enemy targets
4.	Characteristic change tactics and techniques	Consensus, communication among community factions; group discussion	Conflict, confrontation, direct action, negotiation
5.	Medium of change	Small task-oriented groups	Mass organizations and political processes
6.	Orientation toward power structure	Members of power structure as collaborators in a common venture	Power structure as external target of action: oppressors to be coerced or overturned
7.	Assumptions regarding interests of community subparts	Common interests or reconcilable differences	Conflicting interests which are not easily reconcilable; scarce resources
8.	Conception of the client population or constituency	Citizens	Victims
9.	Salient practitioner roles	Enabler-catalyst, coordinator, teacher of problem-solving values and skills	Activist-advocate, agitator, broker, negotiator, partisan
10.	Practice positions	Village worker, neighborhood worker, consultant to community development team, agricultural extension worker	Local organizer
11.	Agency type	Settlement houses, overseas community development; Peace Corps, Friends Service Committee, Model Cities, health associations, consumers' groups	Alinsky, black and brown power, welfare rights councils, cause and social movement groups, women's movement, trade union insurgent movements, consumer's movements, radical political groups, radical groups in the professions

Community development as a consensus building strategy

The term "community development" came into use after World War II in the efforts to improve village life in newly independent developing countries. The emphasis was on stimulating local initiative, self-help projects, and governmental cooperation to provide technical assistance. Although originally applied to programs of "village improvement" or rural development, the model has also been used as an approach to the problems of the city slums as well. Clinard (1970) lists the steps involved in urban community development as follows:

1. Creation of a sense of social cohesion on a neighborhood basis and strengthening of group interrelationships.
2. Encouragement and stimulation of self-help, through the initiative of the individuals in the community.
3. Stimulation by outside agencies when initiative for self-help is lacking.
4. Reliance upon persuasion rather than upon compulsion to produce change through the efforts of the people.
5. Identification and development of local leadership.
6. Development of civic consciousness and acceptance of civic responsibility.
7. Use of professional and technical assistance to support the efforts of the people involved.
8. Coordination of city services to meet neighborhood needs and problems.
9. Provision of training in democratic procedures that may result in decentralization of some government functions. (Clinard, 1970, p. 126)

Eugster (1974) provides an example of community development that illustrates the steps described by Clinard. Working in a black neighborhood called West Heights, Eugster initially found an area of 400 citizens isolated from the rest of the city, with a poor standard of living, few city services and dilapidated and overcrowded homes. Until 1955, the children of West Heights were educated in an all black two-room school house. With the coming of school integration, the children of the area were bused to previously all white schools. Before school desegregation, West Heights children were performing at levels up to 5 years behind their white peers. After integration, the same school performance disparity continued.

Eugster's entry into the area began with a series of educational lectures at one of the local churches. Even this small first step did not occur without fear and distrust, but eventually the educational program was accepted as part of the church's general moral and educational mission. There were some shaky starts and near disasters, the most serious of which was trying to extend the educational program to children of all ages without adequate planning. It required perserverance by Eugster to bring the group together after this crisis. But when it did meet again, the educational committee nominally in charge of the program began to show some group cohesiveness and responsibility for future programming. The meetings became a format for members "to think together" about common community problems.

Eugster's goal was to help the group come together to develop a plan of action to alleviate *one* specific problem. In West Heights, the specific problem was not difficult to choose; everyone was concerned about the poor school performance and disruptive school behavior evidenced by the area children. Yet, since the adults in the community were poorly educated themselves they felt impotent to deal with this problem. Eugster suggested a tutoring program, hosted and supervised by parents but using the services of educated volunteers from the larger community.

As an indication of the degree of alienation and resignation experienced by community residents, committee members predicted that no children would agree to after school tutoring; that community members would not give their homes for group lessons; and that volunteers if found would quickly quit. These early trepidations proved to be unfounded as the program was enormously successful. Children responded "en masse." The group had touched upon a vital concern of all area citizens; they desperately wanted to improve the education of their children. People became quite excited about the project and their enthusiasm was transmitted to the children. Additional tutors and neighborhood homes in which they could work were recruited and the program was on its way.

The larger community, which in the past had tended to isolate and neglect the West Heights citizens, now began to offer help. School principals who did not volunteer their help initially and who believed that West Heights parents were not seriously interested in the schooling of their children were taken aback when the plan actually materialized. However, they quickly agreed to participate once the plan was successfully under way. They urged children to attend study sessions and set up periodic training and coordination meetings between school teachers and volunteer tutors. Other civic organizations also became interested and soon West Heights children were invited to plays, concerts, trips to the zoo and circus, and tours of some local laboratories. After two and a half years of the program, the School Board agreed to incorporate the program into its educational system and hired two full-time field educators to work toward its continuation and expansion.

While the program was an apparent success, what of other aspects of the West Heights community? Were there other significant changes? Eugster reported that over time the original education committee was expanded into the West Heights Citizens Association with members from every clique and faction within the community. The association obtained garbage collection services and successfully fought an effort by a group of businessmen to have part of the West Heights land zoned for commercial use. The school reported improved school attitudes and performance; the probation department reported a decrease in delinquency; and the public health nurse reported improved upkeep of homes and higher family morale. Biddle and Biddle (1965) define community development as "a social process by which human beings can become more competent to live with and gain some control over local aspects of a frustrating and changing world" (p. 78). It is in this sense that members of the West Heights community became competent to do for themselves.

Assumptions of the community development perspective. This example illustrates several of the assumptions and steps previously listed (Clinard, 1970; Rothman, 1968).

1. The community development facilitator may begin the process of bringing people together when local initiative is absent, but withdraws into the background as soon as it becomes feasible to do so. Eugster refused the chairmanship of the education committee once it became organized, and declined membership in the West Heights Citizens Association that developed later.

2. People act when they think they can do something—i.e., when they feel a growing competence. Having problems, or experiencing deprivation by itself, is insufficient motivation for concerted action. If anything, Eugster believes that facing the true depth and extent of deprivation can be destructive. On one occasion, Eugster showed a documentary film of a deprived southern black community similar to West Heights. The reaction to the film was predominantly negative with several residents stating that they "didn't like to think about people who lived like that." The film did not motivate the group to

action but reinforced their resignation that nothing could be done to improve their circumstances.

3. The model assumes that community officials, who in the past were neglecting the needs of a segment of the population they were supposed to serve, can become more responsive to local initiative. This is a crucial point for it implies that isolation and neglect are not purposeful reactions on the part of officials but occur because the problems may seem overwhelming and no effective solution is apparent. However, when a group comes up with an effective program, administered successfully, that fits community standards, the cooperation of others is not difficult to achieve. Eugster points out that civic leaders from the surrounding community had on several occasions made overtures of help to the West Heights community. The deprivation in West Heights was apparent to all who visited. But neither the civic leaders nor the local indigenous leadership could articulate a plan for neighborhood self-help or community improvement. Outside of occasional funds for church repair and the vague promise "call on us any time we can be of help," nothing was done. Only after the program was under way did civic officials provide help and cooperation.

It should be noted, perhaps with some dismay, that there are many times when civic leaders do not lead. As in West Heights, community officials did not take the initiative in helping the neighborhood deal with its problems, but waited until the process started by a community development specialist was under way. As we shall point out in Chapter 9, officials rarely perceive the mandate to innovate. They do so when they believe that there is a consensus for action in the community. Without such a consensus, they function to keep the community on an even keel—in equilibrium. The power of community development is its ability to disturb that equilibrium with constructive action by newly motivated citizens. As a community official, one may not know how to respond to angry outbursts by long-neglected citizens, particularly if one does not have effective solutions available. It is much easier to jump on a bandwagon that is already moving and receive approval for being such a flexible and cooperative person.

Community development assumptions represent an exceptionally optimistic view of human growth and potential. The optimism can be seen most clearly in the list of operational assumptions for community development offered by Biddle and Biddle (1965).

1. Each person is valuable, unique, and capable of growth toward greater social sensitivity and responsibility.
   a. Each person has underdeveloped abilities in initiative, original-

ity, and leadership. These qualities can be cultivated and strengthened.

   b. These abilities tend to emerge and grow stronger when people work together in small groups that serve the common (community) good.

   c. There will always be conflicts between persons and factions. Properly handled, the conflicts can be used creatively.

   d. Agreement can be reached on specific next steps of improvement, without destroying philosophic or religious differences.

   e. Although the people may express their differences freely, when they become responsible they often choose to refrain in order to further the interest of the whole group and of their idea of community.

   f. People will respond to an appeal to altruism as well as to an appeal to selfishness.

   g. These generous motivations may be used to form groups that serve an inclusive welfare of all people in a community.

   h. Groups are capable of growth toward self-direction when the members assume responsibility for group growth and for an inclusive local welfare.

2. Human beings and groups have both good and bad impulses.

   a. Under wise encouragement they can strengthen the better in themselves and help others to do likewise.

   b. When the people are free of coercive pressures, and can then examine a wide range of alternatives, they tend to choose the ethically better and the intelligently wiser course of action.

   c. There is satisfaction in serving the common welfare, even as in serving self-interest.

   d. A concept of the common good can grow out of group experience that serves the welfare of all in some local area. This sense of responsibility and belonging can be strengthened even for those to whom community is least meaningful.

3. Satisfaction and self-confidence gained from small accomplishments can lead to the contending with more and more difficult problems, in a process of continuing growth. (Biddle & Biddle, 1965, pp. 60–61).*

Community developers assume that antisocial motives are situationally determined. In other words, the belief is that people are basically good but are perverted by environmental circumstance.

A problem for community development: The limits of consensus and cooperation. Since there is little literature on the effectiveness of community development aside from reports of uncontrolled demonstration projects, it becomes very difficult to evaluate the extent to which the assumptions listed above are valid. Our own estimate is

---

* From *The community development process: The rediscovery of local initiative* by William W. Biddle and Loureide J. Biddle. Copyright © 1965 by Holt, Rinehart and Winston, Inc. Reprinted by permission of Holt, Rinehart and Winston.

clearly less optimistic than that of Biddle and Biddle. In our view, community development assumptions are *ideals* toward which community workers should strive. By creating positively reinforcing environmental events, one can increase the likelihood for more constructive and cooperative behavior. Much of what passes for poor motivation and selfishness is norm-determined. Finding ways of changing norms and expectations and providing encouragement for new behaviors can drastically alter performance.

Still, there are constraints which prevent cooperation and consensus alone from achieving constructive change. It is not only organized opposition that can grind a people down; interference also can come from the constraints of inadequate time, money, energy, and ability. Even the most optimistic of community developers recognizes that those who would become involved in community development projects are but a handful of the potential participants available from among the citizenry (Biddle & Biddle, 1965). Furthermore, those with severe deficits (a problem in any poor community) may not have the ability to participate.

> Persons outside the normal range cannot be expected to join a process of development that attracts the average. But we do not know what the limits of the normal range are until we have had further experience with encouraged community development that improves individual lives. . . . There will always be a need for social welfare, health, and psychotherapeutic services. Many specialists who supply these services will welcome community development processes, in the hope that these processes will lighten their loads. But more experimentation is needed. (Biddle & Biddle, 1965, p. 271)

Another limitation of cooperation strategies, when practiced exclusively, can be summarized best by the "squeaky wheel" principle. Squeaky wheels get greased; those that are silent are left alone. A strategy of talking to local officials without "squeaking," that is, by keeping everything "nice" and cooperative allows for the interpretation that one's group may not be hurting enough to require official action. Alinsky quotes Franklin D. Roosevelt as having told a reform delegation who visited him to plead for a specific change: "Okay, you've convinced me. Now go out and bring pressure on me!" (Alinsky, 1972, p. xxiii). The power of an intense minority can be quite high, especially if the issue in question is not of concern to the majority. If an official ignores an angry minority on such an issue, he or she can lose votes and gain nothing from the majority if they remain unconcerned. Only when the issue is of concern to both groups is there less likely to be simple acquiescence to vocal demands. But even for such contested issues, a local official must carefully weigh the potential damage that can occur from an angry group whose members appear ready to create embarrassment at every turn. The threat of such a possibility is never dismissed lightly.

Social action and conflict strategies

Conflict strategies have become prominent in the community organization field, not because of sounder rationale or empirical confirmation, but because more than the development point of view, conflict approaches fit with the Zeitgeist of the 1960s, whose hallmark was confrontation tactics in the political arena. Basically, conflict strategies function to stir placid communities by spotlighting the plight of the minority and by raising basic questions about commonly accepted community roles and procedures. Conflict strategies are designed to make people uncomfortable; and there are times when it may be necessary to do so. There are communities in which the major social institutions no longer reflect the values of large segments of the community, yet the majority is rigid in its refusal to become aware of and accommodate in significant ways to the needs of the minority. In such communities, confrontation and conflict seem unavoidable.

Groups working outside the official system of community and governmental structures can force attention on local inequities. By swaying public opinion, localities can be forced to confront difficult problems and develop better procedures for their resolution. If it appeals successfully to national sentiment, "agitation" can be the stimulus for new laws or significant national programs. For example, much of the progress in areas such as civil rights, housing, and urban development has been stimulated by conflict tactics employed by disadvantaged minority groups.

The principal goal of social action is to achieve a shift in power relationships to insure a more equitable distribution of resources. Alinsky (1972) states this goal in simple terms by pointing out that the battle is between the Haves and the Have-Nots.

> The purpose of the Haves is to keep what they have. Therefore, the Haves want to maintain the status quo and the Have-Nots to change it. . . . The Haves want to keep; the Have-Nots want to get. (Alinsky, 1972, pp. 19 and 42)

Alinsky is convinced that since the Haves will not share voluntarily (their orientation is to acquire "more," and they have never done otherwise), the only way to get power is to seize it and convince the Haves by strength that it is in their best interest to negotiate. Ultimately, gains come through negotiation, but "no one can negotiate without the power to compel negotiation" (Alinsky, 1972, p. 119).

Alinsky provides an example of how power, or in this case the threat of power can compel negotiation. It seems that commitments made by Chicago civic authorities to the Woodlawn ghetto organization were not being honored. The Woodlawn group felt it needed a new plan to maintain the pressure necessary for its goals to be achieved. The following plan was devised:

> O'Hare Airport became the target. To begin with, O'Hare is the world's busiest airport. Think for a moment of the common experience of jet travelers. Your stewardess brings you your lunch or dinner. After eating, most people want to go to the lavatory. However, this is often inconvenient because your tray and those of your seat partners are loaded down with dishes.
>
> So you wait until the stewardess has removed the trays. By that time those who are seated closest to the lavatory have got up and the "occupied" sign is on. So you wait. And in these days of jet travel the seat belt sign is soon flashed, as the airplane starts its landing approach. You decide to wait until after landing and use the facilities in the terminal. This is obvious to anyone who watches the unloading of passengers at various gates in any airport—many of the passengers are making a beeline for the men's or the ladies' room.
>
> With this in mind, the tactic becomes obvious—we tie up the lavoratories. In the restrooms you drop a dime, enter, push the lock on the door—and you can stay there all day. Therefore the occupation of the sit-down toilets present no problem. It would take just a relatively few people to walk into these cubicles, armed with books and newspapers, lock the doors, and tie up all the facilities. What are the police going to do? Break in and demand evidence of legitimate occupancy? Therefore, the ladies' restrooms could be occupied completely; the only problem in the men's lavoratories would be the stand-up urinals. This, too, could be taken care of, having groups busy themselves around the airport and then move in on the stand-up urinals to line up four or five deep whenever a flight arrived. An intelligence study was launched to learn how many sit-down toilets for both men and women, as well as stand-up urinals, there were in the entire O'Hare Airport complex and how many men and women would be necessary for the nation's first "shit-in."
>
> The consequences of this kind of action would be catastrophic in many ways. People would be desperate for a place to relieve themselves. One can see children yelling at their parents, "Mommy, I've got

to go," and desperate mothers surrendering, "All right—well, do it. Do it right here." O'Hare would soon become a shambles. The whole scene would become unbelievable and the laughter and ridicule would be nationwide. It would probably get a front page story in the London Times. It would be a source of great mortification and embarrassment to the city administration. It might even create the kind of emergency in which planes would have to be held up while passengers got back aboard to use the plane's toilet facilities.

The threat of this tactic was leaked (again there may be a Freudian slip here, and again, so what?) back to the administration, and within 48 hours the Woodlawn Organization found itself in conference with the authorities who said that they were certainly going to live up to their commitments and they could never understand where anyone got the idea that a promise made by Chicago's City Hall would not be observed. At no point, then or since, has there ever been any open mention of the threat of the O'Hare tactic. Very few of the members of the Woodlawn Organization knew how close they were to writing history. (Alinsky, 1972, pp. 142–144)

The importance of power and conflict in social action strategies.

Alinsky advises community organizers to cultivate the *impression* that they would stop at nothing to achieve their goals. The more the opposition is embarrassed or fears it will be embarrassed, the greater the potential power of the organizer. Thus Alinsky is willing to state that "in war, the end justifies almost any means" (Alinsky, 1972, p. 29). However, as the supreme pragmatist, Alinsky recognizes that some tactics can produce a backlash of attitude that can undo all prior accomplishment.

> "Power comes out of the barrel of a gun" is an absurd rallying cry when the other side has all the guns. . . . When there are people who espouse the assassination of Senator Robert Kennedy or the Tate murders or the Marin County courthouse kidnapping and killings or the University of Wisconsin bombing and killing as "revolutionary acts," then we are dealing with people who are merely hiding psychosis behind a political mask. The masses of people recoil with horror and say, "Our way is bad and we are willing to let it change, but certainly not for this murderous madness—no matter how bad things are now, they are better than that." So they begin to turn back. They regress into acceptance of a coming massive repression in the name of "law and order." (Alinsky, 1972, pp. xxi–xxiii)

In entering a community for the first time, an initial task of the organizer is to become established as an individual of strength who is on the people's side. If the establishment can be baited to attack the organizer as a "dangerous enemy," credibility is gained with the "have-nots." Breaking through years of apathy and rationalizations for inaction is no small task, but in building relationships within an indigenous community, the organizer attempts to find an issue that people can become angry about and that can probably be negotiated successfully even with only a small nucleus of followers. With one success behind it, the group is on its way. Initially it may appear that the people do not know what they want so that the organizer may have reservations about their capacity and the extent to which they can be trusted. But people tend not to think about issues that they cannot change (Alinsky, 1972, p. 105) so that this initial impression may not be at all valid. Once organized with the power to make changes, poor people become at least as capable as others to discuss and decide issues that affect their lives.

Why is conflict a necessary ingredient in the Alinsky approach? Could more progress be made by conciliation and cooperation? Alinsky would answer that one cannot negotiate and compromise from a weak position. Conciliation only occurs among equals who see that it is in their self-interest to cooperate. Alinsky sees people as essentially selfish; not sharing unless forced to do so. Therefore, important gains for disadvantaged groups will not occur without a fight. This is a fact of life that Alinsky argues community organizers should accept. So despite a "middle-class moral hygiene which has made of conflict or controversy something negative and undesirable," He believes "conflict is the essential core of a free and open society. If one were to project the democratic way of life in the form of a musical score, its major theme would be the harmony of dissonance" (Alinsky, 1972, p. 62).

Problems for social action strategies

The possibility of unleashing an attitudinal backlash in the majority community. Despite Alinsky's admonition to "keep the pressure on" (Alinsky, 1972, p. 128) there can be a point reached where the larger community, pushed to the limits of its ability to accommodate, will find itself frustrated by the continuation of disequilibrium. If constructive solutions are unavailable or are rejected by majority community sentiment, more destructive and repressive solutions may be adopted. It is for this reason that agitation "outside the system" works best when there are also those within the system working for change along more traditional routes. As Miller and Riessman note:

> There is considerable concern both within the system and outside it for the humanizing of bureaucracy, limiting bureaucratic discretion,

guaranteeing the voice of the recipients of service, and guarding their dignity and rights. . . . To the extent that the outsiders are effective in their demands for the poor, they move the center of gravity farther to the "left" and thus may provide the insiders with more leverage in mediating the demands of the poor with the traditional agencies and power structures. (Miller and Riessman, 1968, pp. 228–229; 231)*

According to Miller and Riessman, social radicals should not act with disdain toward those who work for change within the system.

As minorities become more organized and begin winning concessions, other groups fearing a change in the status quo that will be to their disadvantage may start organizing a backlash movement. In any showdown between a minority and other groups in the community at large, the minority cannot win by numbers or by force. They must have a moral right on their side that can sway the still uncommitted members of the majority.

The assumption of static resources.   The conflict strategist assumes that communities cannot increase the level of scarce resources to give all citizens a better life. This means that an advantage for one group can be expected to occur only at the expense of another. The poor can get more only if the rich get less; and since the rich will not reduce their consumption voluntarily, conflict is in order.

This view neglects the possibility that with proper planning, an organized community can build its resources to new levels in some areas. For example: with increased motivation, workers may be more productive; increased educational opportunities may widen the base of technical skills available; more productive use of people can mean less money being spent for supervision and control (e.g. police, prisons etc.); and, more constructive use of leisure time can increase the job opportunities in ancillary occupations such as recreation, park maintenance, and the arts.

On the other hand, prolonged community conflict can serve to ensure actualization of the prediction of limited and static community resources. With prolonged conflict, actual reduction in resources is likely as the older, more affluent sections of the community leave in discouragement and new sources of revenue are frightened away by the specter of conflict. If community groups on both sides of a conflict were to accept the belief in static resources, resistance to change by the established groups cannot help but increase. With this belief firmly entrenched, the "haves" will not give up what they perceive as having

---

* Excerpted from *Social class and social policy* by S. M. Miller and Frank Riessman, © 1968 by Basic Books, Inc., Publishers, New York.

been justly earned no matter how righteous the cause of the "have-nots". For example, in describing the conflict between Black and Italian groups on Chicago's Near West Side, Suttles notes:

> In the background, of course, was the oppressive belief that the benefits of social life make up a fixed quantity and were already being used to the maximum. Thus, even the most liberal Italians assume that any gain to the Negroes must be at their loss. On their own part, the Negroes make the same assumption and see no reason why the Italians should give way without a fight. Thus whatever good intentions exist on either side are overruled by the seeming impracticality or lack of realism. (Suttles, 1968, p. 103)

There is a danger then that prolonged conflict can lead to a hardening of attitudes and a backlash of repression if the "haves" are powerful enough, and flight and drainage of resources if they are not.[2]

Power without program is not enough. An additional problem has to do with the neglect of substantive programmatic concerns on the part of those agitating for change from a conflict perspective. Quite naturally, disenfranchised groups will spend a significant amount of time preparing for the assumption of political power. But when the battle has been won, the same complex problems of housing, education, health care, employment, etc., that the majority found so difficult to solve, still remain. After the community organization stage has been passed, what then? Power without program will lead to little improvement in people's lives (Miller & Riessman, 1968) and may simply substitute a new bureaucracy for the old. It would be ironic if the poor who struggled to support the new "people's organization" (Alinsky, 1946) were to find that when the battle was over, only a few of their numbers benefited from the struggle—those who by reason of personality or skill could gravitate toward management, professional, or para-professional positions. Without innovative programs and resources with which to implement programs, the desperate lives of the many will remain untouched. The community organizer who believes that infinite wisdom resides in the oppressed may find to his or her dismay (Pearl, 1971) that programs depend upon knowledge of complex areas (e.g., economics, law, social relations, etc.) and that without this knowledge, the poor are impotent to generate constructive change. Community control does not mean that the right decisions are always made.

---

[2] While natural resources are finite, social practices concerning use and consumption can be changed. There are many situations in which social change is not a "zero-sum" game.

Choosing between consensus and conflict strategies

Some contemporary writers have polarized the choice between strategies by describing them in value-laden terms. Cox, Erlich, Rothman and Tropman (1974) point out that the terms used can lead the unwary into believing that the choice is between "masculine and feminine," "brave and cowardly," or "radical and establishment" modes of operation. Polarization of this sort is likely to be counter-productive. What is more important is to specify the conditions within communities that favor the success of one or the other approach.

Table 8–2 represents a list of factors we think should be considered in choosing between the two strategies. The factors listed are abstracted in part from discussions by Cox, et al. (1974) and Wachtel (1968).

TABLE 8–2
Factors associated with the choice of community organization strategies

	Strategies	
Factors	*Community development*	*Social action*
Majority group attitude toward change	Uncommitted majority	Strongly antagonistic majority
Concordance in majority and minority group values	Agreement on underlying values	Value clash
Availability of resources	Untapped resources	Scarce resources
Structure of community decision making	Pluralistic decision making	Power elites

We should first recognize that the psychological processes upon which community development is based are those of persuasion and influence; while social action relies more heavily upon power and coercion. It is our opinion that all else being equal, the least coercive procedure to induce change is to be preferred, since force often leaves an inevitable residue of resentment, which if it becomes strong enough can trigger a counter-movement that can erase previously won benefits. It can be noted from Table 8–2 that, in general, conciliation is more likely to be successful when: the groups in question share under-lying beliefs and values; the majority is not strongly antagonistic; re-sources are available or new resources can be generated through cooperative effort; and the community already has a tradition of pluralistic decison making in which problems tend to be worked out through negotiation and compromise. On the other hand, political pressure through concerted social action becomes more necessary when: value differences are high and the majority is strongly antagonistic; resources are scarce and increased opportunity for one group can be achieved only at the expense of another; and the decisions by a small elite group in power consistently favor only certain segments of the community. In all of these latter instances there are counter-forces and interests that would nullify persuasion attempts undertaken without sufficient organized power.

Cox et al. (1974) believe that *both* consensus and conflict strategies must be used in community organization, and that total reliance on only one of the two will be unsuccessful in most cases. For example, one might start with a power building strategy to compel negotiation, but a point may be reached in which more can be accomplished by negotiation and compromise than by continued disruption. Unfortunately, it is not always easy to change strategies in the midst of a major organizational effort. If one exaggerates the negative attributes of the opposition, as Alinsky suggests, and paints him as the "enemy" or the "devil," it becomes difficult to convince one's followers that, indeed, it is now time to compromise with the devil. It is difficult to move back from the effects of intense negative stereotypes. Similarly, those who are attracted to a more "genteel" and diplomatic form of development approach may become frightened and withdraw if the strategy changes to more militant tactics. Our own view is that it is preferable to start with the less disruptive strategy and only move toward more coercion when persuasion has failed. If conditions are clearly unfavorable for conciliation (Table 8–2) social action must be considered. The first step in the social action process must involve the organization of a viable constituency. The field of community organization is littered with the corpses of well-meaning, fledgling social action attempts whose leaders were too involved in the politics of confrontation to recognize that their programs had little popular community support.

The limits of community organization: Problems for both development and social action strategies

Does community organization reduce the rates of psychological dysfunction?

A claim made for community organization is that increased political power should lead to improved mental health. For example, Miller and Reissman, in advocating involvement in community organization as a way of improving the mental health of low-income citizens, note that "frequently an individual's psychological difficulties appear to diminish when he becomes involved in some commitment, activity or social movement" (Miller & Reissman, 1968, p. 179). The resultant improved mental health is attributed to a "spread effect."

> . . . a self-generator of positive change is put into motion and it may lead the client to feel a growing sense of power and conviction which transfers to various areas of his life, his family, his friends, and the community, indirectly producing broad behavioral modifications and feedback effects (p. 180).

It should be recognized that the positive effects described above are associated with activity, involvement, and participation in self-determined activity, and are not necessarily associated with *political power* as such. It is possible that the same self-confidence and "generator of positive change" might be expected from the leader of a bowling tournament, the president of the local chapter of the Elks, or the captain of a Mah Jong team. Indeed, many psychotherapists recommend social participation and eventual assumption of social responsibility as a form of "sociotherapy" for patients deficient in social skills and self-confidence.

There is some evidence that rates of reported psychic disturbance go down during periods of war, campus unrest, or other environmental emergencies that mobilize the citizenry. Not only do these events help an individual "take his mind off his troubles," but there is usually an increased need for all forms of manpower. Again, being socially useful and performing socially valued competent behaviors does much to improve self-confidence and psychological functioning. But being socially useful is not the same as political self-determination or political power, as any student of totalitarian societies can document. The point is simply that community participation and community control should not be justified on the grounds that participation can be viewed as a cure for mental and emotional dysfunction—until there is clearer evidence that *political* self-determination does produce improved mental health.

Epidemiological data do show that members of the middle class have a lower incidence of mental disturbance, and also are more likely to be involved in social and community affairs than are citizens from the lower socioeconomic classes. The correlations between poverty, community disorganization, and incidence of psychiatric symptomatology have been repeatedly and consistently demonstrated. However, interpreting the meaning of these correlations has been one of the enduring problems of psychiatric epidemiology. It is just as likely that the correlation between lack of social participation and increased likelihood of mental disturbance demonstrates the disabling aspects of mental disturbance as it does the redeeming properties of community participation.

It should be noted that Reiff (1966), an advocate of community organization and social action, does not assert that self-determination produces self-actualization; only that the former is a prerequisite for the latter. It well may be that low-income communities, responsive to the needs of their residents and controlled by their own elected representatives, will not abolish mental illness; but will simply display the same level of psychological functioning as other socioeconomic communities—a level of functioning that they have not been able to obtain under existing adverse environmental circumstances.

It is our guess that when the research evidence is in, we will find that the relationship between community disorganization, socioeconomic class, and rates of psychic disturbance is actually more complex than many currently believe. If we accept the multifactor etiological model of psychological disturbance described in Chapter 4, we should expect that community disorganization is but one of several interacting risk factors contributing to eventual dysfunction. Even so, the possible effects of community disorganization cannot be predicted at this time. For example, community disorganization may have an effect on eventual disturbance, but the effect may not be as strong as that produced by other risk factors, such as those associated with genetics or family upbringing. Other plausible effects include the following: (1) Community organization may influence the form of symptom expression but not the rates of incidence of disorder. Cross-cultural epidemiological studies have not found any society free of psychological disturbance, but the form and intensity of symptom expression does vary considerably across cultures. (2) Community organization may have its greatest impact on mild-to-moderate dysfunction with less of an impact on severe dysfunction where the genetic loading may be higher. But even for severe disorders, the *intensity and duration* of symptomatic behavior may be a function of environmental determinants such as level of community organization. For example, there is evidence that chronic mental patients can function more adequately in some social settings than in others (Fairweather, et al., 1969).

We have discussed this problem at length because the effects of environment (including the level of community organization) on mental functioning is one of the most interesting and hotly debated issues in psychology today. We view the eventual outcome of this debate with great interest. Those committed to community organization should recognize that theirs is a valuable process, but one that should not be justified as a "cure" for mental dysfunction.

Problems of government-sponsored community organization: The CAP example

The 1960s saw a very curious development: the federal government sponsoring programs that challenged the decision making of local governmental units. In some ways it was as if the government were sponsoring a revolution against itself—at least that was the opinion of some local officials who suddenly found themselves opposed politically by groups receiving federal funds. Why was the government apparently sponsoring their opposition? To understand this development it would be helpful to trace the evolution of the Community Action Program (CAP) in the United States.

The original ideas behind the CAP programs were first developed by the Ford Foundation "Grey Area Projects" (named for the zone of deterioration found in American cities); and later they were taken over by planners in the federal government (Marris & Rein, 1967).

It should be recognized at the outset that except for a few progressive states, the course of social reform in this country tends to follow the pattern of federal initiative to induce local changes. Such was the origin of the CAP programs. However, unlike other social reforms, the War on Poverty did not arise from the pressure of overwhelming public demand (the poor had no lobby) but from presidential mandate (Sundquist, 1969). Dissatisfied with the accomplishments of piecemeal social welfare programs, President Kennedy asked his advisers for a broad new program to tackle the bedrock problem of poverty. The social scientists who planned and drafted the CAP legislation believed that redistribution of power and resources, and the humanizing of social institutions, were basic to any coordinated attack on poverty (Kravitz & Kolodner, 1970). What emerged from the shifts and accommodations necessary to bring a major piece of social legislation through Congress was substantially less than this ideal. Still, great potential remained, though the original outlines were now in reduced and softened form.

A major problem with the legislation was its lack of conceptual clarity. How was the original mandate of the Presidential planners to be put into operation in terms of concrete programs? Did the poor need greater opportunity, more income, increased services, or more political power? The legislation tried to provide for all of these possibilities within the same agency. There was a lack of awareness of the full range of problems to be encountered.

Consider, for example, the hallmark concept of the legislation—the maximum feasible participation of the poor. Even among the original planners, the concept was never clearly understood or agreed upon. For some, the thought was simply of a "process of encouraging the residents of poverty areas to take part in the work of community-action programs and to perform a number of jobs that might otherwise be performed by professional social workers" (Yarmolinsky, 1969, p. 49). That is, the poor were to participate in the administration of programs and services. For others, the local community action program was like a "three-legged stool" (Wofford, 1969) in which representatives of the poor would enter all phases of planning administration, and control as equal partners with local public officials and representatives of traditional social service agencies. For still others, the representatives of the poor were not expected to "necessarily be poor themselves" (Moynihan, 1969, p. 180)! What is clear is that none of the original planners expected that the poor would adopt a conflict strategy and attempt to topple local governmental units. In Moynihan's words, "it was taken as a matter beneath notice that such programs would be dominated by the local political structure" (Moynihan 1969, p. 87).

Regardless of original intent, CAP programs in many communities soon found themselves caught up in a political struggle over who "owned" the poverty program. Without clearly prescribed guidelines and procedures, federal administrators found themselves powerless as local CAP groups adopted the assumption of the social radicals that the enemy was "the establishment"—the very groups with whom cooperation was to be encouraged. As this attitude became pervasive, local CAP groups encountered resistance and a backlash in attitudes even before programs were established. Political groups developed to emasculate CAP programs, led by the very people needed to keep the "three-legged stool" on an even keel—the mayors and the traditional social service professionals.

With the benefit of hindsight, it seems extremely naïve to have expected that social radicalism, primarily effective as an "outside the system" strategy (Miller & Riessman, 1968), could be effectively imposed within the context of a government-supported agency. Even Alinsky would not have supported the proposition that "people's organizations" could be set up by government professionals. He predicted that the War on Poverty would not last long, and reminded those who would listen that "social radicalism is not a civil service calling" (Moynihan, 1969, p. 187). By 1968 the inevitable had occurred. Funds were shut off to the most radical CAP units and their directors were replaced. Those CAP units that survived were the ones that had developed either from a social service model, or from a community development model in which local political units were included in a cooperative fashion. In the former case, the emphasis was on palliative service programs whose impact on institutional change was minimal. In the latter case, innovative, cooperative self-help projects took some faltering but significant steps toward maturity. Consumer cooperatives, credit unions, planned parenthood programs, health maintenance organizations, and parent effectiveness classes became available in some poor neighborhoods for the first time. When imposed from above, they easily could become additional signs that self-generated initiative is futile. As self-help projects, they provided the opportunity for people to see themselves as potent providers for their own welfare.

In analyzing the problems of the Community Action Programs, Marris and Rein (1967) make two telling points. The American system of government is designed to guard against the excesses of government control. The system of checks and balances and divided authority is purposely set to prevent the domination of any one group or any one governmental unit. As such, the system works to protect individual citizens from government interference. But Marris and Rein note that we pay a price for our form of democracy. By the time any piece of reform legislation moves through the web of entrenched interests and constituencies found in our legislatures, it is inevitably weakened and compromised by the coalitions necessary for its passage. The CAP legislation was ambiguous because that was the only way of getting it through Congress. If its planners had insisted on keeping the legislation close to their original vision—a bill to deal with poverty in America by redistributing power and resources—it never would have become law.

The second major problem faced by the CAP programs concerned the difficulty of building consensus in communities that were not ready for concerted, unified action. It was the hope of the CAP planners that the diverse elements in a community (the poor, the social service agencies, and local governmental units) would become more unified by working on common projects. This hope did not materialize. In communities that were relatively unified and cooperative before CAP money was accepted, things went smoothly and much was accomplished. Where unity did not exist, there was competition and jockeying for control of funds. In other words, there were no shortcuts for people to learn to work together. Government programs could not force a community to become unified; community organization could not be imposed by government fiat.

Resources for social change may be unavailable at the local level

Both community development and social action are locally based. Neighborhoods are to be organized to provide increased political power so as to influence decisions concerning the distribution of resources within local jurisdictions. The problem is that even though such programs may be successful locally, they may still be unable to appreciably affect the lives of citizens because the local governmental structure finds itself impoverished. Thus we have the dilemma of battles won at the local level in convincing city government to advocate more responsive social programs only to have progress eroded by bleak city-wide fiscal resources. Cities do not have taxing powers that are in anyway comparable to those of the federal government and most often do not control the amount of tax dollars returned to them through the federal and state bureaucracies.

Some important issues are decided and controlled locally. Garbage collection, police protection, and redevelopment plans (e.g., where to put a projected youth center or elementary school) can be affected by local community organization. Other important issues, such as unemployment, welfare regulations, or fiscal policy, are not influenced as much by local input (Marris & Rein, 1967). Guskin and Ross (1971) concur, and note further that the action of a federal agency such as the Federal Reserve Board, in raising or lowering prime interest rates, is more decisive for employment and unemployment than is any proposal for community organization. Similarly:

> Welfare service and renewal programs all compete with one another in the budgeting process, and they compete as well with health programs, farm subsidies, etc.; that is, they compete within the roughly one-half of the federal budget "left over" from defense allocations. In turn defense

> allocations are the least amenable to public reaction, debate, etc. of all
> the contestants in the federal arena. Community planners have come up
> against the symptoms of this problem again and again: they design pro-
> grams that cannot be funded. (Guskin & Ross, 1971, p. 54)

Increased funding for the cities could help programs of local community organization, but influencing the decision to redistribute federal resources requires action by a unified national constituency.
Community organizations may find it necessary to build a national
program through unified action with other groups of similar interest.
This is often the only way to influence national priorities significantly.

There are two problems that must be overcome for a successful
compaign involving a unified national organizational effort. To begin
with, community organizations are not known for their ability to act in
unison even on local issues. It is asking a great deal to expect them to
come together on a national issue that may not have an immediate
local payoff. Community organizations and their leaders will have to
overcome the tendency to compete with one another for a national
strategy to succeed.

A second problem is that, increasingly, national policy is being
formulated by a "new elite"—professional managers and technocrats
who have emerged in government, as the social order has become
more technical and complex (Guskin & Ross, 1971). These professional planners develop programs for "model cities," urban renewal,
wars on poverty, etc., confident that they have found answers to social
problems that will be acceptable to the public. Over the years they
have found to their dismay that without prior public commitment there
is little hope of implementation. One cannot dispense with the need to
build a base of support in the community for programs that are expected to touch people's lives. Community organizations that have
such a base may find it is to their advantage to develop their own corps
of trained planner advocates—who are technically trained and can
speak the language of government planners, yet who are advocates of
needful constituencies.

Guskin and Ross (1971) believe that the nature of national bureaucratic government is such that professional advocates are indispensable, and are even more important than consensus-building or attempts
at participatory democracy. From their point of view, if consensus
cannot be achieved through group participation, professional advocates should act anyway. Our own view is less optimistic of the eventual success of advocate planners who become separated from their

constituents. Participatory democracy is slow and painful and can compromise any social plan. But people will not support plans that are thrust upon them. People need to get involved in developing programs to meet their needs; more is needed than the involvement only of professional organizers and planners.

Conclusion

The emphasis in this chapter has been on the facilitation of social change through the development of organized citizen constituencies. In simple homogeneous societies where there is direct access between citizens and their leaders, special efforts at community organization are not needed. With direct access to decision makers, citizens can have input into the development of social structures to meet their changing needs. However, in complex heterogeneous communities, competing interest groups exist and accommodating to their needs is more difficult. In such communities, individuals and groups may find themselves bypassed, as social priorities are decided without their input by groups that do not represent their interests. Those who view community life from the community organization perspective feel that the experience of alienation, so characteristic of our modern technological society, can be traced in part to this nonparticipation and lack of opportunity for self-determination. Also indicted as a contributing factor is the frustration engendered by dealing with unresponsive and irrelevant social institutions. Community organization is seen as an antidote to the debilitating effects of powerlessness. It is viewed as a vehicle for renewal and the reestablishment of participatory democracy.

Two perspectives for achieving community organization were outlined—one based upon consensus and cooperation, the other upon power and conflict. Advocates of both views strive for similar goals: increased citizen participation, and the facilitation of community change through unified social and political action. Yet, these perspectives differ on basic assumptions concerning the nature of people in society. Proponents of a community development perspective optimistically believe that community groups can be altruistic—interested in their neighbors and willing to share resources. Adherents of the social action perspective are considerably more pessimistic and assume that people's basic nature is selfish and self-serving. According to this latter view, groups will not be responsive to conciliation unless they are convinced (by force if necessary) that it is in their best interest to do so.

Each of the perspectives by itself probably is incomplete. Both altruistic and self-serving attributes exist, achieving ascendance depending upon environmental circumstances. Thus, it is important to understand the social conditions under which differential characteristics are elicited, since these should determine the preferred community organization strategy. Community development utilizes the psychological processes of persuasion, mutual influence, and conciliation and is more likely to be successful when the groups in question have some basis for negotiation. Similar attitudes and values, sufficient resources for sharing, and a tradition of pluralistic decision-making all favor the success of community development. On the other hand, power and coercion characteristic of social action strategies become necessary when value differences are high, resources are scarce, and decisions are traditionally made by power elites.

Community organization in the United States has had a variable and spotty history. Its successes can be traced from the early Settlement Houses of the turn of the century to more recent community development and militant "peoples organizations." Its most recent failures have involved government-sponsored attempts to *impose* organization on communities with programs that had ambiguous and contradictory assumptions and guidelines. Regardless of specific strategy, both forms of community organization work toward increasing citizen involvement in determining their own affairs. The commitment to expanding the opportunities for self-determination is crucial to a healthy community—and essentially, that is the message of community organization.

References

Aiken, M., & Mott, P. E. (Eds.). *The structure of community power.* New York: Random House, 1970.

Alinsky, S. D. *Reveille for radicals.* Chicago: University of Chicago Press, 1946.

Alinsky, S. D. *Rules for radicals.* New York: Vintage Books, Random House, 1972.

Bernard, J. *The sociology of community.* Glenview, Ill.: Scott, Foresman and Co., 1973.

Biddle, W. W., & Biddle, L. J. *The community development process: The rediscovery of local initiative.* New York: Holt, Rinehart and Winston, 1965, pp. 60–61.

Bradley, D. S., & Zald, M. N.   From commercial elite to political administrator. In L. I. Ruchelman (Ed.), *Big city mayors: The crisis in urban
politics.* Bloomington, Ind.: Indiana University Press, 1969, pp. 9–29.

Caplan, G.   *The theory and practice of mental health consultation.* New
York: Basic Books, 1970.

Clinard, M. B.   *Slums and community development: Experiments in self-
help.* New York: The Free Press, 1970.

Cox, F. M., Erlich, J. L., Rothman, J., & Tropman, J. E. (Eds.). *Strategies of
community organization: A book of readings* (2nd ed.). Itasca, Ill.:
Peacock Publishers, 1974.

Dahl, R. A.   From oligarchy to pluralism: The patricians and the enter-
preneurs. In M. Aiken & P. E. Mott (Eds.), *The structure of community
power.* New York: Random House, 1970.

Eugster, C.   Field education in West Heights: Equipping a deprived community to help itself. In F. M. Cox, J. L. Erlich, J. Rothman, & J. E.
Tropman (Eds.), *Strategies of community organization: A book of readings* (2nd ed.). Itasca, Ill.: Peacock Publishers, 1974, pp. 291–303.

Fairweather, G. W., Sanders, D. H., Maynard, H., & Cressler, D. L.   *Community life for the mentally ill: An alternative to institutional care.*
Chicago, Ill.: Aldine, 1969.

Guskin, A. E., & Ross, R. Advocacy and democracy: The long view. *American Jouranl of Orthopsychiatry,* 1971, *41*,43–57.

Kravitz, S., & Kolodner, R. K.   Community action: Where has it been? Where
will it go? In L. E. Sneden (Ed.), *Poverty: A psychosocial analysis.* Berkeley, Calif.: McCutchan, 1970, pp. 236–245.

Levin, M. B.   Copyright © 1971 The American Orthopsychiatric Association,
Inc. Reproduced by permission.

Levine, M., & Levine, A.   *A social history of helping services: Clinic, court,
school, and community.* New York: Appleton-Century-Crofts, 1970.

Marris, P., & Rein, M.   *Dilemmas of social reform: Poverty and community
action in the United States.* New York: Atherton Press, 1967.

Miller, S. M., & Riessman, F.   *Social class and social policy.* New York: Basic
Books, 1968, pp. 228–229, 231.

Moynihan, D. P.   *Maximum feasible misunderstanding: Community action
in the war on poverty.* New York: The Free Press, 1969.

Pearl, A.   The psychological consultant as change agent, or change: real and
unreal, sufficient and insufficient, backwards and forwards. Paper presented at the meetings of the American Psychological Association, Washington, D.C., 1971.

Reiff, R.   Mental health manpower and institutional change. *American Psychologist,* 1966, *21*, 540–548.

Rothman, J.   Three models of community organization practice. In National
Conference on Social Welfare, *Social Work Practice, 1968.* New York:
Columbia University Press, 1968. Revised 1974 and reprinted in F. M.

Cox, J. L. Erlich, J. Rothman, & J. E. Tropman (Eds.), *Strategies of community organization: A book of readings* (2nd ed.). Itasca, Ill.: F. E. Peacock, 1974, pp. 22–39.

Sayre, W. S., & Polsby, N. W.   American political science and the study of urbanization. In P. M. Hauser, & L. F. Schnore (Eds.), *The study of urbanization.* New York: John Wiley & Sons, 1965, pp. 115–156.

Sundquist, J. L. (Ed.).   *On fighting poverty: Perspectives from experience.* New York: Basic Books, 1969.

Suttles, G. D.   *The social order of the slum: Ethnicity and territory in the inner city.* Chicago: University of Chicago Press, 1968.

Wachtel, D. D.   Structures of community and strategies for organization. *Social Work,* 1968, *13,* 85–91.

Wofford, J. G.   The politics of local responsibility: Administration of the Community Action Program—1964–1966. In J. L. Sundquist (Ed.), *On fighting poverty: Perspectives from experience.* New York: Basic Books, 1969, pp. 70–102.

Yarmolinsky, A.   The beginnings of OEO. In J. L. Sundquist (Ed.), *On fighting poverty: Perspectives from experience.* New York: Basic Books, 1969, pp. 34–51.

Zax, M., & Specter, G. A.   *An introduction to community psychology.* New York: John Wiley & Sons, 1974.

9

INTEGRATION OF COMMUNITY PERSPECTIVES

Toward a theory of community intervention

IN THE PRECEDING CHAPTERS, three groups of intervention perspectives were presented. The consultation perspectives are the most optimistic concerning the potential for change within traditional institutions. Agency personnel are thought to be representative of community sentiments and thus are considered to be the appropriate targets for consultation activity. Neither the alternative institutions nor the community organization positions accept these assumptions. Advocates of the alternatives approach believe that rechanneling of resources and substitution of new personnel (rather than upgrading traditional workers) are the important ingredients in producing change. Advocates of community organization assume that social institutions cannot change to any significant degree without important changes in the distribution of power within a community.

Can these perspectives, based upon such differing assumptions be reconciled? Can rational decisions be made in choosing which approach to use in response to given community problems? At the present time, the choice often is made on the basis of personal preference or style, and the comfort an individual practitioner feels working within a particular orientation. Some are uncomfortable attempting to help organize minority communities; others are equally uneasy consulting to "establishment" agencies. Personal preferences will always be important in deciding professional commitments, but they need not be the sole factors determining intervention strategy. What is needed is a framework for understanding the conditions within communities

371

and within social institutions that both facilitate the change process and help *maintain* innovation once it has been achieved. Therefore, in this chapter we will focus on community and institutional characteristics that influence, shape, maintain, and limit change attempts. Understanding naturally occurring change and the structures developed by communities to deal with change and achieve equilibrium should help us see how planned intervention can complement this process.

Community traditions and social regulators: The forces maintaining community equilibrium

As communities grow they develop any number of formal and informal structures to meet human needs and modulate differences between citizens. These structural arrangements, which in actuality are often carried out by complicated networks of care-giving and social control agencies, become stabilized over time, and as long as they are functioning adequately are extremely difficult to change. The structural arrangements of which we speak will be referred to as *traditions*, which represent the generally accepted rules governing community life. They are carried out and enforced by community representatives or *regulators* who function to preserve the social fabric.

Community traditions involve more than attitudes, in that they represent community sentiments, norms, and mores that have an action component. Traditions offer a frame of reference that allow regulators to function, confident that they are enforcing an accepted mandate from the community. Regulators perpetuate traditions; and, since traditions change slowly, regulators rarely function as innovators in society unless they have specifically come to power with some mandate for change.

Gamson (1968, p. 21) uses the term *authorities* to describe those "who, for any given social system make binding decisions in that system." A decision is binding if it can be implemented without the necessity of review by any other persons. In local communities, we normally think of elected officials as having the binding decision-making power of which Gamson speaks. However, they are not alone in possessing this power. Other social regulators also are in the position of making binding decisions about social conduct. Agents of social control (e.g., police and probation officers) and socialization and education officials (e.g., school personnel)—each in his or her own sphere—have almost final authority in decisions involving others, and usually have the power to carry out these decisions. Thus, our use of the term *social regulators* will be similar to Gamson's term *authorities*, but is intended to more broadly include social control, socialization, and primary-care agents who have accrued the power to enforce control over the fate of other community members.

The conflict between control and support functions within regulator agencies

Cumming (1968) describes social order as arising from a continual compromise between constraint and freedom, between the interest of the individual and the goals of society. This compromise takes place informally whenever people interact, but informal regulation alone is not sufficient to maintain order. Formal systems of social regulation supplement informal controls and are administered by a network of agents and agencies that perform both supportive and controlling functions. The active agents in this network represent the community's social regulators, whose performance of both supportive and controlling functions often occurs within the same agency. In fact, it is the conflict between support and control functions that often blurs the clarity of mission of some agencies. A prime example of the conflict of functions can be seen in the typical probation department attached to a court. The probation worker wins the confidence of his or her clients and in the name of rehabilitation provides helpful suggestions, support, and advice. Yet, at the time of a hearing if further legal action is required, this same worker now must reveal the information collected from the client, even if this information is to be used against the client.

Social strain: The production of disequilibrium in communities

As changes occur in society, new accommodations are required. These may occur in a gradual or in a precipitous manner. Strain develops as changes occur in the composition and value structure of society which are difficult to assimilate into ongoing community life. Smelser (1963), who uses the term *strain* to refer to "the impairment of relations among parts of a system" notes that strain in society can result from several factors. Strain can be produced by the ambiguities associated with unpredictable natural and social forces; the disjunction between participation, responsibility, and rewards (e.g., working hard as a foreman but receiving low pay and no recognition); or by changes in beliefs and social conditions, which in turn can lead to changes in operating structures as old role relationships conflict with new values. In other words, strain can occur in all but the most static of societies. Population shifts, changes in the balance of available natural resources, economic dislocation, increases in automation, changes in cultural values—all have the potential for activating social disequilibrium.

The social forces described in the previous paragraph function as strain elicitors, that is, factors in social life that contribute to the potential for strain to be experienced by community members. *At the level of the individual citizen, strain is experienced as a discrepancy between expected and perceived reality.* This is the common theme in the various descriptions of strain offered by Smelser: as a "disharmony between normative standards and actual social conditions"; as a "discrepancy between social conditions and social expectation"; or as "a disjunction between participation, responsibility and rewards" (Smelser, 1963, pp. 228–290). In each instance, the individual's belief structure and expectation does not match what is seen as occurring in the social environment. Examples might include an older person being forced to confront the new dress styles and conduct standards of a younger generation; a dedicated worker passed up for promotion or being let go after years of service; or the entry of women into the ranks of fire-fighters, an occupation that traditionally had been the exclusive province of males.

Historical examples of reactions to strain

In tracing the history of right-wing extremist groups in this country, Lipset and Raab (1970) develop the hypothesis that the rapid changes in status relationships between social classes, and other changes in American social life more generally, have been responsible for the periodic development of right-wing groups hoping to preserve the status quo.

> The fluidity of the American social structure—the fact that no group has enjoyed a status tenure in the style of European social classes—has meant that the problem of status development has been an enduring characteristic of American life. New areas, new industries, new immigrant groups, new ethnic groups, have continually encroached upon the

old as important and influential. On these occasions, various formerly entrenched American groups have felt disenchanted. These situations have in America been the typical wellsprings of right-wing movements and, indeed, of right-wing extremism. (Lipset & Raab, 1970, p. 24)

Historical examples of social strain are not difficult to find. The last half of the 19th century saw major changes in the United States. During this period about 25 million immigrants came to this country, most of whom were Catholics who settled in the cities and became the backbone of a new labor force. As the Catholic immigrants became assimilated and increased in political power in the larger cities, a steady rise in anti-Catholic feeling also occurred. The contention that the assassination of Lincoln had been a Catholic plot was one rumor that became widely circulated after his death. National leaders spoke out against the Catholic menace and anti-Catholic secret societies were formed in the major cities. The largest anti-Catholic organization of the late 19th century, the American Protective Association, was organized in 1887. It is significant that this same period also saw the development of other organizations such as the Sons of the Revolution and the Daughters of the American Revolution, whose members saw in the increased immigration an erosion of traditional American society as they had come to know it. The most rapid growth of the American Protective Association occurred in 1893, a year of severe economic depression. Unemployment was blamed on the jobs taken by the Catholic immigrants, while the collapse of banks was attributed to a Catholic conspiracy whose purpose was to weaken the country as a prelude to a seizure of power. In describing this period, Lipset and Raab (1970) point out that the largest growth in membership in the American Protective Association occurred in regions experiencing the largest population growth with the greatest numbers of newcomers. The rapidly growing areas were those experiencing the greatest social tensions produced by the strains of immigration.

A similar situation occurred in the 1920s. This time, the campaign against European Catholics was extended to Jewish immigrants. The Jews, being the newer immigrants, were the more visible targets. Lipset and Raab (1970) report that in 1920 the *Christian Science Monitor* printed a lead editorial entitled "The Jewish Peril," in which the troubles of the world were blamed on a Jewish power conspiracy. That same year, the *Chicago Tribune* contended that Bolshevism was a tool for the establishment of Jewish control of the world. From 1920 to 1927, Henry Ford regularly attacked "The international Jewish conspiracy" in the newspaper the *Dearborn Independent*. The flavor of these articles can be seen from some of the titles: "Jewish Gamblers Corrupt American Baseball"; "How the Jewish Song Trust Makes You Sing"; "Jew Wires Direct Tammany's Gentile Puppets"; and, "The Scope of Jewish Dictatorship in America." That Ford's views had wide appeal can be seen in the short-lived campaign to nominate him for President in 1924. William Randolph Hearst, then publisher of the largest newspaper chain in the country, announced in 1923 that he was prepared to back Ford for President. Also in that same year, *Collier's* magazine reported that Ford led all other candidates in their presidential preference poll.

It was not just immigration that was producing social strain. America had just passed through an era of reform that ended in 1914 with the advent of a major European war. During this period, the country had seen the imposition of an income tax, minimum wage and maximum hour laws, and federal appropriations for fledgling programs in education, rehabilitation, and public health. Organized labor reached a peak membership of 5 million in 1920 and the country had been steadily moving its power base toward the more secular and cosmopolitan cities. The extremist movements of the 1920s such as the Ku Klux Klan, which were to experience their greatest growth in membership and influence during this era, hoped to return to the simpler values of a Protestant rural America. Theirs was a reaction against "modernism," which meant a waning church influence, the breakdown of parental control, and "loose" moral values as evidenced by short skirts, public dancing, smoking, and drinking. Although the Klan eventually lost its grip on American politics, partially due to sex scandals from within its own ranks, it was still able to manage a measure of victory in its defeat (Lipsett & Raab, 1970). By the end of the 1920s, the issues with which it had been most concerned had been settled at least partially in its favor. New legislation placed severe limitations on immigration; prohibition seemed firmly established; the effort to bring the United States into the League of Nations had failed; and the country, in Presidents Calvin Coolidge and Herbert Hoover, was again in the control of a very conservative Protestant America.

The main points of the discussion can now be summarized. Community *traditions* develop as a codification of sentiments and mores about social life. As such, they are given the status of rules whose purpose is to preserve the social fabric. *Social regulators* are the representatives of the community who carry out traditions. Since they function to perpetuate traditions, they rarely have the mandate to innovate without a previously established community-wide consensus. It is for this reason that regulators are often aligned with the forces interested in maintaining the status quo. On the other hand, new groups coming into the community, and changing conditions within society require new accommodations. Unless dealt with adequately, the new forces produce social *strain*. The strain may occur first in the new groups, as they find existing arrangements ill-suited to their needs. Or, strain may occur in the community-at-large as new forces continue to disrupt the existing social order.

Strain mounts as the pressures on the community increase. Community groups producing disequilibrium can be called *exciter* groups (Rhodes, 1972) because in producing strain they are exciting or disturbing the status quo. When exciter groups pose severe threats to community equilibrium, the majority's response to that threat can be constructive, seeking accommodation. It can also be destructive, seeking to reduce disequilibrium by uncompromising force. If the grievances of the exciters are legitimate, suppression may gain only a temporary respite, since it does nothing to redress grievances and leaves the community open to further attack by exciters if they grow stronger and more powerful.

While one may refer to some historical periods as eras of reform or of conservative backlash, in actuality, constructive and destructive solutions to social strain often occur simultaneously. Just as the 1890s and 1920s saw the growth of conservative groups, these same periods also marked the establishment of social reform as well. In many states, the 1890s saw the adoption of compulsory school attendance laws, child labor laws and the beginning of special education classes. The first psychological clinic was established at the University of Pennsylvania in 1896 and juvenile courts were set up in Denver and Chicago in 1899. The Henry Street Settlement House in New York and Hull House in Chicago were also products of this era.

The 1920s saw a different combination of reactions to strain. Many reforms had occurred in the previous decade, producing strain in more tradition-oriented groups. Although the country moved toward a more conservative social stance in the 1920s, with a corresponding deemphasis on socially oriented reforms, the period also produced a reform spirit that now turned toward an emphasis on individual expression and personal openness. Women obtained the right to vote by amendment to the constitution in 1920. The decade following this event was marked by freer sexual attitudes, one sign of which was the widespread adoption of psychoanalytic thinking.

The relationship between regulators and community groups

Gamson (1968) approaches the relationship between authorities (regulators) and various community groups by first defining the relevant groups. On any particular issue, "potential *partisans* may be defined as those groups who would be affected by the outcome of any decision made with regard to that issue." The relationship between authorities and partisans is reciprocal. Authorities are the agents of social control and have power over potential partisans. The power of partisans is less formal but just as real. Their power lies in their ability to influence authorities. Thus "authorities are the recipients or targets of influence and the agents or initiators of social control. Potential partisans have the opposite role—as agents or initiators of influence and targets or recipients of social control" (Gamson, 1968, pp. 36–37).

Some partisan groups possess trust and confidence in existing institutions. These are likely to be groups which are confident in the ability of authorities to represent their interests. *Confident groups* are those which have access to regulators, see regulators as sympathetic to their interests, and believe that regulators are potent or capable of reducing strain. On the other hand, *alienated groups* have the opposite relationship to authorities. They distrust authorities because they believe them to be either impotent or unrepresentative. Alienated groups are not confident that regulators represent their views and they believe that they do not have appropriate access to regulators to make their views known.

Gamson notes that confident groups and authorities have a mutually supportive relationship. With each having good access to the other, both parties make their wishes known through persuasion. A confident group believes in the good will of the authorities and it is only a matter of implementing that good will in the particular issue at hand. Similarly, authorities rely on this reservoir of trust to enforce their rules. They need only convince confident groups that their solutions will keep things well in hand to achieve compliance.

The relationship between authorities and alienated groups is not so benign. Since they feel they have no legitimate channels to redress grievances, alienated groups are more likely to use force or constraints to achieve their goals. Such groups may feel that they have little to lose by violence. Members are less concerned about the resentment that such tactics produce among regulators or in the community at large since they believe that others do not care about their welfare. Positive exchange requires a degree of trust, which is absent for alienated groups who believe that authorities are systematically biased against their interest.

How do authorities deal with alienated groups? One possibility is the use of force to quell the demands of such groups. However, Gamson points out that force is not likely to be the most effective strategy in controlling alienated groups, since "it is necessary for a group to have something to lose before it can be subjected to effective constraints" (Gamson, 1968, p. 182). Gamson believes that "insulation" offers authorities the most "satisfactory" protection from alienated groups. Insulation means isolating alienated groups from other community resources or from the community at large. Insulation keeps the potential disruptive capacity of alienated groups low, while at the same time protecting the community from having to deal with the demands alienated groups might make. Trying to move alienated groups closer to the decision-making powers within a community, i.e., giving such groups increased access to regulators, is likely to fail unless at the same time the community is prepared for a more equitable allocation of community resources.

An example of community isolation of an alienated group

Ghettos that isolate alienated minorities can be found universally in our society and are not just characteristic of large heterogeneous cities. However, ghettos can be hard to find in small towns and rural areas. They are not on Chamber of Commerce maps, nor are they likely to be close to the main streets, but they can be found with some searching. In one midwestern town of 50,000 people, known to the authors, the group lowest on the socioeconomic ladder was composed of rural whites who had migrated north from the hill country of Kentucky and Tennessee. They lived in one- or two-room shacks along unpaved and unlighted streets, often with dirt floors and no running water or indoor toilets. For years the city had left this section of town unincorporated, despite the fact that the surrounding areas were annexed into the city as each became developed. The county refused to provide essential services such as paved roads, street lighting, water, and sewer services because they claimed that this section fell within the fringe area that was the responsibility of the city. The citizens of this section of town, which we shall call Deckard Place, did not pursue the matter. They were a proud people, suspicious of outsiders, whose ethic included an unwillingness to depend on others, or to ask others for help. As the surrounding land became residential subdivisions, the real estate developers built high chain-link fences topped with barbed wire along subdivision property lines. As the population of the city grew, the citizens of Deckard Place became increasingly physically isolated from the rest of the community. Fences enclosed their area on the east and north, a stone mill sat on the west with open fields on the south. Access into and out of Deckard Place was available only from a few streets, none of which allowed direct entry into the neighboring residential sections. The isolation of the citizens of Deckard Place did not seem part of a deliberate design. Yet each time some other adjacent area became subdivided and developed, and as the city as a whole prospered, the residents of Deckard Place became more isolated and fell further behind in their standard of living.

After some time, the citizens of Deckard Place became convinced that incorporation into the city could mean the availability of city services. One of the candidates for mayor had suggested as much in his election campaign. The citizens of Deckard Place requested incorporation, which was granted, and the new mayor went forward to redeem his campaign promise.

The mayor found it difficult to find uncommitted funds to finance the improvement of Deckard Place. As he considered the options available to him, it appeared as if a federal urban renewal grant was the only possibility and this became the plan he pursued for the area. However, a problem emerged, in that approximately 20 to 30 percent of the houses in Deckard Place were below even minimum federal guidelines for rehabilitation, which meant that they would have to be torn down. The citizens of Deckard Place, upon hearing that some of their numbers would be dispossessed from their homes accused the mayor of betrayal. They voted out their own citizen planning committee that had been working with the mayor and elected a more militant leadership. They threatened to sue for de-annexation from the city and successfully blocked the Urban Renewal grant since a provision of that act required that renewal plans be approved by neighborhood citizen representatives.

The standoff was now complete. The mayor claimed that the only way he could finance improvements in Deckard Place was with urban renewal money. The majority of citizens of Deckard Place refused to allow any homes in their area to be destroyed. They claimed that over the years there was money for street lights, water, and sewers in other parts of the city without the need for urban renewal grants. They wanted what other citizens of the city received without special strings attached. Tension in Deckard Place rose to an alarming degree as the pro-mayor minority began feuding with the anti-mayor majority.

How did this situation develop? Over the years, dominant community groups (e.g., real estate interests), with the passive cooperation of social regulators (e.g., previous city administrations), had successfully isolated a powerless minority (a poor white Appalachian group). Attempts to rectify the situation met with extreme difficulty because the needs of the minority were great and the new mayor had only limited funds. Perhaps even more critical was that he attempted to achieve reform without building a prior community mandate. Other community groups had not participated in his decision to help Deckard Place and they were not ready to share their resources with a group that they still saw as outsiders—as "shiftless, no-account paupers". The mayor could have used existing community resources but only if meaningful attempts had occurred to reverse the community's long-standing isolation of Deckard Place.

This example does not have a happy ending—but neither did events turn out to be completely negative. After a two-year delay, the mayor found additional federal funds, from revenue sharing and community development sources, that did not require the demolition of existing residences to make good on his promise for essential city services for Deckard Place. But the fences are still up and Deckard Place remains isolated from the community at large.

Toward the enhancement of community life

Perhaps at this point we should make our biases explicit about optimal community life. If one were to describe an ideal community, what would be its characteristics? One can begin by describing the basic functions communities serve in maintaining social order and regulating interchange among citizens. Klein (1968) provides such a list and describes the major functions of communities as follows:

1. Providing and distributing living space and shelter and determining use of space for other purposes;

2. Making available the means for distribution of necessary goods and services;
3. Maintaining safety and order, and facilitating the resolution of conflicts;
4. Educating and acculturating newcomers (e.g., children and immigrants);
5. Transmitting information, ideas and beliefs;
6. Creating and enforcing rules and standards of belief and behavior;
7. Providing opportunities for interaction between individuals and groups. (Klein, 1968, p. 7)

Given these basic responsibilities of communities, all do not perform these functions equally well. Some communities have a difficult time maintaining safety and order, others are crowded and do not provide for an adequate distribution of living space. Communities probably can be rated on their ability to provide essential functions and services. Such a rating would be valuable but it falls short of our view of an ideal community.

The importance of opportunities for active participation

We agree with Sarason (1974) that a community as a geopolitical entity may perform its functions well and yet its citizens may feel little kinship for it. They may work in the community, pay taxes and vote and yet feel repelled by its other characteristics. Most important of all, citizens may feel impotent in shaping its characteristics. For us, an ideal community is one that maximizes citizen input by providing opportunities for individuals to participate and contribute to the welfare of the group. Our ideal is similar to Sarason's concept of "a psychological sense of community," whose characteristics can be stated as follows:

> . . . a sense of community that permits a productive compromise between the needs of individuals and the achievement of group goals . . . the perception of similarity to others, an acknowledged interdependence with others, a willingness to maintain this interdependence by giving to or doing for others what one expects from them, the feeling that one is part of a larger dependable and stable structure—these are some of the ingredients of the psychological sense of community. (Sarason, 1974, pp. 155, 157)

The availability of community structures for building cohesion and resolving conflicts

The psychological sense of community does not require that the population of a community be homogeneous, nor does it imply that communities should be conflict-free. Differences among people and conflicts of interest are part of group life and cannot be wished away. The crucial issue is how differences are handled. Are they suppressed or accepted? Are there attempts to achieve constructive resolution of differences or are alienated minorities isolated from others? Are there community structures for conflict resolution to which all have access, or is conflict allowed to smolder unresolved, causing the further erosion of group solidarity and the development of schisms between community groups? Differences between groups, such as cultural heterogeneity, add to the level of strain experienced by community members. It would be naïve to think otherwise. But the key to optimizing community life and gaining a psychological sense of community resides in the availability of community structures for building group cohesion and allowing for conflict resolution.

The availability of facilitating community structures and the extent of their use can be used to assess the quality of community life. The ingredients in such an assessment include: (1) the availability of behavior settings that facilitate group cohesion; (2) the extent of participation in such settings by different segments of the community; and (3) the relationship between citizen groups and social regulators.

The term "behavior setting" originated with the work of Barker and his colleagues (Barker, 1974; Gump, 1974).[1] Recall that for Barker, a behavior setting is a basic unit of the environment, one in which the behavior of groups of individuals occur in predictable fashion. Its characteristics are such that regular patterns of behavior are called forth, regardless of the particular individuals who inhabit the setting. Thus if we replaced all the individuals at a baseball game with new people to serve as players, audience, and umpire, the new participants would still engage in the same patterns of behavior (Price, 1976).

The availability of behavior settings and the level of participation of individuals within such settings depends, in part, on the size of a community and the complexity of its social organization. But it depends also upon the number of persons who are available to inhabit such settings. For example, research by Barker and Gump comparing high schools of different sizes, indicates that large schools can offer a wider variety of instruction than can small schools. But the relationship between population size and the number of behavior settings is not linear. In the Barker and Gump research, it took a 100 percent

---

[1] Barker's research is reviewed in Chapter 5.

increase in the size of the school to yield a 17 percent increase in the variety of instruction offered (Price, 1976).

A community may have any number of behavior settings that facilitate group cohesion: open meetings of a city council, discussion groups sponsored by the public library, church meetings, bowling leagues, or almost any form of group participation that allows individuals to develop links to others outside their normal family circle. The availability of such groups is not the only important factor. Equally important is the probability with which an individual can become an active participant—which in turn is, in part, a function of the number who are also potential participants in that setting.

In assessing the quality of community life, one needs to determine the availability of settings that foster group cohesion and the manning potential of those settings. A community may have a large number of behavior settings, but these may be overmanned if the number of potential performers is excessively large and if there have been no attempts to enlarge the capacity of the settings. For example, if a high school drama production can only accommodate 15 players but over 50 potentially qualified actors have applied, the play director might consider double casting, enlarging the size of the technical crew, or perhaps changing to a play that calls for a greater utilization of talent. If the commitment to drama is strong among the students, the school administration might consider reallocating resources to support a greater number of productions each year (Wicker, 1973).

An important conclusion from the research on manning is that those most affected are the marginal members, those who might be the very ones in need of extra support from the environment to maintain an optimal adjustment. Overmanned settings are particularly hard on such persons as they are likely to experience chronic rejection.

The relationship between citizens and social regulators

A final factor of importance in determining the quality of community life is the relationship between citizen groups and social regulators. Optimal community life occurs when citizens have access to social regulators who are capable of reducing community strain and who represent a broad spectrum of community interests. Regulators can be effective in reducing strain but not accessible, or representative. For example, a city administration may decide to solve its unemployment problem by inviting a chemical manufacturing firm to open a plant in its area and provide as extra incentive, tax-free land. When confronted with the pollution potential of the plant, the majority of citizens might prefer enduring unemployment for a longer period with the hope of attracting a "cleaner" industry.

Potent actions to reduce strain may have the community's blessing by representing the majority viewpoint, but may still involve poor solutions in the long run if they rely upon suppression of a minority alienated group. As noted earlier, suppression is only effective on a temporary basis. If grievances of an alienated group are not resolved they will remain, and the community will be forced to deal with these same issues again when the alienated group grows strong enough to overcome its suppression. Compounding the problem is that suppression adds a legacy of bitterness, aggravating the original complaint.

Groups can have good access to regulators but still find that their interests are not represented. For example, in a heterogeneous community, a city council might publicize its "open door" policy in which the views of all citizens are solicited in regular public hearings. Still, despite the hearings, the council may be aligned with only a small segment of the community; the hearings providing access but only the illusion of representation.

We can summarize our views about optimal community life in the following way. We would expect a community to perform its basic functions of regulating social life and maintaining order, but such a list of functions is only a beginning point. A community that does not foster a sense of cohesion among its citizens can be a sterile place. The community should not be simply a neutral field upon which other forces play. The community should be structured to add enrichment to daily living. A sense of cohesion develops as an attitude built upon the ability to work toward the fulfillment of common aspirations. We are not talking about a mystical or ethereal quality but one that depends upon the availability of growth-enhancing structures. These have been described in formal terms as the availability of behavior settings, the manning of such settings, and a relationship between citizens and their representatives that encourages an active coping with the problems of community living. We do not minimize the problems involved in creating or maintaining community settings, or the frictions that can be generated by heterogeneous societies; but we do believe that communities can deal more adequately with problems of group living if citizens are provided adequate opportunities to do so.

Implications for social change

The problems of intervention in static communities

Stable communities not experiencing strain might resist the efforts toward change initiated by a community worker. Indeed, there would be some question as to whether system-oriented change attempts should even be considered in such communities. After all, if communities are adequately coping with problems, and are experiencing low levels of disequilibrium and strain, what could the change agent add? Note, however, that artificially low levels of strain also can be produced by communities that are systematically avoiding problems. For example, if the major problems in a community can be isolated successfully in a politically weak, non-vocal minority of a populace, the community can ignore this sub-population. As long as the alienated subgroup remains powerless and not visible to the majority, the community can continue in apparent equilibrium.

In static communities, with low levels of strain, but where significant problems are being avoided, intervention is difficult. Social regulators, by their inaction may be contributing to the isolation of the alienated minority.[2] Fearful of upsetting apparently adequate status quo arrangements, suggestions concerning changes in policies and practices often will be resisted.

Deciding to use disequilibrium tactics

The problem then becomes one of educating the public about the problems in its midst that have been avoided until now. Here the community worker takes the role of a disequilibrium producer, in that education in problem-awareness produces strain in otherwise static groups. Various methods exist for accomplishing this goal, ranging from direct confrontation (marches, sit-ins, etc.) to more indirect means such as public discussions and letter-writing campaigns. If education in problem-awareness is successful and if communities become ready for action, the job of the community worker now becomes one of working toward the constructive solution of problems and grievances.

Klein (1968) conceptualizes the change process in a similar manner

---

[2] Note that the term *minority* is used to indicate a small group with relatively few members and does not imply any particular racial or religious group composition.

to that presented above, taking as his starting point the ideas of Kurt Lewin. Lewin sees the process of change as involving three steps: *(a)* unfreezing; *(b)* moving toward a new level; and *(c)* refreezing at the new level (Klein, 1968, pp. 126–136). Unfreezing, which allows a previously stable state to become amenable to change, occurs in response to some "precipitants," i.e., events or circumstances that raise anxiety and make the status quo intolerable (*strain* in Smelser's terminology). Movement then occurs if there are "facilitants" available that remove previous obstacles to action. Unfreezing can occur through direct confrontation, so that immediate exposure to new input cannot be avoided; or through more indirect and gradual exposure and involvement so that over time the lack of fit between previously held ideas and new information is more gradually realized.

A caution in dealing with resistance to change: Producing disequilibrium is not enough

As Klein suggests, Lewin's force-field concepts also are helpful in considering how change should be accomplished and maintained once the need for change has become apparent (i.e., once "unfreezing" has occurred). Lewin conceives of any stable situation as being a dynamic equilibrium resulting from the action of opposing forces, described as either "driving" or "restraining" in nature. Driving forces are all of those factors operating to move an individual toward an action goal, while restraining forces are those factors opposing action. Positive action can be realized by increasing the driving forces *or* by decreasing the restraining forces, but both strategies are not equally effective in *maintaining* change once it has been initiated. Increases in driving forces typically result in corresponding increases in restraining forces; thus, movement resulting from increases in direct pressure for change also increases the forces of resistance. However, if change can be accomplished by lowering restraining forces it is more likely to persevere, since action that occurs as a result of decreased resistance lowers the general level of tension and strain. In Klein's words:

> . . . if change has been brought about by direct pressure, restraining forces will persist. In such a case the driving forces that produced the change must be maintained in order to sustain the new condition. If, however, change has been accomplished by reduction of restraining forces, there is greater likelihood that it will be sustained without the maintenance of continued vigilance. (Klein, 1968, p. 136–137)

According to this analysis, a dilemma for disequilibrium strategies is that at the same time strain is increased to unfreeze old patterns of thinking and behavior, resistance to change may also be activated. Disequilibrium strategies that only concern themselves with confrontation and direct pressure without at the same time attempting to decrease restraining forces may be opting for quicker but unfortunately more short-lived success.

Intervention hypotheses

Our hypotheses concerning the relationship between strain and the various intervention perspectives can now be outlined. The first step in determining the type of intervention strategy that is likely to succeed is to assess which groups in the community are experiencing strain. The hypotheses link intervention to a prior assessment of strain and are presented as follows:

A. A homogeneous community not experiencing strain → no intervention.

B. Community-wide strain → consultation to existing social institutions.

C. Strain limited to culture-bearing (confident) groups → consultation to prevent punitive solutions.

D. Strain limited to minority (alienated) groups → education of the majority in problem awareness. If unsuccessful, the community organization or alternative institutions perspective should be adopted if the minority has power or resource potential.

Discussion of the hypotheses

A. A homogeneous community not experiencing strain. Essentially, this condition often represents a stable and satisfied community. Expectations of community members match perceived reality, in that established traditions are sufficient to cope with currently impinging life events. No segment of society is experiencing any significant degree of strain and community members are generally unaware of serious problems.

It is possible that the community specialist sees a problem not evident to others in the community. For example, a sanitary engineer or public health physician may become aware of a source of pollution in the public drinking water. If the specialist is a trusted official who represents a respected level of expertise or specialized knowledge, he or she will probably be able to convince others of the perception of danger to the community. A more likely sequence of events is that others will be difficult to arouse if the danger is not clear to them also. The specialist may find little sympathy and understanding and may even be branded as a "rabble-rouser," so that without the power of law that allows action independent of local sentiment, impact might be minimal. When the dangers are less clear cut, as in problems of group relations and human services, arousing placid communities is even more difficult. In this instance the interventionist must question whether further action would be useful. If others are not experiencing difficulty and are relatively satisfied with their situation, it may be presumptuous to continue to attempt to impose one's own views.

B. Community-wide strain. This is the most facilitative condition for the consultation perspective. If communities are experiencing strain, they are ready for action, and community groups are likely to be pressing social regulators to find some solution to alleviate strain. Responding to community pressure, regulators should be responsive to the exploration of alternatives with a consultant. The one danger is that regressive solutions that simply reestablish the status quo are possible if, as Klein (1968) points out, efforts are not directed toward lowering "restraining forces," that is, lowering the resistances and threat associated with change. Consultation then should not move too swiftly toward imposing what may seem to be "efficient" solutions. As a social change strategy, the essence of the consultation perspective is to help organizations and institutions adopt more facilitative problem-solving strategies that allow their constituencies access, involvement, and input into proposed solutions. In other words, psychological consultation should involve two components: improving the flexibility of existing problem-solving structures, and finding effective solutions to human problems. Whenever possible, improving the flexibility of organizations should be the prior goal.

C. Strain limited to culture-bearing (confident) groups. This condition represents a transitory state in which the majority feels strain but specific exciter groups do not. An example might be a small community in which teen-agers, lacking a teen center, congregate in the town square. Citizens of the community are upset by the noise and "rowdyism." The teen-agers are just as willing to meet at the square as anywhere else and are not initially und strain. However, the condition is transitory because the majority makes its wishes known to social regulators (the police, in this example), who produce strain in the minority by their enforcement of community standards. When this occurs we have moved to a situation of community-wide strain, particularly if members of the teen group come from all segments of the community.

The major form of intervention advocated is consultation to prevent harsh attempts at suppression. Punitiveness leaves a residue of anger and distrust that impedes later constructive attempts at solution. Social regulators can increase the minority's sensitivity to strain without such tactics.

D.   Strain limited to minority (alienated) groups.   This condition is frequently found in changing communities. Initially strain is not perceived on a community-wide basis but only in those groups most affected by changing conditions. The tendency in the community at large is to postpone dealing with "hot" issues as long as possible, or to find some solution that involves the least change in the established equilibrium. Thus education in problem-awareness initially will meet community resistance. The community will become sufficiently aroused only when it is clear that the problem cannot be solved easily. When this occurs, normal channels of consultation to social institutions have some likelihood of success.

Unfortunately, attempts at education in problem-awareness frequently fall on deaf ears. The community can successfully resist dealing with its problems if the strained minority is small, unorganized, and can be effectively isolated or suppressed. Both solutions, isolation and suppression, are likely to be attempted before the community will be ready to face the prospect of more massive social change.

What options are available if education in problem-awareness has failed? Consultation is likely to be unprofitable, as the community probably would oppose any accommodating solution in favor of continued isolation or suppression. This gives the "within systems" consultant little opportunity to effect movement.

The most viable alternative at this point is to assess the potential of strained groups to solve their problems on their own. We are interested in the potential for political strength and the access to skilled resources available to strained groups. The possibility of increased political power suggests community organization as an intervention strategy, if feasible. Some groups under strain are so dispersed geographically (e.g., some rural poor groups) or share so few values and traditions (e.g., differing urban ethnic groups) that attempts at building a cohesive political force are not likely to succeed. Community organization to increase political power is more likely to succeed when groups share common values, have sufficient numbers of citizens, and suffer from the same strain elicitors so that at least temporary cooperation is possible.

Examples of these favorable and unfavorable conditions can be cited. Leighton (1959) suggests that an impediment to effective community organization in a rural Nova Scotia area was the geographic dispersion and ensuing distrust of the poor for each other. The stereotypes that poor people had of others of their own socioeconomic group were the same as those held by the more affluent segments of this rural community. Similarly, in a section of New York, Roman (1973) suggests that attempts by black indigenous nonprofessionals to organize a south Bronx community in support of their attempts to gain control of the Lincoln Hospital Community Mental Health Center, failed, in part, because the community was predominantly Puerto Rican and did not trust or sympathize with the black workers. On the other hand, Schiff (1970) provides an example of a Community Mental Health Center serving an urban black community whose programs did generate community support. Issues of power and control of the program had already been settled. The community was fairly unified and the members of the board that controlled the mental health center's operation were representative of community sentiment.

Building alternative institutions is another possible strategy for strained groups in unresponsive communities. Groups in strain may have low power potential, but may still have untapped resources. A minority that is small in number and potential power can develop institutional structures, perhaps even separate communities, under its own control if it can find adequate resources. For example, a little-known chapter of American history concerns the establishment of Jewish farming communities in southern New Jersey in 1882 (Brandes, 1971). These autonomous rural communities represented a divergence from the mainstream of immigration to the United States that saw East European Jews settle in the urban and industrial areas of this country. The settlers who went to the New Jersey communities hoped to avoid the corrupting influences of the big cities with the attendant likelihood of antisemitism. Luckily, they managed to obtain the backing of established Jewish philanthropic societies which were interested in changing the public's perception of the Jew from that of a stereotyped "Shylock" petty trader and peddler to that of a more

noble man of the soil—a farmer. The South Jersey colonies were subsidized by the philanthropic societies that had resources but were not
particularly powerful in a political sense.

Other sources of support can come from nearby sympathetic
friends. For example, communities without resources but in proximity
to universities may be able to draw upon professional talent and student manpower to develop alternatives that would be unavailable
otherwise. Many communities have established their own alternative
schools and community centers in this way.

However, the community without the potential for either increased
political power through community organization, or without the resources available to develop alternative structures is in an extremely
unfavorable position. With low power potential and few resources,
movement is extremely difficult. Therefore, alienated groups must
work diligently to develop their own resources and to make the majority aware of, and attentive to, their concerns, so that ultimately the
truth of Gamson's admonition will be evident to all:

> The best long-run strategy for authorities in building confidence [in
> alienated groups] concentrates on equity in allocating resources and
> effectiveness in generating them and makes social control a secondary
> consideration and by-product. (Gamson, 1968, p. 183)

Implementation of the hypotheses

Complementing naturally occurring change processes

Intervention is most effective if it can complement naturally occurring change processes. The interventionist should remember
that communities are capable of change on their own, and usually
do so without outside help. Communities have built-in mechanisms
for effecting change and are capable of displaying an ongoing
problem-solving capacity. It is important to understand these naturally
occurring processes and be able to follow their operation in any
specific community of interest. Planned intervention is most effective
when it can be integrated into ongoing events.

Naturally occurring processes of change are initiated when strain
elicitors impinge upon a community. If regulators become aware of
growing strain, or are made aware by confident community groups,
they will attempt to cope with the impinging events. However, regulators cannot improvise freely to reduce strain. Their actions must

conform to existing rules that circumscribe their alternatives—rules developed formally from previous laws and decisions by authorities, or informally from the history of policy implementation and standard operating procedures.

Regulators are most responsive when they sense a community-wide mandate. That is why community-wide strain is most likely to produce change. Under these circumstances, the interventionist does not have to instigate change, and has the relatively easier task of channeling coping efforts in a more constructive direction through consultation to existing regulatory personnel. Thus, strain should not be viewed as a negative force. Strain is neither positive nor negative; only the actions that result from strain can be evaluatively labeled. Communities can react to strain in either constructive or destructive ways. Community-wide strain can provide the motivation to deal with otherwise dormant problems.

At times, the interventionist may wish to consider how strain experienced by a minority can be generalized to other community groups. While he or she may act as an advocate for the minority group, what would be more effective is for an indigenous advocate in the majority community to adopt this role. If a respected member of the community can learn to understand and speak up for the needs of a minority group, the majority community is more likely to listen—more so than if the spokesperson is a mental health professional.

Helping regulators change their perception of alienated minorities

As long as strain is restricted to an alienated minority, naturally occurring change is least likely to occur. Isolated from community life, with restricted access to regulators, it is difficult for an alienated group to make its needs known and its plight understood. Isolation produces distortions in perceptions for both sides, so that without contact and access to others, estrangement is heightened by misunderstanding, distortions, and unchecked stereotypes.

Cumming and Cumming (1962) report an incident in which the staff of a mental hospital was asked to train police recruits in the proper handling of mental patients. Since the hospital was run according to milieu therapy principles, the staff used this opportunity for therapeutic learning by asking the patients to conduct the training program with them. The patients initially refused to participate. Many had painful experiences in their previous encounters with the police. It took some time to work through these initial fears and resistances, but when the patients finally agreed, the police arrived at the hospital for their first training session. The patients were surprised to see that the police were as uncomfortable and frightened about sitting in a room with "crazies" as they were about meeting the police. Isolated from one another, and with only limited and formal contact, both groups had relied on distorted and inaccurate perceptions.

The example from Cumming and Cumming demonstrates how the perception of the problems of an alienated minority can be changed through constructive exposure. The police had contact with mental patients but always in the same kind of situation—one in which an anxious and upset patient was disturbing the equilibrium in a community. The hospital meeting was a chance to understand patients as persons with "normal" fears and aspirations, as well as a chance to see them in other more normal roles, as hosts and meeting participants. In one sense, exposure of this type does not change the basic values or traditions of the community at large. The police as well as most other community members undoubtedly still believe that disturbances of community tranquillity must be stopped. However, the police view may be changed as to why the disturbance was occurring, and this change in perception can be crucial in changing how they react to the call for help. If the disturbance is caused by a person now seen as upset, and not as "crazy therefore dangerous," the police are likely to react in a more humane fashion and not in a provocative way that might further exacerbate the agitated behavior (Monahan and Geis, 1976).

This example also illustrates another principle: namely, that the action of social regulators can itself cause strain in target groups. The mandate of regulators is to reduce strain in culture-bearing majority groups; their procedures act as a protection to the society at large. Unfortunately, protection of the majority can mean abuse of the minority. In the example cited, community members seem to want disturbing patients removed from their midst and probably give no thought as to how this is to be accomplished. Closer examination might reveal that the issue of importance to the community is not removal at all, but the cessation of disturbing behavior. Options other than removal might be possible if they were available and if social regulators could be made aware of them and educated in their use.

Helping regulators increase their options for constructive action

An example of increasing options for action is provided by Hansell (1967), who describes a "screening-linking-planning conference" convened by a mental health center whose goal was to maintain potential patients in the community and return them to effective citizenship as soon as possible. A main ingredient of the conference was linking patients and their families to helping resources in the community (e.g., a minister, public health nurse, or homemaker), with follow-up by a mental health "expediter" to make sure that contact was being maintained and help provided. Without this support, the family's tendency was to want their disturbing member hospitalized. With support, the family learned to deal with crisis events impinging on it to which the patient's behavior was a reaction.

By the time the family reached the mental health center it was convinced that its only recourse was hospitalization, and it was ready to undertake commitment proceedings. The judges who signed the commitment orders were also unaware of any other way to help the families who came before them. The mental health center explained their goal to the judges and invited them to observe the screening-linking-planning conference in operation. The judges became convinced that this was a viable option for helping potential patients and their families while at the same time protecting the safety of the community. They agreed that they would refuse to sign a commitment order unless the parties involved had first participated in a screening-linking-planning conference. The judges "came to an appreciation of how the court could become a constructive collaborator toward a community reentry outcome rather than a participant in the process of alienation and deposition in a distant institution" (Hansell, 1967).

To summarize at this point, we have suggested that planned change occurs most expeditiously when it complements naturally occurring community change mechanisms. Since social regulators are the monitors of community life, one place to begin is to understand their functions. Each regulator within his or her own area must find a way of coping with the strain elicited by disrupting events. Regulators can contribute to the strain experienced by alienated groups by their method of operation, so that helping regulators change their perception of these groups or increasing their options in dealing with such groups can go a long way toward rectifying excessive strain.

The possibility of facilitating change by increasing the options for action that can be derived from existing values and traditions deserves special emphasis. In the examples from Cumming and Cumming (1962) and from Hansell (1967), cited above, basic values in the community were not challenged. Not questioned was the need for community members to be protected from potentially dangerous behavior, a basic value in the action of judges and police officers in hospitalizing individuals displaying bizarre or disruptive behavior. In neither example was there an attempt to increase community tolerance of deviance, an action which would have been a direct challenge to community values. The need for public safety was accepted. However, regulators whose primary mission was protection were shown better ways to carry out their mission.

Implementation of the intervention hypotheses described earlier in this chapter is facilitated by an assessment process that should cover three levels of functioning. The sequence begins with the assessment of community characteristics, continues with the assessment of organizations and groups, and goes on to the assessment of persons. Unlike a more clinical orientation that would focus exclusively on the assessment of individuals, note that in the model presented here the assessment of person characteristics is the last stage of the assessment process. Knowing the characteristics of communities and institutions has priority in planning community intervention. Each of the three levels of assessment will now be discussed in turn.

Assessment at the community level

Communities can be described in any number of ways: in terms of geographic spread; population; ethnic composition; growth rate; form of government; availability of transportation; yearly school assessment; etc. Each of these variables can provide important information that can be quite useful in understanding community life, and the factors that have shaped its particular history and character. To the extent that such data are available, the information should be collected as useful background knowledge. However, at least of equal importance are the data that flow from the conceptualization of community life presented in this chapter. In order to consider whether intervention is warranted and what form intervention should take, we need to know about pressures impinging on the community, and the relationship between partisan, bystander, and regulatory groups. For example, can the groups in strain be identified? Are the community traditions that contribute to strain recognized? Are there groups not experiencing strain directly, but still sympathetic concerning the need for change? In heterogeneous communities diverse groups may have access to social regulators—some sympathetic to the problems of alienated groups, some opposed, with a sizable segment who are essentially neutral bystanders. Education in problem-awareness involves reaching this large uncommitted group.

Using social indicator and survey data

Unfortunately, there is no clearly accepted methodology for assessing communities as there is for assessing individuals. The best we can do is to study communities at a number of different levels, collecting data from different sources. Lippitt, Watson, and Westley (1958) describe three methods of obtaining information about client systems that have applicability to community assessment: obtaining information by direct questioning; asking a community representative or guide to point out and help survey community problems; and participating as an observer in an organization's or community's routine activities. Essentially, Lippitt et al. are describing two basic approaches: citizen report collected by survey techniques (epidemiological surveys); and social indicator data obtained by participatory observation. Chapter 3 of this book describes these techniques in some detail. At this point we wish to describe their use in developing a community assessment.

In any given community, we want to know the following:

a.   The major sources of strain, if any, impinging on the community.
b.   The groups for whom the experience of strain is most acute.
c.   The traditions in the community for strain reduction.
d.   The accessibility, representativeness, and power of social regulators for various groups in the community.
e.   The availability and manning potential of behavior settings.

The most accurate picture of community life can be obtained by using both surveys and social indicators. Bearing in mind the caution that one must guard against overinterpreting the significance of any one indicator, no matter how pleasing the result, a useful community assessment can be obtained by inspection of the data obtained from both sources. Since social indicators can be collected unobtrusively it is probably best to start there. One can develop hypotheses that later

TABLE 9–1
Assessment at the community level: Sample indices

Factor	Social indicators	Survey indicators
Strain elicitors	Migration—e.g., changing neighborhood composition Recent economic dislocation—e.g., plant closings Employment records for different groups Recent natural disasters	What are the major problems that this community has been required to face in the last few years? Were these problems adequately solved? In the next few years, what do you think this community's biggest worry will be? Are there people living here who are causing problems for the rest of the community? What words would you use to describe those people?
Groups in strain	Neighborhood and group data for rates of crime, delinquency, divorce, alcoholism, mental hospital admissions, etc. Rates of single-parent families	How long have you been living in this area (neighborhood, community)? To what extent are you satisfied with this area? Would you like it to be different in some way? If you could move to another area, would you? Why?
Traditions for strain reduction	Prior decisions, standard operating procedures and policies of regulators for handling specific community problems, e.g., operating manuals and rules of school board, local police, etc.	Let me show you a list of community problems. For each problem on the list, tell me: If this problem were to occur in this community, how would it be handled? Do you agree that this method is the best way of handling such a problem?

| Accessibility, representative-ness, and power of regulators | Access to mayor, members of the city council, school officials, etc., as indicated by their appointment schedules. Voting records of local officials. Analysis of how local tax dollars are spent. Citizen and group participation in public meetings, voting, etc. | Here is a list of some of the public officials in this community. For each one, tell me: Have you ever been to a public meeting where that official was present? Did he or she have a chance to hear how people like you felt? Have you ever talked to him or her directly yourself? Do you think he or she is doing the job well? Whom do you think that official represents? |
| Behavior settings | Membership composition of organizations and clubs. Number of organized groups serving different neighborhoods. | Here is a list of the kinds of clubs and organizations that can be found in many communities (e.g., church and civic groups, labor, fraternal, and neighborhood organizations, social clubs, etc.) Are you a member of any such organizations? Which ones? About how often do you attend meetings? (If not a member) If someone from one of these organizations were to call you up and ask you to join, would you accept? Which ones? If not, why not? |

can be confirmed using survey techniques targeted toward the problems discovered from the social indicator data. Survey techniques involve sampling public opinion directly. For any issue, one might devise questions that tap the levels of strain, involvement, or cohesion perceived by respondents. Table 9–1 presents examples of data that can be collected by the different measures.

It is important to note that this table does not exhaust the potentially useful questions that can be asked in a community assessment, but is simply illustrative of how such an assessment might be accomplished. The exact questions would be determined by the hypotheses under investigation. Thus, in a study of campus dormitory life at a large heterogeneous university, one might expect that the groups in strain would include those from culturally homogenous rural backgrounds. Questions concerning the size and cultural makeup of the hometown and its high school might be used to help identify such a group. Similarly, in a rapidly expanding college town, those in strain might include the long-term local residents whose cultural values differ from those of the college students whom they now find surrounding them as neighbors. Questions concerning length of residence and satisfaction with the neighborhood would be particularly appropriate in this example. Again it should be clear that the intent of the social indicator or survey questions derives from the assumption that assessment precedes intervention. The goal is to highlight those community concerns for which intervention might be helpful and to provide information to guide the decision about the form that intervention should take.

Assessment at the organizational level

If a decision has been made to offer consultation to relevant community agencies, assessment is again needed to provide information about the focus of consultation efforts. In general, the various consultation approaches are most appropriate when institutions have flexible structures that allow them to respond to changing pressures and conditions. However, an agency may need prior improvement in its problem-solving capacity before direct help with specific problems will prove efficacious. For rigid organizations, those caught up in traditions that allow little leeway for coping with new problems not easily solved by old procedures, an improved capacity for dealing with impinging events is needed. Helping such organizations reduce strain before they have developed such a capacity is likely to leave them vulnerable again to the next wave of stressful events. For example, suppose a consultant is asked by the principal of a local high school to help deal with racial tensions among student groups. Suppose also that assessment of the operation of the school reveals that the inability to solve the racial problem is but one issue in a recurrent and chronic pattern. The school is run in an autocratic manner with poor lines of communication between principal and teachers. In the past, teachers have been censured for deviating from a prescribed subject matter curriculum, and from these experiences they have developed the belief that the principal does not want them to "meddle" in human relations. With poor communication, the principal has not adequately conveyed to the staff a tentative rethinking of educational priorities in the face of the changing racial composition of the school. The teachers and principal have not discussed and worked through the potential role conflicts that might ensue if they broadened their educational focus. In this example, the consultant might be able to present the school with a human relations package administered by members of the consultation team that would defuse the racial animosities. But should the consultant do so if the school's staff has not been helped to deal with its role and communication problems? Not dealing with the staff problems leaves the school vulnerable to future impinging events that require role modification. Furthermore, it fosters dependency on the consultant. Reducing racial tensions initially, and then attempting to deal with staff problems, reduces motivation to deal with these issues and makes the task much more difficult. The sequence we are recommending involves helping the school recognize its staff problems and encouraging work on these problems before closure has been achieved on the racial problem.

Differentiating rigid and flexible organizations

Organizations with rigid problem-solving styles can be identified and have been cogently described by Gardner (1965). Our list differs from his at points, but we will borrow heavily from his analysis. Rigid organizations, those suffering from "organizational dry rot" (Gardner, 1965) are likely to have the characteristics described below.

1. Age. Rigid organizations are likely to be older, with long-established standard operating procedures. Over time an organization's identity is determined not only by its mission but also by its style of carrying out that mission. Organizations with long histories generally find it hard to change both style and ultimate mission. According to Gardner, the danger is that personnel within organizations can become "prisoners of their procedures" as "the rule book grows fatter and the ideas grow fewer."

> Thus almost every well-established organization is a coral reef of procedures that were laid down to achieve some long-forgotten objective. (Gardner, 1965, p. 22)

2. Leadership style. Rigid organizations are likely to have directive, authoritarian leadership and are less likely to be run on the basis of shared decision making. Such organizations may be efficient in performance, but tend to be low on member morale and satisfaction. Lippitt (1961) questions the efficiency of authoritarian organizations by noting that decisions may be reached more quickly in such organizations, but implementation may be much less rapid. On the other hand, with shared decision making, reaching a decision may be more time-consuming but implementation should be more rapid because "members of a group who participate in making the decision feel more responsible for carrying it out" (Lippitt, 1961, p. 434).

Another problem for organizations with authoritarian leadership is that the line staff who are closest to the problem situation and who often develop the best understanding of the factors involved have the least say in the organization's operation. The authors have visited state mental hospitals where the line staff (nurses and aides) communicated to the ward chief responsible for treatment decisions (the ward psychiatrist) only through written notes. The written record was a restricted source of information about patient behavior as staff reporting was influenced by attitudes toward the specific patient in question as well as toward the psychiatrist to whom the notes were written. In the end, it was the patients whose treatment was impaired because their psychiatrist, who had not developed effective channels for staff input, made treatment decisions based upon incomplete information.

3. Communication patterns. As just described, rigid organizations make less use of communication from staff to leader. Vertical communication patterns through lines of authority tend to be one way, downward from leader to staff. A flexible problem-solving capacity is marked by reciprocity of communication patterns in both vertical and horizontal channels. Horizontal communication refers to the relationships among workers at the same level of an organization. Here too, reciprocity maximizes the likelihood that innovative problem solutions can emerge. Thinking of new ways of doing things is fostered in a climate that encourages the open discussion of experiences and ideas.

4. Cross-role movement. Specialization and division of labor are at the heart of modern organizations and are additional factors leading to organizational rigidity. Over time "jurisdictional boundaries tend to get set in concrete" (Gardner, 1965), and it is often difficult to see new problem solutions beyond existing rules of operation for one's own specialty. A more fluid internal structure can be achieved by rotating personnel between parts of an organization; allowing an individual with one role to cross over and see the organization's problems from a new perspective. For example, a hospital ward staff that wanted its dayroom to assume a more homelike atmosphere might find that moving the furniture into conversational clusters was resisted by the janitorial staff for whom the room was easier to clean when all furniture was lined up against the wall. Including janitorial personnel on the treatment planning committee from the start might lead to a solution that is more likely to achieve both treatment and housekeeping objectives.

Good cross-role movement means more than shared decision making, in that rotation of personnel on decision-making committees is also required to achieve fresh points of view. It is true that the potential for conflict increases as new combinations of workers are constantly formed. On the other hand, after years of working together, people can get so used to each other that the stimulus for intellectual interchange drops almost to zero (Gardner, 1965). A fresh combination of individuals enlivens the atmosphere and increases the likelihood of creative solutions.

5. Deviance management. Deviant and unexpected ideas or behavior can occur among the staff of an organization as well as among its clients. How are these differences handled? An organization that emphasizes order and control is not likely to accept deviant ideas or actions from either source. The new ways will not get a fair hearing if they seem counter to entrenched institutional patterns.

One of the authors had the opportunity to consult to a high school whose emphasis on order could be seen in the standards of dress held by a number of its staff. In a private conversation, one teacher reported that he thought that wearing a white shirt, tie, and jacket was important for clear thinking, in that it provided the necessary discipline for attacking difficult academic material. He considered the administration of the school lax for not insisting that students comply with a standard with which he felt most of his teaching colleagues agreed. The other teachers did share his views but did not press the issue because it was generally less important to them. However, their agreement with the standard could be seen when one day the school was visited by a street worker checking on one of the boys with whom he worked, who was absent from school. The visitor was an accredited social worker, who because he worked exclusively with street gangs, dressed informally in a sweater, leather jacket, and jeans. The majority of the teachers who talked to the social worker were offended by his appearance and refused to cooperate with him. They did not believe that he could possibly help teen-agers if he himself exhibited such a low moral standard—a judgment made exclusively on the basis of his dress.

Gardner (1965) notes that "organizations can look straight at their faults and rationalize them as virtues." Thus an individual who sees things differently from the rest and has not developed the organization's "blindness" can be of great value. However, without an atmosphere that encourages the expression of new ideas, constructive critics are likely to remain silent, or worse, may be driven away by the organization. An atmosphere in which anyone can speak up and uncomfortable questions can be asked, is a cherished asset that atrophies if not carefully nurtured.

Summary.   We have described five organizational characteristics that should be assessed during the initial stages of consultation to organizations. The purpose of the assessment is to determine how much help an organization may need in improving its internal problem-solving capacity. As was true for assessment at the community level, the assessment of organizations can be accomplished most expeditiously by a combination of social indicator and survey techniques. Such an assessment is not difficult to achieve; helping organizations become more flexible is another matter and requires a commitment and desire for improvement within the organization itself.

Assessment of persons: Emphasizing capabilities

The last step in planning intervention involves the assessment of individuals within organizations and groups. Unlike a clinical assessment, what we want to know about individuals is not their problems, weaknesses, or pathology, but their strengths. We want to know what they can do on their own without outside help. We want to know the capabilities upon which further action can be based.

Viewing persons in terms of their abilities, strengths, and capabilities has a double advantage. First, the fixity and invariance of behavior is de-emphasized. People are not locked in by their needs, drives, and predispositions. Describing someone as an aggressive person (e.g., controlled by aggressive drives) leaves little room for change—we know little about changing basic traits. Describing someone as having the *capability* for aggressive behavior leads us to look for the conditions under which such behavior might occur. As Wallace (1966) notes: "construing personality as response capability reemphasizes the importance of the stimulus conditions under which behavior occurs." In other words, abilities can be self-monitored more easily, displayed, or held in check under appropriate environmental conditions, than can basic predispositions, drives, or "essence" conceptions of personality.

A second reason for adopting an abilities conception of personality, particularly in community work, has been described by Rappaport, Davidson, Wilson, and Mitchell (1975). These authors note that emphasizing *deficits* in persons, whether attributed to genetic and constitutional factors ("blaming the victim") or to inadequate family life or poverty ("blaming the environment"), places the psychologist in an untenable stance of producing an unending stream of "clients" in need of some form of remediation. The person so described is in a perpetual "one down" position as an unfortunate victim of circumstances. Regardless of how benevolent the remedial program, those in need of help are treated as a segregated class of deficient individuals in need of special services, unable to provide for themselves. The "helpers" and the "to be helped" become part of a status hierarchy.

Emphasizing abilities suggests that people can help themselves; that they can transfer skills from areas of existing competencies to new ones. As Rappaport et al. (1975) point out, so-called disadvantaged groups, or any groups "in need of help," collectively can have a wealth of resources. An important role for a community practitioner is to enhance these positive resources whenever they are found in individuals, organizations, or communities.

Looking for skills and capabilities is also an important stance for organizational consultants. The job should not be to weed out the "bad apples" in an organization; such decisions belong to personnel managers and administrators. The consultants' role is to help the organization and its employees do their jobs better. To the extent that consultants become involved in negative personnel decisions, they begin to lose the trust of those with whom they must work. They may now be viewed as the organization's "hatchet men." On the other hand, expanding job competencies is usually valued by staff and cooperation is more easily achieved because each member has a personal stake in self-improvement. Emphasizing member capabilities opens the possibility that a network of "trainers" can be established within an agency, if a structure can be provided for members to share their competencies with one another.

Argyris (1970) takes a similar position concerning the role of organization development consultants. He believes that the job of OD specialists is not to champion one particular problem solution over another, nor is it to guide the organization. What is important is for organization members to learn to operate more competently, so that when a new set of problems occur, they will be solved without the need to once again call outside consultants.

Rappaport et al. (1975) present an example of how the assessment of member capabilities and skills can be used in a community development project. After six months of meetings with the leaders of a local black community, it became apparent that no one particular set of services could meet their many needs. When the focus changed to a service in the community that could be filled by local resources, with some outside encouragement, a number of realistic possibilities emerged. A day-care center was planned, developed, and staffed by local personnel. Directed by a black community health nurse, the center offered a certification program as "day-care worker" to interested citizens who could then use their training to expand the network of needed child care facilities while at the same time providing themselves with added income. The director was chosen for her skills in working with young mothers and children as well as her ability to attract others with similar strengths into her program. In a similar manner, a monthly journal was set up to serve as a training vehicle for graphic arts and investigative reporting. The director was a black graphic artist with leadership skills and the ability to work with high-school-age youngsters. Plans also included a still-life photography studio and a drug education program run by community residents but assisted by psychology personnel. The key to all the programs involved individuals in the community with heretofore underutilized skills.

Summary of intervention hypotheses

The hypotheses discussed in this chapter can be seen in summary form in Figure 9–1. In two of the four community conditions listed, the cycle of assessment → intervention is short. In the case of a homogeneous community not experiencing strain, the recommendation is to forego attempts at intervention. In general, psychological intervention is most effective when there is an awareness of problems and motivation for change. Both of these facilitative conditions are absent in a placid homogeneous community.

The community condition in which only the majority is in strain also requires little additional comment. It is our belief that such a condition is transitory. A strained majority, with good access to social regulators can produce community-wide strain quickly. Thus only two conditions require sustained attention: community-wide strain, which is described as facilitative for the consultation perspectives; and strain limited to specific alienated groups where our first recommendation calls for education of the majority concerning the plight of the minority.

If education in problem-awareness is successful, the community should become sufficiently aroused to apply pressure on personnel within regulatory agencies to deal with the disequilibrium producing problems. They, in turn, should become more open to consultation efforts. However, success is not guaranteed, since community-wide strain also can lead to punitive solutions.

Education in problem-awareness is unsuccessful when a significant number of citizens remain unwilling or unable to confront the issue in question. Everyone need not be convinced that action is necessary for progress to occur, but the minority must acquire a significant number of allies for the issue to remain "alive" and subject to further discussion and negotiation. Without a mandate to explore alternatives, regulators will be reluctant to act and consultation directed at them is not likely to succeed.

At this point, assessment within the minority group itself is required. As Figure 9–1 indicates, we are primarily interested in two factors: the potential for power through unified action, and access to

FIGURE 9–1: Flowchart of community intervention

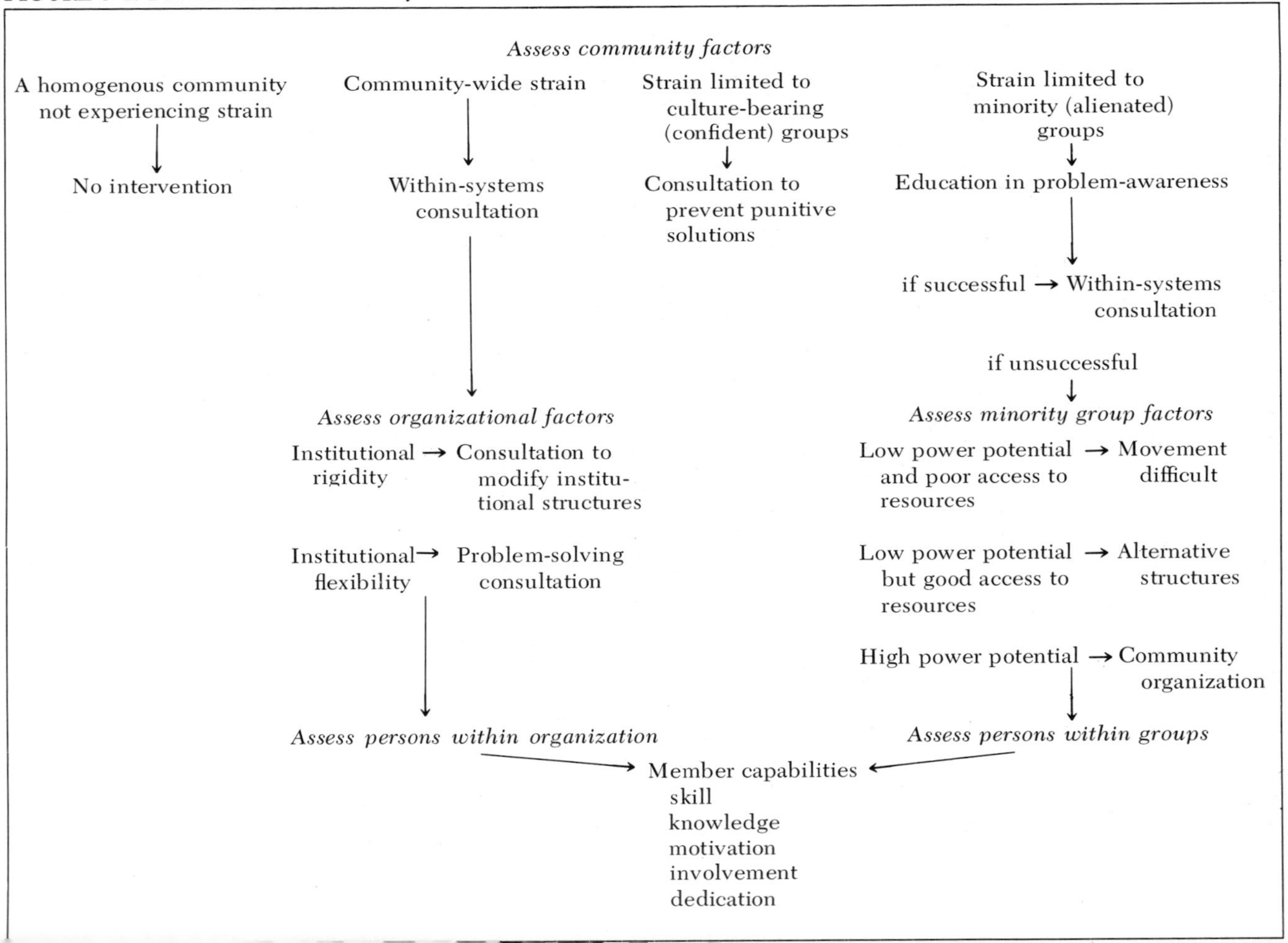

Assess community factors

A homogenous community not experiencing strain → No intervention

Community-wide strain → Within-systems consultation → *Assess organizational factors*

Strain limited to culture-bearing (confident) groups → Consultation to prevent punitive solutions

Strain limited to minority (alienated) groups → Education in problem-awareness → if successful → Within-systems consultation

if unsuccessful

Assess minority group factors

Low power potential and poor access to resources → Movement difficult

Low power potential but good access to resources → Alternative structures

High power potential → Community organization

Assess persons within groups

Assess organizational factors

Institutional → Consultation to modify institutional structures
rigidity

Institutional → Problem-solving consultation
flexibility

Assess persons within organization → Member capabilities
skill
knowledge
motivation
involvement
dedication

resources. Potential power is assessed by noting the geographic dispersion of the minority group; the number of shared values and traditions among group members; the quality of group leadership; the size of the group; and the history of its ability to form coalitions with other similar groups. Access to resources is assessed by noting the frequency of encounters, and the quality of the relationships, between minority group members and social regulators as well as the untapped resources within the minority community. Also to be noted is the group's ability to pull support from sympathetic private sources (e.g., universities, foundations, etc.).

Groups with high power potential can be helped to organize unified constituencies that can compel negotiation toward problem resolution. If necessary, they can negotiate for or create their own alternative structures. Groups with low potential for the development of powerful coalitions, but good access to resources, can decide to cultivate friendly relations with those controlling resources. With support from such friends, alternative structures that are more responsive to their needs become possible. However, little change should be expected for groups without organizational potential or resource access. Attention to unmet needs is least likely for such groups until significant numbers of the community at large become aware of and responsive to their plight.

As indicated in Figure 9–1, community awareness provides a favorable climate for the consultation perspectives. The first step in developing a consultation plan with a particular agency involves the assessment of organizational characteristics. Of particular interest are those attributes that can contribute to an assessment of organizational flexibility, such as age and history of the organization, leadership style, communication patterns, cross-role movement, and deviance management.

The organization's assessed flexibility should provide a guide for the sequencing of consultation objectives. Organizations with a rigid structure need help initially in improving their problem-solving capacity. The focus at this stage is on the organization itself and how it carries out its functions. The recommended sequence is to help improve internal problem-solving capacity before turning full attention to the external problems for which consultation may have been requested. On the other hand, consultation to flexible organizations can move more directly to consideration of particular strain-producing problems.

The decisions involving choice of intervention just reviewed depend upon the assessment of community and organizational characteristics. The last stage of assessment involves noting the specific competencies of persons within the consultee organization or within specific minority groups. With the general form of intervention decided, specific project goals depend upon organizational and member assets. Quite naturally, more can be accomplished when group members have untapped skills and are truly motivated and involved. Also to be remembered is that member capabilities can develop projects that might not be possible if exclusive reliance is placed only on the interventionist's own resources.

Conclusion

In this chapter, theoretical discussions by Smelser (1963), Gamson (1968), and Rhodes (1972) were used as a base upon which implications for community intervention were developed. The model presented stressed the role of equilibrium maintenance in community life, the relationships that develop between social regulators and various citizen groups, and the role of impinging events in producing disequilibrium and strain.

In any community, traditions, reflecting social mores and sentiments, develop as guides for action by regulatory agencies. In this sense, regulatory personnel serve to uphold and perpetuate community traditions. A second function of social regulators is to help communities accommodate to disturbing impinging events. Difficulties can arise when the two functions conflict and produce contradictory mandates: perpetuate status quo traditions while at the same time provide accommodations to changing conditions.

The way social regulators handle this dilemma can have important implications for the quality of community life and the production of further strain. As much as possible, regulators attempt to accommodate to change by maintaining existing community practices. When accommodation of this sort is not possible, a frequent course of action involves "insulation," that is, isolating strain-producing groups from the community at large. Insulation reduces the disruptive potential of alienated groups. It can be used constructively if, in the interim, serious efforts are undertaken to achieve more optimal solutions. Unfortunately, the isolation of alienated groups often is used as a way of ignoring problems and not dealing with the social demands that such groups might make.

Given this analysis, what course of action is open to those seeking to encourage constructive community change? Are the forces sustaining system maintenance and status quo arrangements likely to subvert all attempts at innovation and reform?

We believe that while it may be difficult to establish and maintain true innovation, it is not impossible to do so. Pressures for change are constantly occurring in a dynamic society, and opportunities for intervention often present themselves to the skilled community worker. The most important task, which at times may be difficult to accomplish, is to increase the likelihood that constructive rather than destructive solutions to strain are utilized.

References

Argyris, C. *Intervention theory and method: A behavioral science view*. Reading, Mass.: Addison-Wesley, 1970.

Barker, R. G. The ecological environment. In R. H. Moos and P. M. Insel (Eds.), *Issues in social ecology: Human milieus*. Palo Alto, Calif.: National Press Books, 1974, pp. 255–266.

Bennis, W. G., Benne, K. D., & Chin, R. (Eds.). *The planning of change: Readings in the applied behavioral sciences*. New York: Holt, Rinehart and Winston, 1961.

Brandes, J. *Immigrants to freedom: Jewish communities in rural New Jersey since 1882*. Philadelphia: University of Pennsylvania Press, 1971.

Cumming, E. *Systems of social regulation*. New York: Atherton Press, 1968.

Cumming, J., & Cumming, E. *Ego and milieu: Theory and practice of environmental therapy*. New York: Atherton Press, 1962.

Gamson, W. A. *Power and discontent*. Homewood, Ill.: The Dorsey Press, 1968.

Gardner, J. W. How to prevent organizational dry rot. *Harper's Magazine*, 1965, *231*, No. 1385, 20–26.

Gump, P. V. The behavior setting: A promising unit for environmental designers. In R. H. Moos and P. M. Insel (Eds.), *Issues in social ecology: Human milieus*. Palo Alto, Calif.: National Press Books, 1974, pp. 267–275.

Hansell, N. Patient predicament and clinical service: A system. *Archives of General Psychiatry*, 1967, *17*, 204–210.

Klein, D. C. *Community dynamics and mental health*. New York: John Wiley & Sons, 1968.

Leighton, A. H. *My name is legion: Foundations for a theory of man in relation to culture.* New York: Basic Books, 1959.

Lippitt, G. L.   What do we know about leadership? In W. G. Bennis, K. D. Benne, & R. Chin (Eds.), *The planning of change: Readings in the applied behavioral sciences.* New York: Holt, Rinehart and Winston, 1961, pp. 431–435.

Lippitt, R., Watson, J., & Westley, B.   *The dynamics of planned change.* New York: Harcourt, Brace, 1958.

Lipset, S. M., & Raab, E.   *The politics of unreason: Right-wing extremism in America, 1790–1970.* New York: Harper & Row, 1970.

Monahan, J. & Geis, G.   Controlling "dangerous" people. *Annals of the American Academy of Political and Social Science,* 1976, *423,* 142–151.

Price, R. H.   Behavior setting theory and research. In R. H. Moos (Ed.), *The Human Context: Environmental determinants of behavior.* New York: John Wiley & Sons, 1976, pp. 213–247.

Rappaport, J., Davidson, W. S., Wilson, M. N., & Mitchell, A.   Alternatives to blaming the victim or the environment: Our places to stand have not moved the earth. *American Psychologist,* 1975, *30,* 525–528.

Rhodes, W. C.   *Behavioral threat and community response: A community psychology inquiry.* New York: Behavioral Publications, 1972.

Roman, M.   Community control and the community mental health center: A view from the Lincoln bridge. In B. Denner & R. H. Price (Eds.), *Community mental health: Social action and reaction.* New York: Holt, Rinehart & Winston, 1973, pp. 270–284.

Sarason, S. B.   *The psychological sense of community: Prospects for a community psychology.* San Francisco: Jossey-Bass, 1974.

Schiff, S. K.   Community accountability and mental health services. *Mental Hygiene,* 1970, *54,* 205–214.

Smelser, N. J.   *Theory of collective behavior.* New York: The Free Press, 1963.

Wallace, J.   An abilities conception of personality: Some implications for personality measurement. *American Psychologist,* 1966, *21,* 132–138.

Wicker, A.   Undermanning theory and research: Implications for the study of psychological and behavioral effects of excess populations. *Representative Research in Social Psychology,* 1973, *4,* 185–206.

10

EPILOGUE: STRATEGIES FOR ORGANIZING A COMMUNITY PSYCHOLOGY

THROUGHOUT this book, we have tried not only to present the "state of the art" of community work and to critique the current wis-dom, but to specify the kinds of empirical and conceptual tasks that must be undertaken to advance the field. A major concern of ours has been that while homily, rhetoric, and exhortation may be necessary to launch a new professional movement, they cannot long sustain its growth or vitality. The future of the community field, to our mind, will rest with the rigor of research and the clarity of conceptualization. We have described the individual, organizational, and community levels, and the personal, environmental, and interactional targets at which efforts to prevent community problems and augment community com-petencies must be addressed. We have, as well, detailed the assump-tions underlying various approaches to community intervention, as-sumptions subject to test and analysis.

A final question that remains concerns how best to mobilize and organize the professional behavioral science community to most effec-tively and efficiently carry out the tasks which need to be done. What organizational structures can best advance theory and research in the community fields? While knowledge relevant to understanding and changing communities will undoubtedly come from numerous and disparate sources—from sociology, anthropology, political science, planning, and other fields—we have been most concerned with the contribution of the "mental health" disciplines and, in particular, with the field of psychology.

Organizational structures, however loosely developed, are necessary for several reasons. They provide the reference groups and support systems needed to coordinate information flow among persons with similar interests by formally sponsoring journals and meetings and by informally facilitating the development of the social networks necessary for stimulating ideas. More symbolically, an organized interest area serves as a flag around which partisans can rally to validate themselves and to derive sustenance and support from likeminded peers when the going gets rough. It provides a source of identity and a feeling of continuity when both may be in short supply. On a more mundane level, organizing a field of interest facilitates the development of training programs, the recruitment and placement of personnel, and the creation of a hierarchy of advocates for the area who can fend off the unsympathetic long enough for the field to stand on its own.

Our question, then, is how can a community psychology best be organized to pursue the knowledge needed for generating positive community change. We shall first survey the forms that the organization of the field is currently taking and analyze the advantages and limitations of each in terms of its implications for community research and intervention and for graduate training. It appears to us that psychologists interested in community problems are organizing themselves in four ways: as a *specialty* within clinical psychology; as an *independent area* of psychology; as an *orientation* spanning several areas of psychology; and as an *interdisciplinary profession,* related to, but distinct from, the field of psychology.

Community psychology as a specialty within clinical psychology

The "community-clinical model" of community psychology is probably the most prevalent one in use today. In this organizational framework, students are trained first as clinical psychologists—with expertise in therapy and assessment at the individual and small group level—and later acquire community concepts and experience. This role is also the one most frequently adopted by those whose only formal training is in clinical psychology and who have become exposed to community work by virtue of their employment in a Community Mental Health Center. Those adhering to a community-clinical model can "go both ways" and claim expertise in both clinical and community situations. Since it can be stretched to accommodate many employment situation, it is sometimes referred to as the "bread and butter model" of community psychology.

Graduate education in a community-clinical framework is generally provided by faculty whose major commitments are to clinical work and who teach clinical courses in addition to community ones. Community work is often seen as a "specialty" within clinical psychology, comparable to clinical child psychology or the study of retardation.

Proponents of the view that community psychology is best viewed as a subset of clinical psychology give both substantive and pragmatic arguments to bolster their position. There is a well-established body of knowledge in clinical psychology, they state, that is of direct relevance to community work. It would be foolhardy not to immerse oneself in what is already known about individuals and the treatment of their psychological problems before tackling the thornier issues raised by prevention and community problems. This is especially true, the argument goes, since so little is known about communities and about prevention.

Pragmatically, the ease-of-employment argument is often raised in defense of the community-clinical approach, especially in a time of economic downturn when the public sector is less likely to initiate the funding of new community projects. A second pragmatic consideration is the relative ease with which community psychology can be incorporated within existing clinical training programs, compared with the bitter intramural battles that almost inevitably occur when the attempt is made to set up a community program independent of clinical training. Finally, it is argued that the great majority of the public—including care-givers and agents of control in the community—see psychologists in clinical terms and relate to them accordingly. Rather than attempt to alter this perception, it is more fruitful to initially accept the clinical role as a vehicle to enter community institutions and, after acceptance has been achieved, more system-level interventions can be suggested.

There are many in community psychology, however, who strongly oppose organizing the area as a specialty of clinical work. Rather than providing a useful knowledge base for community work, they see clinical training as undermining a fresh approach to community problems by putting clinical "blinders" on students and practitioners, with the result that they tend to see all problems in individualistic and remedial terms. The critics of the community-clinical approach state that the interventions planned in such an organizational structure often tend to be basically clinical in nature, albeit applied to disenfranchized "community" groups (e.g., crisis intervention to the Spanish-speaking). Laudable and necessary as the extension of clinical services may be, the services are still clinical in nature, and, the critics charge, evince few of the hallmarks of a genuine community approach, such as an emphasis on prevention and on institutional change, or a population focus.

Community psychology as an independent area of psychology

Those who object to community psychology's subordination to clinical work most often propose as an alternative the independence of community psychology as a distinct area within the field of psychology. Under this form of professional organization, community psychology would be a separate and co-equal branch of the field, on a par with clinical, social, physiological, and other areas of psychology. Community psychologists would not be trained first as clinicians, and while they would be aware of clinical theory and research, they would not acquire the expertise to perform individual assessment or therapy, since these tasks are not viewed as integral to genuine community work. Thus freed from the burdens of assessment courses and therapy practica, the student could concentrate on gaining expertise in areas believed to be of more direct relevance to community understanding. According to this view, organizational psychology may be a higher priority than personality theory, and environmental psychology may take precedence over psychopathology. It is not that clinically oriented training necessarily will retard the development of a community psychologist (other than by the possible development of the individualistic biases and blinders mentioned earlier), but that one can only concentrate on so much in graduate education and professional practice, and given these limitations of time and energy, the priority should go to the study and application of sytem-level concepts.

The proponents of an "independent" community psychology tend to see the community-clinical model as a compromised and diluted application of community principles. Without the need to defend the limitations of clinical psychology, and with a strong background in the system-level aspects of the discipline, they view themselves as in the best position to launch genuinely innovative community interventions.

As might be expected, the advocates of an independent community psychology receive as much criticism from community-clinical psychologists as they dispense. It is too early, the clinically trained community psychologists retort, to cut community work loose from its clinical moorings. Community theory and research is in too primitive a state of development to constitute a body of knowledge of sufficient breadth and depth to sustain an independent community field. Independence should be considered at such time when community work has proven its empirical and conceptual mettle. Until then, it should remain firmly linked to clinical psychology. In addition to these substantive criticisms, the opponents of an independent community psychology also hold that the organizational trauma of creating a new niche in psychology department bureaucracies is frequently not worth the considerable energies and political infighting required; and, more significantly, that the employment probability of community psychologists without clinical training is sufficiently bleak (especially outside academia) that clinical training should be offered as a matter of course to all who would engage in community work. To this last point, the advocates of an independent community psychology retort that new and more system-level employment settings (e.g., in welfare systems, government planning agencies, police departments) can and will be found to provide psychologists with an opportunity to effect community change.

Community psychology as an orientation spanning several areas of psychology

While less developed than the previous two organizational models for community training and practice, the notion that community psychology is best viewed as an orientation spanning several areas of psychology is one with a growing number of adherents. According to this model, community intervention should not be construed as the sole province of one area of psychology (clinical), and should also not be distinguished as a separate and independent entity within the field. Rather, community application should be seen as an aspect of the several areas of psychology already concerned with human problems. Thus there would be a community-clinical psychology, a community-social psychology, a community-environmental psychology, a community-organizational psychology, etc. These would not exist as mini-specialties within each area, but rather would constitute an orientation that would span the several established areas that already have a body of knowledge relevant to community work. Psychologists in various relevant areas, according to this view, would employ the principles of community psychology (e.g., consultation) in extending the application of their work. An environmental psychologist who had developed a laboratory-based theory of crowding could pursue his or her research in the direction of reducing strain-inducing crowding in urban communities. Or a social psychologist interested in aggression could extend a theory to encompass community unrest. Psychologists in both examples would maintain their "primary allegiance" to environmental or social psychology, and would be so labeled in academic departments, but both would share a commitment to pursue the community implications of their work. While there might be a need for a few persons to gather together the community aspect of the various areas, or for an organization to provide an occasional meeting-place for psychologists interested in the community application of their work, no training or grouping of people known primarily as "community psychologists" would be necessary. "Community" would be the orientation of many groups rather than the defining characteristic of one.

Those favoring the "orientation" approach would agree with the principal criticisms that the community-clinical and the independent community groups make of each other: there is not yet enough expertise to set up a separate community profession, and clinical training is not a necessary prerequisite for community intervention. They see the creation of a loosely organized community orientation as the way to derive the most benefit from many areas of psychology, with the least organizational baggage.

Proponents of one of the other modes of organizing community psychology hold that more than "interest group" meetings are necessary to forge a solid commitment to community problems in the field of psychology. Without a more tightly organized peer constellation— either as an independent area or a clinical specialty—community psychology, they argue, will be little more than a hobby for psychologists whose principal commitment is elsewhere. When the choice comes between the arduous pursuit of enduring community change and retreat to the laboratory of one's "parent" discipline, those who view community psychology only as an orientation across many areas may feel that following through on community intervention is, after all, somebody else's business.

Community psychology as an interdisciplinary profession

The most radical view of how best to organize the field of community psychology holds that it should be organized outside psychology altogether. More precisely, it holds that understanding community processes and undertaking community change are by their very nature such complex and multifaceted phenomena that only a truly interdisciplinary effort has any hope of success. Psychology as a major intellectual tradition has much to offer the study of communities, but so do sociology, anthropology, urban planning, and the other behavioral sciences. While psychology may have as much to contribute as do these other areas, especially in its knowledge of individual and group behavior and its experimental methodologies, there is no a priori reason to assume that psychology has any more claim to community relevance than many other scientific traditions. Those who view community work as an interdisciplinary endeavor hold that its organizational structure should include psychology, but should be organized independently of any established field.

The advocates of the interdisciplinary approach believe that a science of the community will best be developed by exposing students to the relevant portions of several behavioral sciences on a coequal basis. Only by existing independently of any established field, they state, can the biases and blinders of any one discipline be avoided. In an interdisciplinary framework the biases of one discipline will be counteracted by the biases of another. Thus if psychology emphasizes the individual in the community and tends to neglect the impact of social forces, sociology stresses social forces and tends to underplay their effect on individuals. By providing education in both areas, the student should be freer to conceptualize, conduct research, and intervene at the multiple levels necessary for community understanding and change. The organizing foci of graduate education and professional research and practice, it is held, should be *social and community problems,* rather than traditional disciplines. Thus psychologists and others should cluster together around the problems of crime, alcoholism, or environmental quality, rather than having each discipline cluster around itself and span a variety of problems.

The proposition that community psychology training and practice are best organized outside the boundaries of the psychology profession has been criticized on a number of grounds. The detractors of this approach argue that it may produce a population of generalists, people who know a little about many areas but who lack depth in any one field. They acknowledge that other disciplines may have much to contribute to community work, but state that the way to achieve an understanding of the community is for each discipline to pursue community work within its own traditions, so that there would be a community psychology, a community sociology, etc., rather than a synthesized community science or profession. To the extent that knowledge from other areas is useful to the community psychologist, it can be provided in the form of "outside minors" or interdisciplinary seminars, in the context of a basically psychological education. A fully interdisciplinary education, its critics hold, would leave the student without a clear professional identity or a recognized peer group to which to relate one's research and action experiences.

On a more pragmatic level, the arguments against an independent community psychology within the field of psychology are made more strenuously with regard to a community psychology independent of psychology altogether. The organizational battles necessary to establish a new community discipline, and the alleged absence of employment prospects for members of a new community profession are said to be prohibitive. The reply here is the same as that made by the proponents of an independent community area in psychology. Namely, that the organizational battles are worth it, and that employment settings other than those traditionally inhabited by psychologists can be found on the basis of professional skills rather than disciplinary labels.

The choice of strategies

Each of the four strategies for organizing community psychology is currently in operation. Many professionals working in the community identify with one or the other of the "models," and graduate education programs in the field may be divided into one of the four groups.[1]

[1] Examples of the community-clinical approach would include the programs at the University of Rochester, the University of Colorado, Indiana University, and the University of California, Los Angeles. Examples of an independent community psychology within the field of psychology are at the University of Illinois, the University of Michigan, and the University of Texas. The view that community psychology should be thought of as an orientation spanning several areas of psychology finds expression in faculty and students affiliated with groups such as the Society for the Psychological Study of Social Issues (SPSSI) and the American Psychology–Law Society. The interdisciplinary strategy is illustrated by the Program in Social Ecology at the Uni-

It is our contention that there is insufficient evidence to support a judgment that one or another of the strategies is the "right" one for community psychology, or that one or more of the organizational schemata has proven ineffective. Each of the strategies, we believe, has important strengths not shared by the others and each has equally unique weaknesses. The previous paragraphs have highlighted the assets and liabilities of each approach to community training.

With such a mixture of assets and liabilities, the choice of strategies for organizing community psychology is a difficult one. Perhaps any individual case should be guided by the community psychologist's personal conviction and perspective concerning community work and by the career path he or she desires. It is, we believe, much too soon for any categoric judgments on the various methods of organizing the field. Each of the organizational strategies provides for the supportive reference groups, information networks, and senses of identity and continuity necessary for the development of the field. The choice of strategies is for the individual to make; it does not need an "official" response. In time, when information on the fate of graduates from programs emphasizing one or another of the strategies is available and when the kinds of research, conceptualizations, and interventions produced within each approach can be evaluated, it may be possible to eliminate one or more strategies of organizing the field. But until then, we believe that it is fortunate that several alternative and to some extent competing frameworks are available. Out of this diversity may come the structure most capable of sustaining a vibrant community psychology.

In the introduction to this book in Chapter 1 we stated that the ideal term chosen to denote the community field should have a number of important characteristics. We said that it should suggest:

a. A community and ecological focus.
b. A concern with problems of human functioning that includes a focus on the prevention of disorder, but that also goes beyond problems traditionally designated in "mental health" terms.

---

versity of California, Irvine, the Community Systems and Human Development program at the Pennsylvania State University, and the Wallace School of Community Service and Public Affairs at the University of Oregon. See the volume edited by Iscoe and Spielberger (*Community psychology: Perspectives in training and research,* New York: Meredith Corporation, 1970) for detailed descriptions of some community psychology training programs and comments by some graduates of these programs and also see particularly, the proceedings of the Austin Conference on graduate training in community psychology (Iscoe, Bloom and Spielberger, *Community psychology in transition,* Washington, D.C.: Hemisphere Press, 1977).

c. A stance that includes a concern for coping, adaptation, and competence, not just an emphasis on disorder.

d. A willingness to promote multidisciplinary, collaborative research, since no profession has a monopoly on interest in community change.

e. A commitment to an empirical, experimental approach to social intervention.

f. An avoidance of inappropriate medical overtones.

For us, these are the important themes that we would like to see advanced in the community field. Any number of organizational structures can serve the useful and necessary function of encouraging training, research, and practice. However, we would note with some caution that excessive concern for developing the "correct" organizational structure can serve to inhibit growth in several ways. Energies that could be spent in more substantive pursuits can be diverted to what are essentially administrative arguments. The group can turn inward and spend more time debating how it should be organized than actually carrying out its goals. What can begin as a social movement often can end as a guild, with a rigidity and narrowness that is as stultifying as the arrangements against which the movement first reacted. While we must work to separate rhetoric from theory and to supplant diatribe with data in community work, we must be careful to preserve the spirit and motivation—the social conscience—that first gave rise to the field.

Indexes

NAME INDEX

425

SUBJECT INDEX

A

Adaptation, principle of, 164
Alienated groups, 378–381, 393–394
  isolation of, 379–381
  strain in, 390–392
Alternative institutions
  assumptions, 299–306, 323–326
  Community Action Program, 279–280
  competing bureaucracies, 279–280
  criminal justice system, 285–291
  mental health system, 291–295
  person-environment fit, 277–278
  professional acceptance, 296–298
  school system, 280–285
  tolerance for marginality, 296
Anticipatory guidance, 183–184
Architectural environment, 170–173,
  176–179
Assessment
  community level, 396–400
  organizational level, 400–404
  personal level, 404–407
Attribution therapy in prevention, 184

B–C

Behavioral ecology; *see* Environmental
  psychology
Behavior settings, 187–189, 383–384,
  397–400
Civil liberties, 151–155; *see also* Values
Clinical psychology, 12–13, 113–115,
  414–416
Community Action Program, 279–280,
  362–365
Community development; *see* Com-
  munity organization
Community life, characteristics of, 381–
  386
Community mental health, 20–22

Community organization
  assumptions, 348–352
  commercial elites, 339–343
  Community Action Program, 279–280,
    362–365
  community control, 334–336
  community development, 344–352
  participatory democracy, 334–344
  political factors, 332–344, 354–356
  psychological dysfunction, 359–362
  resources, 356–357, 365–367
  social action, 344–345, 352–368
  strategies, choice of, 358–359
Community psychiatry, 20–22
Community psychology
  clinical specialty, 414–416
  history of, 3–10
  independent area in psychology, 416–
    417
  independent profession, 419–420
  orientation in psychology, 417–418
  perspectives in, 10–12
  research, 71–104
  terminology, 20–22
Competence orientation, 13–20, 404–407
Consultation
  assumptions, 260–262
  behavioral, 225–244
  client-centered, 210–211
  comparison of perspectives, 265–268
  consultee-centered, 211–221
  mental health, 205–225
  organization development, 244–260
  police departments, 25, 221–223
  program-centered, 221–225
  psychotherapy, 209–210
  school systems, 22–24, 133–136,
    213–215, 240–244
  sensitivity training, 252–258
  theme interference reduction, 217–221
Cost-effectiveness analysis, 87–90

431

*This book has been set in 10 point Caledonia,
leaded 3 points, and 9 point Caledonia, leaded
2 points. Part numbers and titles are 24 point
Kennerly. Chapter numbers are 60 point Cas-
lon and chapter titles are 18 point Kennerly.
The size of the type page is 27 by 45 picas.*